MW01140816

NEXUS

TRANSPERSONAL APPROACHES TO GROUPS

M. HONORÉ FRANCE

DETSELIG ENTERPRISES LTD.

CALGARY, ALBERTA, CANADA

Nexus: Transpersonal Approaches to Groups

© 2002 M. Honoré France

National Library of Canada Cataloguing in Publication Data

France, Honoré

Nexus

Includes bibliographic references.
ISBN 1-55059-235-1
1. Group psychotherapy. I. Title.
RC488.F72   2002   616.89'152   C2002-910228-6

Detselig Enterprises Ltd.

210-1220 Kensington Rd. N.W., Calgary, AB T2N 3P5 Canada
Phone: (403) 283-0900/Fax: (403) 283-6947
e-mail: temeron@telusplanet.net
www.temerondetselig.com

We acknowledge the financial support of the Government of Canada through the Book Publishing Industry Development Program (BPIDP) for our publishing activities.

All Rights Reserved. No part of this book may be reproduced in any form or by any means without permission in writing from the publisher. [Parts of this book were originally published under the title: *Expressive Approach to Groups: Dynamics, Methods and Issues.* Published in Co-operation with The Department of Psychological Foundations in Education, University of Victoria, Box 3010, Victoria, B.C., Canada V8W 3N4]

ISBN 1-55059-235-1   SAN 115-0324   Printed in Canada

<u>**DEDICATION**</u>

Mi trozo de pan, mi viejo refran, mi poeta; La fe que perdí, mi camino y mi carreta. Mi dulce placer, mi sueño de ayer, mi equipaje; Mi tibio rincon, mi mejor cancion, mi paisaje....

Serrat, *Poema de Amor*, 1980

I dedicate this book to a special person who has brought me NEW LIFE in a spirit of renewal – Maria del Carmen Rodriguez. *Te amo mi cielo y muchas gracias por tu alma, corazon y vida.*

TABLE OF CONTENTS

PROLOGUE: NEXUS

The events of September 11th, 2001, have forever changed society's sense of safety in a world seemingly gone mad. The sense of normality and optimism about the future has drawn attention to the complacency and materialism that exists in North American society. It is clear that one's existence can be snuffed out at any time. Also, that one's community reaches around the world, when events in the most remote corner of the world can affect what happens in one's neighborhood. What sense can everyone make of the global insanity engulfing the world where a simple letter can contain deadly anthrax or a trip on an airplane evolves into a terrorist weapon? According to Watts (1958) society plays an important role in determining the sanity of an individual. What happens in society shapes how one lives and behaves, which Watts called the social field where humanity lives. There are contradictions in our institutions, which affect who and what one is, and in essence are a creation of what goes on in the world. Thus on one hand, humanity cannot escape the contradictions in the world, just as one cannot escape cultural upheavals that occur a continent away.

Humanity is left with the duality to life that produces energy, yet creates problems. There are solutions in the "game of life," but how does one play the "game" when the fixed order of the world is constantly changing? On an individual level, people are faced with a dilemma of the duality in the order of the universe. In nature there are always opposites, but never good or evil or forces that push and pull. As counsellors, we live with the contradictions in our lives and grope for answers and solutions, which challenge us to go beyond what we have done before. Culture plays a major role in what we are, but also how we help others cope with the new challenges that face everyone in a world growing "smaller and smaller." Approaches that only utilize a Euro-centric worldview cannot explain what happens nor are they comprehensive enough to cover all cultures. Neither can counsellors separate the spirit, mind, emotions and the physical world, as is customary with previous theories of counselling. However, the Transpersonal theory, on which this book is based, does combine all of these elements with "culture friendly" strategies that can work with a variety of people. Vaughan (in Sheikh & Sheikh, 1989) stressed that we "have mapped transpersonal development beyond what was formerly considered the ceiling of human possibility and have found preliminary evidence of common psychological and spiritual developmental sequences across traditions" (p. 94).

Transpersonal counselling has often been referred to as the "fourth force" in psychology, in that it is quite different from the traditional approaches in orientation, scope and strategies (Sheikh & Sheikh, 1989). The literal definition of transpersonal is quite simple – beyond the personal. In a sense, one might say that it is beyond the conventional constructs of traditional psychology's conception of personality. Walsh and Vaughan (1993) stress that the transpersonal is a developmental process in which one goes beyond the self limitation of the physical, psychological, social and spiritual to a point of self-realization of unlimited potentialities. Transpersonal experiences may be defined as experiences in which the sense of identity of self extends beyond the individual or personal to encompass wider aspects of humankind, life, psyche or the cosmos.

The following chapters in this book follow the Transpersonal approach to group work, along with some allied ideas that expand on the theory. The following processes, which you will observe in the following chapters, are incorporated into Transpersonal theory:

- Cognitive processes: (e.g., "How are you thinking about yourself vis-à-vis the problem and environment?");

- Affective processes: (e.g., "How do you feel about the problem, people concerned, and your relationship to them?");

- Action processes: (e.g., "How is your behavior blocking problem resolution in the group?");

- Spiritual processes: (e.g. "How does your spiritual emptiness distance you from your connections with the cosmos and all living things?").

MULTICULTURAL AND THEORETICAL FOUNDATIONS
OF TRANSPERSONAL THOUGHT

Unlike many of the other theories of counselling, there has not been one individual who stands out or who could be considered the original theorist of the Transpersonal approach. The following people have been cited among a large field of writers currently creating, formulating and researching strategies that follow the Transpersonal theory. They are Ken Wilber, Charles Tart, Stanislav Grof, Roger Walsh and Frances Vaughan. Wilber has introduced many Eastern forms of wisdom into Western therapy and psychology by making them more accessible and less esoteric. His writings have helped people better understand Eastern esotericism by recasting them in a logical manner. Charles Tart researched and described human consciousness and modelling/mapping human states of alternative consciousness. Stanislav Grof researched chemically induced states of consciousness and developed a version of archetypes that is similar to Jung's. In addition, the writings of Roger Walsh and Frances Vaughan, published in the *Journal of Transpersonal Psychology*, have clarified transcendental and transformative philosophy into much more practical and understandable therapeutic approaches that are as "substantial, consistent and functional as the ones that are accepted with traditional Western psychology" (Fadiman, in Mahoney, 1989; p. 226).

This model features core group areas of exploration that are based on three fundamental assumptions about the nature and potential of the mind: 1) That our usual state of mind is clouded, entranced, mostly out of our control; 2) That this untrained mind can be trained and clarified; and 3) That this training catalyzes transpersonal consciousness and action. These areas can be grouped into ethical training, attentional training, emotional transformation, motivation, refining awareness and wisdom (Walsh & Vaughan, 1993). This proposed group model adds additional methods to explore intrapersonal and interpersonal functioning. Walsh and Vaughn (1993) voice the paradoxical and multicultural nature of the Transpersonal by stressing that:

Since nobody is perfect and since we can learn from each other's mistakes, it may be useful to regard those who disagree with us as potential teachers from whom we can learn about a different perception of reality. This seems to be a more rational, democratic and compassionate attitude than one which assumes others are either totally right or totally wrong. Furthermore, it enables us to understand and communicate with a wide variety of human beings who have different views of reality and nevertheless share the same human experiences of fear and the same human desire for happiness (p. 133).

The Transpersonal approach is not linear nor even necessarily new. Walsh and Vaughan (1993) stress that the Transpersonal approach brings a "recognition of old wisdom" (p. 1). For example, altered states of consciousness have been a part of many ancient and traditional approaches, from Asia to native peoples from the Western Hemisphere. The Transpersonal approach embraces and incorporates folk medicines and practices from a variety of traditions. Altered states of consciousness can be achieved by focusing on perceptual sensitivity, thus producing more clarity. As such, perceptual processes vary with state of consciousness in predictable ways and it is possible to achieve specific states of awareness not known in traditional psychotherapy. For example, according to Lueger (cited in Sheikh & Sheikh, 1989) developing higher levels of awareness and consciousness in the ancient traditions of "Hinduism, Buddhism, and Sufism [expanded by transcending] in order to connect with the real or cosmic self and to establish a genuine sense of unity with nature" (p. 226). Ordinarily, the usual state of consciousness is less than optimal, thus increasing one's ability to expand the consciousness beyond these levels increases one's knowledge about the forces in the self and the environment. In a sense, one achieves understanding and insight or perhaps "satori" (enlightenment), when one's alienated or false self (maya) is discarded. One might even refer to a neurosis as the illusory distortion of perception, which is not needed and therefore, discarded when one becomes more balanced. Awakening from maya (illusion) and experiencing liberation is the aim of the Transpersonal approach to counselling. Thus, by psychological healing one can become enlightened. In that sense, the transpersonal approach "is not seen as successful adjustments to the prevailing culture, but rather the daily experience of that state called liberation, enlightenment, individuation, certainty or gnosis according to various traditions" (Fadiman, in Mahoney, 1989; p. 227).

The mechanism for achieving higher levels of consciousness is to become more aware of the self and one's surroundings. In addition, meditation helps one recognize the flow of thoughts and fantasies for what they are (this is called de-hypnosis). There is insight into how one's behavior has been shaped by societal forces and so one can "let go" of any illusions that heretofore have conditioned one to act and believe in a certain way. Therefore, the goal is a release of the conscious self and a new knowledge that might be called "enlightenment." There are seven factors of enlightenment:

- Mindfulness: precise conscious awareness of the stimulus;

- Effort = energy + arousal;

- Investigation: active exploration of experience;

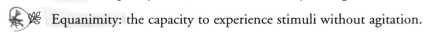

❧ Rapture: delight in the awareness and exploration of experiences;

❧ Concentration: ability to maintain attention on the specific object;

❧ Calm: tranquillity and freedom from anxiety and agitation;

❧ Equanimity: the capacity to experience stimuli without agitation.

ELEMENTS FOR ACHIEVING WELLNESS

There have never been any secrets to wellness or even enlightenment, because these conditions occur by just "living" in a harmonious and spontaneous state that exists in nature. In surveying many healing traditions, Walsh and Vaughan (1993) put forth a number of elements that they called "the heart of the art of transcendence: ethical training, concentration, emotional transformation, redirection of motivation, refinement of awareness, and the cultivation of wisdom" (p. 2). The following are descriptions of how these elements intertwine with well-being, along with several that I feel augment or expand on their ideas: awareness, compassion, emotional transformation, ethical training, meditation and re-focusing, motivation and wisdom.

DEVELOPING AWARENESS

As a process, awareness sounds like it is similar to introspection, but it is different. The difference is that introspection is a way of looking inward to learn something. It is a process whereby one tries to figure out something or to make sense of it. In doing this, there is a review and analysis of behavior. In the end, perhaps one is, as Polster (1966) suggests, distracted:

> by expectations of failure or success. We are so prejudiced in favor of one behavior over another. We are prejudiced…in favor of taking over other behavior, so we are prejudiced in favor of relevance over irrelevance…and given these prejudices, we might not be fascinated with people who don't fit those prejudices (p.9).

This does not mean that people detach themselves from what is going on around them and become introspective. While detachment from time to time is comfortable and even protective, in the end it is very destructive. Awareness is a process of noticing and observing what one does, how one feels it, what one's thoughts are, and what one's body sensations are. These thoughts and body sensations are like a passing scenery, which unfurls like a panorama that people experience as it occurs. Consider the following perspectives on what it means to become aware:

> In Freud's narrow view, it meant calling into awareness repressed impulses and instinctual desires. In Fromm's view, the average individual is only half awake; he or she is conscious of fictions but has the potential to become conscious of the reality behind the fiction. Consequently, to make the unconscious conscious means to wake up, to know reality (Sheikh & Sheikh, 1989; p. 115).

[handwritten margin notes: "detached, withdrawn, analyzing the past"; "awake + observing the here and now"]

In the ordinary movement of life around one, it is possible to observe the silences, which allows us to hear what is not said and to feel the energy flow around unseen. It is all a pattern or process. In the same way, as people listen to what others say to them, they will notice how they say it and experience all the sensations, feelings, thoughts and physical reactions. When this happens, there is total contact, which allows one to be open to all kinds of possibilities. This contact is the process of awareness. Two aspects of this process of awareness that assist in understanding and putting into perspective what is happening are meaning and boundary awareness. The first aspect is that it allows them to keep up to date with themselves. At any given time they know how they feel and what they think. Meaning is not something that has to be processed before they can act. People are people and they act as themselves. The second aspect is the interaction people have with their environment. Boundaries become clear and they react more spontaneously to their environment. They see more, experience more, and are aware of more in their surroundings. If people try to split feelings and thoughts they will find that it is difficult, if not impossible. The focus of the Transpersonal approach is to help people to reawaken to the natural rhythm between awareness and the frequent interruptions that exist in day to day activities in the environment. When one starts to think and analyze, it is impossible to be aware of what is going on. To attend simultaneously to two things with the same degree of awareness is very difficult, because there will always be something missed. If one can just be aware of what is happening and let it flow, one will experience it, not in parts, but as a whole. Arasteh (1984) emphasized that in the healthy person:

> experience and behavior overlap and inner and outer expression are the same; but in many cases, behavior is the rationalization or inhibitor of experience – it is a cover. Experience has an organic and illuminary nature, whereas, behavior is characterized by conditioning. It is experience, not behavior that produces change and, at the same time, strengthens one's sensitivity (p. 150).

This means that if people are more aware, they can learn to trust their natural processes. If they ignore or abuse their body, they know that they will destroy it; but if they work with it and not against it, it will give back to them and help them. As they grow in awareness, they will sense more of the wisdom of their whole being. For example, when people jog they know that once they overcome limitations they put on themselves, their running takes on a natural rhythm. They seem to glide as they run. Their mind is not telling their body what to do, for if they let their mind take over, they will feel tired. They will think about finishing. Their rhythm will falter and finally they will want to rest; but when they run without thoughts, they will become aware of all the things around them. They are now in a state of awareness where they have become open to new insights, experiences and understandings. In the Sufi tradition, awareness is a final rebirth that starts people on the road to living in a new light. "Awareness may come to a person suddenly, or it may develop gradually. Yet awareness is not enough. The seeker must cease unsuitable past behavior: he or she must experience repentance, decide to reform and finally cleanse the self of enmity and cruelty" (Arasteh, 1984; p. 157).

BECOMING COMPASSIONATE

To have an open heart that lets the waters of compassion, of understanding, and of forgiveness flow forth is a sign of a mature person… Then we…will walk towards greater freedom and let waters flow onto others, healing them and finding healing through them (Vanier, 1998; p. 102).

From a transpersonal perspective, compassion for others is one of the most empowering characteristics that we can wish for. To be compassionate means to wish others not to suffer the indignities of pain and sorrow, socially, intellectually, psychologically and spiritually. However, compassion that emanates from the heart and embraces all of nature's creatures is the transcendental sense that unites us with everything in existence. When we empathize we are separate, but when we feel compassion that goes beyond ourselves we are joined with the cosmos. That happens when we realize that we are not a separate ego or self, but part of a collective identity that unites us. Brazier (1995) says that "Compassion is to understand the other person's subjective world without stealing anything. Stealing means taking over…In compassion one sees through the eyes of the other, and feels with their heart, without any private agenda" (p. 195).

In a world that is characterized by oppression, people become burdened by the lack of acceptance, thus they lose one of life's most precious gifts – love. Oppression robs one's opportunities for being compassionate and without compassion there is no love. When one is compassionate, one gains meaning, lives with purpose and has understanding for the welfare of other living things. This is the ability to see one's self in a context of all living things and to understand the birds and the trees. When one is compassionate, every experience is full us that even bad experiences help us along the "road" to greater awareness a part of a great family that loves every member, no matter how small. This is living with the humility that one has survived because another has given to us; it means that to be humble is to receive a reminder of one's humanity. Even disappointments become opportunities for growth. Brazier (1995) goes on to say that compassion:

may begin as a set of observational, empathic and caring skills – thoughtfulness, giving time and attention, listening, helping and generous in action – which we can all improve with good effects upon both our professional work and our private lives. As it grows, it becomes inexorably, a challenge to us to overcome the obstacles to life within ourselves and to flow with the boundless Tao in which we lose our attachment to separateness. The world needs kindness (p. 200).

EMOTIONAL TRANSFORMATION

The truth is everywhere. Wherever you are, it's right where you are, when you can't see it. And you can see it through whatever vehicle you are working with, you can free yourself from certain attachments that keep you from seeing it. The scientist doesn't stop being a scientist, nor anybody stop being anything. You find how to do the things to yourself, which allow you to find truth where you are at that moment (Ram Dass, 1975; p. 2).

The purpose of truth is to sharpen awareness by focusing on the senses, emotions, thoughts and perceptions. People are not their different parts, but the sum total of all of them, and by being more aware of the whole, they can become more responsible and integrated. Thus, the self cannot be examined without looking at the context; it is best discovered by looking at the individual, the group, the environment in which the group lives and the relationship these people have with the cosmos. This is the essence of emotional transformation or to "nurture those aspects that permit a person to dis-identify from the restrictions of the personality and to recognize his or her identity with the total self" (Leuger cited in Sheikh & Sheikh, 1989; p. 228). Furthermore, if people are to live an effective life, they must reduce "destructive emotions such as fear and anger" (Walsh & Vaughan, 1993; p. 4). In other words, it is the enhancement of positive emotions and the development of optimism that help improve one's life. However, possessing humane qualities such as being accepting, compassionate, forgiving, and generous, just to name a few, is not enough. One has to learn to transform one's being to reflect the equilibrium of water and foster a calm demeanor. In other words, one must be open to experiencing things as they are and not what is desirable for them to be. Rumi's (1898) eloquent poem describes this attitude as:

> Keep walking, though there's no place to get to
>
> Don't try to see through the distances.
>
> That's not for human beings. Move within,
>
> But don't move the way fear makes you move (p. 278)

Along with this equanimity, individuals should learn not to put themselves first and they must begin to "unattach" themselves from gross materialism; for only then can they strive to be more humane. Attachment is considered as the conditionings that keep the human spirit down and create petty emotional reactions. Unconsciously, people attach themselves to "things" without realizing that "holding on" is the cause of suffering (i.e., identification with external objects). Once this is accepted, then the potential that exists within everyone can be released. In essence, each human being is a miniature universe. And so practising generosity and forgiveness helps transform each person beyond their material existence. And along with this, there has to be an acceptance of responsibility and the recognition of their interconnectedness. One way to achieve this is building a great sense of awareness of that which is inside the self and outside the self.

ETHICAL TRAINING

The focus on ethical training arises from the observation that unethical behavior both stems from and reinforces destructive mental factors (e.g., greed, fear, anger). Ethical behavior undermines these and promotes factors of kindness, compassion and calmness. As transpersonal maturation occurs, ethical behavior is said to flow naturally from one's identification with all people and life. The simplest technique in a group is to advocate such behavior by the leader and members, to point out that it is both a group ground rule and a method of development for all, and to discuss when it does or does not occur. Ethical conduct in a group helps create a climate of trust, which enhances risk taking and sincere participation. All of this fosters the transpersonal group community itself and imbeds values and standards that enhance the participants' behavior in the surrounding community.

Initial ethical training for a group member involves turning his or her attention inward. In the Sufi tradition, this is considered part of the process of repentance, the first step on the path to integration. This is the recognition of one's lack of fulfilment in life; the observing of one's impulses, wishes and deeds; and the cleansing of oneself from injustice and animosities. To explore this, a counsellor might create situations in which clients see themselves and are shocked with insight into their true conditions, then would offer a variety of practices that move them along a specific line of development. For example, a counsellor changes the meeting time at the last minute. Perhaps clients would arrive complaining about the abrupt change and the lack of respect it offers them. The counsellor then explains that the change was intentional and describes the difference between seeking respect and seeking knowledge. The counsellor notes that when seeking respect, one often behaves in a manipulative way, acting pious or knowledgeable or with a sense of entitlement. This is a very different posture than that which is effective for seeking knowledge, a posture that demands humility and openness and an absence of manipulations. Real world changes in one's surrounding community would also produce such reactions in group members. A distinction could be made between personal impulsive reactions (i.e., apathy, anger) and deliberate transpersonal responses (i.e., attention, collaboration, secret generous acts). The point is that individuals can observe when they are seeking respect from others. If they are at the stage of ego strengthening, this is important. If at the stage of ego transcendence, this gets in the way.

Meditation and Re-focusing

Walsh and Vaughan (1993) used the term "attentional training" to describe one of the important elements of the Transpersonal approach. Attentional training is the process of cultivating or focusing one's mind on mind, keeping it from wandering. Meditation is often misunderstood in the West. It is often exaggerated as something that either has miraculous properties or as a means for withdrawal from life. But there are different kinds of meditation that have the properties of mystical experiences or the heightened skill of awareness. In some ways, forms of meditation are culturally derived. Yet, despite these cultural differences there is a philosophical similarity in the process that goes beyond culture and ends in similar experiences. For example, meditation takes different forms. In Sufism dancing in circles, called a dervish, is a form of meditation; in Yoga the constant repetition of a mantra is another form of meditation, while in Buddhism being attentive to one's breathing or contemplating the message in a koan (riddle) is meditation too. In all of these examples, the end result leads to emptiness or a dulling of one's self and an insight that is quite literally beyond the self. In Buddhism, it culminates in Nirvana or a union with the cosmic all. In Sufism and Christianity, this might be a mystical union with God. The idea is indescribable. Perhaps it is T.S. Elliot (1968) who said it best: "words strain, crack and sometimes break under the burden, under the tension slip, slide, perish, decay with imprecision, will not stay in place, will not stay in play" (p. 12).

Meditation is the process of developing an attitude that is controlled, but not controlled. What happens when someone meditates is an altering of his or her consciousness. In fact, the aim in developing concentration, just as in meditation, is to increase understanding, by realizing and perfecting one's own mind. Yet, paradoxically, meditation strives to release one from the domination of the intellect. According to Humphrey (1968), no person "should go further into meditation who has not found within…a faculty superior to the thinking mind" (p. 154). Thinking is important, but must be abandoned if enlightenment is to occur and truth is to be revealed. In the Sutra of Hui Neng, there is no difference between the enlightened and ignorant person, but what makes these two different is that one realizes it and the other one does not. Thus, one can become a new person by acting in a natural, mindful and skilful manner. According to Ma-tsu (Hoover, 1980):

> *Grasping of the truth is the function of everyday-mindedness. Everyday-mindedness is free from intentional action, free from concepts of right and wrong, taking and giving, the finite or the infinite…All our daily activities – walking standing, sitting, lying down – all response to situations, our dealings with circumstances as they arise (p. 77-78).*

The message in meditation is as old as humanity itself. The process of the meditation experience in the East and West is the openness of the soul or self to God or the divine. Depending on one's culture or perspective, this could be identified in different ways. For example, Saint Catherine of Genoa described it as: "Me as god nor do I recognize any other me except my god himself." While Jallal-Uddin Rumi described it as "the beloved is all in all, the lover merely veils him; the beloved is all that lives, the lover a dead thing" (Rumi, 1898, p. 27). What is inherent in these ideas is that there is an inner knowledge that exists in everyone. The inner knowledge can only be revealed when one achieves oneness with all things or the total illumination of the self with god. Yet knowledge is not the goal, but salvation. Thus, the Christian and Islamic mystics suggest that there is a deliverance from a separate self towards a unity with God. Freedom is the key, for:

> *only one who is ever free of desire can one apprehend its spiritual essence; he who is ever a slave to desire can see no more than its outer fringe…all things depend on it for life, and it rejects them not…it lives and nourishes all things…all things return to it (Happold, 1963, p. 152).*

Notice the themes of humility and love. It seems these elements are required to be receptive, along with a degree of mortification. It is denial of the self by eliminating all attachments, crav- See P. 13 ings, pleasures and self-interests. In other words, the divine within the self can only be gained by losing egocentric impulses and wishing, thinking and feeling. Chuang Tzu (Ramaswami, 1989) emphasizes that a person "without passions…does not permit good or evil to disturb his inward economy but rather falls in with what happens and does not add to the sum of his mortality" (p. 447). Thus, meditation is a process of hearing the music of the inner life, which is mystical and creative. The inner holds the knowledge of the cosmos, waiting to be revealed to us in an entirely new order. Our spiritual world, which is full of symbols, ideas and images, can lead us to enlightenment. The Buddhist mystical experience is correlated with the Christian, Islamic and Hindu path. In the Bhagavad-Gita (cited in Happold, 1963), Krishna said "Resign all your actions to me. Regard me, as your dearest loved one. Know me to be your only refuge. Be united always in heart and consciousness to me. United with me, you shall overcome all difficulties by my grace... for the Lord lives in the heart of every creature" (p. 158).

UNDERSTANDING MOTIVATION

see p. 43

In order to create a balanced self that is free from distractions and meditation, one must be motivated to be healthier. To do this, Walsh and Vaughan (1993) stressed: "desires gradually become less self-centered and more self-transcendent with less emphasis on getting and more on giving" (p. 5). But how does one free the self from self-centred urges? Social conditions do affect how one performs, thus getting beyond this phenomena may go against one's nature. In fact, this is a wide spread condition across the animal world. In an early experiment with cockroaches, researchers found that they went faster if there were other cockroaches present (Zajonc, Heingartner & Herman, 1969). This study compared cockroaches running with an audience of other cockroaches and without an audience down a runway away from a light. Among rats, sexual behavior occurs more often when other rats are present (Baron, Kerr & Miller, 1992). Social psychologists call it "social facilitation," which Forsyth (1999) defines as "improvement in task performance that occurs when people work in the presence of other people" (p. 269).

The social awareness theory is based on the idea of the heightened awareness one has in social situations. When others watch, the performers will become more self-conscious of their actions. In turn, they will become aware of the discrepancies between an ideal and their own performance. This causes them to do better or work harder. Mirrors are often used in physical training to increase personal awareness, thus producing better results. Social awareness can also cause *but* people to be impaired if they feel they are not doing as well as their goal and feel they cannot *⦿* come close to achieving the ideal; physically and psychologically, they withdraw from the task. Therefore, self-consciousness can improve performance, but more than likely, it decreases performance. But how does this translate to redirecting motivation and transcending the need to care about what others think? In Buddhism, this translates into decreasing one's desires as a means of achieving true happiness. Walsh and Vaughan (1993) stress, "the reduction of compulsive craving is...said to result in a corresponding reduction in intrapsychic conflict, a claim now supported by studies of advanced mediators" (p. 5).

GAINING WISDOM

If a person is psychologically secure, they are able to shift from a personal focus to a universal focus. This is what I believe is meant in spiritual practice when people talk about "losing one's ego". I believe that if people have a level of personal maturity and ego integration, they can make the shift from "life is happening to me" to "life is happening". It is a happy shift, a shift from an inside-out, "me-focused" view to a cosmic or universal overview (Boorstein, 1994, p. 101).

Walsh and Vaughan (1993) make a distinction between knowledge and wisdom by stating that the former is something anyone can gain, while the latter is a state of being. Wisdom, then, is a process of "growth" that occurs as one gains personal insight into the self and the environment. From a therapeutic perspective, Brazier (1995) declares that "each time the therapist dies, a part of the client's prison dies with him" (p. 215). The influence of others lessens as one becomes wise and becomes correspondingly more at one with the self and the world around. While one can become aware of the meaninglessness of objects and material things, there is much more to having wisdom. That is, one transcends the nature of suffering in which the intuitive self becomes more focused on the cosmos or the power beyond. What may seem solid is only an illusion and so through wisdom one is liberated from external forces that bind creativity, joy and spontaneity. Brazier (1995) goes on to say that "a deluded person is attracted, repulsed or confused by everything. An enlightened person is enlightened by everything" (p. 222). Walsh and Vaughan (1993) state that this liberating insight is known in many traditions "in the East as jnana (Hinduism), prjna (Buddhism), or ma'rifah (Islam), and in the West as gnosis or scientia sacra. And with this liberation the goal of the art of transcendence is realized" (p. 7).

PSYCHOTHERAPEUTIC TECHNIQUES

The challenge for practitioners is to practice what "they preach" or to embody what they share with their clients. The same vision they have for others is what should be developed inside oneself. According to Walsh (1993) "to share and communicate it where we can; use it to help the healing of our world; and to let it use us as willing servants for the awakening and welfare of all" (p. 136). Transpersonal practitioners differ from other therapists (i.e., behavior-cognitive and psychoanalytic) in that they use less verbal interactions and more action-oriented techniques (i.e., experiments and specific skills promoting action on the part of clients). In addition, transpersonal therapists utilize more meditation, guided imagery (more often with a spiritual focus), dream work and specific books to read than the other groups.

Transpersonal practitioners use a variety of techniques including desensitization, dream work, drama, guided imagery, meditation, nature connecting experiments and practices that develop ethical personal conduct. That is, using the seven elements – awareness, compassion, emotional transformation, ethical training, motivation, meditation, and wisdom – as dimensions for becoming a "whole person." The practitioners help clients work toward creating a sense of balance within and without, a greater sense of connectedness to the environment, and a desire to be a "good" person (spiritual enhancement). Thus, to practice in the transpersonal method, practitioners must have the:

- Openness to the transpersonal dimension, including the belief that contacts with transpersonal realms may be Transformative and of greatest healing potential;

- The ability to sense the presence of, or a report of, numinous experience, whether it should appear in a dream, a vision, a synchronous event or a contact with a spiritual teacher;

❧ Knowledge of a variety of spiritual paths; Activate pursuit of his/her own spiritual development;

❧ Degree of openness about him/herself, his/her own spiritual orientation and experience;

❧ A firm grounding in psychotherapy

CONCLUSION

The most exciting aspect of all the revolutionary developments in modern Western science – astronomy, physics, biology, medicine, information and systems theory, depth psychology, parapsychology and consciousness research – is the fact that the new image of the universe and of human nature increasingly resemble that of the ancient and Eastern spiritual philosophies, such as the different systems of yoga, the Tibetan Vajrayana, Kashmir Shaivism, Zen Buddhism, Taoism, Kabbalah, Christian mysticism or gnosticism. It seems that we are approaching a phenomenal synthesis of the ancient and the modern and a far-reaching integration of the great achievements of the East and the West that might have profound consequences for life on this planet (Grof, 1983, p. 33).

There are some things in life which are riddles that may never be answered or resolved. In the search to find meaning in life, it is easy to despair in this chaotic world. Camus (1947) referred to this as rolling the rock up the hill after it rolls down. In other words, life is a matter of "plugging away" as a way of transcending the "dark" forces that pull one down. If nothing else, the "plugging away" serves as a means for directing energy. However, when self-doubt occurs, and it is inevitable that it will, answers are not easy to find. Camus like many, dealt with this by romanticizing the absurdity of life, but of course, the tragedy for Camus was that the absurdity of it all was too much and he drowned himself in the River Seine one rainy evening. The goal of the transpersonal approach is help others see the impasse as a challenge and refocus one's energy away from selfishness and channel one's energy towards selflessness. Life provides each person with the opportunity to be aware, compassionate and wise. Henri-Frédéric Amiel (2001), the Swiss philosopher and poet, said that "it is by teaching that we teach ourselves, by relating that we observe, by affirming that we examine, by showing that we look, by writing that we think, by pumping that we draw water into the well."

It is not surprising that nature is not only used as a metaphor in Transpersonal psychology, but also as mechanism for transcendence. But, what is it in nature that is such a mystery, because it is not perfect; it is not symmetrical? Nature is something that can never be defined like the ridges of the mountains we have seen at various places in our lives. And if one contemplates the shape and beauty of the mountains, it is impossible to know exactly what it is about the mountains that are so inspiring. And not surprisingly, this can bring similar sensations about the way we feel for someone we love, because they always escape exact definitions. Yet when we let go of the definitions, of the attempt to try and pin down friendship, love and nature, they flow. When we try to define life in our mind, so that we understand and feel in complete control of it, we only get confused. What happens is that we go into our head, because we base our thoughts on the idea that we are different from it. When that happens, we have limited friendship, love, nature and ultimately, ourselves. Perhaps that is an indication that we are trying to master our lives. Yet, when we let go, life has about it a sense of flowing, like water. So as I close my eyes and see the reflection of the water, I stop thinking, analyzing and just accept what is there. It was the attraction of the river that provided wisdom and peace for Siddhartha; and as people move towards one polarity and back again, they must remember that there is no guarantee that there will be no pain in life or in relationships. People will experience pleasure, but also pain. And like water, they always go away, but they always come back. We need to remember that going away and coming back are two sides of the same thing.

CHAPTER ONE
FIRST ENCOUNTER

"When I discover that I am accepted and loved as a person, with my strengths and weaknesses, when I discover that I carry within myself a secret, the secret of my uniqueness, then I can begin to open up to others and respect their secret" (Vanier, 1998; p. 83).

This idea of Jean Vanier (1998) about being open, natural and in essence whole, accepting strengths and weakness, is a good one. For not only does it imply that all parts of the self are what make one unique, but it also has implications for the group. It implies that even the "weakest" in the group is what makes the group unique. And that should be the goal in working with groups regardless of the task – accepting all and everything. It is not easy for people to be accepting of weaknesses, yet that is the way individuals, groups and life are. In the transpersonal group the whole person needs to be engaged. To be expressive means to utilize all of our modes – emotionally, intellectually, socially and spiritually. In essence, it means operating in a holistic manner from the very first encounter. What happens in these first few moments of meeting? For McClintock (1999) there is a making contact ritual: "As I greet them, I comment on something I see and like about them…it is my way of telling them I see you and welcome you" (p. 48). This first impression has a profound effect on how we interact with others. This first encounter of the group reveals a great deal of who people are. This is particularly true for our defense patterns. Therefore, this first meeting is of particular importance.

FIRST IMPRESSIONS

In the movie *K-Pax* (2002), the character that Kevin Spacey played appeared to be insane when first encountered by the police. Despite evidence that he in fact might be a visitor from outer space, the hospital authorities kept him locked up and pathologized his behavior. The first impression was the lasting impression. Why? Was he from K-Pax or was he a traumatized man who lost himself in his delusions? It is not important to know, because this was what the filmmakers wanted us to figure out. When meeting others for the first time, considerable information can be gathered about them. But how valuable is this information in terms of accuracy? In part, most of the information is superficial, for people are more than just their surface. Many people try and categorize others as types (e.g., friendly or hostile, flexible or structured, etc.). Most groups in society are not homogeneous, but a "mixed bag" of different types of personalities, body shapes, variety of communication styles and cultural backgrounds, just to name a few. However, expressions have different meanings in different cultures. Generally, the following factors which influence first impressions are:

1. Physical appearance: type of dress, the hair, teeth, weight, height, level of attractiveness;
2. Facial expression: expressions can convey confidence, fear, happiness or sadness, however, context is important too (e.g., a smiling face looking at a sad face can be viewed as gloating);

3. Gestures: either positive (e.g., open body position, smiling, etc.) or negative (e.g., frowning, yawning, lack of eye contact);

4. Voice: the content, tone (e.g., loud or soft) and speech patterns (direct or circular).

In first encounters people will respond according to their experiences. This is because they create a cognitive construct that is based on social group experience. For example, people will see others in terms of the perceived role they think a person has that may be similar to someone they know (e.g., teacher, parent, occupational role, etc.). Thus, based on the category, people expect that this person will behave in a certain way (e.g., a person dressed as a police officer will be viewed as someone with power and strength). Sometimes this first impression is "right from the start," but frequently it is not. So in the end, most often we will have to gather more information about the person and spend time interacting before knowing the person. After all, each person is unique and always will be.

When meeting for the first time, most people are a little nervous, although most people try not to show outward manifestations of their discomfort. Everyone tries to look confident, natural and relaxed. Even after all these years of facilitating groups, I too am a little nervous. I usually feel my nervousness in a queasiness of my stomach, dryness in my throat, a hesitant manner of speaking and a redness of my face. After such a long time I am still coping with my shyness. Despite the "cool" expressions, I do see some signs of discomfort (e.g., the furtive glances around the room, the awkward physical gestures and the frozen smiles). Many people have their arms and legs crossed as if for protection. Perhaps it is just comfort, but maybe that is an aspect of what protection is all about. Why is coming into a new group a scary situation for most people?

Most people entering a group will try to make eye contact with another person, but an effective group facilitator will try to make contact with every person in the group, if only for a fraction of a second. Many avoid eye contact during a first meeting, while some look back in curiosity. One of my first impressions about people is that if someone avoids eye contact, I wonder, will he or she not want to be in the same group with me? However, this is a superficial impression and I am often pleasantly surprised at the inaccuracy of this assumption. I have often wondered what goes through everyone's mind during this initial meeting of the group. Perhaps some are wondering what they are doing here. To others, the new situation may seem like groups they have been in before. There may be an excitement of getting to know other people more deeply. Whatever the reason, according to Napier and Gershenfeld (1999) "when individuals join a group, they change; they are no longer the same people they were before becoming group members" (p. 5). So, each time people enter a group their behaviors will differ from those behaviors they express outside the new group. And the most common emotion is one of anxiety; a feeling of doubt about how they will be perceived by others in the group. In most cases, this feeling is a natural response to meeting "strangers" or being in new situations that are unfamiliar and thus pose a certain "danger."

In the first encounter of a group that is process oriented, most people are expecting that the experience will be very different from any group they have been involved in. Goals and rules for interacting will have to be formulated and decided upon by the group members. They know that in most cases, the process will be experimental and that the facilitator will stress the affective rather than the cognitive. They probably feel the double bind of wanting to share and being open, but do not want to reveal too much of themselves. Perhaps they wonder how much they can trust others in the group. Carl Rogers (1973) said that if group members wish "to remain on the sidelines psychologically they have my implicit permission to do so (p. 9)." Thus, people have total control over what activities they would like to participate in.

It is human nature for everyone to want to be respected and perceived in a positive manner. This is understandable, for there is nothing more important for people than a sense of dignity – dignity to self-respect and respect for others. If one takes away people's dignity, one destroys their sense of self worth. Even for the most contained person, a group experience is going to be risky. None of the people have entered the group because they have to, but most have entered because they have a desire to become more knowledgeable about group dynamics and more effective communicators. Marshall McLuhan's often quoted maxim, "The medium is the message" is a very appropriate adage when applied to how people respond in group situations, regardless of the setting. It is the consequence of the message that matters more than the contours of the message. This is particularly relevant in communicating emotional material, because there is so little definition in what this may mean. While many of the people have an important and relevant message they want to communicate to others in the groups they work with, their medium of communication is sometimes poor; thus, their message is either not communicated or mis-communicated. So, for most people there is a feeling of obligation to explore in greater depth their means of communication. Some people are more committed to the process and more willing to take risks than others. Like many things, commitment and risk are on a continuum. It seems that commitment or risk to one person often means something different to another person. In the end, it is the group members' decision of what to risk and what not to risk. The hope of the facilitator is to embody in actions, and in the group, the Indian prayer: "The great spirit grant that I may not criticize my neighbor until I have walked in his moccasins."

In most educational endeavors, disciplines are explored using the didactic approach, because it has shown itself to be the most efficient method of communicating information; however, it is an inefficient and ineffectual method for helping people learn about themselves. Why is this? People learn best by being actively involved in the learning process, while the didactic approach puts people in a passive situation. The facilitation has all the answers, but in a group devoted to process it is reversed, for the group members have all the answers. The group simply offers the structure where people can involve themselves in self-exploration and learning about group dynamics. The number and variety of methods in actively involving people in this process is the focus that this book utilizes.

DEFINITION OF GROUPS

Groups with a process focus have become increasingly popular for a wide body of people who have needs ranging from business to education to self-help. This is not surprising, since very few people function outside groups. Therefore, learning more about groups should be an important aspect of everyone's training. The research on group processes has been extensive and enduring since the early research done by Allport (1959) on social facilitation. There is a variety of differing definitions, but Forsyth (1999) has one of the broadest definitions. A group is "two or more interdependent individuals who influence one another through social interactions" (p. 5). In other words, the size, conditions or situation that the individuals are in is irrelevant. What matters is that these individuals act interdependently. And in this day of global communication, the members of the group do not even have to be face to face. They just have to be aware of the others in the group and know they have to work together to achieve mutual goals.

Operationally, groups are characterized by pressures of uniformity, power and influence, leadership and performance in group activities, motivational processes, and structural changes. There are, of course, different types of groups with differing objectives that put the pressure on different aspects of the group (e.g., self-help, encounter, T-groups, work groups, personal growth groups, group therapy, etc.). Yet, I believe that the group process needs to go beyond merely learning about the group process to the transcending of societal roles. The transpersonal approach, which incorporates many of the humanistic group processes, is described as "an attempt to create conditions for learning about what it means to be a member of a group (whether that group be a personal growth group, a work team, a family, or a community), so that the polarities and dilemmas of separateness and unity can be experienced in the context of personal growth" (Kepner, 1980; p. 13). In psychology and counselling in general, there are four operational theoretical perspectives: Psychoanalytic (Freud, Jung, Adler), Behavioral (Skinner, Ellis), Humanistic (Perls, Rogers, Maslow) and Transpersonal (Wilber, Ram Dass). In many ways, the transpersonal approach incorporates many aspects of all the other approaches (mind, body, emotions), but it goes further by embracing the spiritual dimension. In that sense, the transpersonal approach "is not seen as successful adjustments to the prevailing culture, but rather the daily experience of that state called liberation, enlightenment, individuation, certainty or gnosis according to various traditions" (Fadiman, in Mahoney, 1989; p. 227).

BELIEVING IS SEEING

Napier and Gershenfeld (1999) emphasize that "in a group, individual stereotypes apparently feed on themselves, and we rapidly turn for support to those we believe share our own views" (p. 12). This phenomenon seems to occur as a natural habit of people who are always trying to make sense of things and people around them (e.g., "Who will be my allies in this group?"). It seems to be a kind of protection that creates "us" and "them." For example, people look at some older people who walk in a stiff manner and conclude that all older people are slow and not active. This also occurs with their views of different ethnic and racial types (e.g., black people are more rhythmic or Japanese are only adaptive). The figure-ground concept in Gestalt therapy offers an interesting way for examining the dynamics of relationships in groups (Perls, Hefferline & Goodman, l951). When one object is in focus, everything around it recedes to form the background, but what is perceived depends on the needs of the viewer. For example, when one looks at a friend in a crowd of people, the friend stands out because the friend is familiar. When others look at the same crowd of people, they will not focus on the friend who is in the background for them. What is important for some is not important for others. Another factor is the value people bring to what they observe. For example, one person may think that a particular person is attractive, while another person will think the exact opposite. More graphically, the illusions in Figures 1.1, 1.2 and 1.3 demonstrate this. What can be seen? Different people may see different things.

< Figure 1.1

In Figure 1.1 some people may focus on the black, while others may focus on the white. Depending on a person's focus, a different object appears. Some people may see a musician, while others may see a woman.

Figure 1.2 >

In Figure 1.2, depending on a person's perception, the viewer could be looking at either one person or two people.

< Figure 1.3

In Figure 1.3, depending what you focus on, the view could be looking at two different types of animals.

At first, it is difficult to see both objects simultaneously, but in time, the embedded objects become more easily recognizable. Does this mean that the more an object or point of view is explored the easier it is to see diversity? Perception is relative. Perceptions are often colored by their context, if a person is to understand how others see things, one needs to look at the object in context from their perspective. In the same way, one can only understand more about one's behavior by examining it in the total pattern of that person's being. In a group, some people will become the focus (figure), while others will be in the background (ground). Still, if people are to make sense of the group experience, each must be open to others in the group. The crux of the matter is being open without expending energy and worrying about the expectations of others as a more secure way of being.

GROUP MEMBER GOALS

"If you don't know where you're going you will probably end up somewhere else," said the Rabbit to Alice in Lewis Carroll's *Alice in Wonderland* (1946; p. 175). So one has to wonder, where does each group member want to go with the group? The place to start is by examining personal goals for being involved in the group experience. The motivation for entering a group is as varied as people, but primarily people are involved in the process to "grow". What makes the group such a powerful milieu is that it offers the opportunity to learn about the dynamics of community living. Therefore, there are two levels of goals to consider. On the first level are those goals around learning about the dynamics of group interaction, while on the second level are those goals for personal development.

As a member of the group, people might consider some of the following personal goals to:

1. Increase awareness of self in relationship to the group;
2. Learn how to ask others clearly and directly for what they need or desire;
3. Learn how to learn;
4. Increase skills of intervention in groups;
5. Increase understanding of how groups form, grow and develop;
6. Learn how to create a community or group based on trust;
7. Learn how to challenge others to go beyond their boundaries of safety;
8. Learn how to use resources within the group rather than relying on the facilitator.

To enhance an individual's perspective, group members might consider some of the following personal goals by:

1. Identifying personal polarities or different parts of self (e.g., child side and adult side);
2. Integrating personal polarities so they work as a team rather than against each other;
3. Achieving their desired level of contact with others;
4. Gaining support from self rather than getting it from others;
5. Being immediate and in the "here and now" as a choice;
6. Developing a complete awareness using the five senses;
7. Being able to identify the difference between feelings, thoughts, fantasies and actions;
8. Knowing and implementing personal boundaries;
9. Being open to insights and actualizing them;

10. Having a willingness to experiment with risk and with change.

MODELS OF HUMAN NATURE

"Tell me what you find in human nature and I will tell you what sort of man [or woman] you are" (Maslow, 1964). The way that people will develop relationships in groups is dependent on what assumptions they have about what people are like. These assumptions form the foundation of how people will relate to others. Some people interact with others in a suspicious manner, because they assume people are not "good," while others operate in an open way because they assume people are "trustworthy." In observing people in groups I have noticed that those who risk and share more assume that no one will hurt them and they will be accepted. Perhaps the first question group members should ask themselves is: "What are my assumptions about human nature?"

Since the beginning of time philosophers have asked, "What is the true nature of people?" Hipocrates (430-377 B.C.) thought peoples' personalities were determined by the balance between four "humors": blood (courage), phlegm (listlessness), black bile (depression) and yellow bile (irritability). Since the beginning of the twentieth century there has been a shift from seeing the development of human nature, from the physical to the psychological. There has been extensive research done in this area, but no one has been more influential than Allport (1959). One of his contributions has been his work in developing a values topology. In his classic, *Study of Values*, he developed his theory that interest, values and dispositions form distinct personality types.

Allport developed a framework in which human traits could be classified according to three psychological models. In addition, a fourth model has emerged since the Second World War called Existentialism. Since the 1960s another movement influenced by Eastern thought has emerged, called Transpersonal. An overview of the four models and the transpersonal, as they relate to groups, is as follows:

Humans are reactive: People react to the group in accordance to the stimuli present (e.g., someone says or does something and another person reacts to it). Group members respond to the explicit or implicit reward and punishment system of the group. For example, certain kinds of behaviors can be reinforced through praise or criticism. People develop strategies for getting along and living life based on experience (e.g., if a particular behavior gets the desired results, then they repeat the behavior). In essence, people learn to respond to different stimuli according to their everyday experiences. There is little reference paid to unconscious thought or defense mechanisms. According to Skinner (1976), the major theorist of this view, behavior is strongly determined by the environment and the social system people come from (e.g., people are the product of their environment). This approach follows the school of Behavioral thought. *Behaviorism*

Humans are reactive in depth: People react to the group according to how they have been influenced by their unconscious (e.g., no matter what people do, the reaction is based on an unconscious belief). While people react to the environment, it is their drives, will, instincts and other aspects of their personality that determine their behavior. According to Freud, who was one of the most influential thinkers in psychology, few people emerge from childhood un-scarred, which is "the source of most mental, physical, and social suffering later on in life" (Poduska, 1980; p. 42). Therefore, if people are to remain healthy psychologically they should have a clearer image of themselves, which can only come about by exploring feelings and past experiences. Particular emphasis is placed on early experiences with parents and underlying sexual tensions. Essentially, behavior is just a surface manifestation of the inner workings of the mind. For people to understand themselves they must explore the symbolic meaning of their behavior. Freud put forth the notion of the pleasure principle or the meaning that people will seek pleasure and avoid pain. This approach follows the school of Psychodynamic and Jungian thought.

Psychodynamic

Humans are beings in process of becoming: People have a choice to react to situations either in a positive or negative manner. Basically, in this view there is a belief that people are interested in self-growth. People "have an active will towards health, and impulse toward growth, or towards the actualization of human potentialities" (Maslow, 1971, p. 25). People become dysfunctional when they are blocked from becoming who they are. For example, everyone in the group is in the process of becoming more open and nurturing. When angry or joyful feelings are aired, it is all in the process of growth. Rogers (1973), one of the major theorists of this view, stressed that the self has to be considered as a whole. However, many people develop an ideal self or the self they would like to be. The greater the discrepancy between the real and ideal self, the more dysfunctional people will behave. Despite people's development, everyone possesses a self-actualizing tendency. This approach follows the school of humanistic and Client-Centered thought.

humanistic

Humans are what they are doing: In a fashion similar to Gertrude Stein's description of "a rose is a rose is a rose," people are what they perceive themselves to be (e.g., "I am what I am"). They are not destined to be a certain way, but possess the will to create, maintain and change their being. It "is the contact between the person and the environment that defines the person's identity" (Van de Riet, Korb & Gorrell, 1980; p. 12). This contact is called the ego boundary, which determines what is experienced as "me" in my world. People are a part of their environment, but they also possess a totally unique self that is self-determined. According to Frankl (1963), a major theorist of this view, what motivates people is a desire to find meaning in life. For example, people are a result of the relationship between themselves and the group. Neither determines the other, nor can each be considered without the other. This approach follows the Logotherapy and Gestalt school of thought.

Gestalt

Humans are more than what they are and what they are doing: Humans have the potential to be more than what they have inherited or are. In fact, their growth as beings is limitless and higher states of consciousness can be reach if they can only let go of the attachments that limit them. For example, obtaining material goods is a form of attachment that limits people, causing a great deal of suffering, and preventing them from achieving higher spiritual

Transpersonal

needs. Other forms of attachment might be the obtaining of power, recognition or any activity that focuses exclusively on the self. The goal of personhood is living in harmony and balance within the self, with the living community and with the environment. In that sense, transcending "all identification is believed to lead to the experience of a variety of states of consciousness in which perception is described as non-dualistic; the individual feels himself or herself to be connected with, one with, or actually to be the whole universe" (Walsh & Vaughan, 1993; p. 228).

The transpersonal model will be explored in greater depth later in subsequent chapters. It should be remembered that Allport's framework and the existential model are not based on any scientific data. However, these models do provide a simple way of categorizing how people approach relationships. As people explore human behavior and consider their view of human nature, they need to keep in mind the words of the British playwright Oscar Wilde: "the only thing that one really knows about human nature is that it changes and change is the one quality we can predict."

BENEFITS AND RISKS OF LEARNING IN GROUPS

What people can depend on as they embark on the group experience is that there will be many opportunities for learning, and equally as many opportunities to challenge the numerous things taken for granted in human relations. Perhaps this is because the group situation provides the ideal atmosphere for learning about the process of change and growth. Over a period of time as the group goes through changes, people can observe how their fears about the unknown are reduced. They may notice that the personal styles of others that brought on anxiety at the beginning of the group are no longer a factor in determining how they behave. As a result, their awareness of themselves and others will be greatly enhanced. Perhaps they will learn how to respond in situations where there is a high degree of emotion. Essentially, the group is a laboratory where group members can add to their repertoire of communication skills.

Self-exploration is a common thread throughout the life of the group. As a result there will be uncertainty, but on the other hand all explorers experience uncertainty as a companion to discovery. In the group, members will be asked to share concerns and insights as well as provide feedback to others. It does not mean that group members have to reveal everything. The facilitator should monitor what is shared and the participants may monitor what they share; thus, while risks are encouraged, people must be responsible for themselves. If group members are continually aware of what they gain or lose when they share "deep secrets," they will be more responsible. Will this increase self-exploration? (Perhaps yes and perhaps no.) Egan (1986) suggests that emotional disturbance loses its power when it loses its privacy. However, most facilitators are more interested in shared feelings rather than shared information or secrets. Secrets are just that, secrets. Some things are best kept secret.

Unlike many group learning situations, groups focusing on process create a much more supportive atmosphere. After groups have disbanded, sometimes friendships and mutual support remain and develop into much deeper relationships. This should not be a surprise, for with the increased sharing, there is increased understanding and an awareness of similarities between others. This invariably offers people the opportunity to expand their support network. There are risks involved in participating in an intensive group situation. One of the major risks for people in groups is the possibility of "psychological harm" (i.e., buried feelings from the past may be brought into the open). Again, people have to take personal responsibility for what they share. There should never be any doubt that members can choose to do something or not to do something in the group. However, even in the most supportive groups, there can be "casualties" or people who feel alienated from the group and the process. In addition, some people may have so much on "their plate," in the form of stress at work or home that involvement in the group is distracting. Leiberman, Yalom and Miles (1973) suggest that expectations about what will occur in the group and the type of leadership style are responsible for producing most "casualties." This happens when members are seeking "the answers" and facilitators feel they have the answers. Also, it is possible that some members will be rejected by the group because they do not meet the group's expectations or for some other reason. To rectify this, people need to have realistic expectations and group norms should support the diversity among the group members. Simply stated, all group members are entitled to their idiosyncrasies.

MISCONCEPTIONS ABOUT THE "GROWTH" GROUP EXPERIENCE

As with many new modes of learning, there have been many misconceptions about what will happen in the group. These misconceptions have generated unnecessary fear and anxiety, thus when people enter a group experience, they need to reflect on their assumptions about the group process (Corey, 1985). Perhaps if the participants are open and positive, the experience will be personally useful, leading to growth. Some common misconceptions are:

Groups are anti-intellectual: It is true that there is more emphasis on feelings, but there is value to the intellect that should not be overlooked. To understand the process of change in groups, the mind always has to be open. Too much thinking produces distance, but so does too much emphasis on emotion. In fact, the key is balance.

Groups foster impulsiveness: Group members are asked to be spontaneous and open in sharing, and sometimes impulsive actions do take place. Some will have value, while others will not. Some actions will be regretted, but the group can act as a sounding board for untried actions or behaviors. Impulsiveness is not a responsible behavior and group members are asked to be more responsible, not less.

A group is a place to get emotionally high: There will be moments of high emotional tension, but there will also be moments of pure "boredom" and "tedium." A group experience is like life, in which there are always highs and lows. In the end, the group is what the members make of it.

A group is for "sick people" only: While the direction of the group is towards self exploration, the group experience is for those who are not psychologically damaged. The group experience is not for therapy, although there are therapeutic aspects of the group, but most importantly the group processes is for helping people learn about group dynamics and personal development. The group offers an arena for people to learn more about self in relationship to groups.

Groups are a "cure-all": Groups can be very beneficial, but they will not satisfy all the group members' problems. In fact, the truth is that there may never be a "cure-all" or final answer in any question. Groups are one of many approaches that have been successful in helping people grow.

Groups primarily foster closeness: As a result of the group experience many members feel closer to each other than they ever have, yet the opposite can occur. A group is like any other relationship, in which there is intimacy and distance. Intimacy is not a primary goal, but just a by-product of the experience.

Groups are destructive: The group, like some relationships, may be destructive, but is what the members make it. To view it as destructive is difficult if it builds relationships on respect and support. The group does foster change, which can sometimes be painful and sometimes be exhilarating. In addition, its heightening of unresolved feelings may encourage members to re-evaluate some relationships. If, however, members act in a responsible manner, any experience of pain will occur in the most supportive possible atmosphere.

Group experience leads to a "Me" mentality: It is true that the group encourages members to be self-explorative and, through this process, some members will be selfish. However, selfishness usually is a behavior that goes against the group norm. Group members who display selfishness soon learn that it is not tolerated, so in fact group members learn the opposite (e.g., to be a better listeners and more open to others).

Groups are artificial and unreal: Group behavior does reflect how people interact with others in other situations and groups. In a sense, the group reflects life in a microcosm. While members can be different from group to group, there will be consistent patterns. These similar patterns are the source that members can learn from.

Groups make people feel miserable: Many members do feel unhappy or frustrated – yes, even miserable – but there are also periods of pleasure. The point of the group experience is to learn about self and groups, so the process creates at times feelings of pure pleasure and misery. The group is an opportunity to learn the complete spectrum of life's emotions.

INDIVIDUAL PERCEPTION AND GAMES IN GROUPS

According to Eric Berne (1966), people become cultured and enter groups based on biological needs, psychological needs, drives, patterns of striving, past experiences and the desire to experience. From the time of infancy to adulthood, people have a strong desire to belong and be a part of a group. In fact, mental health is defined in terms of social participation. The more people participate in groups, the more socially positive they are regarded. You can probably recall that those who were most popular in school were members of many clubs. While being socially active is positively regarded, the most important mechanism for evaluating personal growth is the quality of the transactions (e.g., personal scripts).

In the development of transactional analysis, Berne (1966) proposed a simple approach to viewing how people develop a position for living life. The first three types are unconsciously made during childhood, while the fourth type is developed as a conscious choice:

"I'm not OK, you're not OK": People are negative, give up, stop hoping and growing psychologically (e.g., "I'm not worth much and neither is anybody else in this group"). In the group, someone with this life script might view other group members in a suspicious or fearful manner, while at the same time feel insecure and anxious about themselves.

"I'm OK, you're not OK": People see all others in a negative and suspicious way and blame others for any difficulties or problems they have (e.g., "I might as well get what I want from others any way I can, because they will never give me what I ask for"). In the group, someone with this life script might view other group members in a suspicious or fearful manner, while at the same time feel superior and confident about themselves.

"I'm not OK, you're OK": People work to get strokes, because that is the only way of overcoming their inferiority. People will develop "games" or strategies for gaining strokes from others (e.g., "The only way I can be any good or be accepted by others is to be competent"). In the group, someone with this life script might view other group members in a positive manner, while at the same time feeling weak and insecure about themselves.

"I'm OK, you're OK": People see themselves as having the capacity to be or do anything they choose. Life is not seen as "game playing" or a series of strategies based on strokes, but a series of opportunities to develop relationships based on mutuality (e.g., "I feel good about myself and many of the people in my life"). In the group, someone with this life script might view other group members in a positive manner, while at the same time feel good within themselves.

As people enter groups, they come with the biological need for stimulation, a psychological need for time structuring; a social need for belonging, affiliation and autonomy; a nostalgic need for transaction; and a tentative sense of expectations based on past experiences. According to Kepner (1980), "on an emotional level, these needs are experienced as issues around identity, power, and influence" (p. 16). How people involve themselves in groups follows a progression, which includes joining, involvement, engagement and separation. Perhaps all experiences in life follow this progression in one form or another. The group experience is an ideal environment for learning and growing compared to individual therapeutic experiences. The following are the important conclusions that reinforce the nature of the group experience (Corey & Corey, 1987; Johnson & Johnson, 1999; Napier & Gershenfeld, 1999; Rogers, 1973):

❀ Social involvement is a fundamental ingredient for survival both psychologically and biologically (no person is an island unto themselves…).

❀ People face two challenges in groups: first, to find a suitable method for structuring time and, secondly, to attain the highest possible satisfaction from the experience.

❀ People form an image about themselves in relationship to a group before actually entering the group (e.g., "I am a person who is open and accepting of others").

❀ Adjustment within groups is based on people's adaptability and flexibility.

❀ Participation in groups is based on the mental image of the group, social customs of the group, personal patterns of interaction (scripts) and long-term goals.

❀ People generally will not fully participate in a group until they feel comfortable with the role they want to play in the group. Their roles will be influenced by their communication styles, cultural background and life experience.

❀ There are well-defined phases of adjustment in the group's image that are unique.

Most group members want to be as objective as possible in their judgments, yet there are some aspects of human perception that are not as objective as is thought. One is the "halo effect." It is defined as "the power of an overall feeling about an individual to influence evaluations of the person's individual attributes" (Napier & Gershenfeld, 1999). This occurs when a person will allow someone to do something without censure, while not allowing it in another. For example, a group member viewed as attractive may not be criticized for habitual lateness by other members, because they may see the group as dull without her. While this may not seem fair, it is not so uncommon. So is everyday life.

Basically, there are four stages of adjustment in the group image. First, there are the tentative rituals of the group, how the group conducts itself. Second is how people develop a sense of adaptability based on past experiences. The third phase is the operational image for games, how people choose to participate in group interaction. The next is people's adjusted image for intimacy or how they wish to express their need for closeness to others. Finally, belonging occurs when people have met three conditions, which include eligibility, adjustment and acceptance from the group.

LEADERSHIP: AUTOCRATIC VERSUS DEMOCRATIC

In the leadership continuum, there are the extremely democratic and the extremely autocratic styles. The extremely democratic style can result in a blurring of the roles of facilitator and group members. While group members may feel positive about a facilitator who essentially joins the group, some goals may not be accomplished because of the low level of direction or control exercised by the facilitator. It does not necessarily follow that a low level of control means little is achieved, but in most cases that is what happens. At the other extreme, the autocratic style, with a high level of control, may allow the group to stay on schedule and accomplish many of the group goals, yet may ignore individual differences and are insensitive to some of the group members. This style of directing and leading may go against the spirit of active learning and may not reinforce positive self-esteem.

A moderate style will incorporate some aspects inherent in both the democratic and the autocratic styles. Control is sometimes at a low level and sometimes at a high level. At times the facilitator may consult or even persuade members of the group, but does not join in or give orders. This does not mean that the facilitator using the moderate style is above participating in activities as a group member, but it means that the facilitator takes on the responsibility not to step out of the leadership role entirely. Sometimes the schedule will be maintained, while at other times the facilitator will take time out to concentrate on process. Despite the number of years of experience working in groups, facilitators have to evaluate their effectiveness. Perhaps, they need to answer these questions on a continual basis:

- ❀ Why am I effective in one situation and not another?

- ❀ How involved should I be in the group?

- ❀ Does increased direction or control decrease the support that group members feel?

- ❀ Is there a point where I can challenge group members and still maintain their trust?

- ❀ When should I push and when should I pull back?

- ❀ Are there some areas or issues that I should explore more than others?

Essentially, facilitators need to have a high awareness of what the different dynamics are in each group, trust in group members' ability to take responsibility, be willing to take personal risks in actions by being a model, be authentic and not worry about being liked, loved, or admired, be honest and open with fears, needs, and fantasies, be approachable, be spontaneous, and willing to self-disclose personal information, history, feelings, thoughts, and fantasies. When people enter a group they are curious about the leadership style that will be used in the group. As a result, they will be cautious until they have a sense of what to expect from the facilitator. If the group is facilitated using a democratic style, the progress of the group is totally in the hands of the group members. The democratic facilitator puts stress on the establishment of a relationship with the group by sharing experiences, feelings, observations, perceptions, thoughts and therapeutic methods. In a sense, the facilitator becomes a "screen" for the group's fears, defenses and polarities. In the initial encounter, the facilitator comes into contact with the group on the outside of their boundary as shown in "A" of Figure 1.4. Some members of the group have already made contact, because of their mutual need for safety and belonging. Some individuals are either on the fringes or outside the group system. As a budding system, the group is beginning to establish norms and rituals. With each new member, the boundaries of the group system will be disturbed, as in "B." Democratic facilitators want to enter the group and individual systems because they want to see and feel what the group sees and feels. This process begins to focus their awareness of their boundaries and contact is now in process.

Examination of the extensive literature on what makes an effective facilitator clarifies only one thing for me: Effective leadership does not depend on a combination of leadership traits, but on the situation in which the facilitator is involved (Napier & Gershenfeld, 1999). Essentially, leadership is based on the goals of the group and the relationship of the facilitator to the group. It has less to do with active participation or any demonstration of the ability to carry out various tasks. Yet no matter what the variables, according to the Roman philosopher Tacitus, "reason and judgment are the most important qualities of a leader."

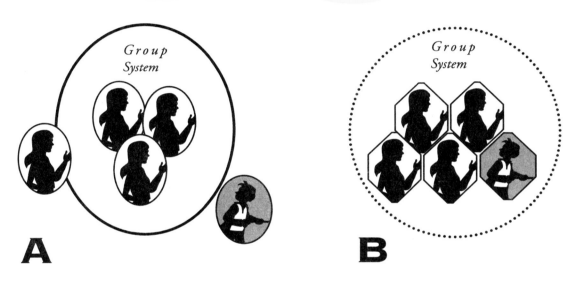

Figure 1.4: Group systems (grey-shaded figure is facilitator)

GROUPS IN OPERATION: MEMBERSHIP, NORMS, DECISION MAKING AND PROBLEM SOLVING

"Two heads are better than one" goes the maxim, which expresses the notion that groups can accomplish a great deal that individuals cannot. Groups permeate society, in which individuals work together to accomplish certain goals. Membership in a group is contingent on several factors. Once the group starts, roles and norms develop that essentially help the group to function. Most groups come together and have to solve problems or make decisions, including those groups that are formed for support and personal growth. Napier and Gershenfeld (1999) indicate that there are five types of membership in groups:

- Formal membership where members perceive themselves as belonging, having common goals and a shared group image;

- Marginal membership, where members appear to be in the group, but do not participate and are not influenced by what goes on in the group;

- Aspiring membership, where there is no formal acceptance, but where aspiring members act as if they were part of the group;

- Informal membership, where members appear to be involved in the organizational structure, but have no power in making decisions or solving problems;

- Non-voluntary membership where members are forced to be involved by some requirement and thus tend to be distrustful.

Norms are one of the most effective mechanisms for social control, because they provide individuals and groups with what is acceptable and what is not. Basically they are rules or patterns of behavior that have been established to regulate the group. They can help groups to accomplish objectives and keep everyone organized. On the down side, norms can keep people from doing anything differently and thereby foster a kind of "herd mentality" (e.g., blindly following rules of the group or society). For example, the group norm may be not to challenge the group facilitator, thus everyone avoids any direct attacks and censures any member who violates the norm. Another example is when members are self-disclosing, there is pressure for everyone to be self-disclosing. Some norms are explicit and some are implicit.

At some time or other, groups will have to make some decisions or solve problems. The cooperative spirit is usually what will foster a climate of positive group cohesion, which, along with the John Dewey's notion of "reflective thinking," facilitates problem solving. Groups emphasizing process use group discussion and problem solving as a means for increasing knowledge, responsibility, sharing and leadership. Decision-making and problem solving are different processes, although there is a close relationship. Decision-making involves solving problems, while problem solving requires decisions. Basic to all group interaction is the degree of power one person exerts over another. There are some complex aspects to why this occurs, but it does occur. Somehow and for some reason there is a conscious choice for one member to follow the other. Perhaps the decision is based on whether one person wants to influence or be influenced by the other. There are advantages and disadvantages for being a follower or a facilitator or both.

In groups, decision-making is more complex as the group consists of people with a variety of different personal and group goals. Together with these differing goals, group members bring a variety of values, beliefs and personal styles that make group decision extremely difficult. As a result, not all decisions in the group will be unanimous or arrived at with a consensus. When majority decisions are made, some may feel left out and not be totally committed to the idea or the group. On the other hand, it is impossible for a group to always reach total agreement and have the same level of commitment. In most of the diplomatic agreements the more general the

process,
maintenance·
oriented

actions, goal directed

wording of decisions, the more agreement there is among differing opinions. On the other hand, the more concrete the decision is, the greater the possibility for disagreement. This means that some group decisions may seem like they are "watered down" to determine a consensus or a decision that consists of elements of all opinions. For example, it is quite common for the group to be split into those who want to concentrate on task activities and others who desire to focus on relationships. In the end, the group usually decides to have a little of both elements.

When a group has fewer alternatives there seems to be a greater rigidity of opinions, the more alternatives there are, the greater the possibility of agreement or consensus. For example, if the choices for the group members are to spend more time in the large group for discussions on theory, or more time on small group activities, there will be a strong feeling on both sides about what is the better choice. However, when the group is presented with a third or fourth alternative, large group activities and small group discussions, the more likely the group will agree.

The manner in which problems are solved in the group can be from the haphazard to the highly systematic. Most experienced facilitators find that the most effective problem solving is when it is done in a systematic manner. The advantages are a saving of time and a thorough examination of alternatives. On the other hand, problems sometimes can be solved accidentally or through intuition. Some of the most successful and satisfying solutions occur at a "gut level" feeling. The problem solving may start out systematic, but somewhere along the way, intuition can lead to the most interesting solution. In essence, one could rely on intuition because one has a system, much like a map that allows one to wander off the "beaten track" when one find something "interesting." Most problem-solving paradigms involve the following steps: problem definition, goal formation, identification of obstacles, point of encounter, alternatives and solutions, and commitment for action (France & McDowell, 1983). Essentially problems can be put into a context of: goal – obstacle – encounter – choice. This allows the problem solver to examine a problem more closely. The problem solver will have to ask some or all of the following questions:

- ❀ What is the problem?

- ❀ What is the goal?

- ❀ Is there any unfinished business?

- ❀ Is there a pattern?

- ❀ Is there introjecting, projecting, deflecting, retroflecting and/or "confluencing" in this pattern?

- ❀ What are the functions and consequences of change?

- ❀ What are the obstacles that stand in the way of accomplishing the goal?

- ❀ What are the circumstances of time and place surrounding the obstacles?

- ❀ What are the different alternatives and solutions?

❧ When are alternatives going to be implemented?

❧ How will the alternatives be evaluated?

CONCLUSION

Jean Vanier (1998) suggested that people who are "excluded" in society have something to teach others about being human, because once we open ourselves to those who are different, then they "change things" within ourselves. Perhaps it is the ability to see things in a different "light" when we open our minds and hearts to those who are different, thus, letting go of the insecure feeling as we enter a group or situation that is different and new. Yet this process of belonging causes change is the most surprising way and affects how the group performs and works together. Consider the second law of thermodynamics "all things tend to go from an ordered state to a less ordered state. Disorder, or entropy, always increased. Always. In one way or another. If you tried to decrease the entropy of something, the energy you created by doing that, was increasing the entropy in another area" (Harstad, 1998; p. 135).

Therefore, as each problem is resolved in a group, there is the potential of increasing disorder or problems in another aspect of the group. In Donald Harstad's (1998) novel, *Eleven Days*, as the police try and catch a suspect, more disorder is created since the amount of time each officer spends doing this, their ability to concentrate decreases since they are getting less and less sleep. One of the best parts of the transpersonal approach to groups is that it accepts confusion and disorder as a means for exploring dynamic aspects of the group. In addition, the transpersonal approach to groups utilizes some of the generic principles of how a group develops and functions. What make it different are the assumptions of what motivates the group members and how the group as a whole can achieve greater awareness. According to Kitzler (1980):

> *Specifically, the group is a here-and-now phenomenon that has no existence except when it meets.... The group has a presentness and force of identity, scattered or astonishingly cohesive that is its form and motor. If we believe, as we must, that each person in the group will work to his best potential, and has within him all the information there is or that ever can be necessary to the group in its presentness, then all members at all times are participating and must have available to them modes for the expression of this information of themselves (p. 28).*

Choosing to join and participate in a group with a focus on process requires commitment because the primary focus is on relationships, conflict, risk taking, sharing, decision making and problem solving. These important ingredients are not easily categorized like tasks, which focus on logic and reasoning. While reasoning and thinking are important, in the words of seventeenth century philosopher Blaise Pascal, "thinking and reasoning must always yield to feelings" in the group process. As a result, it is difficult to remain aloof from the process. To be involved in the process does not mean that people have to give up themselves to be accepted. This will not happen if all group members take the primary responsibility for their actions.

As a facilitator I try to involve myself in the process by modeling openness, risking, experimenting, exploration and challenging. I am there to help group members get the most out of their learning experience. Just as they are responsible for their actions, they are also responsible for the direction that the group takes. However, anything that happens outside the group interests me as I expect the group to affect the behavior of members outside the group. I find that the more I concentrate on what happens inside the group, as opposed to bringing my problems into the group, the easier it is for me to be spontaneous and the greater is my learning about the group's process. This means being in the "here and now" with everyone in the group.

In the beginning the primary focus of the group is on formation of goals, norms and roles. There is a minimum of risk taking, with greater emphasis on awareness. There is a use of structured activities that will help people focus on personal exploration. For example, people will be asked to experiment with using "I" instead of "you" or "we." The rationale for this experiment is to have them speak only for themselves and not for others. This type of experiment makes their communication more immediate and specific. Later, activities will explore the way in which group members communicate with others placing a greater emphasis on the dynamics of the group. There will be confrontations and people will have the opportunity to role play and act out different situations. People will have the opportunity to explore their dreams by reliving them, by acting out fantasies, and by participating in psychodramas. I believe that confrontation cannot be avoided for in conflict there is increased energy that can bring about change.

William Conrad (1962), the English-Polish writer, said that reason is used to "justify the obscure desires that move our conduct, to justify impulses, passions, prejudices and follies, and also our fears" (p. 189). Conrad does have a point: thinking is just as valid as feelings. Each has its place. People's feelings, thoughts and actions form a gestalt, which are not any greater separately than they are as a whole. However, I have noticed feelings are most often controlled and play a greater role in defenses, fears and dreams. In my capacity as facilitator, I work at providing an opportunity for full expression of feelings, thoughts and behaviors. Much has been written about personal growth and how to achieve it. The goal of self-growth according to Rogers (1973) is to become self-actualized. I believe that there are behaviors leading to self-actualization that can make the group experience a more useful one. Self-actualization occurs when people:

❀ Experience fully, vividly and selflessly;

❀ Let go of poses and defenses;

❀ View their choices as processes that are ongoing;

❀ Allow their inner self to emerge through listening to their inner voice and acting at a "gut-level";

❀ Are authentic, spontaneous and honest;

❀ Take risks to be different;

❀ Work hard and utilize their common sense;

❀ Work towards peak experiences;

❀ Identify their defenses and then give them up;

❀ Find out who they are, what they are, what they like and dislike, and work toward a satisfactory sense of personal meaning in life.

As group members reflect on what it may mean to them to be involved in a group, I would like them to consider the wisdom of the French novelist and social critic, Anatole France, who said, "human beings no matter where they live, face the same basic needs: to eat, to work, to love, to play, and to get along with their fellow human beings, but to accomplish great things, they must not only dream, not only plan, but also believe."

ACTIVITIES FOR FOCUSING A GROUP

1. **Forced Choice**: Explain to the group that they will be given pair of words in which they will be asked to choose one. Their choices can be based on a variety of criteria, such as whether they identify with the word or like one better than the other or have had a good experience with it and so on. Once they make their choices, they must find two people, introduce themselves and share with them their rationale for their choice of words. For each set, allow 5 minutes for the sharing. Those listening are asked not to comment. To contrast their choices, ask those choosing (Ocean) to go to the left and those choosing (Mountain) to go to the right.

Ocean – Forest	Dog – Cat
Stick – Ball	Boat – Automobile
Deer – Bear	Blue – Red
Participator – Observer	Night – Day
Horse – Airplane	Mountain – Valley

2. **Fruit and Vegetables**: Ask the members of the group to pick a fruit or vegetable that they identify with. They may choose a fruit or vegetable for any reason. For example, they can make a choice based on a similarity with their name (e.g. "My name is Karen and I choose a carrot, because I like them . . . I feel rooted and it sounds similar to my name") or they can make a choice based on a meaning attributed to the choice (e.g. "My name is Paul and I choose a mango, because it has a mystical quality to it. . ."). Once everyone has made their choice, ask the group to sit in a circle and introduce themselves, their choice and the rationale for choosing it. At the end of the sharing ask if anyone could remember and repeat the names and choices of everyone in the group.

CHAPTER TWO
LIVING AND LEARNING IN A GROUP

By keeping the children at school ten months of the year for 12 years, the residential school system succeeded in separating the children from the Nlakapamux adults and the enculturation process which teach them to be Nlakapamux. This is separation from the cultural self, from parental love and care, from all that is cherished and valued by a hunting and gathering people. (Shirley Sterling, 1997; p. 11.)

The residential school system in effect made it very difficult for people to be themselves. To know yourself is truly a human gift and the tragedy of the residential school system took the gift away. Consider the wisdom of e. e. cummings (1953), who said: "to be nobody – but yourself – in a world that is doing its best, night and day, to make you everybody else – means to fight the hardest battle which any human being can fight, and never stop fighting" (p. 53). Affirming and being true to self is a constant task of personhood that must be kept in mind as people embark on the group experience. This follows the Transpersonal thinking on how people in groups need to take personal responsibility for their actions while at the same time being open to the laboratory approach to learning. As people experiment in the group with their range of feelings, thoughts and behaviors, perhaps each can keep in mind this thought on the value in the Transpersonal philosophy, which "lies in the insight that the whole determines the parts, which contrasts with the previous assumption that the whole is merely the total sum of its elements" (Perls, Hefferline & Goodman, 1951; p. xi). In other words, people need to keep one eye on the whole group, but keep another eye pointing inward.

Whenever people come together and form a group, regardless of its purpose, each member plays a certain role. The role they take may be multidimensional and dynamic or follow a set pattern that has worked for the person in the past. From a global perspective, all of the people in the group have a unique role and function, yet one of the determinants for how the group operates may be the general purpose of the group. One of the hit television shows of the summer of 2000 was the CBS show titled "Survivor." The premise of the show was to see who would be the last one to remain on the tropical island. One catch was that each week one person was eliminated by the group. The show created drama around each personality of the group of "average" people, which probably was one of the reasons why the show was popular. People could identify with the contestants. However, the premise was simple greed – stay on the island and win a million dollars. This Darwinesque idea makes for good television, but in a group where people must cooperate, work together, and learn to be better people, this cannot work. To create a good atmosphere where people are valued and each is supported to achieve their potential, the group members need to be respectful. And that means each person in the group operates dependently and independently within the group. By keeping their attitudes open and being accepting, they can learn from each of the encounters they have together. They can seek feedback from the other group members and provide support for everyone's ideas. By reflecting on one's behavior and with the feedback received from the other group members, each person has the opportunity to experiment and improve human relations skills.

One of the distinguishing characteristics of the transpersonal group is sense of compassion each feels for the other. By giving and helping each other, group members contribute to the "growth" of each member. The direction of the group either by the choice of task and maintenance roles they take is determined by the group through consensus. In the initial stages of the group, where group members are developing an identity and a sense of belonging to the group, there may be areas where people conflict with each other. What seems to bring everyone together is not just a common purpose for making the group productive, but a desire to be a part of something greater than themselves. What cements the group is trust, which is the basis of all relationships. Group members need to answer this question: Does full participation within the group depend on trust, before sharing or risking can occur? They could wait until others show themselves and then risk. On the other hand, if they do, then they may be waiting for quite a long time. Based on my experience with this, trust is established by taking action through risking and not by waiting for others to act. In other words, this is the main reason for being in the group. It is one of the few places people can experiment with new behaviors and explore things they cannot explore in everyday life. When I have done this, I have found that the group becomes a laboratory for greater exploration and, hence, discovery. Kopp (1972) expresses it this way "[people] may only get to keep that which [they are] willing to let go of...the cool water of the running stream may be scooped up with open, overflowing palms...it cannot be grasped up to the mouth with clenching fists, no matter what thirst motivates the desperate grab" (pp. 6-7).

INDIVIDUAL AND GROUP PERFORMANCE

When examining the relationship between the individual and the group, performance cannot be understood without examining the nature of the task. It seems obvious that if the task is a cooperative task, then everyone has a common reason to be together working on common goals; yet, this is not necessarily the case. Consider the early work of Shaw (1932) who gave a classroom problem, called "crossing the river," to find out if the individual or group was better at solving a problem. This type of problem solving is called a "eureka task." That is, once the problem is posed, the solution should be clear immediately, or soon after. According to Baron, Kerr and Miller (1992), only 3 out of 21 individuals solved the problem in Shaw's experiment compared to 3 out of 5 groups who solved the problem.

EUREKA TASK: "CROSSING THE RIVER". THREE MARRIED COUPLES WANT TO CROSS THE RIVER, THERE IS ONE BOAT, BUT IT HOLDS ONLY 3 PASSENGERS. THERE ARE SOME CONSTRAINTS REFLECTING THE CULTURE AT THE TIME: ONLY THE HUSBANDS CAN ROW AND NO WIFE WILL RIDE OR REMAIN WITH ANOTHER MAN UNLESS HER HUSBAND IS PRESENT. [THE ANSWER IS AT THE END OF THE CHAPTER.]

As the old adage suggest, two heads are better than one. But why is this? Shaw's conclusion was that members of the group could catch each other's errors. However, this does not mean the group is superior to individuals in every situation. In fact, while groups may be more effective, they take more time to solve a problem. Thus, individuals can be more efficient. One model for analyzing this phenomenon was developed by Steiner, whose central concept is that the potential productivity of a group is based on the resources of the members and the task demands [resources + task demands = productivity]. To make a group effective, it is important to know everyone's abilities and knowledge in order to for these to be used in the best possible way. Some tasks require specific knowledge or abilities (e.g., knowledge of the terrain or artistic ability). A classroom teacher can increase the reading speed of a class, but there will be a decrease in the level of comprehension. Therefore, a balance has to be struck in which reading is increased, but there is only a slight drop in comprehension. Steiner "suggests that if one knows a group's resources and the demands of its task, one can estimate the group's potential productivity" (Baron, Kerr & Miller, 1992; p. 34). Fundamentally, a group cannot operate without some kind of loss, thus there is some inefficiency. It takes time to process or talk about things, build relationships, coordinate activities and motivate group members whether they be in a class or some counselling group. And the more egalitarian the group, there more process loss there is (e.g., it takes more time to accomplish something). On the other hand, if everyone in the group is committed to the task, while it takes time to get everything ready, there is the potential of doing a better job with fewer errors.

In some groups, one's verbal abilities make that person more influential in the group. As in life, most group members are not totally equal. Thus, a group member's status will affect how the group accomplishes the task. On the other hand, if you have group members with less than adequate verbal skills, which may also translate to lower status, their verbal ability would not be considered as resources. The trick is to use one member's status to increase the group's efficiency. That is easier said than done. But Consider that the more egalitarian a group is, the less efficient it is. Baron, Kerr and Miller (1992) witness this, "if you have ever been in a meeting where you and everyone else politely waited while some dimwit carefully elaborated on an obviously silly proposal" (p. 37). It could be that the group is no better than the "weakest" member of the group, but on the other hand, with group members helping to solve a problem because errors can be caught, this so-called "weak link" phenomenon may be false. In the Eureka Task, only one person, with insight, can help the group solve the problem, thus making the group more effective. Another important factor is the level of motivation among group members. The higher the motivation, the greater the chances that the problem will be solved or resolved (e.g., if you'll only set your mind to finding a solution, you will, regardless of the resources). And, many group members, once in a group, are more motivated.

DO GROUP MEMBERS MOTIVATE EACH OTHER? See p.16

If you have ever been involved in certain sports, you will notice that the presence of an audience, particularly a cheering audience, causes the players to play even harder. Social conditions do affect the way in which people perform, enabling them to act differently in the presence of others. This is known as social facilitation. However, one's performance in certain tasks doesn't necessarily improve if there is an audience. Consider being asked a question in a classroom by the teacher and then not knowing the answer until the teacher asked someone else. You knew the answer beforehand, but once you were "put on the spot," the answer was gone. In other words, certain tasks or certain conditions, with an audience, deteriorate performance. What researchers found that if the task is simple (e.g., weightlifting or jogging), then performance always increases with an audience. If the task was complex (e.g., gymnastics or taking an oral test), then performance could deteriorate. Factors such as competition, evaluation, careful scrutiny or distraction affect performance. Three theories, the learned drive theory, the distraction/conflict theory and the self-awareness theory, attempt to explain why this happens.

The learned drive theory emphasizes reward and punishment to explain performance. This is based on the idea that people respond on the basis of other experiences of a similar nature. For example, if you have experienced negative evaluation from a particular person who will be attending the same meeting as you, there may be anxiety about being there. The anxiety will increase if you have to speak up, because you have learned that this person scrutinizes you in a negative way. This is sometimes called an anticipatory response. You anticipate what will happen and then respond as if it did happen. This can also work the other way. That is, if you have learned that by working harder on a task produces more compliments, then you will try harder, because you anticipate a reward, even if you do not get it. The distraction/conflict theory is based on the idea that by making a comparison with others you respond differently. It could be better or worse, since the comparison may make you try to achieve more. The competition raises the stakes so to speak. Conflict occurs when people have to make a choice as to what to do, which in turn produces stress. If the audience is a critical audience, then it is more possible that one's performance might be effected. As a result, the presence of others on performers' task causes:

> attentional temptation in which they are place in conflict regarding whether to attend to their species mates or to their ongoing task. In such cases, the performer wishes to pay attention to more that he or she can manage, and the resulting conflicts leads to drive/arousal and stress, which internally produces the social facilitation/social impairment effects (Baron, Kerr & Miller, 1992; pp. 22-23).

The social awareness theory is based on the idea of heightened self-awareness. When others watch, the performers will become more self-conscious of their actions. In turn, they will become aware of the discrepancies between an ideal and their own performance. This causes them to do better or work harder. I have mentioned that mirrors are often used in physical training to increase personal awareness, thus producing better results. Social awareness can also cause people to be impaired if they feel they are not doing as well as their goal and feel they cannot come close to achieving the ideal. Physically and psychologically, they withdraw from the task. Thus, self-consciousness can improve performance, but more than likely, it decreases it.

How Can the Group Become Productive?

All people want to ensure that the time they spend in the group is worthwhile, but they may all have a different criterion for gauging productivity. For some, it may be accomplishing a task in a certain way, while for others it may mean spending time with others. Hence, it is important at the beginning of any group to have a discussion on what people want to accomplish. In order for the group to be productive, there are four essential ingredients that can make the group more productive:

❧ A clear reason for being in the group;

❧ Commitment to the group process;

❧ Willingness to be involved in the process;

❧ A mechanism for making the process accountable.

While people will work cooperatively, they will also work independently of the group. This is not a paradox, because each group member has a different reason for being in the group, although all must be committed to the process. This is the only way of arriving at mutually acceptable group objectives. Thus, group members must ask themselves if they can fulfill themselves and utilize their talents as they work towards agreed-upon goals. In experiencing learning by doing, the primary goal of the group is to work at clarifying why it is they are working together, be it a business, a counselling group or any type of group. This means specifying goals that will take the group further. Without clarifying goals and a rationale for being together, the group will fold or end up being frustrated with the process. And what this requires is more than just working together for mutual benefit. Vanier (1998) said that:

> To work means to be energetic, strong, and active, cooperating with others. Communication means to be vulnerable and tender; it means opening one's heart and sharing one's hopes and pain, even all that is failure or brokenness. If my heart is broken, I can quickly feel crushed and fall into depression, unable to work. Or, I may refuse relationships and throw myself savagely into work. If my heart is fulfilled, it will shine through my work (p. 85-86).

Assumptions About Group Functioning

In order for the group to function in an open and mutually beneficial manner, group members must be committed to the process of working together to make decisions rather than making them in an isolated manner. They must ask themselves if their goals can be achieved working with the other group members. It is axiomatic that when group members work together to achieve, there is (Johnson & Johnson, 1999):

❧ A better match of group goals and individual goals, which results in greater acceptance and more motivation of group members;

❦ A clearer understanding of group activities directed at achieving group goals;

❦ An understanding of how group members can contribute to the required group action.

Often, as a group works together to achieve goals, a lot of time is spent on trying to define how group members view the nature of the group. This can have a positive effect as the group defines how the group will work. Some groups have specific tasks they want to accomplish, while others are only interested in the process. In working in a group using an expressive perspective, I have found that there are several assumptions about the nature of groups that need to be understood before the group can operate in the most effective and productive manner.

The first assumption is that only group members know how they want to relate in the group. A part of that is a sense of what they want others to think of them. Members must define and actualize their behavior in terms of what they want it to be and what they want out of the group. Group members need to keep in mind how they stop themselves from doing what they want and how they energize themselves to do what they want. While I may feel that I am confused about what I want, the answer cannot come from anyone else in the group. The great Indian political leader and warrior, Sitting Bull, said that, "each man [or woman] is good in [the Creator's] sight. It is not necessary for eagles to be crows or crows to be equal" (Hifler, 1992; p. 81).

The second assumption is that the atmosphere, goals and actions of the group can be anything that the group as a whole decides them to be. The group is essentially responsible for what occurs in the group. If something happens or does not happen, then the group is responsible. Some things may be given up, modified or even compromised, but such modifications can happen only as a conscious choice of the group. Perhaps people in the modern world have (Van de Riet, Korb & Gorrell, 1980) "through repression of experience…lost their images of themselves as responsible individuals…for when [they] divide the word responsibility into response-ability, suggesting the central importance of the ability to respond of each person for the individual personal experience" (p. 45).

The third assumption is that the maximum potential for effectiveness of the group is limited only by the limitations that group members put upon themselves. Limitations are self-produced and self-imposed. Group members may want to experiment with doing something different as a method of learning something new, but when potential is thwarted by self-imposed limits on actions, then group members have diminished themselves. According to Perls, Hefferline and Goodman (1951), it is "the process of experimental life-situations that are venturesome as explorations of the dark and disconnected, yet are at the same time safe, so that the deliberate attitude may be relaxed" (p. 166).

The fourth assumption is that group members are responsible for themselves only. To take responsibility for others is to diminish the effectiveness of others. This means to be true to the values, beliefs and experience of self. Sometimes in a group, members will take it upon themselves to protect others from the process. Perhaps their intentions are good, for they only want to save someone from the pain, yet the result is a thwarting of that person's opportunity for growth. Self-responsibility is the only way for others in a group to learn fully and completely. All group members need to remember as the group develops what Perls (1969b) said about responsibility: "I am responsible only for myself. You are responsible for yourselves. I resent your demands on me, as I resent any intrusion into my way of being" (pp. 127-128).

The fifth assumption is that the group process is potentially risky and exhilarating. It sounds like it is only through risking that things can be exhilarating. That is not completely true, but it is through tension that learning takes place. Remember that tension is not necessarily something negative. If group members decide to play it safe, then the potential for change may be minimized. If group members decide to experiment and risk, the potential for change is maximized. This means that group members can choose to be spontaneous and authentic. In the group, risk will always be there. It is the way life is and we must always ask ourselves: "Is what we [in the group or work] do worth it?" Nothing ventured, nothing gained is an apt truism. Vanier (1998) said that: see p. 38 (chaos)

> We can find fulfillment only if we all work together to create a society [group] where each of us is moving from narcissistic and egocentric tendencies, where we are closed up in self, to a state of openness towards others; we can find fulfillment only in working together to find a greater fullness to humanity. It is the truthful acceptance of self, and the desire to live in truth, in justice, and in love, that is the basis of freedom (pp. 114-115).

HOW DOES A TRANSPERSONAL GROUP WORK?

There are many methods that facilitators can utilize that will make their approach unique, but whatever the method, one must consider which is most suitable to the task. The nature of the transpersonal group is the desire to consider all the dimensions of humanness (e.g., psychological, social, cognitive and spiritual). Since not everyone in a group is at the same level of personal development, there will be some uneven encounters and differences of interpretation. As a consequence, the sense of compassion, that is, a motivational shift from personal gain to serving others, is appropriate. A part of this sense of compassion is an acceptance of the idea of "nonattachment." In a personal way, it is cultivating what is genuine and true in one's inner nature. Accomplishments, roles, material status and everything that is imposed from the outside can be thought of as not from one's inner nature. Das (1997) describes this idea as being:

> free flowing, natural, and well rounded. It's like Teflon — nothing sticks. On the other hand, the un-awakened, ordinary [self] is rigid, limited, and sticky like flypaper; the ordinary [self] has corners and sharp jagged edges on which ideas get caught, hanging us up. Dualistic thinking is like Velcro; it takes two to tangle. Unitary vision is more like a crystal through which all forms of light can pass unimpeded (p.102).

From a personal perspective, this means not being able to let go of our worries or keeping fixed opinions or ideas that hamper our flexibility. When a new idea is put forth, rather than discarding it, one must approach the idea as if one was "water." Envelop it and examine it before deciding whether it is acceptable to one's inner nature. Just as ideas can attach themselves, memories too can attach themselves and keep people from moving on with their lives. Things happen and one learns from them, but one has to "let go" of the past "hurt," otherwise these things can fester and corrupt one's inner nature. In the same way one lets go of material things, one has to cultivate the notion of letting go of thoughts, feelings and ideas of how things are "supposed" to be and accept things as they are.

CORE AREAS OF TRAINING

Walsh and Vaughan (1993), two transpersonal theorists, proposed a model for group work that incorporates three assumptions about the human condition. The first assumption is that people's minds are so enmeshed with external ideas that they cannot control their thinking. That is, the mind, with decision making potential, is corruptible. For example, the "heart" will want to do something, but the mind intervenes and tells the heart, "wait a minute, what is in this for me?" The second assumption is that the mind can be trained to be open and flexible. Through experience one develops certain set ways of thinking and ways of doing things that become a routine. A routine becomes a habit and one does things without thinking whether they are the "right" things or not. The routine, while bringing comfort, dulls the imagination and stops us from seeing things in a new and novel way. Thirdly, that as the result of training, one's consciousness and actions can be "transformed." It should be noted that it is usually the mind that leads us "astray" and thus one has to train oneself to listen more to the "heart." In other words, seeing is believing, but feeling is God's own truth.

TRAINING METHODS

Unlike traditional theories of counselling and group work, the Transpersonal perspective advocates involving the whole person and his or her environment. Most important though, is the inclusion of the spiritual dimension of human development. To help the individual tap into the spiritual dimension, a variety of unique methodologies are employed. The following categories as outlined by Vaughan (1989) include the following:

Meta-needs, transpersonal process, values and states, unitive consciousness, peak experiences, ecstasy, mystical experience, being, essence, bliss, awe, wonder, transience of self, spirit, sacralization of everyday life, oneness, cosmic awareness, cosmic play, individual and species-wide synergy, theory and practice of meditation, spiritual paths, transpersonal cooperation, transpersonal realization and actualization and related concepts, experiences, and activities (In Sheik & Sheik, 1989; p. 225).

This does not mean that methods that focus on the psychological or even the physical cannot be employed (e.g., dream or psychodrama). Any counselling method that helps the person become a better human being and tap into his or her true nature can be utilized. However, there are unique Transpersonal methods that can be integrated with traditional counselling approaches. These include the following:

Ethical Training: This is the idea that in working with groups, the facilitator encourages people to think in terms of helping and supporting others. There are a variety of ways of getting people to train themselves to be more ethical, but two useful ones is asking group members to demonstrate on an on-going basis "appreciation." This is done by asking participants to tell at least one person in the group what they appreciate about the other. In other words, participants are encouraged to say "thank you" as much as possible. The other technique is to encourage participants to repent for any discomfort caused to another person. The idea is to get people to think in terms of "cleansing" themselves of petty anger, jealousies and animosities.

Attentional Training: This is a form of "mindfulness" that Das (1997) describes as a "relaxed, open, lucid, moment-to-moment present awareness. It is like a bright mirror: non-clinging, non-grasping, non-aversive, non-reactive, undistorting" (p. 300). It is the ability to look at something or someone in a non-evaluative manner. One of the primary means of achieving "mindfulness" is through meditation training. Another way is by simply paying attention to body sensations, the clouds floating across the heavens or the sounds of the waves as they wash up on the shore.

Emotional Transformation: A method for transforming the emotions is by learning to "dis-identify" with them or learn when to react to various external stimuli that bring up emotion. In other words, rather than being reactive to feelings, one learns to put it "aside" and examine it as if it were a "flower." This does not mean suppressing one's emotions, it means learning not to become one's emotions. Once a person trains to separate oneself from emotions, then these feelings, when appropriate, can be expressed at a much deeper way. However, one of the most important ways of becoming emotionally transformed is by cultivating emotions that have positive outcomes (e.g., compassion, joy and love). Prayer, poetry, music and other expressive means of demonstrating positive regard for others, animals and things in the environment is practiced every day (e.g., touching a tree or pet with love in our hearts).

Understanding Motivation: Motivation is often thought of how a person sees his or her world and what the goal in doing various things in life. By understanding why one does what one does, it is possible to not let events control oneself. When events control one, then the locus of control is outside oneself. The goal is to learn to choose when to let things happen rather than to control what happens. This happens when one learns to be an observer and learns how to watch rather than react. This also improves intuition, one's sense of personal boundaries and helps to identify incongruence in words and actions. The latter aspect of motivation is important in learning to be true to one's inner nature. For example, a person uses words that sound "nice," but says the words in an "angry" manner.

Awareness Training: This is a process of learning to use one's intuition by looking at everything as if for the first time. Rather than walking around "thinking," one learns to stop "thinking" and just observe. In that sense, thinking is like talking and when one talks, one is not listening. Therefore, by not thinking, one learns to see at a deeper level or to see with the "inner eye." Meditation is also a good way to train oneself to stop thinking and evaluating.

Evoking Wisdom: Wisdom, unlike knowledge, is not something that a person gains. Knowledge is learned, but wisdom is something that one becomes. A person can have knowledge, but not have wisdom or conversely, have a lot of wisdom, but no knowledge. One way of evoking wisdom is the use of legends, stories and parables that have a deeper level of meaning. Meaning has the power to transform behavior and therefore, what a person is. Stories have layers of wisdom that evoke a higher level of responses that one can have with the cosmos.

FACILITATING GROUPS: ADVICE FOR CONSIDERATION

- Be positive and show enthusiasm all of the time despite how you feel.

- Establish a climate of safety by reinforcing specific cardinal rules (e.g., confidentiality, respectfulness, etc.).

- Maintain clear personal boundaries as a facilitator, including how you communicate verbally and non-verbally, with all of the group members.

- Continually check with group members in terms of how they are feeling and whether their needs are being met (e.g., a group check-in).

- Ensure that everyone in the group has the opportunity to speak by paying particular attention to those "quiet" members.

- Listen to not only what is being said, but also how it is said.

- Maintain a sense of safety and trust in the group.

- Stay focused, despite how you feel or what is going on.

- Ensure that everyone is "present" by trying to connect verbally or non-verbally.

- Pay attention to the roles participants take in the group and encourage them to experiment with different roles.

- Value diversity and encourage everyone to respect differences in others.

- Get into the habit of showing appreciation to all of the group members.

- Never be defensive in dealing with challenges from the group – reflect back the energy and use it to model conflict resolution.

- Observe patterns of communication in the group (e.g., who talks, how long, how often, in what order, style, etc.).

- Strike a balance between task and maintenance functions within the group.

- Expect challenges from group members and be open to criticism.

❀ Encourage sharing by all group members.

❀ Be willing to share your feelings and thoughts on a variety of issues, but be careful with personal informational "things."

❀ Involve the participants as much as possible in decision-making concerning aspects of the group, but don't be afraid to be decisive.

❀ Encourage the group participants to make specific goals that they would like to accomplish in the group.

WHAT KINDS OF PROBLEMS ARISE IN A GROUP?

There will be a number of problems that people will experience as a part of the group process. In most situations, these problems serve to enhance the excitement and reality of the laboratory experience. After all, the group experience is designed to help people anticipate problems and overcome them. Not surprisingly, there are blocks that can stop them from dealing effectively with the problems. There is a kind of confusion that makes them 'blind' to using their senses, to seeing what is 'going on in the group' and prevents them from achieving the fullness of the experience. To paraphrase the Greek philosopher Socrates, if life is not worth examining, it is not worth living.

When people lack awareness and lose touch with "what" and "now" behavior, it is difficult for them to see what is most obvious in their environment. When things happen and people are not aware, they will miss the experience or misconstrue it. Perls (1969b) said that awareness is experiencing and vice versa, experiencing is awareness. "Without awareness, there is naught, not even knowledge of the naught...the omnipresence of God is mirroring awareness...experience as phenomenon appearing always in the now" (pp. 28-29).

If people refuse to take responsibility for themselves as group members and insist on manipulating the group environment, rather than accepting it for what it is, they risk not only the spontaneity of the moment but the richness of creativity. To be responsible means to accept themselves, others and the actions at the moment they occur. If they want to impose control they undermine the immediacy of the group. Responsibility means letting go and flowing with the action. If people lose contact with the environment by not knowing how to shift focus, it is possible they may miss what is actually happening in the group. For example, if people focus on something of little importance and miss what is really vital in an interaction, they will be unable to comprehend the totality of the experience, thereby missing valuable material. Perls (1975b) said that: "the ego boundary is flexible in the healthy person...but rigid in psychopathological states...thus the ego boundary can be thought of as a meeting of opposite sets of emotions, acceptances and rejections, identifications and alienation, positive and negative emotions" (pp. 30-31).

If unfinished business occurs in the group, it is impossible for the group to continue with the same degree of awareness. As a result, needs are unfulfilled, feelings are not expressed, and incomplete situations are left unfinished. According to Passons (1975), when there is a feeling that something is incomplete in the group, there is "an unexpressed feeling, or some other uncompleted situation that is of significance…[thus] the unfinished task dominates…awareness and clamors for attention…being "stuck" in this way severely retards the flow of attention and excitement required to cope with other needs yet to emerge out of the background" (pp. 18-19).

the big pink elephant in the room

Being uncomfortable with emotions, often used synonymously with feelings, is one of the biggest blocks for people in groups. All people are feeling something in the group, yet they may not be comfortable with their feelings. According to Perls, Hefferline and Goodman (1951):

emotions are tools

> *it is important that you become aware of the continuity of your emotional experience. Once emotions are understood to be not a threat to rational control of your life but a guide, which furnishes the only basis on which human existence can be ordered rationally, then the way is open to the cultivation of continuous awareness of its wise prompting (p. 100).*

Accepting personal feelings as a guide can help people negotiate their way through "uncharted areas." They have probably had the experience of feeling that they are interacting only on a certain layer of feeling with others. A good way of understanding feelings is using the metaphor of the "onion" to indicate the layers of feelings that seem to be prevalent in dealing with emotions. As people go deeper there are more intense feelings, which eventually lead to the authentic self (e.g., the "real" and uncensored self). Figure 2.1 demonstrates these dynamic layers of feelings, from the superficial (polite layer) to the authentic layer.

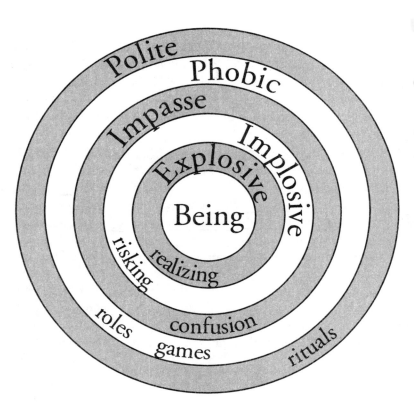

Figure 2.1: Layers of emotions

At the initial stages of the group, members stay at the polite layer rather going to deeper layers of feelings. They use a lot of clichés: "Good morning, handshake, and all of the meaningless tokens of meetings" (Perls, 1969a, p. 59). In the group this may take the form of group rituals that are meaningless formalities – for example, saying: "Let's get to know each other," but sharing only information and few emotions. The second layer, called the phobic layer or sometimes the 'Sigmund Freud layer,' where 'shoulds,' roles, and games predominate, is a synthetic layer, because of its close relationship with dialectical thinking. Translated, this synthetic existence is a compromise between the 'real self' and the 'ideal self' (e.g., naturalness versus posing). In the group, if people are in this layer, they are revealing what they think they 'should be' or what others expect them 'to be,' rather than the 'real self.' Perls (1969a) used the following examples of people acting out "the very important person, the bully, the cry-baby, the nice little girl, the good boy – whatever roles we choose to play…these are superficial, social, as-if layers. We pretend to be better, tougher, weaker, more polite, etc., than we really feel" (p. 59).

The next layer is called the impasse, which is when people are forced to come face-to-face with all their fears and fantasies. Here they experience discomfort with a loss of awareness and a distortion of reality. This is the layer where most people get 'stuck,' because it is painful to feel. Often people simply do not feel and they experience a kind of nothingness. In this layer people want to avoid this discomfort and pain, so they:

> stay immature [and] go on manipulating the world rather than to suffer the pains of growing up…there are many things you can do on your own, but when you come to the difficult parts, especially the impasse, you…get into a whirl, into a merry-go-round, and you are not willing to go through the pain of the impasse (Perls, 1969a; p. 60).

Next comes the implosive layer where there is a realization of errors and the cost people are paying for restraints. People now have to make a choice. They can either collapse in on themselves or experiment with new behaviors. This is a difficult place, for they have to take a risk and experiment regardless of the consequences. Perls (1969a) called this the 'death layer,' because there is a paralysis or confusion in which they "…contract and compress [themselves], imploding" (p. 60).

From implosion comes explosion, where there is a realization of who people really are. Now they begin to move towards getting in touch with their feelings. They 'come to life' with a 'joie de vivre', laughing, crying, expressing anger, and joy. What has happened is a 'breakthrough' and finally a realization that the authentic self or 'true self' is there. 'Doors have been opened' for authentic expressions. According to Tobin (1975b), the authentic people trust themselves, and "they take a stand on what they are doing, whatever it is, and do it openly and directly and completely, they are doing the 'right thing' for themselves and others, and they are more alive and whole…existing sensorial in the present: seeing, hearing, smelling, and touching" (pp. 134-136).

When people have the experience of feeling alienated, they have a sense of not being in contact with their surroundings and themselves. When this happens, fragmentation occurs in which they disown and deny their feelings, actions and awareness. In fragmentation there is a

See Ferrucci

dichotomizing of differing parts of the self. They hold back, fantasize and project catastrophes. For example, according to Perls (1969a) when people do not express resentment, which he calls an incomplete Gestalt, one can neither let go nor have the resentment out. He claims:

> *Resentment is an emotion of central importance. The resentment is the most important expression of an impasse – of being stuck. If you feel resentment, be able to express your resentment. A resentment unexpressed often is experienced as, or changes into, feelings of guilt. Whenever you feel guilty, find out what you are resenting and express it and make your demands explicit. This alone will help a lot (p. 49).*

When people do not feel whole or when their complete self is not engaged, there is a sense of imbalance. In that sense, the aboriginal belief is that people have to engage all aspects of themselves, both psychologically, intellectually, socially and spiritually. Aboriginal helpers such as Rod McCormick of the First Nations House of Learning, at the University of British Columbia, have modified and used the ancient spiritual symbol as a guide to engage all aspects of a person. It is this holistic way of dealing with people, expressed in the Medicine Wheel, Figure 2.2, that can be a guide for addressing all aspects of human nature (France & McCormick, 1997; p. 28). When people do not feel whole, their feelings, actions, hopes and awareness are fragmented. They may feel 'bad', withdraw or even blame themselves. For example, when people feel whole, then they may are able to accept themselves and their feelings. Addressing these four areas helps people to use their strengths to cope with difficulties. And once they "let go of guilt," they will not ruminate about it any more, it's gone, past, filed away, and they are free to experience living without interference.

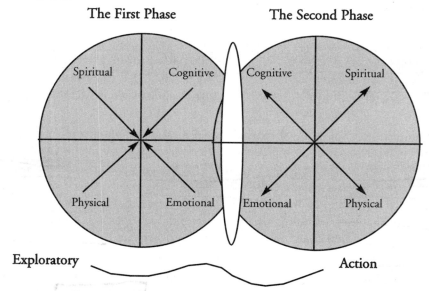

Figure 2.2: The Medicine Wheel

Notice that the wheel is divided into four parts, but also two distinct phases — exploratory and action. While the whole person is engaged, physically, spiritually, cognitively and emotionally, so is the helping process. In the initial stages of any relationship, it is engaging a person by knowing them at a deeper level, hence the arrows are pointed to the center. In the action phase or doing, the arrows point outward. That is, all parts of the person are engaged in assisting in solving a problem.

WHAT ARE THE PRINCIPLES OF CHANGE?

"All things must change, to all something new, to something strange..." wrote the American poet, Henry Wadsworth Longfellow. This is a law of nature. Change is inevitable! In a transpersonal group, changes are not planned, programmed or coerced. Perhaps changes are allowed, although a more precise way of saying it is that they just happen. Group members become more aware and accepting of who they are, and changes become possible that were previously thwarted. This thwarting usually happens when members deny or disown parts of themselves. In other words, good contact is based on authenticity. The Greeks defined authenticity as "aut + hentes" or to master and accomplish. Therefore, to be authentic is to be in control or to be the master of self, which brings about a sense of accomplishment. In order to bring about change, group members must have a sense of awareness of themselves and others. According to Enright, (1975) "awareness is a state of consciousness that develops spontaneously when organismic attention becomes focused on some particular region of the organism" (p. 151). This does not mean that group members focus on one aspect of behavior and try to make sense of it. It means taking everything in, through observing, accepting and allowing. Rather than trying to control events, group members who are aware experience it. In fact, awareness by itself may be curative, because through awareness group members will make choices and take responsibility.

For group members to change, they must take personal responsibility and then make choices about how they will live. Awareness provides group members with insight into their choices. And a necessary ingredient is the acceptance of responsibility. This is an acceptance of the self, a trusting, in the regulation ability of the organism (e.g., the totality of self), without interrupting it with thoughts. Ram Dass (1975) stressed that "we are all prisoners of our own mind [and] this realization is the first step on the journey to freedom" (p. 5). Therefore, being responsible means relying on the wisdom of the organism, that only by acting in a congruent manner with all parts of the self (mind, body, emotions and spirit) we will live a more balanced and harmonious life.

WHAT ARE THE ASSUMPTIONS ABOUT PERSONHOOD IN GROUPS?

The first step in understanding human relations is to get a notion of what people are like. These assumptions of how people can interact are both implicit and explicit. Some people may emphasize their social part, while others may emphasize their spiritual parts. Differing assumptions of people lead to differing ways of interaction. In the Transpersonal perspective the assumptions of a person is that he or she is:

- A whole, with a body, emotions, thoughts, sensations, perceptions and a spirit, all of which function interrelatedly;

- A part of the environment and cannot be understood outside of it;

- Most effective being proactive rather than reactive, when he or she determines responses to external and internal stimuli;

- Capable of being aware of sensations, thoughts, emotions, perception and spirituality;

- Capable of choice through self-awareness of responsibility for covert and overt behavior;

- In possession of the resources to live effectively and to restore the self through personal efforts;

- Able to fulfill maximum potential when she or he is able to experience self only in the present, while the past and the future are experienced only through remembering and anticipating in the present;

- Neither intrinsically good nor bad, because as a person he or she is.

WHAT ARE THE ELEMENTS OF EFFECTIVE GROUP INTERACTION?

Effective group interaction depends on whether the group has accepted the responsibility of being authentic, honest and aware. This means that group members must have a willingness to make contact with the group as a whole. As members of the group people must choose a personally acceptable way of "being" in the group. In doing this, they must be clear about the connection between their functional role and the relationship of their role in the group. The function is the tasks they, as group members, choose to utilize (e.g., consensus taker, stimulator, etc.). The relationship that evolves as a result of their function reflects the quality and nature of their interaction with others. It is possible that people's functional role within the group will change, but as it does, it will also change the relationship they have with the rest of the group. This, however, is an opportunity to experience something new. Whatever direction the group takes or whatever decisions the group makes, there are values that will always underlie what happens in the group. Values are important since they have important meaning for each person. There are three specific values that identify effective successful working groups: task effectiveness, immediacy and the view that conflict is not something to avoid, but is an asset.

Task effectiveness is putting emphasis on doing things right rather than doing things the right way. Essentially, this occurs when the group places value on the process rather than the goal (e.g., it is the journey that is important, not the destination). This value can be reflected in the joy the group feels in being together. Time becomes relative when this happens and tasks become secondary. Immediacy in the group is dealing in the present in thoughts, feelings and actions. When this occurs, group members are more accepting and flexible to what is happening rather than why it is happening. This does not mean that group members do not question, but rather talk about what is occurring in the present (e.g., "When you do that, I feel. . ."). Conflict is viewed as an asset by the group rather than a deficit. Group members accept that conflict is a part of active living, because it is a source of energy and creativity. Conflict is a natural element of relationships and when conflict develops, it creates an opportunity to learn. In essence, conflict is used rather than avoided, resolved rather than suppressed. As groups work at establishing relationships, defining goals and evolving procedures, three important factors contribute to the group's effectiveness. These factors are synergy, interdependence and the basic support demonstrated by the group members. Synergy is the combined energy of the group. It is not just the effective use of the energy of the group members, but an entirely new energy. Sometimes there is a lack of cohesion (synergy) when one or two of the group members are absent. Interdependence in an effective group occurs when there is an amalgamation of group resources rather than a coordinating of resources. The "bottom line" for the group is that there has to be a supportive environment; otherwise, there is no reason for working together.

WHAT IS THE ROLE OF THE FACILITATOR IN THE GROUP?

The facilitator has a very difficult role, because there are a lot of expectations that group members may have about what the facilitator is supposed to do and what he or she is supposed to be. However, whether the facilitator decides to be passive or active, democratic or autocratic, structured or unstructured, in a Transpersonal framework the facilitator has a unique and specific role that is often quite different than other group facilitators. The facilitator continually engages the group members in the "now" and reacts to them from an immediate perspective. Whatever past experiences are brought into the group environment, they are secondary to how group members are behaving in the present. It is not only how the group members relate, but the language they utilize in the group (e.g., use of present tense). In other words, group members are asked to respond to how they are feeling right now with the other people in this group. To do this, the facilitator must enhance their present awareness (e.g., "I want them to see every aspect of their boundaries, not only the starting point, but its furthermost extensions").

The facilitator works at helping group members develop a greater sense of self-support in their actions. When they turn to the facilitator for direction, the facilitator will turn it back to them. This sometimes creates chaos that is often frustrating because many group members are unaccustomed to this practice. An effective facilitator will use strategies that emphasize independence on the part of group members rather than dependence. The goal is to help group members rely on inner support rather than relying on external support from others. As group members focus on their inner support, they will be challenged to come up with an answer to this question: "What specifically can I do without anyone's help or direction to accomplish my goals?" The facilitator will interrupt group members and challenge them in the way they participate in group activities. The idea is to focus on their patterns of behavior and examine closely how they relate to others. This is not designed to throw them off balance, although that happens, but to get them to be more aware of how these patterns either assist them or frustrate them in everyday life. The facilitator acts as an "agent of frustration" and is not dismayed when group members get angry or express their frustration. In fact, the facilitator works towards helping group members express clearly their feelings, regardless of what those feelings are. In other words, it is all right for the group members to express frustration or joy. For example, a pattern of behavior may function in a way that accomplishes individual goals, but comes across as manipulation to others. Group members may not be aware that they are being perceived that way by others, thus they can have an opportunity to develop and experiment with a more effective way of meeting their needs in the group and the real world (e.g., "How can I do this differently and in a way that comes from myself?").

The facilitator often focuses on the discrepancies of the group members. The discrepancies may be between verbal and nonverbal expressions, aspirations and self-perception, insights gained and later actions, how others view them and how they view themselves. This can be painful and uncomfortable, yet it provides group members with an accurate picture of how they relate to others in the group (e.g., "Did you notice that, when you said that, your body did this?"). The facilitator will ask them to try experiments that are designed to focus on these discrepancies. For example, a common practice of the facilitator is to draw attention to verbal expressions and ask group members to experiment with an alternative word or phrase:

FROM	TO
"You"	"I"
"We"	"I"
"It"	"I"
"But"	"And"
"Why"	"How"
"They"	"I"
"I think"	"I feel"
"I know"	"I imagine"
"I have to"	"I choose to"
"I'm afraid"	"I'd like"
"I need"	"I want"
"I should"	"I want"
"I can't"	"I won't"

In short, the facilitator is an initiator and reflector. There is a constant focus on helping people become more aware and, as such, he or she is an agent of awareness. Yet the facilitator must be a catalyst and frustrator of those defenses people may use to stay at the impasse layer. While attending to the obvious, the facilitator is also attending to what is not obvious. As such, he or she needs to be patient, tolerant and possess a sense of humor. This means that as a facilitator one has to be careful not to take oneself too seriously. Thus, the facilitator is observing, attending, challenging and reflecting back what group members are doing.

WHAT ARE THE UNIQUE ASPECTS OF THE GROUP EXPERIENCE?

There are a number of ways to become aware of interpersonal and interpersonal skills. Some people may seek individual introspection, while others will seek out and explore themselves via the group experience. There is no question that the individual approach has advantages and is appropriate. There are, however, a number of advantages in the group experience that make it one of the most attractive methods of self-exploration. According to Johnson and Johnson (1999) some of the advantages of the group experience is that group members are provided:

- ❧ A more heterogeneous experience in which interpersonal skills can be learned, mastered and integrated into behaviors;

- ❧ A supportive environment where they are encouraged to take risks;

- ❧ An opportunity for constructive approval or rewards that would be more limited in an individual therapeutic setting;

- ❧ A safe environment where powerful feelings cannot only be induced, but explored;

- ❧ A greater variety of opportunities to use interpersonal skills with a wider variety of people;

- ❧ An opportunity to help their peers;

- ❧ A variety of different perspectives that can increase insight;

- ❧ A greater opportunity for comparison, with a greater variety of people;

- ❧ A wider variety of feedback;

- ❧ A remedial environment where they can experiment and practice new behaviors;

- ❧ A greater opportunity to establish constructive peer relationships.

HOW TO TUNE INTO SELF TO MAXIMIZE TIME IN THE GROUP

Most of the time group members are not aware of what is guiding them, but just accept and do what others want them to do. In extreme situations people may find that they are living other

autopilot, "default settings"

people's lives and not their own. To be sure, there are a lot of "pay-offs" for doing this: support, approval and protection. However, the price or consequence may be too great, because there can be a sense of dissatisfaction or a feeling that something is missing. Perhaps the tragedy of life for these people is what dies inside them while they live. This can happen when people are cut off from their inner resources, thus undermining their creativity in projects and in enriching relationships. The "bottom line" is that, when people do what others want them to do, they give up their power and lose themselves. When group members begin to tune into themselves, they may experience impasse or a feeling of discomfort. It is not surprising, because it is hard to go against so many years of training. As they contact this impasse layer, they may want to move back to a more comfortable layer of behavior (e.g., the polite layer). This can occur in a variety of situations. For example, in a group it can happen when the group facilitator abstains from directing or telling the group what to do. As this may be an unfamiliar occurrence, group members may be thrown back on to their own resources and may experience a great deal of discomfort.

EXAMPLES OF EXPERIMENTING WITHIN THE GROUP

A valuable way of using the group is to encourage members to look on the experience as a laboratory in which they can experiment with new ways of communicating and relating. For example people can consider the following:

If they relate to others with	They might experiment with
Complying, giving in	Saying no and owning
Being self-effacing	Providing one's ideas
Resisting suggestions	Being open to suggestions
Holding back	Not holding back
Always talking	Being silent
Not sharing feelings	Sharing feelings
Reacting	Initiating
Smiling, even when upset	Talking without smiling
Explaining	Not explaining
Always helping	Asking for help
Deflecting praise	Accepting praise
Being defensive	Not being defensive
Hiding feelings	Openly sharing feelings
Playing it safe	Taking a few risks
Giving advice	Taking advice

CONCLUSION

In analyzing why the TV show "Survivor" was so popular during the Summer of 2000, an Ohio State University professor of psychology and psychiatry, Steven Reiss, said: "People enjoy being mean. It's tough to acknowledge it, but it explains a lot of human behavior. And we need relatively harmless outlets for that" (Moore, 2000; p. C14). While this notion that each person harbors a mean spirit may be anathema to the idea that people are basically good, there is evidence that evil exists within each person. Could it be that evil is a choice? If so, then it means goodness is a choice too. What makes one person do terrible things and another person to do good things? Das (1997) stressed that most people are "sleeping Buddhas." Thus:

> To reach enlightenment, our only task is to awaken to who and what we really are – and in so doing to become fully awake and conscious in the most profound sense of the word. "When I am enlightened, all are enlightened," Buddha said. Help yourself and you help the entire world (p. 17).

If what we are is a matter of choice, the ultimate test for being the way we want to be, is to risk and experiment with positive and constructive behavior. One of the best models for the willingness to experience is Nikos Kazantzakis' (1952) character – Zorba. Despite his age, Zorba was totally free and it meant "to have a passion, to amass pieces of gold and suddenly to conquer one's passions and throw the treasure to the four winds" (p. 30). To risk is to be free and it does not occur by holding on to outdated ideas and beliefs, but by learning through experimentation with new behaviors. It is difficult to do this, but with practice in the group it becomes easier. Then the new behavior can be added to people's repertoire – increasing their total range of options – and it is available whenever they need it. Perhaps it will help if people keep in mind these three thoughts:

> Have you learned lessons only of those who admired you, and were tender with you, and stood aside for you? Have you not learned great lessons from those who braced themselves against you, and disputed the passage with you? (Black Elk Speaks. Neihardt, 1988; p. 141).
>
> To save all we must risk all. (Friedrich Von Schiller, Fiesco, act 4, sc. 6.')
>
> Risk! Risk anything! Care no more for the opinion of others, for those voices. Do the hardest thing on earth for you. Act for yourself. Face the truth. (Katherine Mansfield, 1927; The Journal of Katherine Mansfield; p.87).

People, as members of the group, will have to take risks and will need to experiment if they are to get the most out of the group experience. In groups they will learn to take the theory, what they have learned through reading and through life experience, and translate it into doing, which is the rationale of the laboratory approach. There are always some exceptions to the guidelines and procedures, but group members need to be open to those exceptions. Sometimes answers are beyond what is immediately obvious. Some insights of self and the group occur after a time of thought and processing. In fact, it is possible that some experiences in the group will not make sense until long after the group has disbanded. One aspect of life should be clear by now: There are simply no easy answers. It may seem that the group experience has a false veneer about it, because sharing feelings, self-disclosing, and giving feedback to relative strangers are not an acceptable norm. Egan (1973) refers to this as "cultural permission," because the laboratory environment is "cut off" from everyone's normal way of behaving and a "new cultural climate" has been created. For example, telling someone how I really feel about him or her or about a third person is something that is not normally done. Yet in the group people will be asked to do this. I want the group to experiment with human relations in a manner that is entirely new. Therefore in the end, experience becomes the highest authority. No other person's ideas are more authoritative than direct experience. To discover the truth, people must experience again and again.

It would be easy to back away and discount group process and experiential learning as so much talk, hype and games. It is possible that feelings, thoughts and experiences can be trivialized by staying on the polite and phobic layers. It is also possible, if people stay on these layers, that they are only gossiping or groping and engaging in unethical behavior. If that happens, then that is their choice. People can "play games" or be authentic. If they explore in an open and positive attitude their feelings, actions and awareness they may gain insight that can reorient them toward a fuller and richer life. Group members should think about what Prather (1970) says "[it is]only when my attention becomes fixated that I act like a part rather than a whole. When I favor my conscious perception over my total awareness, I can no longer hear the rhythm of the whole. Calmness accompanies that part. Intuition goes beyond the figure-ground focus of conscious perception" (p. 82).

ACTIVITIES FOR FOCUSING A GROUP

1. **What's in a Name**: Group members are to write down their full name on a piece of paper. Next they should write down what they have been told about their first, middle and last names. For example, they may have been named after a beloved family member who is deceased or they may have been given a name that evoked a certain memory in their parents or their name was modified to adapt to cultural norms (e.g. Anglicizing a Polish name like Bolzynski to Boland). If they have not been told anything about their names, they should write what they feel about their names. Next they should respond to how they like their full name and whether they would change it. Finally, they should write down a totally new name that they feel would fit them. The group can be divided into triads to share what they have written down.

2. **My dreams**: The group should be divided into two smaller groups and get into two circles (inner and outer) in which the people in the inner circle are facing those in the outer circle. The people in the groups will be given topics to talk about and they are to share with the person facing opposite them their "dream." Allow six minutes for a pair to share each topic. Once the time is up people in the inner circle move clock wise to the left to the next person. For each topic there should be a new pair of people. The topics are:

❀ What did you dream about becoming when you were young? Why?

❀ If you were exiled to a desert island, who would you want to share your exile with and why?

❀ If you were guaranteed that you could accomplish one thing in life what would it be? Why?

❀ What three things would you like people to say about you?

EUREKA TASK ANSWER: "LET'S DENOTE THE 3 COUPLES AS H-1-W1, H2-W2, AND H3-W3. H1 ROWS ACROSS THE RIVER WITH HIS WIFE, W1. HE LEAVES HER ON THE OTHER SIDE AND ROWS BACK. THEN HE PICKS UP THE OTHER TWO HUSBANDS, H2 AND H3, AND ROWS WITH THEM ACROSS THE RIVER. H1 GETS OUT AND THE OTHER TWO HUSBANDS ROW BACK. THEY PICK UP W2 LEAVING W3 BEHIND, AND ROW BACK. H2 AND W2 GET OUT OF THE BOAT. H3 ROWS BACK, PICKS UP HIS WIFE, W3, AND THEN RETURNS WITH HER" (BARON, KERR & MILLER, 1992, P. 45).

CHAPTER THREE

GROUP DEVELOPMENT AND GROUP ACTION

"When I must first know myself, I must not be curious about that which is not my concern, but to do this while I am still ignorant of myself is ridiculous." Socrates

It seems axiomatic that people would want to follow this dictate of Socrates and put energy into self-exploration, but many do not. Those who choose to become a member of a group, regardless of the theoretical framework, therapeutic environment or type of the group, stand a good chance of answering a fundamental question: "Who am I in relation to others?" The answer can only be found when individuals come together in a relationship based on "I - Thou" rather than the "I - It." According to Buber (1970), "I - It" is a relationship based on person to object or an unequal relationship in which one is higher than the other, while the "I - Thou" relationship is subjective and based on equality. The "I -Thou" relationship allows each person to explore polarities and the dilemmas of separateness through the process of group involvement. Perls (1969a) stressed that in doing this, people must develop a clear idea of their personal boundaries because:

> *no individual is self-sufficient; the individual can exist only in an environmental field. The individual is inevitably, at every moment, a part of some field, which includes both him and his environment. The nature of the relationship between him and his environment determines the human's behavior. With this new outlook, the environment and the organism stand in a relationship of mutuality to one another (p. 16).*

Explanations on how people respond in groups have a generic quality, which crosses all theoretical constructs. Examples of these basic elements of group process include stages of group development or how group norms are formed. How approaches differ is in their basic assumptions of personal development and learning. As a result, the manner in which groups are structured, which methods are utilized and how individual leadership style is expressed also vary. For example, the humanistic approach stresses the importance of individual perceptions and feelings; thus, the group is unstructured and the leadership style non-directive. The focus of the group is on encouraging group members to verbalize feelings in the moment. In contrast, the rational-emotive approach stresses thinking and belief systems; therefore, the group tends to be structured and the leader specific and direct. While exploration of feelings and thinking is basic, I believe that the transpersonal approach offers the most creative and experiential way of personal development in groups. What makes the transpersonal approach attractive for me is the emphasis on putting feelings and thinking into action. Rather than analyzing the process, wherever possible, action is encouraged (e.g., role playing).

The basic assumptions in the transpersonal approach are that group members are free to make choices and be responsible for their behavior and actions. As group members, they have the power to determine their destiny, despite their heredity and environmental background. In this respect the group experience becomes therapeutic. People are responsible for their feelings and thoughts, while they strive for personal integration. Taking responsibility to develop and mature in a congruent manner is the only way to be, if people want to achieve personal power. To do this people must move to a place where they do not depend on others for direction or protection. The major task of the leader and the group members is to help people discover what is their full potential and how to achieve it (e.g., to go further and do more than group members think is possible). In this regard, the transpersonal approach is described as a place where "Positive energy is "stoked as a fire" and the seeker moves to a different state. Once again it is the experience or passion that remains dominant as seekers move toward rebirth. As emotions peak in the dance, the seeker is filled with love towards all things" (France & Rodríguez, 1999; p. 9).

To be a complete person it is paramount to strive for self-integration. When group members' inner state and behavior match, there is little energy wasted within the organism. They will not block themselves or sabotage their energy and they will be more able to respond appropriately and with a greater repertoire of actions that can help satisfy needs. Yet Perls (1969a) believed that integration is never complete because there is always something to be integrated and always something to be learned. As a result, people in the group are not to be "occupied with dealing with symptoms or character structure, but with the total existence of [being]…for the aim is to make everyone of us a wholesome person, which means a unified person, without conflicts [and] what we have to do is…re-own [our] hidden potential" (pp. 71-72).

It is paradoxical, but before people are able to tune into others, they must be willing to tune into themselves. As group members, they have the choice of experimenting with the full range of behaviors at their disposal as they make contact with others in the group. If the choice is to "sit back" and observe, the consequence may be a loss of connection with the group. People must realize that, only when they are involved in the process, will there be authentic contact with others in the group. Yet there is a risk in the contact with others, for some people may be rejected, get hurt, be disappointed and invite danger. As people get in contact with others, they stretch themselves and their energy radiates outward; but when they do not, they remain rigid and spend their energy inwardly. Perls (1969a) stressed that people: "may all see only catastrophic expectations – the negative side. [They] don't see the positive gain. If there was only the negative side, [they] just would avoid it….risk-taking is a suspense between catastrophic and astrophic expectations. [They] might gain and [they] might lose" (p. 49).

The Helping Relationship within the Group

For a healthy existence, people must become authentic, honest, and open with themselves and others. However, it is a challenge, because people often deny their experience. In most cases this happens in the area of feelings, particularly what is perceived as socially unacceptable, and in the discrepancy between the real self and the ideal self. Another aspect of that is that people get confused about what they should do, think or even feel in relationship to others and themselves. They are individuals, yet they belong to groups. They must be honest with themselves, yet they have a strong need to belong. Which comes first, the self or the group? Perhaps, it is through belonging that our growth for independence becomes manifested. According to Vanier (1998), "it is only through belonging that we can break out of the shell of individualism and self-centeredness that both protects and isolates us" (p. 35).

In the transpersonal model there is a consideration that "the individual and the environment is a unified field or system, in which all parts are interdependent, so that a change in one part of the total affects all other parts" (Kepner, 1980; p. 7). Among many First Nations helpers, there is the view that every aspect of helping is viewed as collective as opposed to individual, as it is in majority culture. This means that when a person has a problem, it can be the community who tries to solve the problem, as if everyone has a stake in the outcome (e.g., one community member's problem is everyone's problem). The healing circle, within the context of a Long House, is ideal for the community to come together and help someone solve a personal issue. However, the problem, once defined, can follow the direction of a variety of problem solving paradigms. The difference is that anyone in the circle can contribute with their ideas and that the problem can be examined using the medicine wheel, embracing the physical, cognitive, emotional and spiritual aspects of existence.

The helping relationship is defined as the process of promoting the growth, development, maturity, and functioning and coping skills in another person. Fundamentally, those helping or healing practices that are used must be consistent to the value system of those one is trying to help. The diversity of First Nations people suggests that understanding how individuals see the world is the best guide to establishing a helping relationship. Yet among traditional healing practices in all cultures, there seem to be two principal phases of the helping process: an inward exploratory phase and a outward action phase. That means that the level of trust one develops will form the way in which one interacts with the person whom one wants to help. Trust is the principle "grease" that facilitates the helping process. The exploratory nature of this phase suggests that the peer support giver listens in an active way, paying attention not only to what is being said, but also how it is being said. The skills that are used to do this are the skills of attending, empathy, questioning, self-disclosure, reflection of meaning and concreteness. The second phase of the helping process is characterized by an outward direction in which courses of action are outlined and implemented. The peer support giver works in a cooperative manner as the problem is being worked through. Helping generally does not move in a direct "line". In this sense, helping is cyclical as compared to a linear mode or moving directly from a statement of the issue to a solution.

Figure 3.1 demonstrates symbolically this interrelationship of all the parts using the classical Muller-Lyer illusion. When one part of the figure is changed, the appearance changes. Both of the horizontal lines in "A" and "B" are the same length, yet they appear unequal. "A" appears longer than "B", because the diagonal lines have been changed.

Figure 3.1: Muller-Lyer illusion

This is an important concept in the development of the group, because what may appear in surface perception may not be accurate. However, part of the illusion is the way that the two are paired; because they are observed together they affect what is seen. In the same way, what one member does affects the perception of other members in the group. When group members have a desire to be liked and do what they think others might want them to do, they end up taking action that denies personal feelings. Living up to the expectations of others, results in disowning the self. If people are faced with a sense that they 'should' be doing certain things, because that is what is expected, then they have lost their ability to make free choices. In order to function at the most optimal level of energy, group members must get beyond those mechanisms they use to deny personal experience. The five psychological mechanisms that block spontaneity are: introjection, projection, retroflection, deflection and confluence.

THE EFFECTIVE USE OF FEEDBACK

Most people who come into a group, whether it be a task-oriented group or relationship-oriented group, have a desire to get feedback on the tasks they are involved in. And most are genuinely interested in knowing how others see them. However, I believe they also have the desire to be psychologically touched as they "touch" others. In a sense it is only through seeing themselves in the mirror of others' eyes that they can understand how they are coming across. This underscores the power of feedback as a process for understanding how everyone in the group is communicating. In a supportive relationship, feedback is a way of sharing with others how they feel, think, and experience the world. Feedback can be positive or it can be negative, but it works best when it:

❀ Focuses on strengths;

❀ Is specific and concrete;

❀ It is non-judgmental (avoiding "good" and "bad");

❀ It is straightforward and precise.

Feedback serves several important functions in the group. First, it is helpful to someone who is considering changing a behavior. For example, when people share with a person how they see his or her behavior, they let the person know specifically what it is (e.g., "When you constantly make jokes about what is going on here, I just stop taking you seriously"). The person may now choose to disregard a behavior because he or she has a better insight into its effect on others. Secondly, feedback helps people to see if what they want to communicate is being communicated. It is like a corrective device that keeps them working towards a goal (e.g., matching behavior with intentions). Finally, feedback can help people share helpful information or personal feelings about what others are experiencing. For example, the active listener can share the person's particular strength (e.g., "I see you as being a very perceptive and friendly person"). In giving this information the active listener encourages the person to feel good about life. In addition, it tells others that people view them in a positive manner.

THE POWER OF ENCOURAGEMENT

Of all the people I have observed in groups, those who have the most difficulty seem to be the ones who project a sense of inferiority. It seems that if they felt more confident about themselves, they would have less difficulty accomplishing goals, working out relationships, and being adaptable to the pressures of the group. Encouragement is one way of helping them feel better about themselves and so I freely give it when it is appropriate. I have also observed that those in the group who are most positively perceived are those who offer encouragement. I can remember so many times feeling that what I did was poorly done; yet when someone gave encouragement, it somehow gave me the motivation to continue striving and feeling good about myself. Surprisingly, it is a skill easily overlooked in the desire to be proficient as a facilitator, but it has been found to be a very powerful factor in overcoming a lack of confidence and in motivating people. On the surface, encouragement may seem not very different than praise and reassurance, yet it is. Praise is a positive reinforcer that is contingent on a behavior and reassurance communicates that an outcome of an act will turn out all right. Encouragement is given not as reward (praise) or to communicate everything is all right (reassurance), but is given to reinforce actions for the purpose of resolving difficulties and overcoming faulty perception. Encouragement is strongest when it is genuine, based on some past history or interaction between two people, and prefaced with an "I" when used. For example, "I am impressed with your perception of body language and how you have used it to lead others."

THE GUIDELINES FOR ESTABLISHING
A SUPPORTIVE RELATIONSHIP

In establishing a supportive relationship, I encourage group members to utilize a number of guides that will help them be more aware of others in the group. First, I want them to be aware of total communication, which means they must pay attention to all the messages – verbal and non-verbal. Since feelings are often the most difficult for people to share, when it is appropriate, I want to encourage them to use empathic responses that can be interchangeable in feeling and meaning. It is primary that they be respectful to each other, open and accepting of differences. When they do not understand something or when coming face to face with a difficult issue, I want them to be as concrete as possible. They should attempt to identify attitudes, be willing to share feelings and be open to exploring the meaning of issues in themselves and others. I also hope that they will always try to use natural expressions and be as spontaneous as possible. I know that this may seem contradictory or impossible to achieve, yet I know that an active listener is able to apply these general guidelines.

I always try to encourage them to take time and listen carefully because often the telling of a concern or problem is therapeutic; therefore, I initially allow people to share what is on their minds regardless of how long it takes. If they desire to tell me only how they feel, this is also all right. I leave it up to them, because the story is not important in the stream of things. The story is always engaging, for it means that people have to blow their cover, drop defenses and stand somewhat naked in their own eyes and in the eyes of others. If this happens, then the story is useful. While group members are exploring their concerns, there is usually a movement towards intensification of shared feelings when active listening skills are used. For example, if one person is sharing feelings of being hurt and said, "I felt really bad after she said that to me." An active listener can intensify the feelings by saying, "It really hurt you when she said that to you." This helps to clarify expressions and allows the person to own feelings. When this happens people are more likely to feel understood and begin to share more of their concerns. "Seeing is believing, but feeling is God's own truth," an English proverb, conceptualizes this idea. Because when feelings are shared, people begin to experience those feelings. This can increase understanding and move people to a point where insight into an issue is gained. For some people it takes longer to build that relationship, thus I want them to take as long as it is necessary for them to get to the root of their issue.

During the second part of the helpful relationship, group members will be most effective when there is a focus on action-oriented skills. As people work at accomplishing group goals, active listeners:

❀ Use open and full expressions that challenge personal awareness;

❀ Ask probing questions that are concrete and specific;

❀ Share observations of others' body language, word usage and coping strategies; and

❀ Apply problem-solving skills in a cooperative manner.

As the action-oriented part of the helpful relationship unfolds, there is a greater use of the listening skills they used in their exploration part. However, the emphasis is now on problem solving. Encouragement and reinforcing positive behavior (e.g., responsibility) on the part of others is a crucial element. In other words, active listeners are continually validating each other's power to change and developing a plan of action that brings about resolution. This involves working out specific, agreed-upon actions that the group will be able to carry out and evaluate.

STYLES AND LEVELS OF COMMUNICATION

In a study to understand the style of people's communication, it was found that 80% of most face-to-face communication was a combination of the following categories in order of frequency: evaluative, interpretive, supportive, probing and understanding (Rogers, 1973). The remaining 20% were statements that were incidental and of little importance. Sadly, the understanding style is the least common of the styles. Rogers found that when a person uses one of these styles 40% of the time, the person will usually be regarded by others as always responding with that style. That means, for example, that, if I respond in an evaluative fashion, I will be perceived as being evaluative. As people communicate with each other in the group they may notice that there are different levels of communication. It seems that people start communicating at the first level and proceed to a deeper level as they talk. Ivey (1983) outlines four levels of communication that people utilize individually and in groups:

Level I: In this level the talk concerns very superficial topics. People may "shoot the breeze," talk about the weather or current events (e.g., "It is a really nice day to go sailing, isn't it?").

Level II: In this level there is philosophizing, intellectualizing and sharing of self-disclosures that are descriptions of activities and thoughts. People talk about others and things in their lives, but without feelings. People will try and explain themselves or talk about personal qualities with little depth (e.g. "I believe that people should be respectful of others").

Level III: In this level people talk about feelings, but do it without a lot of intensity. They are vague and generally "beat around the bush." People may overuse some qualifiers or give messages that are inconsistent with their verbal and nonverbal content [e.g., "I feel kind of upset about what you are saying" (with a clinched fist and red face)].

Level IV: In this level people are at their most intense. Messages are clear, direct, in regard to their feelings. They freely share feelings and are clear in communicating what they want. They are open to giving and receiving feedback and sharing perceptions (e.g., "I really have mixed feelings about what you are saying. I feel angry that you say it, but glad that you are telling me").

LISTENING TO NONVERBAL MESSAGES

Eighty-five percent of communication consists of nonverbal messages (Burgoon & Saine, 1978). Facilitators and group leaders need to particularly pay attention to their own non-verbal language and that of group members. It is entirely possible that group members' manner and attitude demonstrates non-verbally their level of caring and interest in what is taking place in the group. Not surprisingly even when people are not consciously paying attention to how something is being said, they still react to the non-verbal messages. When people are communicating to others who are not looking at them, are looking at a clock or watch, and have a posture that seems closed (i.e., arms crossed), they "turn off." Not only are their messages invalidated, but also they often feel that they are not being valued or respected. In counseling, non-verbal skills that encourage others to open up are called attending skills. I have noticed that these same attending skills used by active listeners in a group, have the same affect as in a counseling situation. Essentially, attending skills are those physical actions and psychological behaviors that say, "You have my undivided attention." Non-verbal messages and body language by themselves may be unreliable, but when taken in context with verbal messages, they have a real impact. In fact, the expressive approach greatly emphasizes body language as a part of the totality of communication.

Physical attending involves the following: eye contact that is consistent (e.g., not staring but looking at whom you are communicating with); being face to face; congruent facial expressions (e.g., not smiling, excessive smiling, or expressions that do not match the topic); tone of voice (i.e., a well-modulated voice); distancing (i.e., 3-5 feet); and an open posture (i.e., sitting in a slightly inclined position towards the other person). Psychological attending is defined as paying attention to the actual internal state of another, by observing the non-verbal behavior along with the verbal message (Egan, 1986). When people are psychologically attending, they are better able to understand the intensity of feeling and underlying messages. For example, if I do not look at people, seem distracted and am lethargic, while saying, "I'm feeling a little sad," the intensity of emotion may mean that I am feeling more than just sad, that I am actually experiencing extreme grief. Finally, it should be remembered that support is communicated through words and actions. It is not enough to say, "I want to be supportive." It has to be said through actions. Therefore, people need to pay attention to the way others say something; otherwise, people may be communicating a far different message than was intended (i.e., a match of message and its delivery). For example, if someone says, "I am very happy," with a face that does not look happy, then there might be more to what is being said. I have also noticed that when people feel balance and comfort with their bodies, there is little discrepancy between feelings and body language.

Group Development Model

Group development usually follows a series of stages that reflect the needs and dynamics of the group. These stages draw people to the group and help the group to function in a satisfactory and productive manner. The first issue for group members is settling relations with the leader before relations with other group members. The stages are not unconnected elements, but are the interpersonal needs at the time. They are in a series of stages that include inclusion, control, affection and separation.

Inclusion Stage

Everyone in the group is striving for acceptance, recognition, and visibility (e.g., "Where do I fit in?"). When group members become anxious, there is a tendency to exhibit self-centered behavior (e.g., withdrawal, defensiveness, over talking). There are, however, behaviors within the group that reinforce a sense of belonging. Group members are looking for what is acceptable and what is not (e.g., "How much can I trust these people?"). The beginning stage of the group is characterized by **"goblet issues"** and **dependency**.

"Goblet issues" come from cocktail party behavior where the guests size up everyone through their glasses. The topics are relatively minor, yet they function as a means of getting to know others (e.g., weather, profession, meeting room, reasons for taking the course). **Dependency** relates to how the group depends on others and the leader (e.g., "give me some advice", "tell me where I'm at", "tell me what to do" or "can I trust you?"). The focus of activities is:

❧ Contracting and setting boundaries;

❧ Encouraging interpersonal contact;

🦋 Giving messages about the approach in the group;

🦋 Encouraging and legitimizing experimentation on all aspects of personal and group development.

CONTROL STAGE *"Storming"*

Once group members have a sense of inclusion, control becomes most important. This could include decision-making, the sharing of responsibility within the group, structure of the group, competition among group members, and the distribution of power. This occurs when there is a struggle for control, which for Corey and Corey (1987) is a common issue:

> *group behaviors include competition, rivalry, jockeying for position, jealousies, challenges to the leadership (or lack of it), and discussions about the division of responsibility and decision making procedures... in order to deal with these control issues, members must bring them to the surface and talk about them (p. 144).*

In order to face the issue of control, open discussion must take place in the present (e.g., here and now). What most people try to do is gain a sense of mastery or control over their feelings and behavior. Sometimes it is manifested in "over-control" of feelings, which ends up in a lack of spontaneity. Group members will characteristically ask themselves, "How much control do I have? Who is going to control me? How much do others influence me?" People are trying to be, in their way, an effective group member. This stage is characterized by **conflict** as group members try to draw meaning from the experience ("Why isn't the leader giving us what we need?"). The focus of the activities is:

🦋 Heightening awareness of the norms that are operating in the group;

🦋 Encouraging challenge and open expression of difference and dissatisfaction within the group;

🦋 Exploring different roles by group members.

AFFECTION STAGE *"performing"*

Once inclusion and control are resolved, group members feel a greater sense of comfort, warmth and trust as they work together (e.g., "We really click together"). However, while there is a willingness to share a task with each other; there may be anxiety over being liked, not being close enough or being too intimate. There is also increased openness, mutual exploration and group cohesion. Group cohesion is an important element in cementing the bonds of the group. According to Johnson and Johnson (1987):

> *Group cohesion is determined by the assessment of group members of the desirable and undesirable consequence of group membership. The more favorable the outcomes members can expect from membership, the more they will be attracted to the group. The outcomes expected from membership in a given group depend on such factors as the nature of the group and*

its goals, how clearly the goals are stated, how clear the procedures are for achieving the goals, how likely it is that the goals will be successfully achieved, the past successes for the group in achieving its goals, how well the group members cooperate with each other, how constructively conflicts among members are managed…with each other and whether membership in other groups would provide greater benefits (p. 409).

As a result of cooperation there is a corresponding rise in group participation, which results in more resources available for the accomplishment of group goals. One of the dilemmas of this phase is the **double bind** expressed by Schopennhauer's notion of the porcupine (e.g., You want to get close enough to feel warmth, but far enough away to avoid the pain of the sharp quills). This stage is characterized by a sense of **interdependence**, warmth, intimacy and even sexual attraction. The focus of activities is:

❧ Facilitating greater leadership from within the group, while the leader maintains a consultant role (e.g., staying out of the way);

❧ Heightening the interactions within the group.

SEPARATION STAGE

Closure

Once the group comes closer to the end, group members have to come to grips with saying good-bye. In addition, they will be working on clarifying the meaning of the experience in the group and what they are going to do about insights, gains and newly acquired behaviors. There will be "unfinished business" and unresolved issues that they will want to delve into. Separation anxieties will develop, which are characterized by withdrawal (e.g., lateness, absences, daydreaming, reduced interactions and a desire to complete unfinished business). Often there is the desire for the fantasy reunion (e.g., "Let's meet next year and renew our acquaintance"). The focus of activities is:

❧ Helping the group to arrive at some closure;

❧ Acknowledging the unfinished business that could not be dealt within the group;

❧ Helping the group integrate the things they learned about themselves and how it will be transferred to everyday life.

Group members must recognize that problems that can develop during this separation stage can decrease group communication. Commonly what happens is that separation is not acknowledged and resolved effectively, despite the fact that separation is one of the most constant parts of personal relationships and group membership. According to Corey and Corey (1987), the group can consolidate the separation experience by reviewing:

their individual changes and the evolving patterns from the first to the final session. Of particular value is…[giving] one another feedback on specific changes that were made from the outset of the group…[and] putting their learning into perspective by looking at ways to apply in-group experiences to everyday life (p. 204).

GROUP MEMBER DEVELOPMENT

There is a progression of phases that group members experience as they learn to tune into themselves and immerse themselves in the group. This progression follows closely the stages of group development, although it may not necessarily correspond.

Phase I: During this phase people may see a lot of **dependence on the leader** and other group members. They may wonder in which direction the group should go and how they will respond to changes in the direction. This phase is characterized by issues of inclusion, defensiveness, waiting for direction, caution, politeness, submission to the leader, attempts at identification, indecision and withdrawal. The questions people should be asking themselves in this phase are:

1. How can I be more independent?

2. How do I become defensive or take flight (e.g., physically, psychologically, and spiritually)?

3. With Whom and what have I identified within the group and how do they or how does it protect me?

4. What are my defense mechanisms in the group (e.g., introjection, retroflection, projection, deflection and/or confluence)?

5. How are those things that are unfinished for me interfering with my involvement in the group?

Phase II: People may feel a sense of **resistance to the freedom** offered to them in this phase. They now must rely on their sense of where they want to go and actualize those behaviors that give them a sense of control. This phase is characterized by conflict over goals, masked hostility, impatience, confusion, mild anxiety, conflict over expectations, conflict between desire for growth and comfort, and the attempt to develop group norms. The questions people should be asking themselves in this phase are:

1. If I am resisting, how am I resisting?

2. How do I get and maintain control in the group (or in my life)?

3. How can I be specific about the goals I have in the group?

4. What are the behaviors I have adopted in the group?

5. Are they also group norms?

Phase III: There is a feeling of **rebellion** by many group members in this phase, because of the challenge to 'take charge and direct' in the group by members. This phase is characterized by leadership struggle, resistance to direction, clearly defined norms, conflict over group and individual needs, ignoring of stated leader, independence, polarization, spontaneity, intimacy, and working out identity within the group. The questions people should be asking themselves in this phase are:

1. How do I rebel or conform in group situations?

2. Are my needs being met? If so, how? If not, why not?

3.   How do I use my power in the group?

4.   What are my roles within the group?

   Phase IV: At this point there is a sense of **independence** from the group and the leader. People follow what is happening in the group, but they are not directed by it; they are 'in charge' of their actions, feelings and thoughts. This phase of the group is characterized by a sense of freedom, greater responsibility undertaken by all the group members, lack of fear of what will happen, reduction in the time the leader takes in the group, less structure, more trust, greater productivity, more self-disclosure, more intimacy, jockeying for position with the group, more acceptance of others who are different, more tolerance, and more confrontation. In effect, people are taking the learning and insights that they experienced in the other stages of the group and applying them in Phase IV. To get the most out of the group at this point, people can take a number of actions that will help. They can experiment with:

1.   Being aware of their needs and how to go about achieving them.

2.   Becoming conscious of the task and maintenance roles that can be used at any given time.

3.   Experimenting with a range of roles within the group.

4.   Being more open and accepting of the diversity of opinions, thoughts, feelings and actions.

5.   Reducing the number of questions, which become a preface for statements.

6.   Paying attention not only to what is being communicated but how it is being communicated.

EMERGING LEADERSHIP FROM WITHIN THE GROUP

   Every group has leaders who emerge from within the group and who capture the attention of people either during the discussion of a specific issue, during a phase of the group or throughout the life of the group. While a great deal of research has been conducted to find out leadership traits, there is no conclusive evidence that one trait is superior to another. What researchers have been able to say is that some traits work best for certain tasks (Napier & Gershenfeld, 1999).

Example 1: **Decisiveness** may work best in situations where time is a factor in accomplishing a task.

Example 2: **Consensus building** may work best in situations where there are many competing factions.

Example 3: A **self-confident** person may become the leader when group members want someone to speak on behalf of the group.

Example 4: A person who is thought of as a **good listener** may become the leader when there are two strong and divergent factions with the group.

THE FACILITATOR AS LEADER

The facilitator, by the nature of the role, is automatically a leader of a group. However, if leadership is not exercised properly, the facilitator can lose influence despite the role. It is important for facilitators to develop a working relationship based on participation and on the ability to carry out the task. Surprisingly, most people expect that these leaders have **magical qualities** that somehow put them above others. Yet probably the most important factor in leadership is actually having the position. In other words, position gives the leader the power to influence. Expectations of leadership also influence how people will respond to the leader. Drory and Gluskinos (1980) argued whether leaders really possess some special qualities or in fact just meet expectations of what people perceive a leader to be (e.g., if you don't act like a leader, then you are not one).

A number of theories have been developed that highlight leadership (Napier & Gershenfeld, 1985). One theory suggests that the one who influences the group the most is the leader, whether in fact that person is the acknowledged leader or not (e.g., leader behind the throne). Another theory views leadership in terms of the situation – that is, when the situation demands someone to lead, someone is chosen to fulfill that need. Once the need is over the effective leadership is changed. Weight in this theory is given to the environment. Another leadership theory is based on function. When the task requires a certain function, that person becomes the leader (e.g., a pilot is the leader in the air until on the ground). Despite all the theories, leadership remains a nebulous element. Creativity and a willingness to experiment are basic elements of the effective leader in a transpersonal group. According to Zinker (1980), creative group leaders are able to move the group because of their innate awareness of the emotional climate of group members. These are some examples of how this awareness is used:

Example 1: A **sense of timing** or knowing when to intervene and when to withdraw. This sense of timing can be observed when a leader utters a word that has the effect of mobilizing the energy of the people in the group to do something that seems right at that moment. It is a kind of capacity in which the leader is able to detect where the group members can be reached, energized or moved emotionally at a particular time.

Example 2: The knowledge of where and how to **push the psychological buttons** of people in the group. This is an ability to shift 'gears' or to let go of something and move on to another issue, topic or another person in the group. In effect, the leader is able to focus the group in a way that maintains their interest, imagination and energy.

Example 3: A **willingness to risk** confronting, pushing, persuading, energizing, cajoling, or motivating group members to do something. The leader has the vision of knowing when to let group members be confused, so that they can move towards clarity when they are ready.

ROLES AND INTERACTIONS IN THE DEVELOPMENT OF THE GROUP

As group members develop, there are a variety of roles that members take in the group to assist it to function. At different times people may take a different role in the group than is either required by the group or appropriate for them. It is vital for them to be aware of the role they take, because some roles will be more effective than others. Thus, effective group membership requires that much be done to keep the work or discussion of the group focused (task), by providing facts or proposing solutions, and yet help maintain interpersonal relations (maintenance). However, according to Underwood (1973) regardless of the type of role in "which members may be engaged, it is important to note that the particular behavior – standing by itself – is neither constructive nor destructive…that is, whether or not a particular role facilitates or inhibits the group and its members at the time" (p. 124).

TYPES OF TASK ROLES

Task roles relate to specific functions that group members take on in a group to help the group work towards common goals and directions in achieving those goals. Task roles focus on those problem-solving mechanisms that move the group towards achieving the desired goal. These roles are not static, so group members can employ one or more of the roles at any time. It is also possible for group members to change roles from group to group. The following are task functions:

- **Information and Opinion Giver:** shares thoughts and experiences that promote the group discussion or interaction;

- **Information and Opinion Seeker:** asks questions or information on others' ideas, thoughts and feelings which promote group discussion or interaction;

- **Starter:** proposes ideas or activities that encourage actions and tasks that get the group focused or directed;

- **Direction Giver:** develops a plan of action, focuses the attention of the group on a particular task, and directs or explains to group members;

- **Summarizer:** reflects, organizes, conceptualizes ideas, and integrates the major points or issues to be discussed or worked on;

- **Coordinator:** synthesizes ideas and actions and harmonizes the activities and relationships of the members in a cooperative working group;

- **Diagnoser:** identifies, explains and interprets inter-group conflicts, difficulties, issues and blocks;

- **Energizer:** injects energy and activates group members towards a given task, goals or direction;

❧ **Reality Tester:** explores the practicality of ideas and directions, and evaluates alternatives and applies them for workability;

❧ **Evaluator:** examines group goals, decisions and achievements for comparison.

TYPES OF MAINTENANCE ROLES

Maintenance roles focus on the level and intensity of relationships among the group members. They assist the group in working together, focusing the members' attention on communication. These behaviors help the group to (Napier & Gershenfeld, 1999):

maintain itself so that members will contribute ideas and be willing to continue towards progress on the group task…these roles help a group maintain itself in order that work on its task can proceed without becoming immobilized by inappropriate social behaviors and so that individuals are brought effectively into the emotional sphere of the group's life (pp. 240-241).

For example, one member may nod his head encouragingly as another member speaks, while another member may summarize what is said by the group, or make sure all members of the group are heard by soliciting responses from them. The following are maintenance roles:

❧ **Encourager:** is open and accepting of group members and reinforces the contributions of thoughts, feelings and action within the group;

❧ **Harmonizer and Compromiser:** tries to reconcile differing opinions and ideas by looking for common elements;

❧ **Tension Reliever:** reduces tension by using jokes, suggesting breaks or some other activities that relieve pressure;

❧ **Communication Helper:** facilitates communication by being empathic and concrete;

❧ **Evaluator of Emotional Climate:** self-discloses and checks out feelings of group members;

❧ **Process Observer:** observes group dynamics and shares insight into how the group is functioning;

❧ **Standard Setter:** makes group members aware of the group norms, direction and progress towards achieving goals;

❧ **Active Listener:** listens with interest to others, is open to new ideas and goes along with the group when not in disagreement;

❧ **Trust Builder:** is accepting and open to risk taking and individual differences;

❧ **Interpersonal Problem Solver:** promotes togetherness by discussing conflicts as a method of resolving group conflicts.

Types of Non-functional Behavior

Sometimes people in the group intentionally and/or unintentionally behave in such a way that disrupts or blocks the function of the group. Sometimes group members have "hidden agendas," conscious or unconscious, which are different from the stated agenda of the group. Or they may want the group to go in a different direction. People are often surprised when it is pointed out that they are engaged in non-functional behavior. The following are some examples of non-functional behavior:

- **"Mugging"** is the criticizing or blaming of others or showing of hostility against the group or some individual, by deflating the ego or status of others.

- **"Rugby"** is the blocking and interfering with the progress of the group by going off on a tangent, citing personal experiences unrelated to the problem, arguing too much on a point, rejecting ideas without consideration.

- **"Confessional"** is using the group as a sounding board, expressing personal, non-group oriented feelings or points of view.

- **"Kentucky Derby"** is competing and vying with others to produce the best idea, talk the most, play the most roles, or taking actions to gain favor with the leader.

- **"The Victim"** is seeking sympathy and trying to induce other group members to be sympathetic to one's problems or misfortunes, deploring one's own situation, or disparaging one's own ideas to gain support.

- **"Horsing Around"** is clowning, joking, mimicking and disrupting the work of the group.

- **"Hero/Heroine Syndrome"** is attempting to call attention to one's self by loud or excessive talking, putting forth extreme ideas or engaging in unusual behavior.

- **"Flight"** is acting indifferent or passive, resorting to excessive formality, daydreaming, doodling, whispering to others or frequently wandering from the subject.

- **"Red Crossing"** is going to the aid of someone who is experiencing pain or discomfort for the purpose of getting that person off the "hot seat."

- **"St. Sebastian Syndrome"** is asking pointed questions or offering remarks that "sets" a person up and has no purpose, but to hurt and humiliate.

- **"Three Monkey Syndrome"** is using protracted silence or not bothering to respond to someone who is self-disclosing.

- **"Advising"** is responding to another by giving advice directly or indirectly.

- **"Flattering"** is responding in a way that is designed to make people feel better rather than giving them help or insight.

- **"Cracker Jacks"** is a type of responding that is aimed at giving a surprise and has no benefit except hiding an issue.

In examination of non-functional behavior, it is more useful to regard such behavior as a cue to the group's ability to satisfy individual needs through group-centered activity needs. However, it should be remembered that some behaviors could be interpreted differently by different people in the group. It must also be remembered that some behaviors, which can be labeled as non-functional can create an atmosphere that can contribute positively to the group process (e.g., aggressiveness).

FORCE FIELD: A STRATEGY FOR ANALYZING BLOCKS IN GROUPS

Everyone who joins a group, regardless of whether it is work or growth oriented, desires to have effective and satisfactory interactions with other group members. The end result or the product of the group always depends on the quality of the process, whether anyone is conscious of it or not. All group participants eventually come to the conclusion that they will have to work together, regardless of their perceptions, independent goals or work habits to accomplish their goals. Yet just agreeing to work together is to risk conflict, either by covert or overt actions. Joining together is a process of opening up a Pandora's box. It is the unknown that creates hope, but also created is fear, particularly if the group moves beyond the polite stage creating conflict at times. Thus, conflicts are inevitable and part of the group process.

As the group begins working towards its goals, tensions emerge as different group members assert themselves. Just like crossing a river, some may risk the deep part and some the shallow part. Tensions develop in the form of competition, passivity, hostility or confusion, just to name a few. Yet anything that affects the dynamics of change in the group represents an obstacle to be dealt with regardless of the direction. Not surprisingly, many members are fearful of conflict, lack experience in dealing with it or are unskilled at giving or receiving feedback. Naturally, they often choose a course of avoidance when tensions arise. While it may seem strange to "embrace conflict," the fact is that conflict is a natural part of group membership, so it should not be avoided. The greatest difficulty is getting beyond the impasse of confusion, indecision and passivity. It is here that people feel and experience a kind of nothingness. The first step in moving beyond the impasse is to define it as specifically and concisely as possible. For example, if the group is languishing because there is a lack of flexibility, the group can examine the factors that support change in that direction. In many respects, this first step of voicing a concern is the most difficult for group members because it is human nature not to want to "rock the boat." Effective membership requires that the group process be constantly monitored for "cracks" or other issues that impact on its effectiveness. If the group adopts the norm that they will constantly do this, then it is more likely the questions will be voiced (e.g., "How are we doing?").

Force field analysis is used to analyze any issue that impacts the group or affects the group's drive to achieve specific goals. What the leader does is facilitate the group in answering the questions: "How are we doing?" and "What can we do to function better?" The strategy is to help the group diagnose those forces that stop effective group functioning. For example, if the group members were looking at those factors that inhibit the drive towards more flexibility, they would also examine those forces that restrain the drive and brings about rigidity in the group as demonstrated in Figure 3.2. Notice that the flexibility is on a continuum with one end being very flexible, with a high climate of sharing, while at the opposite end the group is closed with a low risk climate (rigid). Events will occur that can move the group towards more risk taking or conversely can move the group towards less risk taking. The process is always pushing and pulling. The driving and restraining forces are the environmental conditions, group member behaviors and situational pressures. Driving forces lead to more personal risk taking, while restraining forces lead to low risk taking.

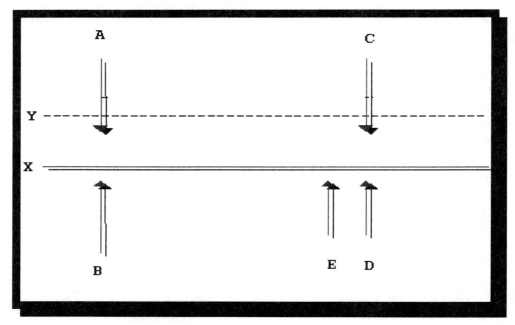

Figure 3.2: Force Field

There is a multitude of driving and restraining forces that can affect the level of openness in a group. At this point, the leader(s) can facilitate the group in voicing those conditions, behaviors or pressures that affect the group process. All conditions voiced by the group should be included in a list regardless of what they are. These can then be prioritized for analysis. For example, an environmental condition that is a driving force in a group is the placement of chairs in a circular design or subdued lighting. Group member behaviors that are driving forces that lead to a more open climate are honest feedback and self-disclosure. A situational condition that is a driving force might be an open ended and flexible time schedule.

Examples of environmental restraining forces might be tables that act as barriers that separate group members. Group member behaviors that can restrain risk taking are submissiveness and indecision. Situational restraining forces might be a structured organizational design, authoritarian leadership or their opposites. Since the forces are working against each other, the push and pull creates a force field that is in constant flux. Mitigating factors are the relative strength of the driving and restraining forces. As demonstrated in Table 3.2, driving force (self disclosure) and restraining force (fear of negative evaluation) are represented as opposing arrows. These forces counterbalance each other, keeping the level of openness at status "X". Both driving force "A" and restraining force "B" are stronger than driving forces (circular formation of chairs) and (small group), retraining forces (windowless room) and (large group). Eliminating or reducing restraining forces might change the group's behaviors by helping the group members to relax, thus creating a warmer atmosphere that brings about more sharing and thereby influencing driving force (self-disclosure). The result could be a movement towards a more flexible group. The force can also vary, as group members get closer to either end of the continuum of openness.

THE NATURE OF THE GROUP EXPERIENCE

Groups, no matter what kind they are, are like people with their own needs, values, norms and practices. Nevis (1987) stresses that for a group to be healthy it requires "a means of tuning into its needs and of mobilizing energy" (p. 30). Groups, like people, seek equilibrium to bring about change, thus it is necessary that there be a willingness to change accustomed patterns of behavior. This is why groups utilize the experimental or laboratory approach. This involves learning by doing, experimentation and the constant examination through the use of feedback (e.g., "How am I coming across?").

IMMEDIACY

There are certain rules of immediacy that can intensify the experience and help the group members understand the dynamics. First, group members can concentrate on being in the here and now rather than talking about things from the past or outside the group. The present and "here and now" always need to be emphasized. Secondly, they can choose to cooperate, despite the fact that there will always be disagreements, because nothing will be accomplished if the group does not. This does not mean there will not be conflict or disagreement, but that group members will involve themselves with others and work at resolving their disagreements. Avoiding confrontations or disagreements is not cooperating; on the contrary, cooperation means facing and dealing with all issues, regardless of what comes up in the group. Thirdly, they can avoid using generalities when they communicate. They can do this by trying to be concrete and specific and using "I" statements. As much as possible they should avoid abstractions, intellectualizing, story telling, or rambling. Finally, they can commit themselves to working through issues in the group rather than independently with the leader or individual group members. Whatever affects one member of the group affects all members of the group; thus, all issues need to be worked through using the arena that the group offers. While it may be easier to deal with an issue people have with another member outside the group, there is the potential for the group to learn and gain insight from the issue.

INTERACTIONS

In order to get into contact with others, group members need to be open to experiencing the full dynamics of the group. It is vital for people to explore and experiment with the way they use language, the differing emotional states, fight-flight response and a variety of core responses. Exploring the way people use language, can help them understand how their thoughts and feelings are translated in their communications with others. People's language reflects how they see the "world" in relationship to themselves (i.e., the words and manner people use reflect their personality). The way people use language is not always spontaneous, for they use expressions and patterns that reflect their cultural background and life experiences. For example, people often use depersonalized expressions, such as using "it" rather than "I". People can experiment with contrasting "it with "I" (e.g. "it is good of you to do that" to "I feel good that you did that").

Exploring how people express their emotions can help them gain knowledge about how they feel about themselves and how they interact with those in their environment. After all, emotional responses begin in infancy and are the basis of people's energy. Through maturation, people learn what types of emotional response help them meet their needs and which do not. Eventually, patterns develop and people begin to use those patterns that are helpful ("good") and drop those patterns that are not helpful ("bad"). To become more aware about their patterns, people can monitor and share their feelings about various issues or practice expressing various emotional states. They can become more cognizant about those emotions that "spark" the group to action or "dull" the group into passivity. For example, people can experiment with "feeling bombardment," in which they use a stream of consciousness to share their emotional states (e.g. "I am feeling confused"; "Now I am feeling fear"; "I feel my fear in my stomach," etc.).

Experimenting with how people use fight or flight in anxious situations can help them maintain greater responsibility and use their power in a more satisfying manner. The group is an ideal place to experiment with this, because fight or flight is the most common reaction to situations that are anxiety producing in a group. When people choose to face an issue or person (fight), they may do this in a way that does not meet their needs. They can explore how they can take a stand, without being obstructionist or engaging in constant "warfare." The other side, avoidance (flight), also has positive and negative sides that can be experimented with. Flight is a good way of controlling or escaping negative situations, yet people may also avoid situations that produce fear or loneliness and deny their feelings. A method of counteracting this trend is exploring the issues or feelings that they want avoid. As a group, people can identify those issues where there is tacit agreement not to talk about something (e.g. "this is a contentious issue that we can't agree on, let's avoid it").

Experimenting with utilizing the core responses or active listening modes can help people build a more effective communication style within the group. Knowing when and how to use various levels of self-disclosure can increase people's communication repertoire. In addition, people can practice using other active listening modes such as confrontation, reflection of meaning, feedback, and encouragement. For example, people can offer self-disclosures to others in the group who they feel most comfortable with and share the specifics of why they feel that way. The group can then offer feedback to each member on what has been shared (e.g. "I am not surprised that you value_____ because I see you as _____").

RESISTANCE

"Much of the frustration that accompanies working within a... group... results from an inability to understand and accept as perfectly natural much of the resistance within a group" (Napier & Gershenfeld, 1985; p. 305). Basically, people organize their lives around reducing stress, which is reflected in the patterns of behavior and rituals that reinforce the familiar (e.g., going to the pub on Friday night). Problem solving and decision-making can create a disruption of people's and group's state of equilibrium, which is one reason for resisting new ideas (e.g., sit in the same seat, tell the same jokes, and maintain prejudices and the same work habits). People need to be reminded that there are stressful situations that have positive outcomes (e.g., job promotion, graduation) as well as negative ones. When people work in a familiar framework of accustomed behavior with those in authority, they know what is expected, but when people take on new responsibilities or change to a new authority, they immediately become more vulnerable and less sure of their position. Unless people feel personally secure and relatively safe within the group, they will tend to respond with their own characteristic patterns of defense (which can be important sources of diagnosing behavior).

What people seem to fear most is being inadequate or impotent (they don't want to have it publicly affirmed). It is, however, an illusion of impotence that reduces the desire for risk (e.g., "That's been tried before"). Thus, it should be remembered that a group's sense of potency will affect its attitude toward problem solving and decision making. People may fear a loss of power because of the traditional gender stereotypes in our society; women, because they might have been conditioned to be powerless for so long, and men, because there might be an ingrained attitude that "to be a man, one must act powerful." Men must learn to get in touch with their sensitive side and realize that strength is not in how much "power" they have, but how they use it. The struggle in the group for women is a "two edged sword," for they "often enter [the helping environment] with a sense of powerlessness, lack of trust of self direction, and permeable "I" boundaries. They may adhere to numerous "shoulds," fail to nurture themselves, and have difficulty communicating suppressed emotions" (Enns, 1987; p. 93).

Groups build security by establishing standards and rules of behavior (traditional values). Most conflicts and resulting tensions in groups can be traced back to four areas of concern: conflicts arising from personal goals; problems arising from personal identity and acceptance; problems generated from the distribution of power and influence; and the question of intimacy that takes in trust and openness. Thus, what was troublesome or fearful before does not have to continue to be so. People are constantly changing, because "flux is basic to experience, so if one can allow each experience the reality it seeks, it will fade into the background in its turn to be replaced by whatever next has the force to appear in the foreground" (Polster & Polster, 1974; p. 48). The dilemma for group members is that, as long as issues remain unresolved, much of the group's energy will be directed toward self-oriented behaviors, and the accomplishment of tasks will be disrupted. Despite the group's best intentions, all problems cannot be erased, but it is important to try. Resistance is a natural reaction to that which is uncomfortable and a form of protection; however, it often blocks awareness and understanding. The Gestalt view is to identify resistance as it arises and to use it as a focus for resolving personal and group issues. Perls (1969a) stressed that if people resist actions because of fear, the best way of dealing with it is by going with it. In other words, take what is fearful and experiment with becoming fearful (e.g., when in terror, become a terrorist).

COGNITIVE DISSONANCE

A poll conducted in the United States after the shooting down of the Iran passenger airplane in the summer of 1988 showed that over 75% of the people did not blame the military for shooting it down, nor did they feel any remorse. Yet people felt that the United States was a moral and caring country. An American military review of the situation laid the blame for the tragic accident on the military. This is cognitive dissonance, in which people's beliefs are at odds with an established attitude. Cognitive dissonance seems to be a common behavior in groups where, despite the facts and feedback, people cannot understand what may be obvious. In some situations, it is a mechanism to help people avoid pain and dislocation, where the most terrifying experience will be suppressed. People go into a kind of shock (e.g., "It never really happened"). Accepting the perception of others in the group will be difficult, for the group could be wrong; on the other hand doubting, suspicions and skepticism can color the truth. In Charles Dickens' novel, *Great Expectations*, the bride is a classic example of cognitive dissonance. She waited for 50 years for her lover to come, keeping the banquet table set and wearing her wedding dress while it disintegrated. The truth was more painful than the reality of a wasted life, because learning new ways of coping in society does not always insure that these strategies will be effective. According to Polster and Polster (1974) the:

> *effect his actions will have…increase experience as he grows more sensitive to the requirements of new learning. With continuing support for growth, errors can be assimilated, and the need for previous self-destructive and crippling props diminishes, and the opportunities for trying out new methods all join together to consolidate the new experiences and transmute them into fresh reality (p. 193).*

ETHICAL ISSUES

I have wondered how people decide that a particular way of doing something is the 'best' way. When I say 'best,' I mean what is ethical. Some people may also call them moral injunctions or general principles. Group members need to consider this and it may be helpful to think about it in these general terms:

1. Consider it 'real,' now, and specifically, rather than what is a symbol or even reality.

2. Experience events in terms of awareness as a yardstick of what is valued, rather than what others value.

3. Consider it a personal responsibility for completing a gestalt or integration of self.

Ethics are guides that help group members be more responsible for themselves and to work more productively with others. While everyone wants to be ethical and do what is considered "right," perhaps all of us fail or are unethical at some time. The following are rights that all group members should be able to exercise at all times:

1. To withdraw from the group at any time.

2. Not to share some issue, problem or information.

3. Not to be verbally abused.

4. To know the psychological risks of involvement in a group experience.

5. To be aware that the group environment is more intense than any other, because change and damage are accelerated.

6. Not to experience any judgmental behavior from the group.

7. To have personal integrity respected.

The "funny" thing about ethical considerations is that what is ethical to one person may not be to another person. So as people interact in the group they must be sensitive to what others consider ethical. As a guide, the group can consider some behaviors that have the affect of being slightly unethical, but sometimes occur in a group regardless of the safeguards. Often these actions and pressures are ignored or played down because they are so subtle. However, if the group honestly addresses them, these subtle behaviors can be minimized. Consider the following:

There should not be any pressure on people to participate in an activity unless they want to participate, yet the very fact that people are involved in a group experience puts pressure on them to participate regardless of what is said. Nothing they say will leave the group room, but often group members will share with their spouses or friends what took place, either by sharing after saying "this is confidential, but ___." While positive statements are fairly easy for people to respond to, their negative feelings are more difficult to bring forth. It may be unethical for people to tell others that they feel negatively towards them without an effort to do something about those feelings. Messages that have double meanings or are interpretive are sometimes provided to group members that are unhelpful or even hurtful: "I bet your mother was a meticulous housekeeper" is an interpretation that does not help the group member, but confirms a personal diagnosis; "I know I can help you…" may be an exaggeration of what can be delivered; "it'll take care of itself" may be a kind of "placebo" that avoids the issue; "everybody in this group will be treated equally," yet it is very difficult to do this in practicality, because one person may be liked better than another.

CONCLUSION

"By our stumbling the world is made perfect." – Sri Auribindo

In the transpersonal approach, immediacy and personal responsibility are emphasized. Thus, rather than just talking about feelings, group members are asked to experience or actualize them through action. Essentially, the goal is to help group members to reintegrate all parts of themselves. The leader "wears bifocal lenses" by paying attention not only to the development of the group as a social system, but to the development of individual group members as well. The leader intensifies the experience and alerts the group to their verbal and non-verbal messages. The group is a dynamic psychosocial environment that affects the attitude, feelings, thinking and actions of the group. As a system, there is a simultaneous interaction between the levels with the group members and leader focusing on the following questions:

Levels	Group Members	Leader
Intra-personal	"How do I relate to my different parts?"	"How do I tap their resources?"
Interpersonal	"How do I relate to others?"	"How can I promote relationships for learning?"
System	"How am I developing in this group?"	"How can I help them learn from each other in the group?"

The process of personal development of people in the group is extremely important, and yet the development of the group is equally important (e.g., the whole is not any greater than its parts). While this may seem like a dilemma, it is in fact another polarity: the individual's needs versus the group's needs. An important element that people in the group must consider is how they will involve themselves in the process. The effective development of the group is everyone's responsibility, so the question for each member is: "How far must or can I go to fulfill my goals and add to the development of the group?" According to Johnson and Johnson (1991), the most important consideration for group members is whether they are committed to a cohesive group by adhering to:

the group's goals, accept assigned tasks and roles more readily, and conform to group norms more frequently. With more cohesion there is an increasing rise in participation of all group members, [that results]…in more resources available for the group to enhance goals accomplishment (p. 409).

In addition, the group must decide on its goals, but the dilemma for individuals is how to satisfy their needs that dovetails the group's goals. Rogers (1973) says that he usually has no specific goal for a particular group and sincerely wants the group to develop its own directions. There are a number of actions that group leaders can utilize to be more effective in the group. However, the group members can also utilize these modes of action to be more effective in the group and ultimately the world at large. They can:

1. Direct their attention to what they want, yet be open to change;

2. Be active when it meets specific needs, but be passive and receptive to the wonder of things in the environment;

3. Examine particulars, but look at the whole or gestalt;

4. Be in control, yet be open to the process;

5. Be specific to what is desired and be open to experiencing confusion;

6. Be humorous and open to laughing at themselves, but know when to be serious;

7. Be curious and open to experimentation, yet look for patterns;

8. Name things, but attend to spatial imagery;

9. Be open to intuitions and gut reactions.

The paradox challenges people in the group, including the leader, to transcend personal freedom and develop by being cooperative, disciplined, and responsible with others in the group. Thus, freedom is not doing what the impulses demand, but achieving a sense of self-awareness, responsibility and spontaneity regardless of the group or situation. Moondance (1994) offers an interesting perspective: "Granddaughter, listen to the wind tonight. There you will hear the song of patience. Each breeze blows a teaching. With each breath you take draw in confidence, peacefulness, endurance" (p. 85)

ACTIVITIES

1. **Enacting Group Roles**: Write an equal number of task roles, maintenance roles and non-functional behaviors and put them on small pieces of paper, fold them up, and put them in a basket. Make sure that there are equal number of roles that fit the number of people involved in the activity. Group members are to participate in a discussion, but act out the roles that they have drawn from the basket. Have 9 or 10 people choose a role from the basket. If the group is larger, have some members sit outside the group and observe one or two members role-playing. Later, feedback can be offered to those observed on their actions. Give the group some topical subject, which they are to make a decision about (e.g., should

self-disclosure be required). Allow 15 minutes for the discussion to develop and then process the activity (20 minutes). In processing the activity, ensure that everyone can share the difficulty in role-playing and how the role fits or doesn't fit a pattern they exhibit in a group.

2. Divide the group into triads and give each triad five maintenance roles, five task roles, and five non-functional behaviors. The triad members should take turns playing one of the different roles (e.g., one member is role playing a task role, another a maintenance and another a non-functional role). One of the triad's members is to discuss some topical issue that has some personal relevance (e.g., "should I buy a new car"). Allow five minutes for each of the 5 cycles. An open-ended discussion of the experience should follow.

CHAPTER FOUR
AWARENESS:
<u>SELF-PERCEPTION IN THE GROUP</u>

If you wish to enter the Way of Tea, you must first be your own teacher; only by careful observation can one learn. A fool is one who gives an opinion without suitable experience. Sen-no-Rikyu

After making the fire, the tea master returns to the tearoom with a water jar that she places next to the hearth. From the tea caddie she takes out the ladle and sets it near the hearth with a small sound ("ponk"), which signifies that Chanoyu is about to begin. All focus is on the ritual movement of the master, but the guests are not looking only at what the tea master does. They are taking in all aspects of the ceremony: the shape of the utensils; the scroll on the wall; the shadow of light reflecting the pattern of the branches on the window screen; the aroma of the finely ground green tea; and the slight sounds emanating from the tea master's movements. As the participants in the Chanoyu ceremony focus their attention, their awareness level increases to a point where they become one with their environment. They are not trying to make something happen; they are just looking and are open to what is there. This oneness matters if the organism is to grow and become fulfilled. Therefore, the only way to growth and oneness is to abandon any idea that you are differentiated from your environment. In groups that foster awareness, an individual has to:

abandon the ongoing flow of communication, turn his attention towards himself, identify what was indeed happening therein, and finally be able to report to another person about processes which might ordinarily remain unobtrusively underground or unattended (Polster & Polster, 1973; pp. 207-208).

The purpose is to sharpen awareness by focusing on senses, emotions, thoughts and perceptions. People are the sum total of all of their parts and, by being more aware of the whole, they can become more responsible and integrated. Thus, the self cannot be examined without looking at the context; it is best discovered by looking at the whole, that is, the individual, the group, the environment in which the group lives and the relationship these people have with the cosmic. This is the essence of the transpersonal approach or to "nurture those aspects that permit a person to disidentify from the restrictions of the personality and to recognize his or her identity with the total self" (Sheikh & Sheikh, 1989; p. 228). Furthermore, if people are to live an effective life, they must be open to experiencing things in the present. This does not mean individuals put themselves first, for unattaching themselves from gross materialism for example, allows them to strive to be greater than themselves. Along with this, there has to be an acceptance of responsibility and the recognition of their interconnectedness. One way to achieve this is building a great sense of awareness of that which is inside the self and outside the self.

Being aware is focusing on what is there and what is not there. What is not there is also a part of what is there. For example, the silence occurring is just as important as our verbal and nonverbal communication. This notion of what is not there is also a vital part of Chanoyu. Even the place in which the tea ceremony takes place suggests emptiness, it is called the "abode of vacancy." Just as participants in Chanoyu try to experience all aspects of the ceremony, they try to become aware of all the things, people and movement around them. It is focussing on what is "flowing" without trying to make awareness happen, but to letting it come freely. When it does, participants opened all their senses to the sensations around them. As a skill, being able to experience awareness can help clarify problems, discover new answers, and understand any experience. In the words of Aristotle, "it is the flowing together of the senses that produces such self-awareness, as well as the images of memories, thought and dreaming" (Hunt, 1995; p. 180).

WHAT IS AWARENESS?

Most dictionaries define awareness as having or showing realization, perception or knowledge. As this definition states, awareness is an all-encompassing concept. In a Transpersonal approach, awareness has a very vital place as an agent of change. Simkin (1974) states that awareness is "the capacity to focus, to attend. Thinking is not awareness, feeling is not awareness, sensing is not awareness. I need awareness to be in touch, to know that I am sensing or feeling or thinking…If I am unaware of what I am doing, I am not responsible for what I am doing" (p. 89).

A broader and more interesting explanation of awareness is provided by Stevens (1971) who divides it into three kinds of awareness, called awareness zones, that always occur in the present. The first zone is awareness of the outside world, which is the experience of sensory contact with things and events going on around you. As I pay attention to this zone of awareness, I look out my window. I see the bamboo as it shakes in the wind, changing into different shades of green, and I hear it rustle as it bends against neighboring stalks. I smell the aroma of the earth, musk like and pungent as nothing else could be. I still have the acrid taste of morning coffee in my mouth. The second zone is awareness of the inside world, which is the sensory experience with inner things and events that are going on. As I pay attention to this zone of awareness, I feel the tension in my leg; it begins to shake in a rhythmic fashion, faster and faster. There is a tingling on the skin of my left arm; I feel excitement building. As I move, the shaking and tingling go away. I lean back on my chair and feel a heaviness coming on…The third zone is awareness of images, ideas, and fantasies going on inside that go beyond the present. This occurs when a person anticipates, explains, guesses, interprets, imagines, plans, or remembers. As I think about what I see, I imagine that the bamboo needs water; perhaps I should go out and water it. Will the bamboo break if the wind becomes too strong? Perhaps my body is telling me to exercise. Am I becoming too inactive? Perhaps I was always destined to go through life like this. I remember that, as a child, I really enjoyed watching things. As I go on, I wonder what I should write next. I want people to understand what I am trying to say. I want my efforts to be something worthwhile and meaningful to others.

AWARENESS AS A PROCESS

As a process, awareness sounds like it is similar to introspection, but it is different. The difference is that introspection is a way of looking inward to learn something. Introspection is a process whereby people try to figure out something or to make sense of it. They review and try to analyze their behavior. For example, people may ask themselves, "What did she mean when she said that?" What they do in their minds is go over what she said, how she said it and possible meanings. Perhaps they go so far as to play out scenarios in their heads. They might end up, after a lot of thinking, with what they take as her meaning. But do they really know? They may guess right, but they will never know. It becomes confusing when one tries to do this, because one does not know what is right. In the end, perhaps one is, as Polster (1966) suggests, distracted:

by expectations of failure or success. We are so prejudiced in favor of one behavior over another. We are prejudiced...in favor of taking over other behavior, so we are prejudiced in favor of relevance over irrelevance...and given these prejudices, we might not be fascinated with people who don't fit those prejudices (p. 9).

This does not mean that people detach themselves from what is going on around them and become introspective. While detachment from time to time is comfortable and even protective, in the end it is very destructive. Meursault, the protagonist in Albert Camus' (1946) novel, *The Outsider*, lived life in a detached and introspective manner. Even when convicted of murder, he reacted indifferently and allowed himself to be pushed by events, instead of making choices of what he should do. It is only by acknowledging existence, that people have essence, and their essence is expressed when they make free choices. Awareness is a process of noticing and observing what one does, how one feels it, what one's thoughts are, and what one's body sensations are. These thoughts and body sensations are like a passing scenery, which unfurls like a panorama that people experience as it occurs. Consider the following perspectives on what it means to become aware:

In Freud's narrow view, it meant calling into awareness repressed impulses and instinctual desires. In Fromm's view, the average individual is only half awake; he or she is conscious of fictions but has the potential to become conscious of the reality behind the fiction. Consequently, to make the unconscious conscious means to wake up, to know reality (Sheikh & Sheikh, 1989; p. 115).

So, when people observe with meticulous precision the tea master whisking the tea, they see the magic of the dancing movements. In the ordinary movement of the tea making, they observe the silences, which allow them to hear the water boiling and the pine branch brushing the roof of the building. It is all a pattern or process. In the same way as people listen to what others say to them, they will notice how they say it and experience all the sensations, feelings, thoughts, and physical reactions. When this happens, there is total contact, which allows them to be open to all kinds of possibilities. This contact is the process of awareness.

Two aspects of this process of awareness assist people in understanding and putting into perspective what is happening. The first aspect is that it allows them to keep up to date with themselves. At any given time they know how they feel and what they think. Meaning is not something that has to be processed before they can act. People are people and they act as themselves. The second aspect is the interaction people have with their environment. Boundaries become clear and they react more spontaneously to their environment. They see more, experience more and are aware of more in their surroundings. If people try to split feelings and thoughts they will find that it is difficult, if not impossible. The focus of the Transpersonal approach that I use is to help people to reawaken to the natural rhythm between awareness and the frequent interruptions that exist in day-to-day activities in the environment. When they start to think and analyze, they cannot be completely aware of what is going on around them. To attend simultaneously to two things with the same degree of awareness is very difficult, because there will always be something missed. If people can just be aware of what is happening and let it flow, they will experience it, not in parts, but as a whole. People will know where they end and where other things begin. When this happens, they are more self-supporting and responsible.

The ceremony of Chanoyu brings peace to its participants, who feel renewed and invigorated with the heightened sense of awareness. Awareness has a curative quality because, as people's awareness levels increase, it will become clear that the organism (e.g., body, mind, emotions and spirit) is self-regulating. Those things that people do naturally, sometimes even the smallest, are done without planning or considering how others might view the action. The action is done because it seems to need doing, so our mind is alert to what is being done, and so is our spirit. Arasteh (1989) emphasized that in the healthy person:

experience and behavior overlap and inner and outer expression are the same; but in many cases, behavior is the rationalization or inhibitor of experience – it is a cover. Experience has an organic and luminary nature, whereas, behavior is characterized by conditioning. It is experience, not behavior, that produces change and, at the same time, strengthens one's sensitivity (p. 150).

This means that, if people are more aware, they can learn to trust their natural processes. If they ignore it or abuse their body, they know that they will destroy it; but if they work with it and not against it, it will give back to them and help them. As they grow in awareness, they will sense more of the wisdom of their whole being. For example, when people jog they know that once they overcome limitations they put on themselves, their running takes on a natural rhythm. They seem to glide as they run. Their mind is not telling their body what to do, for if they let their mind take over, they will feel tired. They will think about finishing. Their rhythm will falter and finally they will want to rest; but when they run without thoughts, they will become aware of all the things around them. They are now in a state of awareness where they have become open to new insights, experiences and understandings. In the Sufi tradition, awareness is a final rebirth that starts people on the road to living in a new light. "Awareness may come to a person suddenly, or it may develop gradually. Yet awareness is not enough. The seeker must cease unsuitable past behavior: he or she must experience repentance, decide to reform and finally cleanse the self of enmity and cruelty" (Arasteh, 1989; p. 157).

The Outer Zone of Awareness

When people have awareness of the world around them, using the senses becomes the most concrete method of expanding boundaries. As they interact in the group and they are stimulated by what they see, smell, touch, taste and hear, they will notice that each of these sensory channels determines how they relate to others. What is surprising is how people have been influenced by their environment in what they have experienced and how they have been conditioned. This does not mean they do not have the choice to change the conditioning; but once they have been trained to perceive something in a particular way, it becomes extremely difficult to change. For example, cultural upbringing has a very strong influence on what people will consider as tasting good. Many people from China have a preference for "anything but fresh vegetables or cheese." These foods are nourishing, delicious and certainly preferable to a North American, but it is just the opposite for people from China. Consider these assumptions about the senses as they affect people's awareness.

The sensory organs differ in the amount and type of information they can receive. Consider an instance of looking at some pictures of food in a magazine. The food may look delicious, but how does it taste? Just seeing something does not give people any indication that they will like the taste. When I lived in the Philippines, I would often hear the voice of a man selling a delicacy called "bulut". This is an egg, which has been allowed to age before it is cooked (it contains the embryo of the chicken). I went out to buy one, but my Filipino friends always laughingly warned me that this delicacy should be eaten only in the dark. One day I brought it inside, sat down with a glass of lemonade, opened the egg, and became really sick. What I saw was a perfectly formed little chicken, complete with feet, head, and feathers. My senses of taste and smell never prepared me for this. This does not mean that I should not trust my visual awareness, but that some senses are more developed than others. Through practice one can increase the level of awareness of certain senses and learn to discriminate between different tastes or sounds or what is being touched. All the sensory channels are interrelated. All of the senses work together as one interacts with others. What one sees is affected by what one hears; what one hears is affected by what one smells, and so on. If a person interacts with others in the group only as they appear to him or her, that person will not get the full benefit of who they are. People are more than just those parts that can be observed with the eyes. As one becomes aware of others and things in the environment, all the senses start working together in the discovery of new things. This occurs because the senses screen how people perceive various stimuli. Unfortunately, all the things they look at are not seen. It could be argued that, if they were able to take in all the information that is there, they would suffer an overload of information. If they are using only one channel of their senses, they may only be aware of certain things, but if they are able to access more channels of awareness, their repertoire increases. In the group, people may see that one person is wearing a motorcycle jacket and react to him in a stereotypical way, assuming that motorcycle jackets are worn by people who are "rough." Sometimes I have observed that people in groups react to their facilitator only as such, rather than as a person who happens to be a facilitator. As a result, they see the facilitator in a capacity that not only dehumanizes the person, but projects enormous power on that person (e.g., that person's insights are more meaningful than their own).

The senses influence the messages, particularly non-verbal messages that people transmit to others. If one is close to someone, he or she cannot see that person's whole body, but only some things, such as a face and upper torso. Conversely, if one is far away, one may not be able to smell the scent of a person or hear that the person is breathing heavily when speaking. Yet those parts one does not see could be crucial in what is being said; but since one is not aware of them, one may misunderstand the message. This could affect how one perceives the messages. When someone comes close to a person, he or she notices that there is a much stronger feeling of connectedness. It is easier to speak in more intimate tones and with more warmth. In fact, most people never realize how powerful this sense is to helping people learn. Odors are full of memories and may be processed in the brain differently than are sights and sounds (Schab, 1990). Finally, all people do not have the same level of sensory power. Some seem to have a superhuman capacity to hear or see, while others seem to be very limited. Sometimes loss of sensory power is due to no fault of our own, as in the case of age, accident or illness. According to Burgoon and Saine (1978), the "loss of the use of one sensory organ places greater dependence on the others. The potential power of our sense generally exceeds our capacity. Blind people…tend to develop auditory power two or three times greater than that of seeing people" (p. 45).

The implication is that one can also learn to develop the senses and awareness to a greater capacity than what is used at the present. As awareness develops, one can be better able to utilize all of the senses. As a result, the person will be able to discover aspects of the environment that he or she never knew existed; and things that were taken for granted, such as the breeze or the smell of flowers, now make the environment more colorful and meaningful.

THE INNER ZONE OF AWARENESS

Meditation has long been associated with inner awareness and, although it is vital to be aware if people are to meditate, awareness, like meditation, is not a passive process. Buddhist thought emphasizes the "complete view" of living in the world. The aim is to see the world not as it could be or as it is going to be, but as it is right now. This comes about through a process of awareness called yathabhutam or "just as it is." Awareness, according to Watts (1957), is:

a lively attention to one's direct experience, to the world as immediately sensed, so as not to be misled by names and labels…and the last section of the path, is the perfection…signifying pure experience, pure awareness, where there is no longer the dualism of the "knower" and the known (p. 52).

Meditation, or inner awareness, is the core of the Zen Buddhist way of enlightenment, called satori. It has often been described as a state of no-mindedness that comes when there is no thinking or analyzing. When this happens there is an "aha" experience. This is a process of suddenly becoming aware of something that was not understood before. Everything falls into place and that which was a confused jumble of thoughts and feelings now has meaning. Suddenly, the separation of self and world, of subject and object, or any other such polarities is no longer there. Leggett (1978) describes the power of inner awareness, expressed in the Zen form, zazen, as the:

> gate to the great liberation; all Dharmas flow out of it, and the thousand practices come from it. The divine powers of wisdom arise from within it, the way of man and of heaven opens out from it. All the buddhas come and go through this gate, and the Bodhisattva enters his practice by it. Those of the Hinayana stop halfway, and those on the outer paths do not get on to the right road at all despite all their efforts. No doctrine, open or secret, leads to Buddhahood without this practice (p. 43).

The inner zone of awareness is an active process of living that is not just contemplation. Although meditation in the Zen form occurs when you sit in a cross-legged Buddha posture (double lotus) called zazen, it does not have to be that way. Suzuki (1962), describes Zen as "not sinking oneself into a state of torpidity by sitting quietly after the fashion of a Hindu saint and trying to exclude all the mental rippling that seems to come up from nowhere, and after a while pass away – where nobody knows" (p. 90).

In fact, there are many different forms of meditation that exclude the classic zazen posture. Suzuki (1962) tells the story of the seeker who wanted to find enlightenment and went to great lengths to find a master, who responded to the seeker by saying, "Before enlightenment, chop wood and carry water. After enlightenment, chop wood and carry water." While many answers to life's problems can be found by developing an inner awareness, it does not have to be found through deprecating your body. The rationale of developing inner awareness, as Suzuki said, is that all people are endowed with a Buddha-like nature. They have a choice to develop this natural process or let it lie dormant. However, if they become more aware, the inner dimensions of themselves crystallize and allow them to experience more. Suzuki (1962) calls this:

> the business of the Yogi who is therefore to bring out his self-nature, which is the Buddha nature, in its original purity. But...in practice this is apt to lead the Yogi to the conception of something separate, which retains its purity behind all the confusing darkness enveloping individual mind (p.159).

Meditation may lead to an inner awareness that may result in clearing up the consciousness in such a way that people can see the image of their original pure self-being (i.e., what was before all of the socialization). The problem is that this may separate them from life, rather than increasing their inner awareness to help them function in an expected manner. However, it continues to be an important strategy from the Transpersonal approach to counselling and psychotherapy.

Awareness of the inner zone of being can assist people in keeping their focus off distant things that can distract and throw them into confusion. When they focus in on nothing, where there is no thinking or analyzing, thoughts do not rush about and the body and mind become one. There is no why or how or when, just what. What happens is a state of clear awareness, where even the emotions concerning life and death are not pressing on the self. Just as in the Chanoyu, whether the focus is on the beauty of what is eaten, or if it is the taste of the tea, the sight of the bowl, or the fragrance of the flowers, all thoughts of past and of future are forgotten.

When people are aware, there is no sense of time because, when they try to put what is around them into any form of organization, they are explaining it. In other words, when people try to categorize and explain things logically, they limit them. Suzuki (1962) stressed that there is no separation, "where time has not come to itself; that is to say, where timelessness has not negated itself so as to have a dichotomy of subject-object, Man-Nature, God-World" (p. 240). This timelessness of awareness is expressed in Zen as having no dichotomy, since it is the beginningless beginning of all things. In the self-actualized person, there is no beginning or ending, only a present "here and now" existence. The aim of the Transpersonal approach is to end this dichotomy or to split and integrate all the parts. When people become aware, they are just "being" with their environment. Everything is immediate, concrete and without any illusions. There is no analysis or judgment. Experiences are accepted for what they are. Through awareness they center themselves and move towards self-realization, self-reliance, self-actualization and transformation of the self.

AWARENESS OF FANTASY

Fantasies are often thought of as being useless activities, because fantasizing usually involves things or experiences that people want, expect or even fear happening. It is obvious that fantasy is a process that is unreal, but fantasy by no means is useless. For me, fantasy is a method of going beyond myself and dreaming of past events and things to come. Sometimes it is both satisfying and anxiety producing. It has given me pleasure, but also pain. However, if the process of imagination is only used as an escape, it is wasted, because it has the potential, according to Stevens (1971), of flowing into a state of:

> awareness that interacts with existing reality, and something new grows in the world. A creative person is aware of the qualities and characteristics of his surroundings, and responds to these surroundings with awareness of his own individual process – his own feelings, needs and wishes (p. 37).

Imagination is the source of creativity, because there is an integration of the awareness of self, the environment and fantasies. Fantasizing is a satisfying and useful endeavor as long as it is not split off from awareness. When it is, worry and anxiety occur and people's imagination creates all kinds of fear. The unreal becomes the real, creating a disruptive influence. The fear of negative evaluation is an example. If people fear to try something new because they are afraid of how they will be evaluated, then they will never try anything. Early in the group this is quite a common fear for some people. They play it safe, because they may have fantasized that others may ridicule them if they say what is on their mind. What people have to work towards in order to use their fantasy power to its fullest, is to become more aware of themselves in relation to the environment.

When there is acceptance, acknowledgment and identification of experiences in the present, full awareness results. There are times when even the unpleasant must be acknowledged, because it is a part of living. Perls (1969a) felt that the "avoidance of unpleasantness and risk is both a reduction of my awareness and an alienation of my experiences. This alienation is the process of saying that's not me, that's something different" (p. 38). The power of fantasy is infinite. Fantasy is a process where people can go forward, backward, or to strange and unusual situations. While they are using their imagination, they can utilize awareness to experience what is not real. In the group experience, this process can be used to activate people's imagination in dreams and guided imagery. According to Tyler (l979), the self:

> *grapples with the tension of opposites directly while experiencing polarities within oneself, and confronts archetypal images in the here and now…there is an insistent focus on experiencing such integrative processes in the presence of and, importantly with participation of the therapist (p. 107).*

As members of a group, people are exposed to fantasy situations in which they can make contact and experiment with artful decisions. While the situation is contrived, the awareness that they have about themselves and their environment is real. Besides, fantasy may be projected reality or just another way of seeing something in a different form. Polster and Polster (1973) suggest that what people are working towards is the best use of the awareness zone of fantasy activities, in which:

> *everyone manages his energy so that he makes good contact with his environment or he resists the contact. If he senses that his efforts will succeed – that he is potent and that his environment is capable of nourishing return – he will confront his environment with appetite, confidence and even daring (p. 70).*

A MODEL OF AWARENESS

The Johari Window was developed as a mechanism for understanding degrees of self-awareness (Figure 4.1). It is called a Johari Window after its originators, Joseph Luft and Harry Ingram (Egan, l970), who divided people's life awareness into four parts. In groups the Johari window is used as a means of getting people to look at each of the four categories and think of what would fit into each part.

Reading the box horizontally are the parts dealing with the self, while reading vertically are the parts dealing with how people appear to others in their environment. In both parts, there are things they and others freely know, but there is also a blind spot or unknown part. These are parts hidden from others and unknown to themselves. For example, I freely let others know that I did not like sky diving, but I hide from others that I am afraid of being thought of as incompetent. My single-mindedness in the way I do some things in my life sometimes blinds me as to

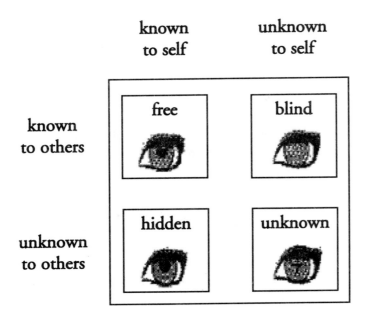

Figure 4.1: Johari Window

how I annoy others. Certain aspects of my conduct, unknown to others and me, block me from full participation with some people and in some activities in my daily life.

The more aware people are, the smaller are the hidden, blind and unknown parts that they have (Figure 4.2). As a result, they are apt to be more open, spontaneous and willing to be self-disclosive and to offer feedback to others in the group. The less aware they are, the smaller is the free part (Figure 4.3). Therefore, they may be more closed, rigid and guarded in the group. While all people have behavior patterns that

reflect their degree of awareness, few people remain totally static. Thus, they are constantly changing to accommodate circumstances. Figure 4.3 may well represent group members' awareness levels during the initial stages of the group; but as they establish closer relationships, Figure 4.2 will be more representative. According to Stevens (1971) the best way to be aware is to learn to focus, which is described as a:

> search light. Whatever you focus
> your attention on is pretty clear
> but other things and events tend
> to fade out of awareness. If I ask
> you to become aware of what
> you hear, you can probably hear

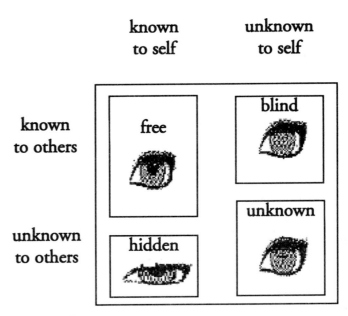

Figure 4.2: Openness

known
to self   unknown
                 to self

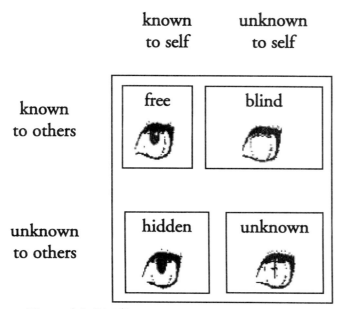

known
to others

unknown
to others

Figure 4.3: Rigidity

quite a few different sounds and noises...And while you are doing this, you are mostly unaware of the sensations in your hands...As I mention your hands, your attention probably moves there, and you become aware of the sensations in your hands (p. 9).

While people's awareness is constantly shifting, by focusing it, they can move at will to the three awareness zones outer, inner and fantasy. Here are some factors that affect how they will focus their awareness. These include:

❦   The selection of the object they focus on;

❦ Any generalizations they make about the object;

❦ Any avoiding of unpleasant or fearful things;

❦ The length and duration of the focus;

❦ How connected they are with the object of focus;

❦ Any interruptions while they are focusing;

❦ Any pleasant or unpleasant aspects brought up as a result of the focusing;

❦ The physical attributes of the object of focus.

To get an idea of how these factors affect people's awareness, consider this example. A facilitator asked one group member to look around the room and let his focus go anywhere he liked. After letting him take everything in, the facilitator asked him to respond to whatever he focused on. He shared that he first saw a number of things, then his gaze focused on one. He began to make some generalizations about it in his mind such as the spots on the wall. A noise from outside occurred, and his focus shifted. "What was that?", he thought. He thought it was someone skateboarding, then he thought, "I can hear various conversations going on in the room." Then his thoughts began to come in a quick fashion. As he focused on a chair, memories flooded into his mind and he was pushed back into the past. It was something uncomfortable and he quickly pushed it away. Next, some physical attributes held his attention, the foot of a man sitting across the room. He could have gone on and on because the process of awareness, like learning, is endless. Of course, the difficulty is to be able to shift on choice to something desirable rather than something unpleasant. Imagine the power, if people were able to go to bed at night and literally put everything out of their head except the task of getting a good night's sleep. Perhaps most people could not do this, but those with a highly developed sense of awareness could easily shift their awareness and focus on anything, including sleep.

ACTUALIZING AWARENESS PRINCIPLES IN EVERYDAY LIVING

Awareness is the process of seeing completely all that there is to be seen. Awareness breaks down into what people are experiencing or being and what they are doing. It is possible for people not to be able to experience things completely, because they try to understand why, rather than being attentive to what is said. This happens, for example, because people are thinking about why someone is talking, rather than listening, observing and feeling what is being said. This distorts the message and creates interpersonal problems. When people begin to evaluate, make judgments or ask why, they cease to be aware. When people are aware, they are able to experience things at deeper levels. All of their senses are engaged. They can make full contact only if they enter a realm of being in which they are accepting of themselves, which means they must also take total responsibility for their actions. They do not have to explain or meet the expectations of the world. They are! As they become more aware of people and things in their environment, contact is made. This contact is supported through their breathing and the manner in which they experience sensations, textures, colors, images and sounds. People can now give a voice to what they are experiencing. For example, when a person is intimate with a loved one, that person becomes aware of the feel of the loved one's skin. The person feels the softness, the downy hair that gently brushes the face, the different shades in the colors reflected in their hair, the gentle breathing of the loved one's body as the person strokes their soft skin. Perhaps, the person will become aware of rising excitement and of the possibilities... it is all a matter of awareness. In intimate situations, many of the senses seem to be engaged, but in fact in a person with a high sense of awareness, the senses are engaged in all situations.

When there is an absence of awareness it is usually associated with avoidance. People separate themselves from their environment and are avoiding many potential benefits including risks. Not taking any risks will reduce the chances of making mistakes, which could make existence boring, uneventful and lacking in vitality. If people take the time to focus, they will notice that there are things that they never saw before. In groups I like to ask people to look around the room and share what they are aware of, for example, "I am aware of _____." A facilitator will want them to fill in the blanks and try to mention as many things as they can and notice where they focus their awareness. As they do this, the facilitator wants them to consider the following questions: "Is it through the senses? Is it through the inner self? Or is it through thoughts or fantasies? What are the zones of awareness? What are those factors that affect their awareness?"

There is a continuum of awareness between these differing zones (Figure 4.4). In addition, there is an aspect of self where there is no awareness, which Perls (1969b) called the DMZ. He borrowed this term from the US military that referred to the area separating North and South Vietnam as the "Demilitarized Zone," because there was no action between the two warring sides. They saw each other, but pointedly ignored each other. It is an apt term, because the DMZ is a place where there is not only no action, but little energy to integrate or to understand – it is a kind of dead zone. Problems arise because of the fragmentation of self, life, and experiences, which is reinforced through the mind. In the DMZ, there is only judgment, control, comparison, analysis, rehearsal, and memory. According to Van de Riet, Korb, and Gorrell (1980), the DMZ:

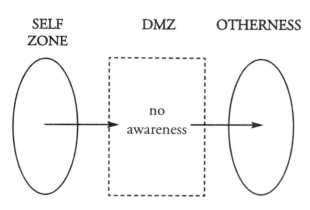

Figure 4.4: The "DMZ"

is a meta-experience —experiences about experiences — that mediates, improves, destroys, biases, organizes, but profoundly influences the quality of the inner and outer zonal experiences. The capacity in individuals for meta-experience entails the separation of cognitive functions from other experiential functions (p. 42).

A person truly aware can focus awareness on self and on others and can use fantasies for creative and satisfying experiments. The DMZ is to be reduced or eliminated. The following are some activities that can help people focus on various aspects of being. In the activities, using the context of the Johari window, people are to write in each of the areas what they focus on. The activities are divided up into areas of: body structure, movement, body process, sensations, feelings, thinking and fantasy.

Body Structure: The body image reflects how people feel about themselves. The image they have of themselves has been influenced by their early experiences. If there is a negative body image, then it will influence one's self-esteem. When people focus their awareness on their body, particularly their posture, they will get an indication of how they feel about it. I ask group members these focusing questions: "What is your posture? Do you slouch or do carry your body in a straight position? Are your legs or arms crossed? How open is your body? Does it feel heavy? Or light? Does it take up a lot of space or very little? How energetic do you feel? Look at your body in a mirror and begin to record your awareness, without judging. If your body had a voice, what would it say to you?"

Movement: In Western culture, dance has not been generally considered healing or therapeutic. This has begun to change as dance and art therapies have demonstrated their potential for healing. Most people have had the experience in dance where they expressed a variety of feelings such as love, desire, joy and anger. As a stimulus for awareness, the movement of the body is very encouraging. Often I ask people in the group not to verbally describe how they feel, but to put their feelings into movement. Afterwards I will ask them these focusing questions: Be as free or restrictive as you desire and, "what are you aware of? What was the pattern of your movement? How does each of the body parts match or mismatch each other (e.g., face with torso)? Do you feel comfortable using your body as a modality of expression? Do you feel powerful or weak? What are the patterns of movement that you use to express your feelings?"

Body Process: It is impossible to put aside the value of the body process in communication. In fact, according to Kepner (1987) people "who are feeling the kind of distress that prompts them to seek help are often intent on getting rid of some uncomfortable body experience" (p. 6). Many people have split themselves off from their body, so they do not feel what is there. Yet there is a very high correlation of the body with language and emotions. Getting people to put movement to their words helps them become more attuned to what their bodies may be telling them.

CONSIDER THE VERBAL IDIOMS OR WORD PICTURES ("RED FLAG EXPRESSIONS") THAT HAVE EVOLVED, AND THE CONNECTION CAN BE READILY SEEN. FOR EXAMPLE, IF ONE LISTENS TO HOW PEOPLE DESCRIBE THEIR FEELING, ONE WOULD HEAR THESE PHRASES: BUTTERFLIES IN THE STOMACH; TURNED OFF; BOILING POINT; THIS IS THE PITS; STEAMED; PISSED OFF; DOWN IN THE DUMPS; THE BLUES; TIGHT ASS; CHARGED TWO-FACED; KNUCKLE UNDER; BACK TO THE OLD GRIND; TON OF BRICKS; BROKEN HEART; GRIND YOU DOWN; PAIN IN THE NECK; CHILLS DOWN MY SPINE; NO BALLS; CHOKE UP; SUCKS; SHRUG IT OFF; TIGHTWAD; LILY LIVERED; UNDER THE WEATHER; AND CRUSHED.

Movement, combined with exaggeration, can be used to help people become more aware of their bodies in relationship to their communication patterns. To increase their awareness, a facilitator can ask them to try a few experiments. One experiment that can be used is to have the person think back to a time in life when he or she felt lonely. As the person imagines this, the facilitator can ask him or her to describe the feeling. A facilitator would probably notice that when people do this, they usually have idioms to describe themselves (i.e., a broken heart). Next, the facilitator can ask the person to physically represent the idiom that was used. It would not be surprising that the descriptors will closely follow some bodily process. Afterwards, the person could be asked to focus the feeling on a body part (i.e., where do you feel your loneliness?). This could be followed by asking the person to become that body part (e.g., "I am a broken heart...I feel weak and in pain...").

Sensations: In my experience one of the most effective methods of being more aware of self and the environment is utilizing all of the body sensations. Many people, who have disowned their body, need help in re-sensitizing themselves to their senses. Some people have even stored emotions, like hurt, in their posture. It is sometimes easy to recognize someone who is fearful, because their posture reflects it regardless of whether they will admit it. Essentially, people's perception of reality is guided by sensations, because sensations are always immediate. When people open their awareness to their sensations, they take a risk. According to Leggett (1979), the Chinese philosopher Hui-neng stated the mind: "could only be apprehended in the process of its working or functioning and not in its repose, in its stillness. Only by plunging into life rather than evading it, could dynamic intuitions abolish all distinctions, categories, and boundaries" (p. 67).

Yet if people are to live life to the fullest, they must take risks and allow the self to experience through sensations. To get people in the group to take a risk -something they hesitate doing- a facilitator could ask them to try experiments that might be silly but help them become aware of all of the sensations available. For example, the facilitator could ask them to take an orange, cut it in half, and smell it, taste it, look at it closely, and squeeze it to hear how it sounds. Next, they could be asked to rub the orange on their cheek. As they do each of these things the facilitator asks them to pay attention to their awareness. Most people are surprised at the many different sensations they experience. After this activity, people are asked to experiment in the group using more sensations. What they discover is that there are more channels of sensing open to them, because they notice more details, textures, and so on.

Feelings: Feelings occur at a visceral level, a "gut level," a point that is felt in the body. In Western society, feelings are often where people may be most blocked. Perhaps they have introjected feelings by thinking that, if they share how they feel, people will think of them as immature. Yet, it is the feelings that bring the most intensity to life and experiences. According to Lathrop (1976), feelings are: "the refined products of emotion, and emotions are like the climate. Feelings are like the living creatures that inhabit the climate. They are defined and limited entities, unlike the emotions" (p. 104). Obviously, feelings are expressive because they are colorful and lively. Without feelings there is no excitement. Feelings literally drive people and help them be more aware of their surroundings. Passons (1975) states that feelings serve people by providing energy that drives them and directs behavior that fulfills their needs. Yet, feelings come on a continuum from low levels to high levels of intensity. However, it is crucial that people be responsible for their feelings. Once they become responsible, then they can create them in a never-ending repertoire.

Language: It is through language that people express their personal style, philosophy and outlook. This relationship of language to being, according to Perls, Hefferline and Goodman (1951), is useful:

> to define "personality" as a structure of speech habits and consider it as a creative act of the second and third years; most thinking is sub vocal speaking; basic beliefs are importantly habits of syntax and style; almost all evaluation that does not spring directly from organic appetites is likely to be a set of rhetorical attitudes. To define in this way is not to belittle or explain away personality, for speech itself is a profound spontaneous activity (pp. 320-321).

To raise group members' awareness about the power of their language, a facilitator could ask people in the group to try experimenting with changing words such as "can't" to "won't" or "need" to "choose." Next, people are asked to think of something they feel that they have to do in the next week. For example, a common response revolves around having to go to work or doing some task that people find onerous ("I won't do that…" or "I need to go to work"). The person would be asked to change the "won't" and "need" to "choose" and then reflect on how the two differ ("I choose not to do that…" or "I choose to go to work"). To help them focus, the facilitator could ask these questions: What are you aware of as you make these changes? Do you feel more emphatic? Precise? Clearer? Stronger? Suzuki (1962) emphasizes this dynamic power of language: "Living experiences ought to be told in a living language and not in worn out images and concepts" (p.56).

Thinking: Thinking often interferes with awareness, because it inhibits it. According to Suzuki (1962), if people are to get the most out of their inner awareness, they "must forego all the ordinary habits of thinking which control…everyday life, they must try to see if there is any other way of judging things, or rather if their ordinary way is always sufficient to give them the ultimate satisfaction of their…needs" (p. 83).

It is helpful for group members to try to experiment with thinking. A facilitator could ask them to let their minds wander for a few minutes. The following questions could be used to focus them: "Did your thoughts skip to many different topics or did you dwell on one topic? What did you think about? Was there a pattern in your thinking? Were you thinking about the past, present, or future? What does your thinking help you to avoid? Now, see if you can stop thinking. Stop after a few minutes and what are you aware of?" This could be followed by some sort of homework, such as asking them once each day to experiment with meditating or not thinking.

Visualization: Art in its visual form is a unique method for exploring experiences, feelings and thoughts. Paintings, sculptures and pottery are only a few ways through which people down through the ages have communicated their hopes, dreams and ideas. Group members can be presented with a variety of situations that they have observed in the group or in their daily lives, then be asked to visualize the physical scene and the emotional climate. Closing their eyes to picture it, they are then asked to draw the scene. However, it is their awareness of what they have visualized that is important and not the actual reproduction of the events. Often pictures have a distorted and uneven quality that is the opposite of a photograph. Color and shape stand out and the concrete fades. What seems to happen is that their imaginations are stimulated, because "truth" is not in the obvious, but in what the experience meant. In the sharing that follows the drawing, the group becomes aware of how different events mean different things to people. Even drawn pictures of the same scene produce a variety of different images. Suddenly, a landscape, for example, is not a place of beauty, but a "living place" with a history that is simultaneously past, present and future oriented.

Fantasy: Fantasies have played an important part in creativity. According to Passons (1975), fantasies "follow the question 'what would happen if…' [and] have resulted in some of the most startling and profound inventions and discoveries in history…a person can learn a great deal about himself through fantasy" (p. 132) Subjects or objects that come up in fantasy tell people how they are perceiving the world. If there is some "unfinished business," it will come out in their fantasies. When they take a fantasy and put it into action through role playing, the fantasy comes alive and can make them aware of happenings in the past, aspects of behavior in the present, and an opportunity to experiment with future plans and actions. One experiment that can illustrate this is taking any daydream and role-playing it. Some useful process questions are: "What scares you or brings you joy about role playing it? Where do you feel the fear or joy?" The facilitator can also ask them to take each part and be that part. As a warm-up activity, the facilitator could ask them to take an object (or person) and share what they are aware of.

MEDITATION AS A PROCESS

Meditation is the process of developing an attitude that is controlled, but not controlled. What happens when someone meditates is an altering of his or her consciousness. In fact, the aim of Zen is to increase understanding, by realizing and perfecting one's own mind. Yet Zen meditation strives to release one from the domination of the intellect. There is a paradox here. According to Humphreys (1968), no person "should go further into meditation who has not found within…a faculty superior to the thinking mind" (p. 154). Thinking is important, but must be abandoned if enlightenment is to occur and truth is to be revealed. In the Sutra of Hui Neng, there is no difference between the enlightened and ignorant person, but what makes these two different is that one realizes it and the other one does not. Thus, one can become a new person by acting in a natural, mindful and skillful manner.

Meditation is a process of hearing the music of the inner life, which is mystical and creative. The inner holds the knowledge of the cosmos, waiting to be revealed to us in an entirely new order. Our spiritual world, which is full of symbols, ideas and images, can lead us to enlightenment.

STAGES OF MEDITATION

According to Willis (1979) meditation has four distinct stages: preparation, attention, receptivity and higher consciousness. The stages are linear and overlapping, with the preparation and attention stages as devices for centering and quieting oneself. Meditation is essentially receptivity and higher consciousness, with preparation and attention as a means for being receptive.

Preparation: Like having a nutritious dinner, one must make proper preparations. One method of preparing is to empty oneself by a process of purification. Some means of purification may be fasting or any other ascetic practices or monastic training. Not everyone agrees that this is necessary to go to these lengths, but all agree that proper preparation must precede meditation. The methods of clearing one's mind and heart are numerous.

Attention: LeShan (1974) divides attention into 4 types: the body, the intellect, the emotions, and actions. The body is used to focus all the energy, which then allows the mind to be free of itself. Two examples of using the body are the Sufi dance and yoga postures. Zazen stresses this notion in prescribing how one should sit and place the hands during meditation. The intellect can be focussed by prayer (a newbutsu from the sutras), or by repeating a mantra, such as "om mani padme hum" and through dialoguing either with oneself or with another using a koan. The koan is a brief story that holds some meaning for contemplation. The koans are at the heart of Zen, which are called the Mumonkaan and the Hekganroku. It should be noted that the koans were invented in China, but refined and developed further in Japan. Interestingly, when a koan is studied, one must not look for an answer, but let it develop on its own:

> *Just steadily go on with your koan every moment of your life…whether walking or sitting, let your attention be fixed upon it without interruption. When you begin to find it entirely devoid of flavor, the final moment is approaching: do not let it slip out of your grasp. When all of a sudden something flashes out in your mind, its light will illumine the entire universe, and you will see the spiritual land of the Enlightened One (Hoover, 1980; p. 179).*

Regardless of the intellectual strategy, the goals remain the same – satori. That is through discursive reasoning or some other impossible mental task, through monotonous repetition or minute awareness, the mediator's intellect eventually is quieted. There is no object. The world is to be ignored. The intellect ceases and non-intellectual awareness supersedes everything (Willis, 1979). Another strategy is to use emotions to achieve a loving union with God. Once again, one is advised not to be intellectual, but to be immediate. In Zen Buddhism one gives undivided attention to the insignificant and mundane. According to Ramaswami (in Sheikh & Sheikh, 1989) one's attention is banished with "egotistic desires and vain imaginings; [to allow itself to] heal the split between thought and affect and informs the current moment with a benevolent presence" (p. 439).

Reception: Finally but most importantly, one must be open like a vessel. Krishnamurti (1954) called it passive awareness or "choiceless awareness." Receptivity is characterized by three qualities: heightened inner awareness; physical and psychological quieting in which thoughts and physical reactions slow down; and a mix of energy and passivity. Another way to describe this passivity is when you don't work for the fruits of your labor, but for the work itself, or if you travel somewhere not for the destination, but for the travel, then you are receptive. In a sense, thinking ceases, yet one becomes intuitive to what is inside and outside oneself. Everything takes on a heightened quality because each sensation is felt individually until the moment of higher consciousness.

Higher Consciousness: Higher consciousness occurs when ordinary thoughts or consciousness awareness is transformed into something that allows the meditator to see into the void. The Buddha nature appears and the potential for growth is energized. A person can then be transformed into something else that is more fulfilling. It is also referred to as a jhanic state. It is more than an altered state of consciousness, but a way of seeing, feeling and being that unites the self with the cosmic. In Japanese it is called satori, which according to Lueger (cited in Sheikh & Sheikh, 1989), is "a waking up. In waking from an intellectual trance, one can see all that one is. Thus one begins to shed the maya (alienated, false self) in favor of awareness of being in one's environment" (p. 221).

Thus there is a shift in what is experienced in the world. In Zen meditation the sitting facilitates the process of satori. The Buddha inside emerges from the self as a moth from a cocoon and we become mindful our Buddha nature (our godliness), which results in Nirvana.

CONCLUSION

As I remember different groups I have facilitated in the past, I have always been aware of how each person had different levels of awareness. Perhaps each may have been focusing on different zones of awareness. This mix of awareness has the potential of creating infinite possibilities of communication, which make contact with others stimulating and exciting. Individuals have the choice to pay attention to whichever zone of awareness they desire. If they choose to go into the inner zone, they can, and if it is their choice to go into the outer zone of awareness, they can. As a result, the potential for discovery becomes infinite, for they have increased their field of awareness. In the Transpersonal approach, awareness is the starting point for all interactions. As a process, it is the primary vehicle for coming to grips with problems. Once people do this, things that were not there before are now there, so it can be said that the level of awareness has increased dramatically. People have illuminated differing aspects of the things around them and are now experiencing them more completely. As in Chanoyu, people must focus all their senses without thinking, rationalizing or making any judgment.

True awareness, as epitomized in Zen, is reached in a state of satori, and enlightenment, which is non-discriminative. No element is valued over any other. To become enlightened, people must start by not clinging to any concept or preconceived notion about what they should or should not do. Suzuki (1970) emphasizes that once people become enlightened, they are more aware and in synchronicity with reality, thus they can respond in a much more sensitive manner. Consequently, rather than facing the world in an exploitive way, they face it in a creative manner. Mahatma Gandhi once said that his life was his message. In the same way, there should not be a separation of self into different parts; body, mind, spirit and emotions. However, the basic practice of awareness starts in the body, for the body epitomizes the natural process of living. Perls (1969a) often said that the body does not lie and people need to be continually asked what they are aware of. For example, they may be asked to get into contact with their breathing by being aware of how their body is moving, noticing physical sensations, feelings, thoughts, images and attitudes. The methods used in the Transpersonal approach are not just weighed with sensorial behavior, but the complete spectrum of human nature: mind, body, emotions and spirit. Contact with the environment is made, not by seeing with one's eyes or hearing with one's ears, but by understanding with one's spirit. Or as Shirley Sinclair, a Salish writer and educator, stressed: "we must remember that we have three ears, two on our head, and one on our heart (*Courageous Spirit*, 1992).

ACTIVITIES

1. **Awareness Hot Seat:** With the group sitting in a circle, each person in turn has the opportunity to share their immediate awareness. The facilitator can focus them by asking questions. For example, a person can start out by saying: "I am aware of the rapid beating of my heart...I am aware of the shortness of my breath...I am aware of the blood rushing to my face..." The facilitator can then ask: "What are you feeling?" or "What are you afraid of?" or "Where do you feel your fear?" The dialoguing can continue, following up on the response of the group member on the "hot seat".

2. **Fire and Ice:** The group is divided into two smaller groups with one group being "ice" and the other group being "fire." The groups are first asked to physically and vocally represent "fire" or "ice" (e.g., the "fire" group could jump and move around the room and verbally roar, while the "ice" group could form into a solid unmoving statue and make crushing sounds). Then have the two groups meet each other and respond to their opposite. Allow 10 minutes for this part. Next, have the two sides reverse their roles. Finally, have the members share what it felt like physically to be ice or fire. Some process questions might be: Is "fire" or "ice" most like you? How do you "fire" up? How do you "cool" yourself down? Which was most comfortable? Where in your body did you feel the "fire" ("ice")?

CHAPTER FIVE
ART, IMAGERY AND FANTASY:
METHODS OF GROUP FACILITATION

although the eye of the art connoisseur may judge forms esthetically, the eye of religion passes through and sees — or at least strives to see — not stone, not wood or paint, not bronze, but a ground of seven jewels supporting a lotus of innumerable lights...Joseph Campbell (1962; p. 318).

Art, imagery and fantasy are often viewed as superfluous activities; endeavors that are full of beauty and creativity, but with little relevance to the real world. Many in the art world have reinforced this notion of art as art for art's sake, yet art does offer a very powerful medium for expression in therapy and group dynamics that might otherwise be overlooked. The arts provide people with images that they might not otherwise have. Images seem to excite, inspire and frighten people. It is through these images that they can view things and people in an entirely different way. Fantasies, like imagery and art, have also given people new ideas and brought them pleasure vicariously. Art has always played a kind of therapeutic role in the spiritual, practical and community life of people from the beginning of time. Most early art revolved around people's relationship with nature and the cosmos, although today, art, especially "avant garde" art, has become a more general expression of creativity. Unfortunately, many people do not tap into their artistic creativity, and are thus cut off from increasing their self-knowledge. The power of art, imagery and fantasy is its power to literally soothe a person's soul. Is it the freedom that is suggested in artistic things that makes it so inspiring? Dostoyevsky described art this way: "What is the good of prescribing to art roads that it must follow...? To do so is to doubt art, which develops normally according to the laws of nature, and must be exclusively occupied in responding to human needs." There are many aspects of art, but the way that I think of it is that it is anything that is creative from painting to therapy. Thus, in this chapter, I have interpreted art very broadly, involving anything that utilizes the imagination. In addition, art, imagery and fantasy are powerful therapeutic tools that use multidimensional modes and are always in the "here-and-now." According to Perls (1969b), the essence of expressiveness is covered in two words – now and how:

Now covers all that exists. The past is no more, the future is not yet. Now includes the balance of being here, is experiencing, involvement, phenomenon, awareness. How covers everything that is structure, behavior, all that is actually going on – the ongoing process. All the rest is irrelevant – computing, apprehending, and so on (p. 47).

The way people perceive visually or through auditory means is directly related to how they feel and think. While a description of a sunset gives an idea of what it was like, seeing it or reproducing it in a painting gives the viewer or maker a sense of seeing it again. However, the "sun" becomes more "personal" than it is in "real life." It may take on a strange color or shape that reflects how it was perceived. The beauty of the painting is that it "captures" an individual's perception of what is felt rather than what is. Pablo Picasso said that a painting is not designed to be an esthetic operation, but rather a mediator between the world and us. Art is indeed a kind of melange of the common and the strange. The cliché "a picture is worth a thousands words" is an apt expression. Any art object, such as a picture or painting, is very immediate – it is a now experience. It is simple and straightforward, evoking images and feelings that continue long after seeing it.

It could be said that art is a process of only feeling rather than thinking, yet art seems to combine both, and more. According to Zinker (1980), the artist is anyone involved in the process of creating. Thus, all people are artists, because art taps into a deeper self, perhaps even a more spiritual side of humankind. When this happens, people become aware of their creative potential, and as such, art provides them with a way to bring meaning to their existence. The French writer, Anatole France, reinforces this power with his idea that "to know is nothing at all; but to imagine and dream is everything." Art and imagery have been utilized in a number of therapies including the Psychodynamic, Jungian, Gestalt and Transpersonal approaches (Corsinni & Wedding, 1989). Sigmund Freud and Carl Jung first saw the potential of art in therapy and used it as a mechanism to probe into the unconscious part of their patients. Their work inspired the Thematic Apperception Test and the Rorschach Ink Block Test, which are only two widely used examples of the use of art and imagery in standardized diagnostic testing. These tests use a combination of colors, designs and pictures as a method of getting people to project meaning of the images. The pictures and images are ambiguous enough that people have to project their way of seeing, feeling and generally expanding their life view. Art therapy is a relatively new approach to helping that offers practitioners a structure for utilizing expression as a form of helping. While it is not a conceptual theory of psychotherapy, it has adapted itself to existing psychotherapies and is used as an adjunct within various theoretical frameworks. It is used in a wide variety of settings from education to rehabilitation, and even as a mechanism to help people who are dying. Its success with people suffering from moderate to severe sexual and physical trauma or abuse has been widely documented (Krammer, 1971). It is the nonverbal aspect of art that helps people to release material that might otherwise be held back. Somehow the spontaneity revealed in the imagery of art shows far more about people than is shown in what they say. Perhaps art has its most enthusiastic supporters in the personal growth movement and Transpersonal approach to counselling. The natural appeal of art in Transpersonal is that it emphasizes creativity, spontaneity, immediacy and awareness. In fact, the earlier students of Perls (1969b) were artists and writers. Perls often felt that those trained in psychology were too cautious and restrictive and that the best therapists might be those unencumbered by a narrow education in psychology. Artists appealed to him because of their sensitivity, creativity and willingness to take risks. First and foremost, Perls thought that the helper needed to be creative. This attitude on artistic modes is underscored by Laura Perls (Bernard, 1986), who said that "the wider and deeper the education of the therapist, the more he or she can work with all kinds of people on a deeper level...just learning all kinds of techniques and a "bag of tricks" is not...a good preparation to be a therapist or anything else" (p. 370).

THE FUNCTION OF ART AND IMAGERY IN GROWTH

Conductor and composer Modest Moussorgsky contends that "art is not an end in itself, but a means of addressing humanity." The imagery in art captures not only the beauty of creation, but speaks directly to the heart. It is not just an intellectual exercise in form and patterns, but an immersion into emotions. The result is an integration of all aspects of being, which is the assumption behind using art and imagery therapeutically. I believe that the process of growth is the integration of all parts of the self from the biological forces to the cosmic forces within. Somehow it seems that art, imagery and fantasy challenges people to bring themselves into a more harmonious relationship with the universe. Art can provide a process that creates a kind of "oneness" that unites the self, with the environment and the cosmic world. Surprisingly, this kind of harmony does not occur by analyzing or looking for reasons, but by simply being immediate and spontaneous. While projecting often leads to problems in everyday life, it is a process that most people do on a continuous basis. As people think about what might happen next or reflect back to what has happened, they may be projecting. Since they are projecting all the time, why not use it to their advantage to learn more about themselves? Zinker (1980) said that:

In a sense everything is a projection…culture would not exist without [humankind's] lofty projections. Nor would it be in danger of disappearing without his destructive projections. I am deeply grateful for the projections of Copernicus, da Vinci, Shakespeare, Jesus, Einstein, and many other fellow human beings who leaned on their projections (p. 259).

There is a kind of universality in using projections that allows group members to go beyond what is obvious and use the creativity of art and imagery to understand what can be expressed in talk. According to Enright (1975), using the imagery of art as a means of examining projections:

is a method of harnessing this basic human\process; instead of wasting energy opposing or criticizing it, 'go with it' as an exercise that can enhance awareness and develop feelings and perceptions more vividly…it is not a new technique. Artists – particularly Japanese sumi painters – have been using it for centuries (p. 149).

When people talk out their problems and issues, they may be able to express what they are feeling and thinking, yet could they do it without censoring or holding something back? When people think about something, they are quite logical. They want to understand. However, art can get people involved by doing rather than thinking and talking about it. People often censor things they feel and think which results in their actions always being a logical and predictable consequence. When this happens learning becomes dull and automatic.

As the British novelist, Aldous Huxley (1936), once said, "logical consequences are the scarecrows of fools and the beacons of wise men" (p. 45). The artistic process does not follow logic nor reason, but emerges from inner emotions that are pumped forth from within. While talking can be good for the 'soul' and gives people an opportunity to 'get something off their chest,' it is still 'talking about.' They can draw it and use the drawing to focus on the feelings expressed in the drawing. What makes drawing the picture different than just retelling the story is that the retelling is just that and tends to be more informational. According to Sheikh and Jordan (1983) "…the linguistic mode is limiting because it subtly forces us to exclude from consideration and even from consciousness those aspects of our subjectivity that evade easy articulation" (p. 391). When people only verbalize something, they are forced into dividing the experience into preconceived categories and are thereby separated even more from the experience. Drawing the picture gets them involved in reliving the whole experience (i.e., in the here and now). It is very easy to see and understand what the experience was like in a graphic way. In addition, people are able to access more aspects of the experience because the drawing structures the process. In their example, the student is using art as a method of conveying the imagery of the situation in a much fuller way. Landy (1984) suggests that the process is:

> not analytical. However, [a person] both thinks and feels through the creation of imagery…[it] is in the act of exercising…creative imagination, in living through a dialectical moment of simultaneously thinking and feeling. It is a moment of balanced esthetic distance, of simultaneously playing creator and observer roles. Repressed feelings are available, but as clay to be molded, raw substance to be given form (p. 88).

Feelings come out because the experience is closer. In fact, one of the goals in using art therapeutically is to lead the person to a point of catharsis. Catharsis is an emotional release and is seen by many helpers to be a way of healing. Art releases people from verbal restrictions by allowing them to graphically represent strong feelings that are difficult to express. In effect, the person is offered the chance to explore those feelings, learn to accept them, and develop strategies for dealing with them. However, it takes a very sensitive and skillful person to assist another in actualizing the experience. The experience has to be structured in order for the person to derive expression and meaning from the activity. In addition, it helps the person to be more open and receptive to further exploration. As a diagnostic tool, art reveals much about the person's idiosyncrasies and coping styles in life. There is more spontaneity in the process than there would be in using only verbal responses. Mind pictures have the capacity to create details that are richer in color, texture and form than any verbal message. If allowed to develop, these images produce a "story" that tells far more about life than anything else. Narrative fantasies or the exploration of symbols from dreams are just a few examples of how imagery can help bring meaning to thoughts and emotions. Therefore, if people are (Sheikh & Jordan, 1983):

> experiencing something in imagery, [your] experiencing is in many essential ways psychologically equivalent to experiencing the thing [or person] in actuality…thus imagery and perception are experientially and neurophysiologically comparable processes and cannot be distinguished from each other by any intrinsic qualities (p. 393).

THE PROCESS IN USING ART, IMAGERY AND FANTASY

While there are some variations in utilizing art, imagery and fantasy, the basic approach involves four distinct steps that follow Moreno's (1953) Psychodrama approach. Each of the steps overlaps each other in a flowing pattern.

WARM-UP

In the warm-up people share their issues and how they feel and think about it. It is possible that they may feel uncomfortable about working with art materials, because they feel they are not very skillful artists. However, since the outcome is only a means to an end, participants have to feel relaxed about whatever it is they are making. The facilitator needs to de-emphasize the mechanics of doing while emphasizing the spontaneity of the process. Putting this in perspective serves to reduce anxiety, build trust and provide a structure for the activity. Once this done, everyone relaxes and usually gets into the spirit of the activity. One effective way of getting group members to share how they see themselves in the group, is to ask them to imagine and create what they are in the group or to identify with an object as a method of sharing. The warm-up provides them with the energy for getting into the spirit of the drawing or clay piece or whatever artwork activity is being used.

ACTION

In the action phase people use the medium selected to create something. Generally the creation will be directed by the facilitator, focusing on some experience or image where the participants can express their feelings and thoughts. For example, in one past group, everyone was asked to make a clay object of how they saw themselves in the group. Sharee, one group member, made a clay figure of a fish.

SHARING

Once the action concludes, people share their creation, describing the object in the first person or as if they were the object. For example, Sharee shared that she felt like a fish that was alone, surrounded by water that separated her from connections with others. While she said the water provided comfort and the aloneness helped her to be more independent, there was a down side – loneliness. The sharing about the clay object with other group members confirmed that they saw her quickly moving as soon as anyone came close. The making of the clay object and the feedback revealed her feelings and attitudes in such a powerful way that the rest of the group saw her as being "slippery" and hard to get close to. She was surprised at their perception and touched by their desire to get closer to her or have her "swim with them." Despite this, she seemed unable to go beyond descriptors and the sharing of her dilemma. She spent a lot of time getting into the details of the scales of the fish, trying to create a sense of movement (e.g., swimming).

DIALOGUING

The purpose of this step is to lead the participants to a sense of feeling rather than just thinking. The role of the facilitator is to work towards a catharsis, an emotional climax, in order to break through the impasse symbolized by the object created. In the following interaction Sharee was asked to describe herself as a "fish" and talk about what it is like being in her group.

Sharee: "I am a fish. I am a fast and strong swimmer. I have the ability to out swim the strongest fish in the sea. I am never fooled by other creatures or people who try and catch me. That is why I have grown so big and strong. I can get away at any moment. I .. . (silence)."

Facilitator: "What are you aware of right now?"

Sharee: "I am aware that my body is posed to dart away . . . and escape. . . and I realize it is so very tiring ..."

Facilitator: "Does it make you tired to hold yourself in a ready position to swim or get away?"

Sharee: "It is the only way if I am not to be caught and hurt."

Facilitator: "How do you hurt yourself?"

Sharee: "I hold myself in a position to make an escape and isolate myself in... (with tears)."

Facilitator: "And you isolate yourself from others, which on one hand provides protection, but on the other hand the price is discomfort and separateness from others in the group. You have a choice to live alone always on the move or to join with others. What do you want?"

Sharee: "To be more open to others...."

DISCUSSION

The imagery that Sharee created with the clay provided a backdrop for the facilitator to use in focusing and engaging her. Everything was reflected back to her because the imagery is concrete and very clear. As a result, the dilemma was put into perspective and she is put in a position to see the price that she paid for her freedom. Afterwards, she had a choice to live life differently. Once everyone has an opportunity to reflect on their object, I get the group to share and elicit more feedback on what they saw, felt and heard from the experience. To be sensitive to those participating in this type of activity, it is necessary for facilitators to be constantly in touch with their own projections and those of the group. Facilitators have to watch out for projecting their fears, anxieties, desires and wishes onto the group. Essentially, facilitators act as screens for the projections of group members. It cannot be otherwise if people want to make changes, because "therapeutic changes occur when pathological projections are converted into creative ones" (Zinker, 1980; p. 261).

IDENTIFICATION THROUGH IMAGERY

I shall use the following case to illustrate the process stages that individuals go through as they project themselves onto an object. In addition, this example demonstrates another approach in using imagery to create a mood and structure for self-exploration. I have asked members of the group to project themselves onto a number of objects that I have brought. My basic instructions were to look at the objects in the box and choose one "that speaks to you and that you can identify with."

CASE BACKGROUND

Joyce is a thirty-five-year-old secretary, who has expressed a desire to do something exciting and different in her life. She is sincere, industrious and conservative in appearance and manner. In an earlier self-disclosure she expressed anger at having to take responsibility for caring for her invalid mother.

ANCHOR STAGE

Joyce looks around the room, appearing very awkward as she examines the various objects. She tentatively chooses an object after looking everything over very thoroughly. During this stage, group members are usually a little self-conscious wondering what others will think. There is a little humor from some as a way of easing tension. Joyce shared later that she had the following thought as she examined the objects.

Joyce: "I feel a little silly. What can I choose that will not reveal too much? I don't want to be ridiculed and negatively evaluated. Hmm, this looks interesting."

IDENTIFICATION STAGE

Once the objects are chosen, group members are instructed to be each object by describing themselves as the object in the first person (e.g., "I am a pencil . . . I am . . ."). I always have to keep everyone from talking about the object rather than being the object, by having them say "I" rather than "it." At this point people become more confident and bolder as they get "lost in the object." They start being creative and their figure relationship is revealed. Zinker (1980) suggests that when there is confusion between figure and ground. "There is a lack of purpose and focusing, so that as they look at a particular situation they are not able to pick out that which is central for them. From one moment to the next, they are unable to separate the important things for themselves from the unimportant things" (p. 93).

Joyce: "I am a clay lid from a small tea pot...I made of brown clay, and while I have maintained my shape over a long period of time, I am very brittle. I can break easily so I have to be very careful. I have a small round handle that can easily be pulled or pushed (with a far-away look in her eyes)."

Facilitator: "You look very functional, but you can easily break."

Joyce: "Yes (pause). I'm used to covering and containing things. I have this little hole here that lets out steam when everything gets too hot. I'm really very useful, although I am overlooked because I'm so small. People often overlook me because I am not as colorful as the pot."

Facilitator: "How do you feel?"

Joyce: "I feel misused and not noticed (with a downcast face)."

Facilitator: "That must make you feel sad and angry. Yet when things boil over, you have a way of releasing your feelings."

Joyce: "Yes, my talent is letting things pass through."

IMPASSE STAGE

There is resistance at this stage as the interaction increases the awareness that something is under the surface. There is a double bind at this point because to bring what is below the surface, the person will have to let go and lose control. There is a resistance to giving up control. Impasse, according to Perls (1969b), is "the crucial point in therapy, the crucial point in growth …the position where environmental support or absolute inner support is not forthcoming anymore, and authentic self-support has not yet been achieved (pp. 28-29).

Facilitator: "That is a powerful talent."

Joyce: "I guess so (with a deep sigh)."

Facilitator: "You sigh…and let out a little steam. It must make it hard for you to focus and concentrate on anything other than containing all that steam?"

Joyce: "Yes. I don't know…."

Facilitator: "You don't know? (after some silence)…You seem stuck? Can you tell me that it isn't my business any longer?"

Joyce: "It isn't your business to know what I think. Get lost (with an explosive voice). Stop it!"

Facilitator: "That is very powerful! Strong! How would you answer that?"

AWARENESS STAGE

The impasse is past and there is a connection of actions and meaning. There is an "aha experience" or an awareness of something not known before. The person "sees and understands" something that is new. There is a higher energy level as this understanding takes place. Things are clearer now, and a choice and commitment can be made. In this stage, according to Perls (1969), there is a sense that:

> *suddenly the world is there. You wake up from a trance like you wake up from a dream. You're all there…the growth aim is to…come more and more to your senses. To be more and more in touch…with yourself and in touch with the world, instead of only in touch with the fantasies, prejudices, apprehensions (pp. 53-54).*

Joyce: "It's safer…(still angry, but with a surprised look on her face) Hmm…It is easier not to do anything. Letting off steam helps me contain my anger. I am repressed by…then I explode…"

Facilitator: "It's like you've suddenly been shocked…"

Joyce: "Yes. I'm shocked. I can't believe what has happened to me. I've made myself insignificant by not risking. Not breaking the bonds."

Facilitator: "How do you feel?"

Joyce: "I feel quite good about being angry. It's all right. But a little tiring."

Facilitator: "That must be painful for you, because you've worked up to now to contain things around you."

Joyce: "Yes. I'm tired of repressing (putting the object down). I'm scared to be me. I've used my mother as an excuse. Now look at me…"

Facilitator: "It's scary not to be in control."

Joyce: "Yes,… but… (tears in her eyes)."

Facilitator: "What are you going to do about it?"

Joyce: "I've got a choice to do something or let things continue. I want a change (speaking in a firm voice)."

DISCUSSION

Joyce has been able to talk about herself via the object because it seemed more remote. She was experiencing doubt because her mother does need care, yet she has never seriously explored other options that might have satisfied her and her mother's needs. Using the object she applied to herself all the characteristics that she saw in it. She projected her feelings, which I helped her to identify and intensify. This gave her the opportunity to verbalize something that heretofore was impossible. The more she internalized her feelings, the worse she felt. Using the object, she was able to talk about what was not comfortable. The Gestalt approach of projecting herself onto an object allowed those repressed feelings to surface. She was able to talk about the feelings and thereby gained an emotional release and greater understanding of her needs.

THE MAGIC OF FANTASY: A NATURAL LEARNING

All people have grown up with the experience of fantasy that "make believe world" where spirits, knights and maidens, magicians, and the unicorn roamed freely. Fantasy "refers to suggestions for make-believe involvement, not subject to reality" (Lamb, 1982; p. 266). As a tool for learning, fantasy still has the power to increase self-awareness and assist us to make a variety of personal changes. Professionals of all types are using fantasy for improving concentration in sports and for overcoming fears and phobias. Through the use of fantasy, people have the power to go back in time or forward in the future, or to leave the present and simply lie on the beach at some tropical island. Although fantasy can distort reality or even produce anxieties and phobias, it can, if used in a positive manner, bring a lot of relief. As a therapeutic tool for psychological growth and learning, fantasy has a great deal to offer. Fantasizing is something that everyone can do and it takes very little time and energy. On a hot day I have had the experience of wishing to be in the mountains skiing. As I begin to fantasize, suddenly I am there, vicariously enjoying the "ski slopes." It is not the same, but the value may be that it gives me an idea of making the decision to take a winter vacation or plan out something I desire to do.

As a mechanism for adaptation fantasy is very powerful, for it makes time irrelevant. Using fantasy, people can anticipate or rehearse for future activities. This is one reason why sports psychologists are using fantasy in training athletes. Athletes can go through all the required moves on the playing field, and using fantasy, anticipate where they will have problems at any time. This mystery of time is voiced eloquently by T. S. Elliot (1968) who wrote:

> *Time present and time past*
>
> *Are both perhaps present in time future, and time future contained in time past*
>
> *Time past and time future, what might have been and what has been*
>
> *Point to one end, which is always present (p. 83).*

Fantasy is like having a whole library of videos of past experiences that can be played at any time for any reason. Through fantasy people can go back and finish things that they never had the opportunity to do. They can go back in fantasies and "say good-bye" to a long dead friend or relative. By examining their fantasies they can learn a great deal about themselves (e.g., attractions, avoidance and a host of messages). Fantasies are highly correlated with creativity. When people fantasize they create ideas and scenarios, because they are thinking outside the realm of possibilities or probabilities. Fantasizing is often used in problem solving to bring fresh thinking to a situation. Creativity is often said to be thinking the impossible, which is pure fantasy. The fifteenth century playwright, William Shakespeare, emphasized this when he wrote *The Tempest*: "We are such stuff as dreams are made of, and our little life is rounded with a sleep." As an instrument for self-discovery, the use of fantasy (guided imagery) helps to create images that people might not otherwise tap into. The following is an example of how to used guided imagery in a group. "The Forest" is a guided fantasy in which group members are led into the forest to confront someone they are fearful of. The rationale is for them to explore what they typically do in situations involving anger. After first relaxing the group, through deep breathing exercises, the facilitator says the following:

> *Imagine yourself as an animal...What would you choose?...Be that animal and imagine yourself going through the forest...hear the forest sounds, the smells, and the wind blowing across your body...It is very peaceful there...you feel relaxed and comfortable in the cool shade of the trees...up ahead there is light, where the forest ends...there is a meadow, with brightly colored flowers waving in the wind...At the edge of the meadow you look around, smell the air, and now you make your move across the meadow...Suddenly, in front of you is someone that has made you angry...imagine that person as an animal...What kind of animal is that person?...As you face that animal...what do you do?...Finish the fantasy.*

Once group members finish the fantasy they share their fantasy with the rest of the group. While mutual sharing may be enough for some, others need a little help in resolving the fantasy. If the fantasy remains a mystery, it can create a lot of confusion. Resolution is "coming home instead of wandering around in circles. As in all things the main barrier to resolution is ourselves" (Perls, 1975; p. 69). Because of some unfinished business in regard to the issue bringing more stress, I want to work towards a resolution. Unfinished business occurs when there are unexpressed but still contained feelings around some past event. The unfinished business is still disrupting interpersonal communications and growth cannot occur. The following is an example of a fantasy that has some unfinished business in it:

Martha: "I am a hawk and I feel very comfortable in the forest. As I come to the meadow I feel fear. I'm not comfortable with the light. Just before I get to the other side I meet a big black raven. It is bigger than me. It begins crowing, which sounds like a laugh. I try to fly away, but I can't, and it is still laughing and laughing. I now look only at the ground, "out of sight, out of mind" is my motto. I look around and I realize I've turned into a chicken."

Facilitator: "How do you feel?"

Martha: "Numb. No feeling."

Facilitator: "Let us experiment. Let's have a dialogue with these two birds. Can you sit in this chair and be the raven? Later I will ask you to sit in this chair and be the hawk/chicken."

Martha: "I am a raven. I'm big, black, and very powerful. Nothing scares me."

Facilitator: "Are you aware that you are sitting up straight and your voice sounds so strong?"

Martha: "Yes…it's true (with surprise)."

Facilitator: "How do you make yourself strong and powerful?"

Martha: "I puff myself up, do what I want, say what I want (with a strong and firm voice)! And damn the consequences."

Facilitator: "What would you like to say to the hawk/chicken?"

Martha: "You make me laugh (as the raven). Why do you cower? What are you afraid of? (laughing) Me? What the hell do you want anyway?"

Martha: "You frighten me (as the hawk/chicken). I don't want you to laugh at me. It really hurts me when you do that."

Martha: "You make me laugh (as the raven). You're so insignificant (beginning to cry deeply)."

Facilitator: "Who are you?"

Martha: "I am my mother (sighing). Always she told me I was never going to amount to anything."

Facilitator: "Let's put your mother over there. Choose any chair. What would you like to tell her?"

Martha: "Mother, I love you, but I am not going to take that kind of bullying any longer. I'm grown up now, so stop (choosing the raven's chair and speaking in a very strong and firm voice)!"

SUMMARY OF THE REMAINDER OF THE SESSION

The two-chair method was utilized in the session in separating two types of messages coming out of Martha's fantasy. Martha had never told her mother how she felt about the early experiences. Using the two-chair method helped her speak to her mother, to express her hurt and angry feelings. This was something she had never done before. As Martha worked through the fantasy, she discovered that she was the raven just as she was the hawk/chicken. She has learned that she does have a powerful side and a sensitive, caring side.

Strategies for Using Art, Imagery and Fantasy

The basic process of using art, imagery and fantasy with groups is the same as using it with individuals. The difference is the dynamic interaction occurring with members of the group reacting to the activity and to each other. The group is not only able to share how they feel and think about each other's projections and fantasies, but are able to get an alternative perceptual view. For example, one member sees a "hawk" with attributes of power and aggression, while another gives attributes of independence and freedom to the "hawk." These shared views tell a great deal about each of the members as they bounce back and forth their differing perceptions. There are a variety of strategies for using art, imagery and fantasy in groups. Only people's imagination and creativity will limit the use of all the mediums in art from drawing, sculpturing, paper folding, painting, photography, making music, dance and movement. The following are only a few strategies that I have used in previous groups.

Eidetic Images: One novel method of using imagery is suggested by Shorr (1978), who uses what is called eidetic images. This is a process for using empathy, paired with an image, as a vehicle for interpersonal development. One member describes an image while the other members of the group make empathic statements. This is followed with sharing and a discussion of the possible meanings, feelings and actions that the person might take as a result of the feedback. According to Shorr (1978), this teaches group members to use empathy as a means of understanding how people view themselves and others. Often resolutions evolve spontaneously as group members share images and empathy statements. For example, the activity may resemble the following:

Person 1: Today I feel like a big ripe tomato.

Person 2: It seems like you feel fruitful?

Person 3: I see you as being nourishing to me in the group.

Person 4: You often blush when talking about your feelings. How does that fit?

Image Feedback: Group members are asked to first write down an image of themselves and everyone in the group as an animal or fruit. Next they share with each other what they have written. To facilitate the group processes the facilitator clarifies and reflects feelings or underlying meaning of each of the images and any discrepancies between the self and others.

In Your Parents' Shoes: Group members are asked to first think of their parents and with their eyes closed stand as one of them would stand. The purpose is to get group members to put themselves "in the shoes" of someone else. Group members might be able to explore how they have incorporated some styles of relating or projections based on their parents' body image, "My mother always carried herself in a tight manner, which reinforced my discomfort in being around her." This activity can be expanded to include spouses, employers or other people in the group members' lives.

Body Part: When group members are voicing strong feelings, but are not able to fully feel them, I ask them to become a part of their body as a means of separating feelings from thoughts. In addition it helps people accept and voice feelings that otherwise might be difficult. This enables group members to separate themselves from their feelings in order to identify and later reintegrate them. The range can be physical parts, a scar, heart, or foot to psychological characteristics, stubbornness, humor, softness and aggressiveness. For example, if one person states that he or she has no feelings, the facilitator or another member of the group could ask the person to experiment in becoming a body part (e.g., heart):

Person: "I am a heart. I pump blood around the body. I give life. Without me there is death."

Facilitator: "How do you feel as a heart?

Person: "I am warm and loving."

Facilitator: "What does it mean to be warm and loving?"

Person: "It means to be nurturing and protective."

Facilitator: "It seem like there is a lot of energy in being that for you?"

Person: "Yes. And power."

Facilitator: "As a member of this, how do you make yourself warm, loving and powerful?"

Stump, Cabin, Stream: Stevens (1971) developed a fantasy activity in which people are asked to take turns being a stump, a cabin and a stream. The rationale is that people will explore what it feels like to be different things and be able to make a comparison of different aspects of self. In a group people are often comparing and judging themselves in relationship to others. This activity allows them to explore a different aspect of themselves from three different and interrelated parts. For example, as the stream one person may feel free and flowing, but as the stump the person may feel "cut down" or "pushed down." As the cabin, the same person may have mixed feelings like a feeling of belonging and being over protected. Since the purpose of this activity is to explore the different aspects of the self, a dialogue can be created in which the different parts talk to each other. To increase levels of self-awareness, the facilitator or another member of the group could focus the person with reflections or questions, for example, "How are you "cut down in the group?"

Self-Object: When people become stuck, the facilitator could ask group members to use the two chair method and have a dialogue with an object. This is a method for examining projections of self onto an object. For example:

Facilitator: "You say you feel enclosed by a wall. Could you be a wall? Start by saying, "I am a wall, I…" and finish the statement describing yourself."

Person: "I am a wall. I enclose everything. Nothing can get in or out. I'm tall, gray and made of thick concrete."

Facilitator: "How does it feel to be a wall?"

Person: "I have no feelings."

Facilitator: "You are as solid as a wall – with no feelings! How about your thoughts? Do you have any?"

Person: "Sure!"

Facilitator: "What would you like to say to yourself?"

Person: "I want to protect you from making a fool of yourself (speaking to self). I don't want you going overboard or doing anything wild."

Person: "Listen, I don't need your help (moving to the other chair). With you, I never feel anything but safe, but I'm never able to experience things fully and spontaneously."

A variation of the self-object dialogue is the object-object dialogue. This involves having two objects speak to each other (e.g., pencil and paper). According to Passons (1975) this "way the person can project two personal aspects which tend toward opposites and heighten awareness of both sides" (p. 151).

Role Playing: Role-playing is a method for exploring situations using drama to enact real or imaginary situations in people's lives for problem resolution, problem solving, decision-making, and leadership training. The rationale for doing this is based on the idea that everything in life, no matter how mundane it may seem to some, has the potential for being dramatic for others if put into context. People in the group are given roles and a script in which they enact some experience from the past for the purpose of rehearsing alternatives or previewing alternative scenarios. Short episodes or full dramas with several scenes can be used to re-experience situations for completing unfinished business, increasing self-awareness or rehearsing new ways of being in life.

THE IMAGERY IN MOVEMENT METHOD [IMM]

Tart (1975) has pointed out that there are certain experiences not available to ordinary waking consciousness, and in order to investigate them, one must enter an altered state and explore dimensions of that domain from within that experience. In order to achieve this, the method not only must access particular spiritual and phenomenological experiences, but it must be a catalyzer for the development of a transformative journey through many levels of awareness. The Imagery in Movement Method (IMM) is a four step process used to explore any topic or question of concern or to simply open investigation into the structure of one's consciousness. It is generally a facilitated process, but people can be trained to work alone.

STEP ONE: EXPRESSION

Even though any kind of self-created art may be used, drawing is the usual method of choice due to the availability of the materials (paper and crayons), the outcome (a tangible product) and the ease of this form of expression. The purpose of expression is to make the implicit explicit and that the nonverbal experience through images; that the feeling in the "guts," an intuition, "on the tip of my tongue," or my sense of things are brought into the light of our consciousness, transforming the entire gestalt of the momentary ground of being, into a view. Even when the participant thinks that there are no images in his or her mind to draw, the feeling quickly fades and everyone is able to create. People must be reminded that this is not art, so all they are doing is letting their hand do whatever it wants. Of particular importance is that the facilitator does not suggest anything to draw, nor express his or her own emotional reactions to the unfolding drawing.

STEP TWO: MAPPING

Mapping is an exploration of each element of the drawing and the overall organization of the drawing itself in order to guide the client through his or her own inner landscape revealing the dynamics of the psyche by implying the direction of growth. The facilitator asks the person to look for a particular shape, pattern or color in the drawing and the person is then asked to report on any body sensations, feelings, images or thoughts that might speak to him or her. The facilitator helps the client to explore the full sensory experience associated with the drawing, not only in terms of visual images, but also in olfactory, kinesthetic and perceptive images. Sometimes, the client might be asked to "step into the drawing" and report what is happening. The next step is to encourage the client to be receptive to the symbolic meaning of each element of the drawing by asking himself or herself what the symbolic meaning of a particular part of the drawing is and to pay close attention to the answer. If the client should answer "I don't know," it is suggested that the facilitator give a simple instruction to access the appropriate mode by saying something like: "That is your verbal mind and it does not know, ask your imagery mind what it means." The facilitator must comment on or interpret the associations (in the drawing) reported by the participant and must be really careful on the kinds of questions utilized to trigger ideas, thoughts or sensations.

STEP THREE: FANTASY ENACTMENT

The purpose of fantasy enactment is self-transformation. When memory and waking dream experiences have been accessed, the client understands the source of an issue, has become aware of how the body has participated in holding that specific issue, and has seen the solution to the issue within the larger context of his or her life. First, the group member or participant is asked to identify the most charged part of the drawing. He or she is asked to step into it and report what is "happening." One major role of the facilitator is to focus the participant's attention on the sensory details that first present themselves. Based on information given by the participant, the facilitator can ask questions such as: "What color is the floor?", "How does your body feel?", "What do you smell?" or "What do you hear?" As the scene becomes more and more vivid to the group member, it might begin to unfold and evoke sensations, feelings and thought. It is then that the facilitator might want to begin the enactment process by asking the participant to role-play the scene as it unfolds.

The facilitator acts as an aid for the participant by performing any roles that he or she might request. Typically, if there is bodily engagement in the exploration process, a dramatic shift occurs in the person's experience: there is an experience of being at an edge and fearing the unknown. The participant often experiences his or her body moving spontaneously and without any conscious forethought. The client becomes the process, becomes the fantasy unfolding itself; and as he or she experiences catharsis and insight that is at once intellectual, emotional and embodied, the experience finds its own path for resolution. A participant might find himself or herself reliving a memory in very vivid detail recalling aspects that have been long forgotten. Once one scene is retrieved in full sensory detail, the entire memory usually unfolds. Waking dreams that emerge when the client enters a particular color or shape of the drawing express the issue represented by that part of the drawing and attempt to resolve it. With the conclusion of the fantasy enactment work, the client moves from accessing material to utilizing the methods of verbal translation to understand the relevance of that material for use in daily life situations.

STEP FOUR: VERBAL TRANSLATION

The goal in this last step is to help people understand the experiences that have been unfolded through the drawings and their explorations. Because they have experienced very vivid emotions through the enactment of the fantasy, they might be in an altered condition. At this stage, the facilitator's role is to ask general questions about the process in order to move the participant back into his or her everyday situations (e.g., How was that for you? How do these images relate to your reality? What in your life reminds you of this memory and fantasy?). After this last part of the process has been completed, the participant is given a writing task as homework divided into three major parts. The first part is a section for reflecting on the graphic elements of the drawing and the emerging experiences during the mapping; the next section is dedicated to reflecting on the major events of the fantasy enactment, and the last part of the assignment includes various summary sections about the impact that the overall experience has in the participant's current life. Verbal translation returns the client to his or her ordinary life situations with renewed insights derived from the journey into imagery and fantasy; there is a new and expanded sense of self. The experienced reported is one of feeling at a shimmering edge; the edge of connection and communication between what the client experiences as two very different things.

Used over time, IMM catalyzes the development of a vocabulary of color and form that brings forth a new "something" that is felt and experienced differently by each person. As the old images, memories, fantasies and feelings associated with a color become fully conscious and integrated, the color may become engaging in and of itself because of the qualities of light and energy that it possesses. This new "something" appears to be self-healing; it presents key issues, works on those issues and resolves them, and then the new something moves on to present the next issue. As the drawings change, so does the behavior. Despite the idiosyncrasies in the way in which each person's process unfolds, the process appears to move towards increasing joy, freedom, and capacity.

CONCLUSION

Nineteenth century French writer Honoré de Balzac captured the power of art when he wrote, "What is art? But nature concentrated." Art, imagery and fantasy are natural processes that everyone possesses and responds to, no matter what their background or orientation. These are activities that everyone has grown up with and has used extensively. According to Sheikh and Jordan (1983), the value of art, imagery and fantasy is that they not only free group members:

> but also the therapist from verbal logic...communication through images may lead the therapist to be more creative in his or her interpretation and quicker to establish empathy...a shift to the imagery mode may make the therapeutic interchange more interesting...[for it] eventually feeds back into the therapeutic relationship (p. 414).

Using art, imagery and fantasy as mechanisms for exploring feelings has a great many advantages over some of the more traditional approaches. According to dictionary definitions, art is a form of human activity that is the product of imagination and skill. Art, imagery and fantasy, unlike other methods, are projections from the mind and soul of others and, as such, bring a perspective that is unusual; the reality in art depends on your perspective. When I view art I may feel one thing, but someone else may feel something entirely different. Art allows the person free reign over what is imagined. What came up for the person were those feelings under the surface; often those which were repressed. Using art as a medium has many advantages over verbal interaction because it is indirect. For those group members who have experienced the power of art, imagery and fantasy, the use of these mediums allowed them the opportunity to talk about what was difficult. Art activities are enjoyable and generally less stressful. Art has been particularly helpful in counseling hyperactive people, because it redirects their excess energy in a constructive way (Krammer, 1971). It seems to be an especially therapeutic approach to use with children. Enright (1975) stresses the:

> over-all sense of excitement and playfulness [this] method generates. The realization that fun can be profound, and profundity fun; that we can laugh till we cry and cry till we laugh in the same few minutes; that knowledge of a highly useful sort can be generated by such light-hearted sport, helps a group move rapidly away from a heavy, problem centered orientation toward something much more rich and full (p. 155).

Art, imagery and fantasy are being used in a wide variety of therapeutic approaches from Behaviorism to Transpersonal psychotherapy. The results have been very positive in numerous diverse routes from helping people overcome stress to losing weight. It not only taps creativity, but helps to desensitize people in the helping process. It does not matter whether the events occurred in the past or are anticipated, for art, imagery and fantasy transcend all boundaries. I once heard someone in a previous group say that it is only through art that a person can experience life. While this may overstate the case, for me art, imagery and fantasy evoke feelings that I do not sense in other endeavors. Art is not only esthetically pleasing, but emotionally satisfying. While I am not an artist, I find a lot of satisfaction in drawing or working with clay. I use fantasy a great deal in my everyday life; although I sometimes frighten myself with it, I find it to be relaxing, enjoyable and generally helpful. My daydreams, like my life, are sometimes frightening and sometimes pleasing. However, art is not just an esthetic process, but a kind of magic which shuttles me from the mystical to the hostile to the peaceful. There is a plasticity about things artistic that brings forth energy, creativity and spontaneity. It somehow brings the inner and outer world together in a way that unites the physical, psychological and cosmic senses. Eventually they become myths once people have gained insight from them. All people have an inherent artistic and creative ability that viewed separately from society's definition of art is mystical in proportions. According to Campbell (1986), the:

> *fact that the nature of the artist (as a microcosm) and the nature of the universe (as the macrocosm) are two aspects of the same reality (respectively, as a minute part of the whole, experienced from within, and as the whole, viewed from without equivalent, respectively, to Schopennhouser's "world as will" and "world as spectacle or idea") accounts sufficiently for the creative interplay of discovery and recognition which alerts the artist to the possibility of a revelatory composition in which outer and inner realities are recognized as the same (p. 121).*

ACTIVITIES

1. **Clay Projections:** Take a handful of clay and make whatever comes to mind (allow 30 minutes of uninterrupted activity). Once the object is made, group members can share the object with a small group in the first person (e.g., "I am…My function is to…And what I feel is…"). Allow 15 minutes for group members to share their art. Some variations can include making an object that: reflects present feelings, self or group perception, object that symbolizes life, etc.

2. **Pawn Shop:** After deep relaxation, imagine going into a dusty old pawn shop full of strange and exotic objects After looking around, what you focus on is something that looks like it came out of "1001 and one Arabian Nights." The object that attracts attention is an old Persian type lamp that is dusty. After rubbing the dirt off the brass lamp, it shakes precipitously and a puff of smoke appears and after the smoke dissipates, a turbaned genie bows and asks: "Master, what is your wish? You will be granted 3 wishes. Anything you want." After thinking about it for 10 minutes, the reply is: "_____" Group members share their replies in a small group, paying particular attention to what the objects signify, how the objects will change life, etc.

CHAPTER SIX
ALTERNATIVE DIMENSIONS OF SELF:
DREAMS AND GROUP WORK

And there are only two states for the person: the one here in this world and the other in the next world. The third, the intermediate, is the dream state…And when he [she] dreams, he [she] takes away a little of the impressions of this all-embracing world…In this state [the person] becomes self-illumined. The Upanishads, (1962)

Since the beginning of time all cultures have regarded dreams as having some special power that goes beyond the past, present or future. All of the major religions have given dreams spiritual significance. In groups where process is emphasized, dream work offers people the opportunity to explore a unique aspect of themselves with the group as a backdrop. The Greek proverb, "the net of the sleeper catches fish," emphasizes the power that has been ascribed to dreams. Dreams somehow link the past with the future and somehow explain the present. For many they open the door to the unknown. In group facilitation, dream exploration is a way of going beyond the physical world into the spiritual world. As a process, dream exploration allows individuals to examine their unconscious in a symbolic manner. Dream exploration in essence is a means to transcend the "public" part of ourselves in a "private" existence unfettered by the rational.

What makes dreams such a powerful medium is that there are no limits to the real and imaginary. Dreams are intuitive in nature, yet dreams bridge the conscious and unconscious. The beauty of dream work is that it transcends the physical, social, psychological, and metaphysical realms of human nature. This metaphysical aspect reinforces the cosmic and spiritual needs of people, which are often missing in group work where the social and psychological parts are primarily stressed. Essentially, it is the transcendental nature of dreams that makes exploring them so attractive in groups. Since dreams are an important part of everyone's lives, it is only prudent that dreams be explored. From the earliest beginnings of history, the Greeks and Egyptians believed that a dream was a message from the gods, while the Chinese felt that a dream was an internal manifestation. For the Chinese there was a "material soul," which ceased with death, and a "spiritual soul," or hun, which left the body and continued in another form (Van de Castle, 1973). Among First Nations people of North America, dream sharing was an important part of community life, such as the Iroquois nation who had a dream sharing in the Long House every winter. In ancient Jerusalem, it was quite common to find people who would interpret a dream. However, even in life, the hun could temporarily leave the body and communicate with souls of the departed and bring messages back through dreams. Today many believe that the messages of dreams are the vehicle through which God can speak. Hunt (1995) states that in societies which have a shamanistic tradition and live close to the land, they often do not see a separation between what is conscious or unconscious. Meditative practices are at the heart of these societies and are part of their community identity. Consider the Senoi tribe of Malaysia, who believe that:"the dream is a spiritual experience, in a sense as real and important as physical experience in his or her waking hours…few important decisions are made by a group without one of its members having had a dream that points to a certain course of action" (Noone & Holman, 1972; p. 80).

The open attitude of the Senoi tribe about dreaming is not universal in majority society, but in the Transpersonal approach exploration of dreams is a vital method for exploring the unconscious, providing insight and empowering the individual. In Western society the dream or the dreamer has sometimes been feared, sometimes respected, and sometimes ridiculed. However, dreaming has always offered people something beyond the self that is mysterious, yet emanating internally. Kopp (1975) describes the value of dreams this way:

> I have long trusted my dreams as prophetic visions. I do not mean that they foretell the future, only that they illuminate the present when my eyes are closed enough so that I may see clearly. Unhampered by reason, far from the distraction of conventional wisdom, free of the distorting protective rituals of social interactions, in my dreams I can see most vividly who and where I am.…Openness to my own dreams puts me in touch with the oldest, most human aspects of who I am, helps me to find my place in the community of man (p. 255).

The Relationship Between Sleep and Dreams

The nineteenth century British poet Thomas Beddoes said that "if there are dreams to sell, merry and sad to tell, and the crier rang his bell, what would you buy?" This sentiment evokes the mystery of dreams, yet there is definitive scientific research that demonstrates that dreams have not only a physiological but also a psychological basis. Before dreams can be understood it is necessary to understand the role dreams play in sleep. There are two processes that have been identified; they are called REM – rapid eye movement sleep and NREM – non rapid eye movement. REM sleep is also called D for desynchronized or dream sleep. Brain waves produced during this sleep are very similar to the brain waves during wakefulness. The eyes dart about as if something is being watched. NREM sleep, called S or synchronized sleep, is characterized by a gradual desensitization of the body. The senses do not relay messages to the brain. It is as if the body had disconnected itself from the brain. Sometimes the body will move in a violent and jerky manner that the sleeper is totally unaware of during NREM sleep.

Sleep is divided into four stages that are repeated in a cyclical manner, in which the sleeper gently moves from wakefullness to deep sleep and back again. These stages are measured by comparing brain waves via an electroencephalogram (EEG). The brain waves move from low frequency (stage 1) to high frequency (stage 4). Early in sleep people are in phase 4, but by the end of the night they are in phase one. The movements of the eyes are also recorded behind closed eye-lids. In addition there is a transitional phase, called hypnagogic sleep, which is part wakefulness and part sleep. Some people can remember things occurring around them during this period when they have just closed their eyes and the body has started to relax. It is like gently walking into shadows where the environment slowly recedes into the background. During this sleep cycle people are experiencing different states of consciousness called ego states. The ego states consist of: **intact ego state (IES)** with discrimination between what is internal and external; **de-structured ego state (DES)** with no contact to external stimuli; and **restructured ego state (RES)** with the reconnection of the internal and external. These states are generally present at all stages of sleep, but are more prominent in certain stages than others. The four stages of sequential sleep are from light sleep – stage 1 (high frequency and low voltage) to deep sleep – stage 4 (low frequency and high voltage). The sleeping states consist of:

Alpha/REM: Alpha waves are present with a rhythmic eight to twelve cycles per second activity of a normal waking EEG and occasional REMs in which the eyes seem to be watching something. There is a high level of IES present in this phase. A typical response of a dreamer if woken up during this phase might sound like this: "I was thinking about whether I closed all the windows since it was getting cold." The content of the dream consists of a realistic perception of things and surroundings.

Alpha/SEM: The EEG alpha rhythm is still present, but there is a decrease in the movement of the eyes. This is a transitional stage, with slow eye movement, somewhere between REM and NREM or sometimes called (SEM). There is a decrease in IES and an increase in DES, which becomes accelerated as the sleeper enters the Alpha – Stage One Phase. A typical response of a dreamer if woken up during this phase might sound like this: "The door seemed to shake, followed by loud noises, then suddenly it flew open." The content of this dream consists of a loss of reality mixed with the bizarre.

Alpha – Stage One: The EEG has slowed down considerably with a more irregular pattern and no eye movement (NREM). DES is at its highest, often characterized by bizarre and implausible elements of the dream. A typical response of a dreamer if woken up during this phase might sound like this: "The door seemed to go in on its self as if swallowed up by a black hole that seemed to expand and swallow up the house." The content of this dream consists of a complete loss of contact with reality and implausible dream elements.

Alpha – Stage Two: The EEG shows bursts of activity called "spindle waves" that come in 14 cycles per second, along with random slow activity with no eye movement (NREM). There is a rapid rise in RES and a rapid drop in DES characterized by more realistic elements, but with little contact with reality. A typical response of a dreamer if woken up during this phase might sound like this: "The loud thumping seemed to come towards me up the stairs, so I tried to tell my friends that I didn't have any more time to spare." The content of this dream has plausible elements, but still lacks contact with reality.

In all the phases mental activity and dreaming are taking place; however, the different ego states along with the corresponding brain wave affect the content of the dream. The brain waves in REM sleep are very similar to wakefulness, which are primarily alpha waves. All four stages last about 90 minutes before the whole process is repeated (Shulman, 1979). If sleepers are disturbed the whole process starts all over again. When sleepers are deprived of REM sleep they can experience hallucinations, irritability, paranoia, or aggressive behavior. In animals, sleep deprivation can cause death. Dreams occur most often in REM sleep, but activities like sleepwalking occur in NREM sleep. While sleepers are dreaming they lose all contact with the sensory world.

If they are awakened right after a dream, no external stimuli will be included in the dream. When external stimuli occur, such as a telephone ringing, they are incorporated into the dream. Thus, dreams are a natural part of sleep, although some people do not remember their dreams, and therefore, conclude that they do not dream.

In general, REM sleep is about 25% of sleep in adults, while in infants it accounts for 50% of sleep. Interestingly enough, premature babies experience REM sleep 75% of the time. This brings up the question of the healing effects of REM sleep and dreaming. Naps have a higher percentage of REM sleep than do night sleeping. Some psychologists see naps as a way of lifting depression and increasing energy. It is also thought that disturbing a child in REM sleep can produce a nightmare. This might support Perls' idea that a nightmare is a dream that has not been completed. William Shakespeare reinforced the soothing effects of dreams in the play *Macbeth* when he wrote, "the death of each day's life, sore labor's bath balm of hurt minds, great nature's second course, chief nourisher in life's feast."

JUNGIAN APPROACH TO DREAMS

The early dream work of Sigmund Freud influenced a generation of psychologists, with some building on it and others totally rejecting it. Carl Jung, a student of Freud's, developed a theory of dreams, based on Freud's ideas of the unconscious and the influence of the past. Fritz Perls, on the other hand, minimized the idea of the past and its influence on dreams. Up until the time of Sigmund Freud, the scientific community discounted dreams as being worthless and meaningless. Freud shocked the scientific community when he published his classic *Interpretation of Dreams* in 1900, in which he explored the relationship between dreams, psychopathology and normal functioning. For this, he was criticized as being nonscientific. At that time, viewing dreams as meaningful aspects of the dreamer's personality was quite revolutionary. For Freud, the dream was a process of integrating the internal with the external, a process that could take the dreamer back to an archaic heritage with which the dreamer was born (Corsini & Wedding, 1989). Most importantly, he felt that dreams were only a facade that covered what was in the unconscious. Dreams consisted of manifest content or those parts of the dream remembered and latent content or aggressive or sexual wishes. The dream served as a mechanism for discharging sexual and aggressive behavior. Everything in the dream could be explained and therefore interpreted, translating the latent content into manifest content. Once the dreamer understood the dream, through interpretation of the symbols, insight and resolution would occur.

Carl Jung added to Freud's theory, but he viewed dreams as a natural occurrence whose purpose was to restore psychological balance. He felt that dream material in a subtle way re-establishes the total psychic make-up of a person. The dream becomes a form of compensation for establishing psychological balance and illuminating the dreamer's situation. Jung (1964) believed dreams were a part of a collective consciousness in which the dream could be interpreted by examining mythology and legends. Dreams were in essence influenced by ancient legends and the dreamer's ancestors. Critical dreams occur during early youth, puberty and at the onset of middle age. Accordingly, personal experiences were secondary to archetypes and the cultural past. "Archetypes are innate energy clusters within the psyche which reveal themselves most clearly in dreams and other visionary experiences" (Williams, 1982; p. 27). To help the dreamer understand the dream, Jung used the symbols and myths of the past to interpret the archetypes; a horse symbolizes wild, uncontrollable, instinctive drives, and the sea could symbolize the mother's womb. Since the unconscious has a life of its own and is a storehouse of energy, dreams are particularly valuable in not only shedding light on present living, but also past experiences. Like Freud, Jung believed that insight into a dream could help dreamers understand their feelings, actions and behavior. Choices and decisions in their personal lives could be made based on this insight. Common themes that occurred were dreams of examination, falling, finding, flying, losing, nudity and sex. Jung (1964) felt that people:

feel [themselves] isolated in the cosmos, because [they are] no longer involved in nature and have lost [their] emotional unconscious identity with natural phenomena. No river contains a spirit, no tree is the life principle of [humanness], no snake is the embodiment of wisdom, no mountain cave the home of a great demon. No voices now speak to [people] from stones, plants, and animals, nor [do they] speak to them believing they can hear…this enormous loss is compensated for by the symbols of our dreams. They bring up our original nature – its instincts and peculiar thinking (pp. 45-46).

SENOI-JUNGIAN DREAM WORK

Williams (1982) took many of the principles and concepts of Jung and fused them with the Senoi dream approach to create a very accessible methodology that is very much in the spirit of transpersonal psychology. The core of the Jungian-Senoi approach is to uncover the meaning of the dream. Since the "dream world" is also part of the person, though at a more unconscious level, just as thoughts and feelings in the conscious state are a part of the person. The potential of dreams are that they can help in transforming the person by expanding his or her awareness of the unconscious. However, it is not the interpretation of the dream that is important, but actualizing the dream; that can bring meaning. It is thought that once interpretation takes place, the real meaning becomes more distant, but when the dream is actualized, the meaning is closer. What is actualization? According to Williams (1982):

Actualization is the re-experiencing of the dream, or some aspect of it, with similar or greater emotional intensity than that of the original dream. Actualization also refers to gaining meaning from a dream by doing specific outer life project, which embodies some part of the original dream. Thus we include under the term "actualization" both re-experiencing the dream in itself and transforming the dream specific out-life experiences (p. 20).

Actualizing or re-experiencing dreams borrows the Senoi method by taking aspects of dreams and using them to "create projects [which] directly contribute to individual and community life" (Williams, 1982; p. 27). This could be as simple as sharing the dream with someone or using some of the messages to compose a song or find a solution to an everyday problem. The process of the Jungian-Senoi approach uses the following format:

- ❧ dream task (hearing the dream, obtaining feelings about it, objectifying the dream, focusing on one aspect of the dream, actions to take that can clarify meaning and reflecting on all of the above);

- ❧ dream incubation;

- ❧ objectifying the dream (analyzing the dream structure, elements, symbols, issues and qualities of the dream characters);

- ❧ key questions;

- ❧ following the dream ego (defining attitudes, feelings, and actions behind the dream);

- ❧ dialoguing (visualizing the character in the dreams and asking it questions and then waiting for the reply, examining questions concerning outer life, and expressing the dream in an art form);

- ❧ symbol immersion (amplifying the symbols by analyzing their meaning in the outer life, meditating on the symbols);

- ❧ bringing resolution to the dream state;

- ❧ direct dream re-entry;

- ❧ outer-life dream actualization or outer dream tasks.

TRANSPERSONAL APPROACH TO DREAMS

One of the particular characteristics of the transpersonal approach is to honor not only that which is from within, but that which is from outside the self. That which is within has always been a part of the psychology of the self, but including outside phenomena that has a very "magical" element to it. In a sense, the dream can transcend reality. The Transpersonal approach uses dreams to relate to source experiences that do not have their origin in the ego or conscious self. In other words, it is working with the non-decision making part of one's self and letting go of the rational self. In the unconscious self, the boundaries of the individual go beyond the physical manifestations of the body. This layer of the unconscious self that reaches beyond is not only a psychic phenomenon, but is transcendent of reality. While some therapies will look at dreams that relate to the past, the transpersonal looks at the dream in relationship to the future. Williams (1982) states that "the transpersonal emphasizes not only human potential, what a person is, but also the transformation of personality based on the 'never-before-manifested'" (p. 216). Thus, one's future is in the here and now, although a mystery; or to paraphrase Rilke: the future enters long before it happens. What happens in dreams are solutions to present day problems or confirmations of one's choices. While the source is a mystery and may remain so, the symbols of the dream are concrete. The idea is to discover what the meaning is to oneself by dialoguing the dream. What comes up in dialoguing are our fears, joys, attitudes, foibles and so on. Through the dialoguing, either through the help of another person who takes on the role of the dream or with another part of the self, one seeks answers by actively engaging the dream. When this happens the ego and the non-ego create a kind of contrasting energy field that can provide meaning or insights into what one is experiencing. In addition, the symbols in the dream can provide meanings that are reflective of one's culture. By reflecting on these symbols, an answer comes to the conscious self. It is much like when an object buried at the bottom of a pond floats to the surface. It may take moments to discover what the symbols mean or it may take years, but eventually the answer comes.

> *Often, the experiencing of these symbols is accompanied by feelings of awe, or fear of the tremendous. Such symbols might include any of the primary archetypal manifestations, such as dream landscapes of vastness, climbing mountains or plunging into dark abysses. Thus, transpersonal does not mean experiencing only the light and bright. Hell's imagery is as much transpersonal as Heaven's. God is everywhere and nowhere visible (Williams, 1982; p. 217).*

A FIRST NATIONS PERSPECTIVE

One of the principal philosophers of the First Nations tradition is Black Elk, who was a Lakota [Sioux] born in the 18th century. Exploring one of Black Elk's early dreams or visions provides an excellent example of the transcendent experiences. Before one of the battle of the Little Big Horn (1867), the young Black Elk saw a vision of two men descending with flaming spears. They kidnapped Black Elk and brought him to a great plain on a cloud. There, horses of differed colors greeted him: black [West: releases water from the clouds], white [North: cleaning, endurance and courage], red [power of the sacred pipe and the power of peace, to awaken others, through knowledge and wisdom] and yellow [South: growth and healing]. From there, Black Elk went into a rainbow-covered lodge of the Six grandfathers. These are the powers of the four directions, father sky, and mother earth. The first grandfather, of the West, gave Black Elk water to sustain life, and then handed him a bow and said he could use it to destroy. The second grandfather of the north gave sage, cleaning power, and a white wing, cleaning power of the northern snow. The third grandfather gave the power to awaken others by bring wisdom peace and knowledge. The fourth grandfather of the south gave him the power to heal others. The fifth grandfather, the spirit of the sky, became an eagle and told him that all living things were his relatives. The sixth grandfather, who was really mother earth spirit, gave the power to obtain salvation by providing the ability to make connections with the earth (nature). Later Black Elk was shown the hoop of the world that was made of many hoops, representing all people, but that they were one and the same. When Black Elk actualized his dream upon awakening, he spent his life using his powers to help his people. In the end, as an old man, well into the 20th century, he thought that the dream had failed. He was wrong because much of what was predicted came true, perhaps through his efforts, but the real gift was what he said and did to inspire the spiritual revival of the Lakota, and all First Nations people. It was just a dream that Ed McGaa, *Eagle Man* (1990), stresses, which has become a blooming tree with the:

> *bright rainbow, symbolic of the flowering tree...now blooming among the environmental and spiritual gatherings of enlighten peoples that have begun to flourish throughout the land. The rainbow-covered lodge of the six Grandfathers is a strong symbol of the old holy man's prediction [dream] that, someday, the flowing tree would bloom. The blooming has begun and will continue – if only some blue man (creed, corruption, and user of the land] doesn't push the wrong button (p. 17).*

THE DREAMS OF THE CHEROKEE

Among the Cherokee First Nation people, dream sharing is a vital part of their lives, because it links them to the real world that they experience to the world beyond themselves. It is where the conscious self meets the unconscious self. Thus to talk about dreams after they occur is important, since some dreams are gone shortly after one awakes. Dreams "talk" about strange actual events that have impacted them and events past. And some dreams are not just for one-self, but might even foretell the future. These dreams are about unusual happenings and they transcend life as it really is and can provide a sense of awareness about things that might otherwise be unknown. The history of the Cherokee people, whose language was one of the first indigenous languages to be written, shows that dreams were a pathway to other spiritual dimensions. However, not many of the ancient Cherokee signs, presages and dreams have pleasant associations; in fact, it seems as if they are fixated in death, illness and misfortune. In the study of such portents and dreams, there are four important characteristics to consider:

- Some of the dreams are about things that seldom happen, they caused little concern among the observers;

- Through dreams and signs, people found ways in which to deal and come to terms with unexpected deaths without accusing the Above Beings of being unfair to them;

- Signs and dreams prepared people to accept death as a natural consequence of living. It was better to be ready than to be suddenly seized;

- People were kept from attempting to solve their problems on their own by seeking the help of a priest for cleansing and restoration and they believed that this action pleased the Above Beings [the Creator].

For the Cherokee, dreams and signs were thought to be among the causes of things happening. To see in a dream the sign of death was to cause the death, the illness or any other matter; and even when most dreams defy recall, the Cherokee utilize seven ritual stones to help in this important act, since this is a vital practice in their lives. These are some examples that foretold sickness or death among the Cherokee:

🌿 Seeing anyone with an eagle feather in his hand or to dream of possessing such feathers was a sign of death;

🌿 Seeing a person with very clean clothes meant that the person would not live long;

🌿 Dreaming of a living person or an animal that was dead in the dream was a certain sign of sickness to come, and those who dreamed of seeing a woman would have fever and the ague.

Other dreams had to do with good fortune, good luck and greatness. If hunters dreamed of having bread, peaches or any kind of fruit, they were told they would kill a deer and if someone dreamed of flying, it was implied that a person would live a long life. In addition, there were dreams and signs that had to do with strangers and visitors. For example, if a little bird called Tsi ki lili flew over in the direction of someone who was traveling, that person would soon meet a stranger; if a bird flew into the house, it announced that a visitor was coming. There were also signs that had to do with enemies and warfare. If a Tsa wi sku bird was heard singing very loud and fast, it meant that enemies were in town and if an owl rested on a peach or any other tree in town and sang, enemies would approach shortly after. And yet, not every aspect of the Cherokee dreams have a negative connotation; there is a lingering belief that dreams do speak of positive human attributes and of how people must be centered in religion and the Above Beings. In the transpersonal sense, the traditional way that Cherokee people embraced dreaming and then incorporated the messages and signs into their everyday life illustrates how the unconscious world can be a part of everyday existence.

THE GESTALT APPROACH TO DREAMS

In the Gestalt view, dreams were a "royal road" to integration of divided selves (Perls, Hefferline & Goodman, 1951). All parts of the dream are essentially projections of the self. The dreamer, by role-playing each part, helps to unlock the existential message in the dream. Unlike Freud and Jung, reliving and not analyzing the dream is the most important aspect of dream work. For Perls (1975) the dream is neither a fulfillment of a wish nor a prophecy of the future. The dream simply tells the dreamer what is going on in life and how to change potentially "nightmarish" thoughts to an awareness of present existence. Faraday (1974) echoed this idea, because she saw dreamers as:

> the painters of dream pictures, and learning to understand dreams is a matter of learning to understand heart's language... [someone] may suggest all manner of interpretations, but unless they resonate with your own bones and move you to change your life in some constructive way, then they remain useless speculations on his or her part, which logically is the same as saying they are just plain wrong (p. 201).

There cannot be any interpretation of the material in dreams in the Gestalt approach. For Perls, a person's body is full of inherited wisdom and it is more or less adjusted to the environment from birth. The body is to be trusted, because it is the other side of the mind. The body has the raw materials to make new wholes, and in its emotions it has a kind of knowledge of the environment. The body, in effect, expresses itself in a well-constructed and purposeful way. Perls (1969b) felt that "the organism if left alone to take care of itself, without being meddled with from the outside…would heal itself…you can let the organism…without interrupting…you can rely on the wisdom of the organism" (p. 35).

All of the different parts of the dream, whether objects or people, are fragments of the dreamer's personality (Perls, Hefferline & Goodman, 1951). Since the aim of the transpersonal approach is to help everyone become a whole person, which means a unified person without conflicts, the facilitator has to assist the dreamer in putting together the different fragments of the dream. The dreamer has to re-own those projected, fragmented parts of the personality and discover the meaning of the dream. The difference in Perls' thinking, as opposed to Freud's, was the view that the dream is a process to understand reality. The dream is a better reflection of reality than life itself. While people can pretend or cover feelings in their conscious life, they have more difficulty doing so with dreams. Dreams are the way to reality, because unfortunately it is precisely in trying to live up to the expectation of others that they have lost themselves (Perls, 1975). In Gestalt dream work the dreamer can gain both emotional and intellectual insight, but the methods focus on promoting the former (James & Jongeward, 1973). Emotional awareness is that moment of self-discovery when a person says "ah-ha." The "ah-ha" experience is what happens whenever something "clicks" or falls into place. In other words, each time a gestalt closes there is this "ah-ha" click, in which the shock of recognition occurs. Perls (1969a) said, "I believe that in a dream we have a clear existential message of what's missing in our lives, what we avoid doing and living, and we have plenty of material to re-assimilate and re-own the alienated parts of ourselves" (p. 67).

Thus, instead of discounting a dream, the Gestalt approach is to "go with it." Energy is not wasted by opposing or criticizing it. As an exercise, exploring a dream can only enhance awareness and focus feelings and perceptions more vividly. Dreams are attacked when they are interpreted, rather than seen as parts of vitality. For Perls, working through a dream is essentially a creative operation. This notion is reflected by Latner (1973) who said, "It is only as an artist that man knows reality" (p. 67). In fact, the Gestalt views dreams as the most spontaneous expression of the human existence. Dreams are like a stage production, but the direction and the action are not under the same control as in waking life. The major difference between Gestalt and Psychoanalytic dream work is the emphasis on the present or "here and now" in Gestalt. The dreamer relives the dream by becoming each of the objects and people in the dream. In doing this, the dreamer becomes more aware of the meaning of the dream. Doing this also puts the person in the "here and now," which makes it easier to relate the dream to present personal experiences. Now the message of the dream becomes the responsibility of the dreamer. The choice is to act on the message or not.

STEPS IN GESTALT DREAM EXPLORATION

In the exploration of a dream it is not essential to know the whole dream to understand its meaning. For example, Monique, an eight-year-old, told me a dream about her mother beating up her father. As she told the dream she began to cry and related her feelings that her parents were angry with each other and with her as well. The telling and reliving of the dream reflected her own fear of being the cause of the anger. Although she did not remember any more of the dream, the retelling of it allowed her to share her feelings about being caught in the middle of her parents' difficulties and acknowledge her anger about what might happen. The Gestalt dream work made it possible for her to understand the dream in a more concrete way than if it had been interpreted or analyzed. By integrating and not analyzing the dream, she was allowed to express her feelings and what she was going to do about her feelings.

Perls (1969b) felt that every part, no matter how small, contains important elements of the story that can be used. As the dream is explored:

> the difficulty is to understand the idea of fragmentation. All the different parts are distributed all over the place. If you are capable of projecting yourself totally into every little bit of the dream – and really becoming that thing – then you begin to re-assimilate, to re-own what you have disowned, given away. The more you disown, the more impoverished you get. Here is an opportunity to take back (p. 78).

There are four interrelated phases of the Gestalt therapeutic process: identification, differentiation, affirmation and integration. This process is easily adapted to a group environment, whether it involves one group member exploring a dream with the group as a backdrop or a number of group members role playing parts of a dream. As shown in Figure 6.1, the facilitator, acting as a screen for one group member's feelings, thoughts and actions, creates a dialogue in which the group member can gain insight into how he or she is avoiding responsibility for making the choices that will bring resolution. The facilitator can utilize a number of therapeutic methods with slight variations, but essentially the four-phase process is followed.

STEP ONE: EXPRESSION OR TELLING OF THE DREAM

Person 1: I dreamed that I was awakened by a noise…as if the door had opened. I could hear someone walking up the steps…a muffled sound. My body felt frozen and I wanted to cry out, but I couldn't move. The door slowly opened and there was a shadow of a man, whom I couldn't see, I tried to get up…do anything, but I couldn't. Slowly he came forward and he had an ax in his hands…he raised it and I again tried to scream. As the ax came down I woke up hearing a strange peeping sound…it was my voice…(he looks down, with his body hunched over).

Facilitator: How are you feeling?

Person 1: I am afraid (he folds his arms around his chest).

Facilitator: Are you aware of folding your arms around your chest?

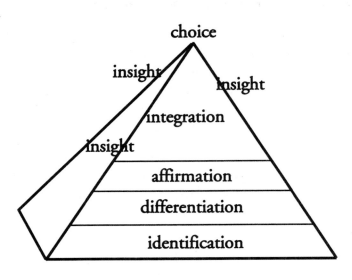

Person 1: Yes. I'm really afraid and I feel so helpless.

The facilitator focuses on verbal and non-verbal expressions of the dreamer. The dreamer tells the dream and, if it is necessary to bring out more material, the facilitator will ask clarifying questions. According to Perls, Hefferline and Goodman (1951), the facilitator wants to separate "verbalizing" from experience, because the dreamer may try only:

to be objective about his personal experience – which largely means to theorize in words about himself and his world, meanwhile, and by this very method, he avoids contact with feelings, the drama, the actual situation. He lives the substitute life of words, isolated from the rest of his personality, contemptuous of the body and concerned with the verbal righteousness, arguing, making an impression, propagandizing, rationalizing – while genuine problems of the organism go unattended (p. 105).

In addition, the facilitator finds out how the dreamer feels "right now" about the dream. This brings the dream to the "here and now." Perls felt that it is vital that the facilitator attempts to identify each part so it is "real" and in the present. It may be necessary to slow down the telling of the dream so that the dreamer can experience the parts. By using the first person present tense, the dreamer becomes the dream.

STEP TWO: DIFFERENTIATION

Facilitator: In your dream the intruder had an ax? What other objects or people were you aware of?

Person 1: Only me and the intruder. And I was in my bed...

Facilitator: I would like you to choose members of the group to work with you as the various objects and people in your dream. Can you choose someone to be your bed and the intruder? To give the person you've chosen to be the bed an idea what it is like would you be your bed and speak as if you are a bed. Start off by saying, "I am a bed, I..." and go as far as possible with this.

Person 1: I am a bed. I give comfort and rest. I am soft and warm.

Facilitator: (Speaking to Person 2, who will be the bed) Now you have an idea what it is like. Can you add to this and don't be afraid to "ham it up."

Person 2: I am a bed. I can take you all in and give you sweet peace…You never have to be afraid.

Facilitator: (Speaking to Person 1) Can you continue…

Person 1: I am afraid…(looking down at his hands) I…am alone.

Facilitator: You are alone. How do you feel right now?

Person 1: I don't like being alone. People need others…

Facilitator: Try saying, "I need others."

Person 1: I need others (slumping down with eyes moist, making a fist).

Person 2: I need others and I am angry about that…

Person 1: Yes, I am angry about that…

Facilitator: What do you want?

Person 1: I want to be with others. To have someone who…

Person 2: Someone who will be there for me…

Facilitator: (Speaking to Person 1) You need others or you want others?

Person 1: (smiling) I want others.

Facilitator: Are you aware that you are also making a fist?

Person 1: (looking down) Yes. I'm angry?

Facilitator: Do you feel sad and angry?

Person 1: Yes.

Facilitator: Now I would like you to choose someone to be an ax. (Speaking to Person 1) Can you tell her what it is like as an ax.

Person 1: (Speaking to Person 3) You are an ax that is old, sharp and strong.

Person 3: I am an ax. I am old, sharp and strong. I can maim, kill, or make things.

Facilitator: (Speaking to Person 1) Can you continue that and add or subtract anything you want.

Person 1: I am an ax. I'm not one of those long handled ones, but shorter and easily carried. I am sharp and hard. I can really hurt and cause pain…

Person 3: I have no feelings or thoughts.

Person 1: Yes. I only carry out the wishes of those who use you…

Facilitator: You? Please repeat that, but substitute me for you.

Person 1: I only carry out the wishes of those who use me…(making a fist again).

Person 3: Why do I let them get away with it, without doing anything?

Facilitator: (Speaking to Person 1) What's happening to you right now?

Person 1: I guess I'm angry...

Facilitator: You guess?

Person 1: No. I am angry. The thing I hate most is to be used by others.

The facilitator takes the least significant object, and using present tense begins a dialogue. Asking other group members to help actualize the objects makes it easier to intensify the feelings and thoughts. In addition, those people participating in the dream process can offer insight and support to the dreamer, while being able to explore parts of themselves. However, person 1 must be the one who gives meaning to the objects. The facilitator keeps person 1 in the "here and now" by reflecting feelings and making him aware of nonverbal behavior. Perls (1969b) says it is often those objects or non-human parts "...in a dream that hold the key as in some way they are more disowned. The object's relationship to other objects, humans, the dreamer can be explored in dialogue after the existential existence of that object is explored" (p. 97). Also, notice how the facilitator moves the person to be more exact in language (e.g. " I guess I am angry" to "I am angry").

Each part of the dream, a unique and separate aspect of the dreamer, is identified and differentiated. So far there is a soft comforting side (bed) and a hard unfeeling side (ax). Each part of the dream is likely to hold a message about the person dreaming with the alienated personality being "re-owned" and thus integrated. Perls (1969a) emphasizes that "every part is me... instead of being incomplete and fragmented. And very often the projection is incomplete, but it's obvious. If we have a staircase without railings it's obvious that the railings are somewhere in the dream but they're missing. They're not there...this is a hole" (p. 99).

STEP THREE: AFFIRMATION

Facilitator: Now I would like you to be the Intruder.

Person 1: I don't know, its really scary...

Facilitator: Can you pick someone from the group to be the Intruder?

Person 1: (Choosing Person 4 to be the Intruder) It's OK to be the Intruder?

Person 4: Humm. Sure, but why me?

Person 1: You scare me the most in the group.

Facilitator: How does he scare you?

Person 1: He's unpredictable, powerful and unknown.

Facilitator: (Speaking to Person 4) Can you be unpredictable, powerful and unknown.

Person 4: (Growling Person 4 moves around the room taking large jumps, flailing his arms and contorting his face.)

Facilitator: (Speaking to Person 1) What could you tell the intruder to say to make him even more scary?

Person 1: (Speaking to Person 4) You should say: "I am an intruder. I want to destroy."

Person 4: (Growling and jumping around the room, he comes up and faces Person 1 and speaks in a loud voice) I AM AN INTRUDER! I WANT TO DESTROY! I WANT TO DESTROY...

Person 1: Me?

Facilitator: Can you be the Intruder now and answer that?

Person 1: Yes. I want to destroy you!

Facilitator: Louder!

Person 1: I WANT TO DESTROY YOU! KILL YOUR SOFTNESS! YOUR SMUGNESS! (looking down and rubbing his hands on his knees).

Facilitator: Are you aware of what your hands are doing?

Person 1: Yes. I'm rubbing them on my knees.

Facilitator: What are you trying to rub out?

Person 1: (after some silence, with tears in his eyes) The feeling part of myself...the pain...the hurt...

Facilitator: I would like you to continue rubbing until you've rubbed it away.

Person 1: (slowly rubbing harder and harder, until he pounds his knees).

Facilitator: (giving the dreamer a pillow) Hit this!

Person 1: (hitting the pillow until tears come, he now cradles the pillow).

Facilitator: (touching him after the tears have subsided) What are you aware of?

Person 1: I feel that I am the intruder and...

Facilitator: You seem surprised?

Person 1: Yes...I scare myself...God, it seems so very strange.

The dreamer has expressed two opposing feelings about different parts of himself. With the help of Person 4, the facilitator has asked him to exaggerate those feelings, even if it means expressing them in a way that he would never do. The Intruder seems to represent everything that the person finds abhorrent in himself. It is quite a surprise to feel the power that is in the Intruder. In a sense, the darkness of the Intruder and the lightness of the bed complete the wholeness of being. Essentially, there is no wholeness without the "dark" and the "light." They are just opposites that are incomplete without each other. Exaggerating the Intruder, feeling the power, helps the person to experience the fullness of the feelings and makes him more aware of the polarities that exist. This process of exaggeration helps in the differentiation of feelings. In accepting the different feelings and the parts of self the dreamer can achieve a more integrated personality. Zinker (1977) concludes that the way to understand conflict is to identify the polarities, because:

each person is a conglomerate of polar forces, all of which intersect, but not necessarily at the center…a person has within him the characteristics of kindness and also its polarity of cruelty, the characteristic of hardness, and its polarity of softness…a person possesses not just one opposite, but several related opposites, creating 'multi-polarities' (pp. 196-197) .

Step Four: Integration and Choice

Facilitator: In your dream there seems to be two parts of you: a hard part, who is angry and doesn't mind inflicting pain, and a soft part who is comforting, yet lonely. What is your dream telling you?

Person 1: In my family anger was something never expressed. I have always found it difficult to be angry. I'd really be disliked if I expressed my anger. It seems that the two parts…

Facilitator: I would like you to begin by saying, "My two parts…"

Person 1: Yes (laughing), my two parts need each other. If I don't protect my vulnerable part from time to time, I get hurt; yet when I pull back, become angry, all I want to do is hurt.

Facilitator: Whom do you hurt?

Person 1: Maybe myself…

Facilitator: Maybe? You're not sure?

Person 1: Yes. Basically I do hurt myself! Somehow it seems that, if something bad happens, I figure I'm to blame.

Facilitator: You turn on yourself.

Person 1: Yes. I'm my greatest enemy.

Facilitator: Would any of you who participated in this dream like to share anything?

Person 2: I'm glad you found me soft and comforting, because that's what I like about you. You have been very supportive of me in this group. I hope it doesn't stop.

Person 3: I can't say I was happy to be an ax. Yet I found myself getting into the role and enjoying being sharp for a change. You are sometimes a powerful person to me. You can be sharp when you want. But, I want to be sharp and powerful more often in the group than I am.

Person 4: I wasn't surprised that you chose me to be the Intruder. I could sense you felt distant from me. I hope as the group continues, you will share with me how I do that.

Facilitator: (Speaking to Person 4) Thanks. I hope we can explore that further in future sessions. (Speaking to Person 1) How do you distance yourself in this group?

Person 4: Well…By not feeling…and sharing my fears.

Facilitator: What are you going to do about it?

The dreamer has become aware of differing parts of himself and how he, in his daily life, turns his feelings back onto himself. This is a mechanism that Perls (1969b) calls retroflection. Rather than expressing anger towards others, the dreamer turns them back in on himself. In the process, he wanted to "disown" the angry part of himself, which he found unacceptable. The feedback and sharing of the other group members who participated in the dream work helped the dreamer see how they view him. The choice of the people involved seem to have some significance for the person, so exploring those feelings adds immediacy. The group now becomes an arena for experimentation by using the insights gained in the dream work. Through the dream awareness and by use of the last question, the facilitator focuses the dreamer on his choice and responsibility. Perls (1969b) said that what was unclear has now become quite obvious, because it is a process of "re-owning power by becoming those images which are most vital and powerful aspect…Don't forget that it is just as important to own the beauty and goodness of some symbols as it is to focus on the ones that seem frightening or complex" (p. 101).

LEARNING FROM DREAMS ON AN INDIVIDUAL BASIS

A person can work on a dream outside of the group, although it is always better to do it with someone. I have found that another person can point out what I am avoiding in the dream. The only danger is that this other person might come too quickly to the rescue and tell the dreamer what is going on, instead of giving the dreamer the chance of discovering his or her own message. However, it is not always possible to have someone to help do this. James and Jongeward (1973) suggest the following format in working on a dream.

1. Write down the dream, make a list of all the details and record any feelings or thoughts related to the dream.

2. Get every person, thing, mood, no matter how trivial, and then work on these parts by becoming each one of them (e.g., speak as the tree or the river).

3. Ham it up and transform each of the items by becoming the thing, whatever it is – become it (e.g., turn into the form or whatever it is) and do not try to make sense or interpret.

4. Take each one of the different items, characters, and parts, and let them have encounters between each other by dialoguing (e.g., the desk speaks to the chair and the tree to the ax).

5. Write a script of an encounter between two important elements in the dream (e.g., have a dialogue between the two opposite parts).

6. After working through the dream address the following questions:

   Was I avoiding something in the dream?

   Was I running away? Hiding?

   Was I able to use my legs or voice?

   Is there a similar pattern of avoidance?

CONCLUSION

The good road and the road of difficulties you have made me cross; and where they cross the place is holy. Black Elk (Cherokee Feast of Days, 1992; p. 161).

Two characteristics that take dreams beyond traditional personal development is that dreams go beyond physical laws and no matter how bizarre the dream is, the events in the dream are taken as real. In this regard, dream work is a creative process of the imagination, very much like a painting. Secharist (1974) stressed that to "the individual who desires self-improvement and communication with his or her divine self, dreams will show the way... for they are the magic mirror of the soul" (p. 12). This is the essence of the Transpersonal approach. And the Jungian-Senoi approach embodies this idea. It utilizes input from dreams as disguised messages full of symbolism, while the Gestalt approach to the parts of the dream, no matter how insignificant they appear, reflect the different parts of the dreamer. In other words, both approaches look for hidden meaning in the dreamer's existence, but differ on how to find the meaning. In the First Nations tradition, the dream world is not separated from the everyday world of life, but incorporated into daily living. Essentially, a dream contains two elements:

- A statement of who the dreamer is; by playing each part people can become aware of their feelings and the meaning of their existence; and

- A mechanism for "re-owning" of parts or aspects of the self that have been denied, by accepting attributes of the self, it is possible to become whole.

Human nature is composed of various parts, which when integrated result in a healthy spontaneous person. While there is a multiplicity in everyone, each part is not more important than any other part. In working on dreams people must get "in touch" with alienated aspects of self, and work on "re-owning" those parts. The process of "getting in touch" consists of identification, differentiating and integrating the differing parts of the self. What follows is self-acceptance, which allows people greater personal choices in how they want to live their lives. All people are in a never-ending "battle" with their polarities, which sometimes are mutually supportive and sometimes alienating. These opposites are illustrated in Herman Hesse's (1971) novel, *Narziss and Goldman*, in which one character represented the spiritual part and the other the physical aspect of the writer. Hesse presented them as two different characters, but in reality they were the two parts of the same person. Without each other they become self destructive, but together they produce a complete person capable of a multitude of responses.

When one aspect or part of a person is in the foreground, the other part is in the background, but because there is a "see-saw" effect, the person can become easily confused. Differentiation of the conflicting parts eliminates this effect. The task of Gestalt is to resolve these polarities so they aid each other. When it is time to be tough, be tough; when it is time to be soft, be soft. The following are examples of common splits that Gestalt attempts to resolve: mind/body; emotional/real; subjective/objective; infantile/mature; biological/cultural; and personal/social. Perls personified these splits by calling them "top-dog" and "bottom-dog." "I believe that in a dream we have a clear existential message of what is missing in our lives, what we avoid doing and living and we have plenty of material to re-assemble and re-own the alienated parts of ourselves" (Perls, 1969b; p. 76).

The dreamer takes the part of the dream that he or she least identifies with, no matter how vague, and "gets in touch" with it. It is thought that the part, which the dreamer is least in touch with, has the greatest likelihood of an "ah-ha" (insight). However, there has to be some action to actualize the dream in order for it to have significant effect. It is one thing to know, but more powerful to do something as a result of what you know. When there is difficulty, the facilitator can switch the dreamer to people or places. An important role of the facilitator is to ensure that the dreamer does not talk about the dream, but re-experiences it. It is vital that the dreamer be encouraged to explore the relationship between the parts of the dream and their current life situations. Perls felt that the process of dream work could increase awareness, help identify all parts or aspects of the self, and complete "unfinished business" from a person's past. Perls stressed the importance of process in dream work, which he felt could sometimes reinforce personal identity and self-responsibility; for example it is not the destination that is important, but the trip. Perhaps it is good to keep in mind Kopp's (1975) idea on dreams: "Again and again I find that my own inner counselor, my secret dreaming self, is not only wise and helpful but usually amusing as well" (p. 35). Finally, dreams along with sleep bring another dimension of living that help people be more responsible because:

> whatever you do in life, you will have some kind of control or deliberate interference. Not so with dreams. Every dream is an artwork, more than a novel. A bizarre drama. Whether or not it's good art is another story, but there is always lots of movement, fights, encounters, all kinds of things in it...We have to re-own these projected, fragmented parts of our personality, and re-own the hidden potential that appears in the dream (Perls, 1976; p. 75).

ACTIVITIES

1. **Nightmare Party:** Think about the worst nightmare ever experienced. Now, write a description of the scariest person or object from the dream (e.g., villain), giving it a name, age, personality and mannerisms. Next, everyone is asked to become the villain and participate in a party. The more people are encouraged to "ham it up" the more interesting and fun the role-playing can be. Allow about 20 minutes for the interaction. Everyone is to imagine that they are the villain and they are attending a party or reunion with other villains. They introduce themselves, share past experiences, and whatever "small talk" they can think of. At the end of the interaction participants are to share aspects of the role they played. This can be done in the large group, in small groups or in dyads. Some of the topics that can be shared are:

❧ What qualities are most disconcerting?

❧ What qualities, if any, were attractive?

❧ Similarity or differences between the "villain" and self?

❧ What characteristics were active, interesting, scary, etc. in others?

2. **Dream Sharing:** Record a dream during the coming week and share it with the small group. In the sharing, the dream should be described in the first person. Group members are to help each other find any "messages" in the dream. To do this, by:

❀ Placing an easily reached notebook by the bed;

❀ Reminding yourself before retiring that a dream is to be remembered;

❀ Writing down everything, after getting up, including dream fragments;

❀ Recording any words that reflect feelings and thoughts about the dream.

CHAPTER SEVEN
USING PSYCHODRAMA IN THE GROUP

Imagine that you have received some insult in public, perhaps a slap in the face that makes your cheek burn whenever you think of it. The inner shock was so great that it blotted out all the details of this harsh incident, but some insignificant thing will instantly revive the memory of the insult, and the emotion will recur with redoubled violence... if you possess such sharp and easily aroused emotional material you will find it easy to transfer it to the stage and play a scene analogous to the experience you had in real life. Constantin Stanislavski (1969; p. 176)

Stanislavski, the great Russian actor and director, knew the power of unfinished business and translated it into a powerful technique for getting the best performances out of his actors. Psychodrama has borrowed these methods and utilizes theatrical techniques, but applies them to real situations that are replayed as a means of bringing resolution to problems and issues not resolved. Psychodrama is based on the premise that drama occurs in everyday life. As a therapeutic approach it takes the creative acting ability inherent in everyone and applies it to the helping process. Psychodrama is a flexible and creative approach to problem solving that can be utilized in a variety of settings, such as educational, industrial and therapeutic, and could be used in individual and group counseling, personal growth groups, leadership training and mediation, just to name a few.

The Greek word *drama* translates to "action or a thing done." A creative and therapeutic intervention that actualizes this meaning is Psychodrama. "Psychodrama can be defined, therefore, as the science which explores the **truth** by dramatic methods" (Moreno, 1953). It was developed by the Romanian born Jacob Moreno at his clinic in Beacon, New York, in the early 1920s. Moreno felt that the stage could help patients actualize their problems by making them real and immediate, thus providing a concrete direction for change and wellness. According to Langley (1983) "Psychodrama is directed towards emotional catharsis, while drama therapy does not necessarily demand deep emotional involvement" (p. 20). Moreno, like William Shakespeare, felt that "all the world is a stage and all the men and women merely players"; thus, Psychodrama developed as a natural method of actualizing situations in a realistic manner.

RATIONALE FOR USING PSYCHODRAMA
IN GROUP PSYCHOTHERAPY

One of the aspects of helping that prompted Moreno to develop the theory and procedures of Psychodrama was the undemocratic aspect of therapy he found in Freud's approach. As the dominant theory at the time, the Psychoanalytic approach is a process whereby the helper interprets the behavior of the client as a means of bringing insight and change. Moreno felt that this approach stifled spontaneity. He felt that in a group it was better to get people to physically act out their problems, as opposed to talking about them. He noticed that this process not only activated the group, but also helped those with problems better extract emotions far more realistically and with more clarity. Moreno taught that problems arise in society because people lose their spontaneity and become more anxious. He noticed that, when clients became more physically active, their anxiety was lowered. The differences between Moreno and Freud were expressed at a conference in Vienna in 1912 when Moreno told Freud (Corsini & Wedding, 1989) "I start where you leave off. You meet people in the artificial setting of your office; I meet them on the street and in their home, in their natural surroundings. You analyze their dreams. I teach the people how to play God" (p. 458).

Psychodrama's most important characteristic is its emphasis on spontaneity and creativity. Moreno noticed that anxiety decreased with the increase of spontaneity in a person's behavior. He found that in most spontaneous situations, there seem to be lower levels of thinking about self. To capitalize on this observation he used a stage where people could act out scenes from their inner world or past experiences. The goal was to lead them to an emotional catharsis. Re-enacting situations through drama created tension, which Moreno (1953) felt was the most effective way of getting people to explore their attitudes. In his work, Moreno could see that tension, if channeled in the right direction, could lead to heightened awareness and sensory receptivity. The stage and drama was a simple mechanism to breach the dualism of reality and fantasy. The problem could be a real or even an imagined situation. It did not matter if the psychodramatic content were a past, present or future dilemma. As an approach to personal growth, problem solving and group process, Psychodrama is attractive, because everyone can be involved. Involvement of the group members follows a set sequence: presenting a problem to act out (protagonist); assisting someone in the group working on an issue by role playing someone from a past situation (auxiliary ego or as a double) or participating as a member of the audience. The double becomes a mirror for the protagonist by either providing support or acting as a voice. Some people have a hard time saying they are angry; thus, the double says it for them (e.g., "You are really pissing me off"). The double works at intensifying emotions and clarifying feelings and thoughts. The facilitator is the director, whose function is to assist in setting up the scenes and structuring the drama. The rest of the group serves as an audience who observes and offers feedback to the participants.

By offering the group an opportunity to totally involve themselves in the process, Psychodrama is one of the most innovative and creative therapeutic approaches to resolving problems. It relies on group members to participate in each other's lives through acting out their thoughts and feelings, rather than just talking about them. It draws on everyone's need to play, as children enacting life. The drama is not limited by time, space or even reality. Perls (1973) felt that by helping people recognize the relation between fantasy and reality: "We can make full use in therapy of fantasizing and all its increasing states of intensity towards actuality – a verbalized fantasy, or one which is written down, or one which is acted out as Psychodrama" (p. 86).

THE SPIRIT, SOUL AND CONSCIOUS
SELF IN THE PSYCHODRAMA PROCESS

Many of the tools and methods used in the Psychodrama process get the participants to focus beyond their conscious selves. Time and reality become relative and participants can use fantasy or even magic or spirit beings to help and support them. Moreno was very aware of the spiritual dimension that was often overlooked in the therapeutic process, yet terms like the "spirit" and "soul" are vague terms. What is the "spirit?" In his book, *The Spiritual Universe*, Fred Alan Wolf (1999) describes the spirit in metaphorical terms. He uses a violin string (matter or the body) that is plucked and vibrates. The vibrations (movement of the spirit) produce energy that cannot be seen, but it's there and stays there long after normal eyesight or ears (conscious self) sense the vibration. Energy is infinite. "What is the soul?" The reflection of the vibrations is the soul in a vacuum in relationship to time. In that sense, Wolf stresses that the soul exists from the beginning into infinity. Like the reflection in a mirror, the soul is merely a reflection. The material embodiment of the soul is the conscious self. The main goal of the soul is to help the body survive in its material existence. In Psychodrama the spirit and soul can be actively engaged, in which either can assist, support or teach the conscious self. From a transpersonal perspective "The goal of therapy is not that the person establishes a strong and predictable self. The goal is that the person becomes flowing, flexible, responsive, and spontaneous: they move from the stasis to the process" (Brazier, 1995; p. 173).

PSYCHODRAMA FROM A CROSS-CULTURAL
PERSPECTIVE: SPIRITUAL HEALING

The therapeutic benefit from dramatizing or acting out the inner and outer state of being, a core component of Psychodrama, is quite well known in a variety of cultures. It is even possible that Moreno's development of the psychodrama techniques came about as a process of going back to older rituals that formally characterized European culture. What Moreno did, it can be argued, was to stylize his method to utilize acceptable dramatic expression and incorporate psychological beliefs concurrent with his time. In fact, Moreno (1959) was influenced by the Shamanistic tradition of First Nations people of North America. Hence, the dramatic stage fused with Humanistic psychotherapy and ritualistic healing processes.

In the same context of Moreno's philosophy is the use of psychodrama, along with other methods, in other cultures to help rid people of alienation, depression, some psychosomatic illnesses and a host of other problems. The psychological literature is filled with the therapeutic benefits of Santeria [among Hispanic peoples] and Voodoo [among Haitians] to help people feel better about themselves, be more productive, and develop a closer, more positive, relationship with their family and community. In China for example, illnesses not only have their causes in the physical being, but in the spiritual and psychological realms as well. That is, illness, to be treated properly, must included healing of the spirit too. This is one of the basis of the centuries-old Chinese Medicine, which incidentally has not only been grudgingly accepted by the Western Medical establishment, but by government health departments (e.g. the B.C. Ministry of Health now accepts certain practices of Chinese Medicine as a legitimate Medicare expense). In a study of dramatic acting out among Hong Kong Chinese to deal with "possession syndrome," it was found that "the powerful psychological effect on the audience of the mythological dramatis personae entering the stage of the Chinese popular opera through the so called "ghost door", and relates a tradition of actors being possessed by the spirits they impersonate" (Jilek, 1992; p. 92).

Among Salish spirit dancers, from the coast of the Pacific Northwest, each repeats the first possession during the annual winter ceremony. By re-entering a trance-like state, there is a re-experiencing of the spirit power acquired originally in an altered state of consciousness induced during the initiation ceremony. As in the fashion that Moreno developed, ritualized movement helps the person feel in the present, exactly what they felt the first time. Not only does this reproduce a sense of well being, but it also reinforces the archetypes, or cultural energy sources, that empower. Hence, the winter spirit dance is very much in the keeping of positive therapeutic methods that are proven to be helpful and culturally relevant. Consider Jilek's (1992) description of what happens in the spirit dance :

> *Some dancers are experienced virtuosi in achieving such a state; they work themselves up with loud hyperventilation and vehement commotion, to pass into song and dance when dozens of deer-hid drums strike in. The dancer's spirit finds its dramatized expression in dance steps, tempo, movements, miens and gestures: in the sneaking pace, then flying leaps of the ferocious yelling "warrior," or in the swaying trot of the plump, sadly weeping "bear mother," in the rubber-like reptilian writhing of the "double headed serpent" as well as in the desperate wailing and gesticulation of the "mother seeking her child"; just as in the "lizard" who sheds tears over his devoured offspring or in the mighty "whale" who grabs smaller fish (p. 92).*

Furthermore, Psychodrama and the winter spirit dance include the following characteristics. Both are cathartic, since it leads people to a point of expressing their feelings and fears, while at the same time Binding strength in the experience. Clearly the dramatic format, the group support, and the careful direction that the spirit dance occurs in is very similar to Psychodrama. In the psychodrama, there are specific roles and methods, with its protagonist, auxiliary egos, director and audience. Psychodrama is very specific, following a set pattern, in which everyone involved has roles to play. In the same way, the winter spirit dance is choreographed, with specific rhythms and actions. Finally, both need the group setting, in which there are participators and an audience. Everything is controlled and involves a safe setting with a facilitator (director and ritualist); as Jilek 1992) declares "in the spirit dance are present the dramatis personae of Moreno's clinical psychodrama: protagonists [the dancers], auxiliary egos [babysitters or assistants], director [ritualist], and group [audience] (p. 93).

A very important aspect of the comparison of the winter spirit ceremony and psychodrama is that psychodrama is a psychological technique, albeit transpersonal in many respects, but it is not a spiritual ritual. One has to be extremely careful in over-analyzing the winter spirit dance.

The significance of Jilek's discussion is to demonstrate that this and many other First Nations' practices have a method and philosophy that is complex and people in the larger society need to recognize, respect and honor what is being done. This is the beauty in Black Elk's dream of the return of traditional beliefs and practices. In addition, this ritual and many others clearly are beneficial and thus should be a part of cross-cultural counselling with First Nations people or other people with traditions that can clearly be therapeutic. In discussing the positive effects of the spirit dance "clinical experience…would suggest that [the]…'Indian treatment' compares favourably with Western therapeutic or correctional approaches" (Jilek, 1992; p. 97).

THE RELATIONSHIP OF PSYCHODRAMA
AND THE TRANSPERSONAL APPROACH

The Psychodrama model is quite adaptable and can be used with other theoretical modalities, including the Transpersonal approach. The similarities in the theoretical orientation of Psychodrama and Transpersonal are the values placed on spontaneity, immediacy, catharsis and the search for wholeness. In Psychodrama the self "emerges from role-clarification expression and movement" (Orcutt, 1977; p. 98). This occurs through experimenting with different roles as the protagonist increases awareness and provides a more concrete and acceptable style of being in the world. In the Transpersonal approach, not only is the person searching for greater fulfillment; additionally, he or she is trying to find how to transcend attachments and self-indulgence. In essence, to be able to re-connect to nature and to learn to live in harmony with others. The flexibility of Psychodrama is helping to break through the impasse through experiencing differing roles, polarities and increasing one's awareness of personal boundaries and a greater reliance on self.

The plots and roles in Psychodrama reflect the experience of the protagonist rather than the director or anyone else. Paradoxically, while the protagonist projects the self onto the dramatic script, the goal is to liberate the self from it. Healing occurs through catharsis brought about by the bond (tele) between the director and the protagonist. The role of the facilitator is to be challenging, empathic and creative, while attempting to focus the participants' healing power back to themselves. As in the Transpersonal approach, methods such as dream work, imagery, art, bodywork, and role-playing can be used. Psychodrama has a very clear role for the members of the group in each phase of the process (e.g., warm-up, action and sharing). The rules of Psychodrama are structured to the point where it varies little (e.g., protagonist, director, auxiliary ego and double). In the opening, the director in the Psychodrama warms up the audience to bring out the drama. It could appear that a Psychodrama of some past event recreates what happened, yet no matter how much the protagonist tries to go back it is only a projection from where he or she is at now.

Theoretical Concepts of Psychodrama

Psychodrama, unlike other forms of therapeutic intervention, is able to immerse all of the group members in each other's issues. As a dramatic recreation, spontaneity, immediacy, tele and catharsis are usually present. These concepts are not only crucial to the success of a Psychodrama, but are also seen as goals that each person can work towards as a means of achieving a full life. In Psychodrama it is assumed that everyone has the "key" and the means in bringing about resolution. What the Psychodrama is focusing on, according to Goldman and Morrison (1984), is for the person "to see and feel the truth of his [or her] own actions...for it is essential that the protagonist be aware of feelings, thoughts, and actions. The link between the affective and the cognitive is necessary for the protagonist to integrate the session" (p. 32).

There are four major aspects of the person that the Psychodrama, from the Transpersonal approach, deals with.

❀ Cognitive processes: (e.g., "How are you thinking about yourself vis-à-vis the problem and environment?");

❀ Affective processes: (e.g., "How do you feel about the problem, people concerned and your relationship to them?");

❀ Action processes: (e.g., "How is your behavior blocking problem resolution in the group?");

❀ Spiritual processes: (e.g., "How does your spiritual emptiness distance you from your connections with the cosmos and all living things).

Spontaneity

Moreno (1953) emphasized that "spontaneity is the essential principle of all creative experience." People become anxious and neurotic when their spontaneity is blocked. The principal aim of Psychodrama is to help people bring back into their lives a continuous flow of spontaneity. All participants are encouraged to experiment with their roles and a means for enlivening their character. The reason for this is that "hamming it up" and becoming "playful" with their roles can stimulate the protagonist. By spontaneously acting-out roles, people will motivate the protagonist to be less restrictive and more natural. Moreno (1953) stressed strong relationships among spontaneity, creativity and anxiety, for there is no "distinction between conscious and unconscious... in a psychology of the creative act. The unconscious is a reservoir which is continuously filled and emptied by the individuals" (p. 59). When there is an increase in spontaneity there is a decrease in anxiety. Essentially, anxiety is with the person, because spontaneity has been lost. When creativity has no spontaneity, it has no life or substance. Spontaneity is life's catalyst, the energy that makes everyone in the group come alive and be uniquely creative as human beings.

↑ Warm-up

CREATIVITY

← conscious | unconscious→

spontaneity

_____

anxiety

conscious→ | ← unconscious

UNIMAGINATIVE

Figure 7.1 graphically demonstrates Moreno's principle of moving the group from anxiety to spontaneity with warm-up activities. The anxious person tends to be unimaginative, while the spontaneous person tends to be more creative. Notice that the spontaneous person does not separate the conscious from the unconscious; it is one continuum. When the person stops to separate the conscious from the unconscious by asking questions, anxiety develops. There is no questioning about behavior in the spontaneous person, just action. The director uses all means available to encourage the group to be more expressive. Since many people are fearful of spontaneity, perhaps because it means a loss of control, the director encourages participants to experiment with different roles. The aim is to help group members learn to be as spontaneous as they were as children. What group members discover is that the:

> *psychodramatic process tends to facilitate the expansion of a person's role repertoire so that everyone can learn more precisely in action what it is like to be another person in another role. Being this way in Psychodrama can help resolve a personal problem, but a more general impact can be the enhancement of communication and compassion in the larger society (Yablonsky, l981; p. 25).*

IMMEDIACY

In Psychodrama the addressing of problems in the "here and now" is vital to spontaneity. To be in the "here and now" is to be able to relate to a problem or issue in an immediate manner or "it is you and me, here, now." This is important in actualizing issues, feelings, and thoughts, because as a "process the manner in which the individual responds internally to the content of the Psychodrama is how he acts in life" (Goldman & Morrison, l984; p. 40). The benefits of communicating in an immediate manner are numerous. I have found that in a group immediacy promotes direct communication, helping to resolve immediate tensions, discomforts, or faulty perceptions. It offers a means of dealing with incompatibilities by clarifying issues around trust and creating a climate of honesty and mutuality. When this happens it is less likely that people will act in a dependent manner.

Tele is the process of two-way flow or transference of feelings and energy between two participants in a Psychodrama. Moreno's motto of Psychodrama is also a good description of tele, which is "a meeting of two: eye to eye, face to face, and when you are near I will tear your eyes out and place them instead of mine, and you will tear my eyes out and will place them instead of yours, then I will look at you with your eyes and you will look at me with mine" (p. 280).

In most situations, tele occurs between the director and protagonist, but it can occur between any of the participants in the Psychodrama. It is a crucial ability for the director to be able to have a sense of the protagonist's emotions. For example, if the protagonist is feeling isolated, through tele the director realizes this and whispers to the auxiliary ego to say: "You are all alone." Tele heightens the feelings of the protagonist, by bringing him or her into a more spontaneous mode. Tele is like empathy, but rather than one person's feeling what the other feels, both feel each other. With tele, not only does the protagonist feel it; so does the director. Zerka Moreno describes it as the sense on the part of the protagonist (Goldman & Morrison, 1984) that for:

> *[the director to] be genuinely* with him, *the director is free to move again into a more objective position, hence he can survey the needs of the protagonist and those of other group members. The delicate balance of the subjective-objective relationship is one of the most crucial sine qua non demanded of the director for effective achievement of his [her] task (pp. 90-91).*

According to the Greek philosopher, Aristotle, a catharsis is "defined as an experience of release that occurs when a long-standing inner state mobilizes and finds its outlet in action" (Kellermann, 1984; p. 1). Catharsis occurs when feelings that have been stored and localized in the body, mind and spirit of the person are released. It is a process that includes the emotional, cognitive and behavioral. Every aspect of a person's physiological self (respiratory, cardiovascular, nervous, intestinal) and psychological self (communication, information processing and imagination) is affected in a catharsis. It is used "to induce participants to purge themselves mentally from whatever morbid content was stored inside them" (Kellermann, 1984; p. 2). Ginn (1973) says that catharsis plays a pivotal role, for it "is both the main event as well as the aim of action in the Psychodrama. For Moreno, every element in operation in a Psychodrama works towards achievement of catharsis that affects not only the protagonist, but also the audience, director, doubles, and auxiliary egos" (p.12).

Emotions do not develop and reside within the person as static stages that occur as different experiences happen, but occur more like a "river" that flows. Past, present and future experiences are present simultaneously in the emotions. As a "river," emotions can become a trickle or a raging torrent that continuously threatens to "overflow." When emotions do erupt there is release and relief. Kellermann (1984) states that, when catharsis occurs, it comes like "a sudden tidal wave of illumination, an explosion of energies finding an outlet...and when it comes, there is a sense of inward unfolding of a kind of 'oceanic feeling,' followed by small ripples of release, which are experienced over a long period of time" (p. 5).

While logic is quite straightforward, emotions can neither be induced nor inhibited, but can only be allowed to emerge in their own time and place. This happens because there is a desire for resolution, a need for freedom of expression and a spontaneity that occurs because of the action. In the Psychodrama the catharsis is a desired goal of the drama, for it is the high point or the most dramatic part of the drama. It is a catalyst where conflicts are personalized into action. The catharsis is not limited to the protagonist, but can occur in the Psychodrama in the double, auxiliary ego, audience and the director (Karp, 1968). According to Blatner (1985), there are four separate categories of catharsis: abreaction, integration, inclusion, and significance or spiritual catharsis. The catharsis of abreaction is the emotion that comes with a "... recognition of feeling that has previously been disowned" (p. 160). There is intense feeling in an abreaction, which must be followed by a catharsis of integration. This type of catharsis comes when the protagonist has an awareness of previous experiences and former roles. Here there is an integration of feelings, thoughts and behaviors, which produces a sense of relief and expansion. The third type, catharsis of inclusion, is the recognition that there is a need to love and belong. The sense of belonging, acceptance and the realization that the group can be influenced by a person, are very validating. The fourth category, spiritual catharsis, is the experience of feeling a oneness with God or the cosmos. Blatner (1985) suggests that recognizing these four categories of catharsis reinforces the "multi-dimensional and multi- leveled process. Over emphasis on just one area, such as the cliché practice of "getting in touch with anger" can be misguided. Individualism should be addressed in its fullness, and, indeed, this is part of the educational task of therapy" (p. 164).

FIVE INSTRUMENTS OF THE PSYCHODRAMA

THE STAGE

The stage is the "world" where the action takes place that allows the characters and the audience to interact in a free and flowing manner. They do not have to be props, although they can help create a realistic atmosphere. The notion that a stage does not have to be elaborate to evoke reality is not a new idea in drama. The innovative play by Italian Luigi Pirandello (1943), *Six Characters in Search of an Author*, symbolically used only a few chairs and tables to create reality. He said that the stage is a place where fantasy and reality are joined and it does not depend on what is concrete, for on the stage as in life:

reality doesn't change: it can't change! It can't be other than what it is, because it is already fixed forever...ours is an immutable reality which should make you shudder when you approach us if you are really conscious of the fact that your reality is a mere transitory and fleeting illusion, taking this form today and that tomorrow, according to the conditions, according to your will, your sentiments, which in turn are controlled by an intellect that shows them to you today in one manner and tomorrow...who knows how? (p. 659)

DIRECTOR

The director is the facilitator of the action, whose main task is to loosen up the participants, prepare them for the drama, shape the scenes, and structure the elements of the process. The director is continually helping the protagonist to define his or her purpose and goal for bringing about resolution in the drama. The director uses auxiliary egos, as projections of the protagonist, to act as extensions of the director. Rather than the director creating tension, the auxiliary egos create it. The director may whisper to an auxiliary ego to raise his or her voice at a given time or offer advice. During the drama the director must be sensitive to the feelings of the players and audience. It is vital that the director fosters a state of intensity and excitement by ensuring that everyone is prepared through the warm up. He must also ensure that there are open channels of communication among the participants. The key is good timing, rhythm and the ability to keep the participants in character. When resistance develops the director must be able to use that energy to further expression. In Psychodrama there is a tremendous trust in the ability of the participants to create the right mood and identify with their roles.

THE PROTAGONIST

The protagonist is the star and producer of the drama, identifying the story, characters, time, place and actions in the scenes. A group member becomes the protagonist when he or she wants to spontaneously act out a situation, which is totally subjective to the world of the protagonist. What is right or true is what the protagonist says it is, for he or she embodies norms. To do this the protagonist is encouraged to come face-to-face with the issue, acting it out rather than talking about it.

It may seem that the best way to choose a protagonist is to see who wants to work on something, yet the selection of a protagonist must be chosen on the basis of whether the drama will benefit the group (Kumar & Treadwell, 1986). It is not necessary that someone who is a "star" or active member of the group be the protagonist, for even the most isolated and quiet person can intensely focus the group. I have found that questioning potential protagonists, followed by confirming my selection with the group works best. Not only is it an effective method in getting the person to make a commitment, but it also brings the group into the selection process. For example, I may say to the potential protagonist, "It seems from what you said that you have a lot of deep feelings about this…Would you like to explore it further?" I would follow this with a question to the group, "Does anyone have any objections or comments about the selection of Françoise as the protagonist?" It is possible that there may be some objections from the group, and if there are, they should be dealt with immediately. Most often, objections occur when group members are perceived as monopolizing the group with their issues and problems, or when they are oblivious to what is obvious. Sometimes "problems," like a television rerun, become tiring to the group if they are presented again and again without resolution.

According to Kumar and Treadwell (1986), there are six factors that affect the selection process. Each of these factors is influential in the selection process regardless of whether or not the protagonist volunteers. It should be remembered that not everyone desires, needs to be, or is a good choice as a protagonist. In each of the factors the director should consider the following criteria:

- The **type of people** in the group should include members who have both experience with Psychodrama and dual relationships (e.g., spouses, employer-employee), as well as having undergone a satisfactory degree of group warm-up.

- The **size of the group** determines the possible potential number of protagonists available (i.e., generally the larger the group, the more time spent on selection).

- The **amount of time** available for a typical Psychodrama may be from 2 to 4 hours, but considerations affecting time are the level of awareness of the protagonist, intensity of the emotions, and the complexity of the issue (e.g., murder, rape, suicide).

- The **types of conflict** that are shared by more group members produce greater interest and bring more meaning, yet idiosyncratic issues should not be ignored (e.g., Carl Hollander will not work with situations involving murder or suicide, while Krishna Kumar will wait for a time lapse to work on relationship break-ups).

- The **characteristics of the potential protagonist** are crucial, for the more ambivalent the group members the poorer the choice, while those with a high awareness level are generally a good choice. Everyone, however, should be given the opportunity.

- The **director's preference** is very important, because there must be tele working between the director and protagonist; thus, there needs to be some thought on the part of the director as to preferences.

AUXILIARY EGO

Once the protagonist is determined, he/she will choose auxiliary egos that will play various characters required in the drama. The auxiliary egos are responsible for vitalizing and sharpening the spontaneity of the drama by assuming the projected image of the protagonist. The auxiliary in the role of the significant other becomes a moving force in the Psychodrama. They are extensions of the director, in "the sense that they are social investigators, emotional catalysts, and co-therapists" (Hollander, 1971; p. 1). In the protagonist's drama the auxiliary ego acts as a substitute for missing people who are defined by the protagonist. For example, if a protagonist needs a father, mother, sister, wife, lover, daughter, monster, friend, dog, or the voice of an automobile, the auxiliary ego becomes that character or part. Factors such as age, body size, emotion, politics, race, religion or sex are added or discarded, as they are required. While the protagonist gives the role along with a description of how the role is to act, the participant as auxiliary ego is free to use "gut feelings" to intensify or de-intensify feelings. For example, the auxiliary ego feels that more intensity can be added by playing the role of an authoritative father by standing on a chair to make the son feel really "small." Then as the son tries to explain why he had not made the hockey team, the auxiliary ego begins stamping his or her foot. The protagonist might feel more distracted and become angry. The intensity increases and the protagonist can explore what it is like to feel helpless and how he or she might deal with such a "powerful" figure.

DOUBLE

The double is a person who physically and emotionally identifies with the protagonist. The protagonist may have difficulty expressing some feelings or doing some things, thus it is the double's responsibility to externalize thoughts, feelings and actions. In a sense, he/she assumes the identity of the protagonist and can intensify or de-intensify emotions. He/she is a supporter of the protagonist by being there with him or her when no one else is there. The double can also influence the protagonist not to act impulsively or destructively, and basically, is focusing on three separate and cooperative levels:

❧ Mirroring by imitating body language, responding verbally to non-verbal messages, and clarifying mixed messages.

❧ Providing the **social implications** of actions and behavior.

❧ Providing the psychological counterparts of **interpersonal meanings** of the protagonist's dreams, conflicts, fantasies, self-esteem and values (e.g., being the aggressive part of a mild-mannered person).

The double may mirror the body language, such as voice, posture, movement and gestures of the protagonist. On the stage the double goes where the protagonist goes, speaking to the protagonist when necessary or when directed to do so. The double always speaks in the present tense and first person singular. For example, saying: "I am getting really pissed off with her..." rather than saying: "we are getting really pissed off with her." Early in the drama the double emphasizes emotions. In the latter part, thoughts and concrete data are emphasized. There are a variety of ways in which the double can be utilized. The double can play the protagonist at an earlier age or the "older adult" part of the protagonist. There can be more than one double for the protagonist during the drama. For example, if a protagonist is experiencing conflicting feelings of anger and love, one double can become the angry part, while the other becomes the loving part. In addition, the double can be loving or confrontational for the protagonist, particularly if the double has tele and good rapport with the protagonist.

A double is used when the protagonist: is **in need of help** in expressing thoughts, feelings, and actions; is **unaware** of how he or she is acting; needs heightened **spontaneity** or to be warmed up; needs **support**, understanding and warmth; is unclear and **confused**; and needs assistance in **accelerating or decelerating** the drama in the scene. There are times when the director has to intervene, especially when the actions of the double begin to interfere with the "flow" of the drama. The following scenarios are a few of the reasons why the director will either remove or correct the double:

- The double's actions **interfere** with the protagonist's drama because of his or her needs (e.g., the double has a personal need to be aggressive in a situation that requires sensitivity).
- The protagonist becomes passive and lets the double **do** his or her "work" (e.g., the double is providing all the actions in an angry confrontation).
- The protagonist has **alienated** and lost rapport with the double because of his or her strong feelings or actions (e.g., the double cannot relate to using angry and vulgar words in a situation).
- The protagonist selects a double who is **preoccupied** with a personal issue that interferes with the issue of the protagonist (e.g. the double is experiencing his or her grief at the expense of the protagonist).

AUDIENCE

Although the audience may seem passive, it exerts crucial influence by providing silent support, a pool of potential participants and feedback to the protagonist. According to Yablonsky (1981), the director must take responsibility not only for the needs of the protagonist, but also for those of the group. The Psychodrama must be of interest to the group as a whole; otherwise, the needs of the audience will not be met. Paradoxically, I have found that when this occurs, the protagonist and other "players" react to them. While the drama is not to play to the audience, the audience, as it is in the theater, is a determining factor in whether the drama will be "successful." Essentially, the audience brings a sense of reality to the Psychodrama, which is invaluable because they are observing the preparation for the drama and the "final production." Hence, their insight is valuable. The protagonist learns about his or her behavior through the reactions of the audience, while getting reassurance, encouragement and feedback. A drama that does not involve the audience's interest generally influences the action of the "players" and they can be negatively influenced. Willis (1979) said it best: "people on the stage can 'last' only until they take themselves seriously or their audience takes them seriously" (p. 49).

THE PSYCHODRAMA PROCESS

The Psychodrama, like any play or story, has a beginning, middle and an end. In some psychodramas these stages of development are clear, while in others there seems to be a merging of the parts, in which several climactic episodes occur. The clearest way of understanding the psychodramatic process is through the Hollander Curve (Hollander, 1978). This process looks horizontal, yet there is a circular aspect to it, in which the Psychodrama moves in content from "the periphery to the core and [yet] the session should come full circle; back to the present" (Goldman & Morrison, 1984; p. 39). There are three parts to the Psychodrama as outlined in the Hollander Curve (Figure 7.2). The warm-up (A) that involves the whole group getting in touch with their feelings and the selection of a protagonist. The action (B) in which the various scenes of the drama take place, usually culminating shortly after a catharsis. Finally, the sharing and dialoguing (C), in which the audience, director, and other participants share feelings, thoughts and feedback with everyone involved. Notice that the catharsis is the most climactic part of the Psychodrama.

THE WARM-UP

The warm-up involves preparing the group for the drama that is to take place (see Figure 7.2). The director may use an activity that focuses the participants on some issue, which has some dissonance for someone or may ask for a volunteer who wants to act out the drama. The director helps the protagonist set up the scene to be played, choosing the auxiliary egos that are to be utilized and the place and circumstances to be focused on. Shaffer and Galinsky (1974) provide the following example:

Once the protagonist is on the stage, the director begins to set the scene. Let us take an example of a problem whose central focus is a work difficulty, a conflict between the protagonist and his immediate supervisor. The director should rely as much as possible on the protagonist to give directions on how to play the scene, making certain that the latter provides a description of the situation in which the conflict manifests itself with as much specificity as possible about the setting, how the furniture is arranged, and what other people, if any, are present... The auxiliary ego should be chosen by the protagonist whenever possible, but may be chosen by the director, if he [she] knows the members of the group well enough to decide who might fit the roles as prescribed; or they may be selected in consultation of the two. Once all the participants have been chosen, the plot needs to be outlined in somewhat fuller detail. The roles of auxiliary egos have to be explained by the protagonist or the director (pp. 112-113).

There are a number of methods in warming up the group: encounter and the sociometric process. In the encounter part, called "begegnung" by Moreno, the director uses a number of techniques that provide for encounters with issues that have some emotion or dissonance for someone. The director could simply ask, "Who wants to work on something?" or he can focus on someone in the group who appears to be experiencing some dissonance. Hollander (1978) says that what the director must be sensitive to in others is the:

"me-me" encounter... The individual spontaneously becomes aware of his [her] physiological and psychological readiness. He asks, "What's going on with me?" or "What am I warmed-up to?" the director as a catalyst...asks "Where am I with you?" and "Where are you with you?"...If the director experiences optimal spontaneity at the "me-me" and "me-you" then he [she] is prepared to investigate the sociometry of the group (pp. 2-3).

If there is no spontaneity from the group, the director, in the warm-up phase, can use a variety of activities to create interaction that will focus the group. Like a "film," a psychodrama needs to interest the group (e.g., "what's going to happen"). The type of activity depends upon the type of group and the creativity of the director. I have used guided fantasy and a number of structured activities such as the "magic shop," "life-boat" and "the family portrait." For example, "the family

Figure 7.2: The Hollander Curve

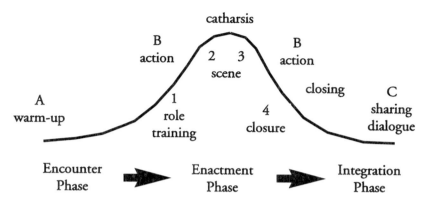

portrait" involves someone in the group recreating a family portrait with members of the group portraying the aunt, mother, son or best friend at a "wedding." However, the characters are given voices and actions that bring the portrait to "life." If there was any underlying tension, the activity brings it into the open. These types of activities are action oriented, tension packed and have a tendency to confront people with unusual dramatic situations (e.g., "living - dying" or a "life change"). As a result, anxiety or tension that is under the surface generally comes to the forefront.

The sociometric process is a way to find out what the group wishes to do and how to focus on a theme. It also helps to uncover a protagonist in the group. This is done by starting a discussion and getting feedback from the group on what their goals, needs and desires are in regard to the Psychodrama. It is similar to the phase warm-up, but does not entail using structured activities. For example, the director could ask the group, "What really 'bugs' you about working in organizations?" From the responses, the director could focus on people for whom there seems to be some dissonance. Until a protagonist is chosen, this type of warm-up closely resembles traditional counseling; "What is the problem and can you tell me about it?" As the person describes a situation, a story begins to emerge, which will be translated into a script that is acted out.

Prior to the action part, the stage is set, chairs become an auto or a bed, the auxiliary egos and double(s) are chosen, and everyone has become reasonably comfortable with their roles (see Figure 7.2). The protagonist positions objects on the stage and makes the choice of auxiliary egos and double(s). Without a proper warm-up the emotional level of the audience will be low and people may be bored or disinterested. The protagonist and auxiliary egos will be chosen and the scenes set up for the action stage of the psychodrama. In the beginning the auxiliary ego can be a stereotype or exaggerated character designed to get everyone into the drama. Finally, the warm-up addresses the circumstance of the Psychodrama before the action begins, "What are they doing in this place?"

As the first scene gets under way, the director is assessing the emotional situation of the protagonist. The scene will last until the director has an understanding of the problem and creates an atmosphere of freedom, trust, and experimentation. The information from this initial scene will determine what happens next. In the action part, there may be from one to ten scenes or only one scene to work through the issue. The director uses soliloquy, role-reversal or dream enactment to develop the drama and move it toward a climax with the goal of helping the protagonist experience a catharsis. As the script proceeds, the protagonist, according to Moreno (1953):

> warms up to the figures and [in this]…private world he attains satisfactions which take him [her] far beyond anything [yet]…experienced; he [she] has invested so much…limited energy in the images of his perceptions…which live a foreign existence within;…delusions and hallucinations of all sorts, that he has lost a great deal of spontaneity, productivity and power …they have taken his riches away and he has become poor, weak and sick…[in the action, there is] reinvestment…by actually living through the role of father, employer, spouse, enemies…and [learning] from them letting go of their power and magic (pp. 447-448).

There may be resistance to working through the issue or repeating some of the scenes, but the director continues to work for that elicited moment in which everything starts to fall into place. Everyone has a need to play – we need to enact life. Once the apex or climax of emotion has been reached, the director works towards closure. No further exploration occurs, only the integration of feelings, thoughts and actions from the presented material. The direction of the scenes depends on the creativity of the director, who chooses the methods that lead to further exploration of the protagonist. Thus, the director needs to "feel" and "see" what the protagonist has difficulty feeling or thinking. During the action the process is sometimes confusing, because everything is constantly in flux. The scene changes, participants are given new lines and new roles may be introduced into the "story." Therefore, it is important that the director not only be flexible, but also aware of the limitations of the script. Once the climax, at the final stage of action, has been reached, some kind of resolution should take place. The psychodrama doesn't necessarily have to have a positive ending, but it should have an ending that provides hope, insight and a means for living life in a more satisfactory way. The director confronts the protagonist who must discover answers and bring about some kind of resolution. The best way to do this is through debriefing the protagonist and the other "actors." Feelings, thoughts and particularly meanings need to be addressed. While the protagonists will review and think about the experience later, they should not be left with intense feelings. Often, letting everyone express how he or she felt during the process rectifies this. The protagonist, however, needs to answer these questions:

❀ What is he or she going to **do** with what has been learned?

❀ Is any **rehearsal** or practice scene required?

❀ Are the corrective and **alternative** ways of behavior clear?

SHARING

The sharing is the final closure for the group as well as for the protagonist…this takes place when the action portion has concluded for the protagonist…who returns to the group…who is now asked to share something of themselves, of their own lives, their own feelings, as they relate to the experience of the protagonist (Goldman & Morrison, 1984; pp. 6-7).

Sharing or feedback is the place where everyone, particularly the protagonist, can get another view of the drama. Even those who played "bit parts" in the "story" may get feedback on something that they did or said that had meaning. In a sense, the sharing is like "drama critics" who provide feedback to the protagonist, not on the performance, but meaning on the actions. The director helps the group share their feedback by paraphrasing or clarifying what is being said. The director draws out meaning, supports those sharing, and encourages responses, "You seem to be moved by something in the script, is there anything you would like to share?" The director does not necessarily have to ask for volunteers, although that is best. He or she may ask for feedback from some members of the group or audience who seemed particularly involved. Sharing is an important part of Psychodrama, because it not only provides the opportunity to give and receive feedback, but it also instills a sense of personal responsibility. Goldman and Morrison (1984) go on to stress that sharing also reinforces the idea that everyone:

is responsible for his/her choices in life…for people avoid talking about the good they do, the values they hold, the aspirations they have. Perhaps one of the principal reasons…is that the good men do is often not unadulterated good. We have goals but we fall short of them…Thus it is very difficult to talk about the "best in me" without also talking about the "worst in me" (p. 69).

Once the group has completed its sharing, the director contributes by entering into a dialogue with the protagonist, a summary of the feedback from the group, the memorable aspects of the Psychodrama, and his or her observations. The purpose of this is to help the protagonist integrate the insights gained from the Psychodrama into a new way of being and living. The director has to be careful that the ending of the Psychodrama is not contrived so it is a happy one, for some situations are painful and difficult. The task of the director is to help the protagonist make sense of the Psychodrama in a supportive and encouraging manner.

PSYCHODRAMA METHODS

Soliloquy, mirroring, role reversal, physicaliation, future-projection and surplus reality are the five primary methods used in Psychodrama (Figure 7.3). These methods can be used at any time during the drama when the director feels that something needs to be highlighted, stressed or explored further. The **key** in using these methods effectively is expressed in Moreno's (1953) dictum: **don't tell what happened, show me!** The director can also use other methods such as non-verbal interactions, art activities, awareness activities, dream enactment, guided imagery or dialoguing with a significant person in the protagonist's life.

SOLILOQUY

Soliloquy is a method in which the protagonist steps out of the role and scene and speaks directly to the audience. It can be useful for expressing hidden feelings or thoughts about a particular person or situation. Yablonsky (1981) says that it is "often parallel to his overt actions. For example, a person overtly expressing love and affection may be feeling love and affection. At other times, however, a person expressing love overtly may be feeling subjective hatred, and this will be expressed in the soliloquy" (p. 121).

I have found the soliloquy useful when the protagonist expresses some feelings or thoughts that have some incongruence or if he or she has a need for immediate feedback. For example, the protagonist may be expressing some anger towards a parent, yet there does not seem to be any anger in his or her voice in a current scene. When the protagonist speaks to the audience, he or she may be freer in expressing thoughts or feelings, than in a face-to-face encounter with the auxiliary ego role-playing the parent. The soliloquy serves to emphasize and bring the anger to the forefront.

MIRRORING

Mirroring is the method of doing everything the protagonist is doing, including using body language (e.g., posture and voice tone), verbal language and action. The purpose of mirroring is to provide the protagonist with an idea of how he or she is coming across. Mirroring can be used with one behavior or a whole scene. For example, all the actions are mirrored, thus providing the protagonist an image of what he or she may be doing. This is a useful method when the protagonist is sending double messages, saying one thing, but doing another, needs a model to practice a new behavior or is unsure of what to do in the scene. It can be done by anyone, including the director, someone from the audience or the double.

ROLE REVERSAL

Role reversal is the **heart** of the Psychodrama process, because it helps the protagonist develop empathy for others and reduces egocentric behavior. A role reversal occurs when the protagonist changes roles with someone else. In a sense, this method is a skill that is taught to the protagonist in everyday life. The art of effective communication is being able to put oneself in the "other person's shoes." For example, in a past group Sheila and Kathy had a disagreement, which seemed very much on the surface. The more they discussed the issue, the more they smiled, and seemed to mask their differing points of view. I asked Sheila to role-play Kathy and take her point of view and Kathy to role-play Sheila. Kathy (in the part of Sheila) began to be overly critical and put down Sheila (in the part of Kathy). In turn, Sheila (in the part of Kathy) began to return anger, and told Kathy (in the Sheila role) to stop being so "pushy." As a result, both Kathy and Sheila were able to be more expressive in their roles and were able to say things that they were unable to say in their original discussion. Both began to have a better understanding of each other's point of view and speak in a more open manner. It seemed that the emotion expressed in the role reversal made it easier for them to express feelings. A role reversal can be used for a number of reasons:

❀ A protagonist plays the role of the relevant other (e.g., daughter becomes the mother)…in order to **understand the other person's position**.

❀ Role reversal may be used to help the protagonist see **himself [herself] as if in a mirror**…the daughter playing the role of the mother will see herself through the mother's perception.

❀ Role reversal is often effective in **augmenting the spontaneity** of the protagonist by shifting him [her] out of defenses…that changes the conflict and produces new insights.

❀ Role reversal is often used simply to help an auxiliary ego to **better understand how a role** is perceived by a protagonist (Yablonsky, 1981; pp. 116-117).

PHYSICALIZATION

Physicalization is a method of heightening the awareness of the protagonist by portraying the interactions in a physical manner. For example, if the protagonist is conversing with a demanding and authoritative father, the director could ask the auxiliary ego to stand on a chair when talking. The protagonist would always have to look up and be in the position of a "small" and weak child. This intensification can make it easier for everyone to visualize and understand the feelings of the protagonist. Another way that Physicalization can be used is by having someone be an object (e.g., a mountain that has to be climbed or books that have to be read). When the protagonist is "torn" by conflicting feelings or thoughts, the director can have the doubles be the conflicting parts, with each part trying to pull the protagonist in different directions. This can result in a catharsis, as the protagonist has to do something about the dilemma.

FUTURE-PROJECTION TECHNIQUE

The future-projection technique is valuable when the protagonist wants to rehearse a newly learned behavior or experiment with a different way of acting in situations in which he or she expects to be in. For example, I have used this technique to help a protagonist try out her assertiveness skills with people who use "put-downs." As a result she was able to have a better sense of how to use her new skills in a variety of ways. The group assisted by playing out possible scenarios that were novel to her and the rest of the group. It turned out that a very assertive approach worked well with one kind of person, such as an insensitive type, but a more open approach worked better with a more sensitive type (e.g., "When you do that, I feel really sad. I just don't want to be around someone like that"). She had not thought of assertiveness as being open with feelings, only as having a strong retort.

SURPLUS REALITY

Surplus Reality helps transcend the boundaries of the "real world" of the protagonist. Anything from dialoguing with the "unborn" to dialoguing with the "dead" can be enacted. In a sense, Psychodrama is based on the idea that truth is not only what happens, but what the protagonist thinks happened. Surplus Reality takes the protagonist to situations that provide insight or to experience what could be. It is used when the protagonist wants to transcend what is real and do something which is impossible. A person can go back to the past or forward into the future and talk to someone. The purpose of the surplus reality is to help the protagonist experience new insights by doing or being something totally different. Surplus reality can be an act fulfillment or re-enactment of a traumatic situation in which the protagonist can take corrective action. An abused person can "face" the abuser and take actions that are more protective. Outcomes to situations can be changed to bring about more satisfactory results.

CONCLUSION

But don't you see that the whole trouble lies here? In words, words. Each one of us has within him a whole world of things, each man of us his own special world. And how can we ever come to an understanding if I put the words I utter the sense and value of things as I see them; while you who listen to me must inevitably translate them according to the conception of things each one of you has within himself. We think we understand each other, but we never really do (Pirandello, 1943; p. 631).

Once again the insight in Pirandello's play, *Six Characters In Search of an Author*, is accurate because what he emphasized was so true – it is impossible to really understand others. Consider, even in one's most empathic manner, do facilitators really understand what it is that people are trying to say in therapy? Words by themselves are inadequate, but with action and drama, one has a better idea of what others might mean when they communicate. The technique of role-playing is one of the most powerful methods for understanding what people are communicating. This is what makes Psychodrama such an exciting and creative method of resolving interpersonal and group problems. Since Psychodrama is a fluid process and accepts the notion of surplus reality combined with a creative process, it allows participants to act or dance their way into realms of the "spirit world." The process, in the spirit of the Transpersonal approach, is open and accepting of anything that can be helpful. Accordingly:

the psychological systems which invent terms like "disorder" for conditions [such as depression]…are essentially repressive. They carry the constant implication that whatever does not conform must be stifled…the goal is the liberation of the spirit. We must always be careful that we do not inadvertently foster those trends, which would reduce people to machines (Brazier, 1995; p. 174).

From a cross-cultural perspective the Psychodrama process parallels the Salish Winter Spirit dance in format, structure and outcomes. Consider that in the Spirit dance, the ritualist declares after the initiation dance that: "now everybody knows him, before nobody knew him" (Jilek, 1992; p. 94). The dancers as protagonists have been reborn, with awareness and knowledge that they did not possess before. From now on, the dancers are more in touch with their "guardian spirit," who provides protection, good luck, success and support. The "spirit guardians" have as one of their powers, the ability to guide people in following the rules of "good" behavior. That is, those who act in an irresponsible manner will be punished, while those acting in a responsible manner will be rewarded. And by being active as dancers, the body stays fit, and helps lift depression. Finally, the dance promotes not only spiritual well being, but also physical well-being.

While it seems like a lot of emphasis is on problem resolution, the Psychodrama theater can also be "a simple direct session in a microcosmic form of a macrocosmic philosophical issue in a society" (Yablonsky, 1981; p. 25). The process of resolution does not have to be dramatic either. Sometimes people need to process what has happened in the psychodrama by thinking it through outside the group. While something may seem obvious to the group, the protagonist may need time to draw meaning. This is the nature of working issues through by creating their own stage, actors, props, direction and expression. This provides people with an opportunity to realize that everything fantasized can be owned and gives them a chance to see conflicts inside.

The variety of issues and methods that can be used in a psychodrama depend on the director, the level of functioning of the protagonist, and the type of group. Yablonsky (1981) emphasizes that "techniques and methods are adapted as the group dictates; they do not dictate to the group" (p. 127). It is possible in psychodrama to create or alter situations, because experimenting is one of the best ways to increase understanding. The strength of psychodrama is the emphasis on re-enacting and re-experiencing traumatic and painful experiences that still burden and stifle spontaneity. By reliving past events, they can be "put to rest" and resolved, then new behaviors can be practiced and rehearsed. Pirandello (1943) felt that for many people this:

self-binding seems much more "human"; but the contrary is true. For people never reason so much and become so introspective as when they suffer; since they are anxious to get at the cause of their sufferings…to learn who has produced them, and whether it is just or unjust that they should have to bear them (p. 659).

ACTIVITIES

1. **Mirroring:** After choosing a partner, stand facing each other (approximately 2 or 3 feet apart). After deciding who goes first, portray a variety of feelings and accompanying actions, which have to be mirrored by the partner. No words or dialogue should be used. For example, a person could portray a series of events like the birth of an imaginary child (e.g., the first 5 minutes of life might consist of peace – pain – surprise – shock – anger – satisfaction, etc.). After 5 minutes, switch places and mirror the actions. Feedback should follow in which the partners share their feelings, thoughts and perceptions of what they were trying to portray and mirror (approximately 15 minutes). A variation of this activity is providing the group with topics to mirror (e.g., getting fired from work, a marriage proposal, death of a friend, winning the lottery, etc.).

2. **Life Boat:** Make a circle on the floor, which represents a lifeboat, adrift in the middle of the ocean. Set the scene by telling the group in the lifeboat that they have only enough food and water for all but one of the group. In order for the group to survive another day, one person

will have to be sacrificed otherwise no one will be saved. The group can come up with any number of solutions to the problem. After the decision, the group is informed that they survived another day, but because of the deteriorating weather they will have to decide once again who will be sacrificed. Other circumstances can be injected into the scenario to produce the same effect (e.g., someone has to be eliminated). This can be continued until half the group is left or until only one person is left. This activity works best with approximately 9 people maximum and 3 people minimum. After the activity, a discussion should follow. The discussion can explore a number of issues: decision making process; leadership; or personal feelings (anger, fear, rejection, distrust, depression, etc.). There is a great deal of tension in an activity like this, so a great deal of sensitivity should be exercised.

CHAPTER EIGHT
GENDER ISSUES:
IMPLICATIONS FOR THE GROUP

But there is nothing so beautiful and beautifully human as to be held, hugged, loved. To feel the warmth and sincerity of another person. To give, in turn, comfort, strength…words can often deceive; but an embrace – the truth is conveyed by something other than sound… Carl Rogers (1973; p. 63)

Love and intimacy are fundamental needs that all humans have; yet the most frequent problems that crop up in group work and psychotherapy are issues having to do with intimacy, love and relationships. Western society is in the midst of a gender revolution that some think is unfolding too slowly, while others are shocked at the radical changes. The women's movement has had a profound structural change on the family, marriage, education, the work place and most of the institutions in society. Many people have become angry, cynical and tired that the changes have not been fast enough, while others feel the same way because they have been too fast. What began as a movement to redress the gender inequities has forced men and women to redefine their roles. Again and again the "gender battle" is an issue that challenges every group either overtly or covertly. When gender issues are brought up, the reaction of many group members is typical to most controversial issues where there are "strong" or "ambivalent" feelings. Facilitators will notice that some men and women angrily deny its relevancy as an issue, while others treat it cavalierly if at all. Predictably, like many contentious issues in the group, it will remain in the "background" like "the Hulk," troubling, until it is addressed. It cannot be explored to everyone's satisfaction in the group, but the group is a fertile place to address gender issues and its close cousin, intimacy, if personal growth and empowerment is to take place.

Not surprisingly, gender issues cannot be separated from sexuality. Sexuality has often been the arena that the sexes have played out their differences and similarities. Some people feel that sex has been used by men to dominate women. Rape, prostitution, spousal battering and pornography are only a few examples in which sexuality has been negatively used. Despite this, sex is one of the most "talked" about topics in society. It is a source of great fascination for people today and throughout the ages. From time to time it has been pilloried as the root of all evil and praised by others as a vehicle for spiritual expression. People are bombarded every day with sexually explicit or implicit advertisements, films, books and magazines. While society has gone through a period of sexual openness, there is a lot of societal conditioning about how men and women should behave. Often, this sets the "tone" for how people interact with each other on other levels. Many people suffer needless guilt, shame, worries and inhibitions about sex. Yet sex can maim and even kill! Venereal diseases like chlamydia and herpes are increasing and now AIDS (Acquired Immune Deficiency Syndrome) is undeniably a factor to consider. And all of the conflicting messages about sex in the media only add to the confusion and the "double bind" facing people. "Do it! but practice safe sex!" "Is there only safety in abstinence?" Yet sexuality is the core of humanness – a way many people express their deepest emotions. Maybe it should not be a surprise to people that they will have to continuously define and redefine sexuality as they grow. During different stages of growth, there are differing rules of conduct and behavior. While some of the initial questions that plague people as they were growing up have been resolved, new ones have emerged to challenge them. Whatever people's beliefs and values are regarding sexuality, the capacity to express oneself sexually adds a tremendous depth and complexity to being human.

Sexuality: Gender "Flashpoint"

According to Eastern tradition, sex is one of the highest of the five centers of energy (Ramaswami, 1989). There are only two others above sex: emotions and thinking. Despite the high place in life that Kundalini Yoga has for sexuality in Eastern philosophy, for many it is a source of shame. Sigmund Freud felt that the problems people encountered emanate from unconscious repressed sexual desires. Interestingly, most of the recent "media scandals" have something to do with sex (e.g., President Bill Clinton, the "Hollywood Madam," Michael Jackson, to mention just a few). While people will laugh at the foibles of those in the limelight, I suspect many people would fare no better if their private life were held up to scrutiny. Perhaps sexual issues should be kept in the "closet"? However, it is my belief that the group experience offers an arena to begin a dialogue that can reduce the gender gap. If people can become more fully integrated, they can learn to live in harmony with their polarities and have a larger repertoire of feelings. What will follow when the inner guide is accepted will be a fuller and more vital existence.

Accepting the sexual part, or any part, of self is believing in its essential good. Because sexuality is primarily related to relationships, it also means trusting that people will be able to successfully fulfill their needs, relate more effectively with others and establish a code of morality that is personally satisfying. Research and surveys indicate that sexuality is considered to be one of the most important aspects of life. What many group members have shared was their curiosity and excitement about sex as they were growing up, yet they also felt the confusion and shame about their sexual feelings. Many say it was the fear of rejection, but basically it was the ambivalence of acknowledging and expressing their sexuality. Perhaps shame is the indication of guilt, of failure, or the exposure of lost potential of the self to oneself. Shame is not moral guilt, but existential guilt. If it had a voice it would not be, "Lord I have sinned," but "I never thought I would do this."

Perhaps by overcoming shame in everyday living it is possible to live a freer and more open existence. If people can confront shame with regard to their sexuality and gender identity, they can better understand how they interact with others. Once people feel free to express an intimate part of themselves, they no longer fear losing control nor do they need external sources of control to regulate behavior. According to Corey, (1985) as members of groups, people need to be encouraged to "speak about and explore sexual feelings as openly as [they] express and explore

[all] other feelings. Sensuality, touching, and physical displays of affection, which often occur in groups, are an important part of the group dynamics" (p. 30).

THE RELATIONSHIP BETWEEN LOVE AND SEXUALITY

On many occasions, the Buddha taught that joy and happiness are nourishing to us, while indulging in sense pleasures can cause of suffering...the practice of the Dharma does not exclude the enjoyment of the fresh air, the setting sun, a glass of cool water, and so on...(Brazier, l995; p. 171).

Dharma, or the way of living (truth), does not exclude being human, only in living self-indulgently. The message is that to be truly human, one must feel, sense and be at peace with the body that one has. However, part of the dilemma is that one's urges sometimes block the development of one's spiritual part. One of the many provocative yet insightful attitudes that are reflected in Shere Hite's (1987) *Women and Love* is the overwhelming dissatisfaction many women have with men and marriage. As I ponder the discontent I hear from many group members about the opposite sex, I am reminded of Denis Arcand's 1987 film, *Le dèclin de l'empire Amèricain*, which illustrates the disappointment, differing values, problems and issues that surround sexuality and gender identity. The story centers on a group of university people who, while preparing for a dinner, share their sexual experiences and philosophies. The personalities of these characters are very different, but as the film progresses, their sexuality can be seen as an extension of their self-image. All of them have secrets that are revealed as the evening unfolds, but there is a lot of hypocrisy in what the dinner guests do and say. When Louise expands on her idea of women's needs, Dominique angrily discloses that she has had sex with Louise's husband, Remy, along with his friend Pierre. Louise is devastated, for her notion of love and sexual excitement is pleasing her husband. Remy, on the other hand, shares that he has continuous affairs as a method of adding variety to his life and keeping excitement in his marriage. "For me," he says, "because I have had sex with others does not mean I love my wife less, actually I love and desire her more as a result."

Dominique, who had devoted herself to her career, displays a lot of cynicism about people's sexual behavior: "When you live alone, you stop thinking about sex." She says, "words are cheap, don't listen to me, but touch me." Meanwhile, Diane views sex as a way of expressing her power over all men. The problem for her is that she enjoys sadomasochistic sex and as her lover debases her in more frequent and bizarre acts, the more she feels she has power over him. Marcel, who is homosexual, views sex as a way of adding excitement and danger. He says "I feel alive when I'm cruising. It's dangerous, but I can't help it. When it hits I need someone, anyone, and I never know how the day will end." While these characters represent stereotypical views, perhaps there is a little of Louise, Dominique, Remy, Pierre, Diane and Marcel in all people. Positive or negative, perhaps these film characters are not very different from most people's experience. Whatever people say and feel about their sexuality, their sexual behavior is really an expression of the self, their relationships and the way they view the world. Thus according to Krantzler (1979), there is:

> *more confusion, unrealistic expectations, misunderstandings, vulnerability, disillusionment, and fear expressed by men and women…when they discuss how sex fits into their lives than when they discuss any other subject…the sexual dilemma…[nor does it have anything] to do with intelligence or intellect…the most highly intellectual people often evidence the greatest blind spots (p. 178).*

While there is a lot of talk about sexuality, there seems to be more talking about sex than a genuine openness about it. Perhaps there is a fear that to explore it is to "open a Pandora's Box." Or on the other hand, so many people seem to have a low level of awareness about sexual practices. According to Hite (1987), more than two-thirds of all marriages experience severe problems when dealing with sexual differences. Many women are simply "turned off" to sex because it is such an explosive issue. For many men in society sex is often equated with love and to be sexually attracted is to be in love. This view, voiced in Arcand's film by the character Pierre, typifies a common attitude. When asked what love is, he replies: "when I get hard, I'm in love, but if I don't, I'm not." As the sexual revolution enters its fourth decade, the emphasis on sexual arousal might equally apply to women. The beauty of the group experience is that men and women, homosexuals and heterosexuals, can have an open discussion about their attitudes. When group members can share, and in a sense educate others on those attitudes that have contributed to these issues, misunderstandings, sexist conditioning and homophobia can be better understood.

However, the group experience can also raise more issues than it can resolve, because the relationship of love and sex is a complicated one. For Pierre, love is physical, but for others, like the sixth century Christian Saint Augustine, love is spiritual: "Sometimes I am so crazy with love that I do not know what I am saying, it is bewildering and I am intoxicated with love" (Mohler, 1975; p. 2). St. Augustine was referring to his love of God, yet the passion and excitement is almost physical. There are many types of love, and sexual intimacy is just one way of expressing it. While some may argue that passion is a manifestation of sexual expression regardless of direction, I am not so sure. It is simplistic to view everything in relation to sex; however, the suppression or sublimation of the sexual part of self is unnatural. Thus, people will have to make a judgment about how they are going to express their sexuality. Kelly (1980) states that:

> *healthy behavior is defined in terms of the quality of contact, which includes, naturally, the context within which it occurs. It does not depend on the form which the behavior takes… for the achievement of a strong gestalt is itself the cure, for the figure of contact is not a sign of, but is itself the creative integration of experience (p. 220).*

SEXUALITY AND NEEDS

The assumption in the transpersonal approach is that satisfaction of needs is a primary motivating source in all of us. To understand sexuality people must examine why they are motivated to involve themselves with others. Sexual expression is a need for most people that results either in pleasant or unpleasant feelings. People's desire to avoid unpleasantness, discomfort and tension is an expression of people's need to take action. Once their awareness of that need is fulfilled, they climb to the next need and/or wish. In other words, as people experience their needs, it:

> rises – comes to a foreground – and recedes progressively as [it] receives attention...once ful-filled; [it], in turn, recedes from prominence when fulfilled. In perceptual terms...[you] will, in effect, acquire blinders...and not see the other aspects of the environment that do not relate to the dominant need of the moment...[for your] behavior will be directed towards the dom-inant need (Van de Riet, Korb & Gorrell, 1980; p. 7).

Need satisfaction, according to Maslow (1971), is an ascendant progression which if stopped results in the surfacing of lower needs. For example, once people satisfy their basic biological need for sexual fulfillment, they seek a sense of safety with self and others in their sexual needs. However, if safety is blocked, they may return to an order of need by forsaking all but the bio-logical aspects of sex. On the other hand, if that need for safety is satisfied, they strive for belong-ingness as that need manifests itself. To explain the interrelationship of needs, Maslow developed a hierarchy of needs (Figure 8.1). As people move from level to level, they grow in maturity. Basic needs are on the first level, which involves physiological and survival goals. These needs have to do with eating, drinking, clothing, shelter and all the other aspects that sustain life. In Western society these include physical comforts, a pleasant working environment, a higher income, and all external conditions that are considered basic for living. This basic need is expressed sexually through fulfillment of cultural demands of sexual identification and procreation such as the pres-sure people receive to have children.

The safety level includes the need for security, orderliness, protective rules and general risk avoidance. This level involves having a home and relationships that are safe and secure. Perhaps interpersonally the safety need results in what the philosopher Lucretius called "love, which comes from habit." Other needs include a decent job, salary, insurance and any other aspect of life that helps people feel safe. Safety needs have often been cited by women in past years as a reason for getting married. In most cases love, sexual intimacy and personal happiness were sec-ondary in the past, because marriage offered security and an acceptable position in society. In a sexual realm, involvement in a relationship often alleviates loneliness and brings a feeling of secu-rity. Albert Camus' (1957) novel, *L'exil et le royaume*, depicts this need in the character Janine who wonders "is there another love other than that of darkness...she didn't know, but she did know that Marcel needed her and that she needed that need, that she lived on it night and day, at night especially – every night, when he didn't want to be alone..."(p. 28).

After basic and safety needs are met, the need for belongingness moves to the forefront. People are less concerned with self and more interested in others. This need is the level that forms the basis for interpersonal relationships. This includes belonging to a family and having friend-ships or important group memberships. If people are successful in fulfilling this need, they will have feelings of being accepted and appreciated by others. What people are doing is making an

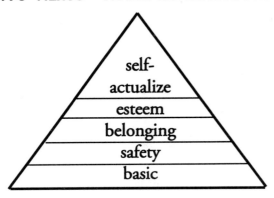

Figure 8.1: Hierarchy of Needs

identification with another person or group. They reach out, give, accept and want to be with other people in an intimate way. Erica Jong (1977) voiced this idea in her novel, *How to save your own life.* "Living with someone you really share things with is not only wonderful, it's actually better than all the love songs, all the silly movies say it is. It really is worth fighting for, being brave for, risking everything for" (p. 265).

Once people feel successful in fulfilling their need for developing relations within groups, they develop ego needs. Ego needs relate to the desire to feel good about the self (self-esteem). People have needs to achieve satisfaction, feel competent about their work, feel positive about themselves and what they have accomplished. They are motivated to succeed and excel. However, there may be tension at this level because they are ambitious and seek social and professional rewards. They will spend a great deal of energy working to succeed. Sexually, they may manifest a desire to achieve orgasms and feel successful as men and women. At the apex of the hierarchy is the self-actualization level. Here people want to grow personally and to be better people. It does not matter what others say, only how people feel about themselves. There is a high awareness level. People feel creative, inner directed and responsible. Self-actualizing behaviors are risk taking, seeking autonomy and developing a personal sense of freedom to act in their best interest. Perhaps it is thinking of pleasure not for pleasure's sake or music for music's sake, but as a vehicle for personal growth or even spiritual ascendance. Sex for the self-actualized person is neither a necessity, habit nor duty, but a choice. Once people become self-actualized, sexual expression involves more than a physical need or emotional support. Thus, they may reflect: a desire to **experience** vividly, with full concentration and without self-consciousness; a willingness to make **choices** that are a progression, rather than making choices that move them to a lower level of need; **listening** to integral messages or tapes that encourage them to do what they want, rather than messages of what they should do; acting with **honesty**, when they are in doubt; and taking **responsibility** and making growthful choices, rather than choices out of fear. Perhaps fulfilling self is synonymous with accepting sexuality as an integral part of who people are. Maslow (1971) says that the ultimate goal for both men and women:

> is to…*become a human being, as fully human as…can possibly be…with a shift away from devaluation of…sex…towards an accepting and loving attitude…a desexualizing of the status of strength and weakness, and of leadership so that either men or women can be, without anxiety and without degradation, either weak or strong, as the situation demands* (p. 353).

MEN, WOMEN AND GENDER ROLE DEVELOPMENT

Despite all the challenges men and women have faced, gender role stereotypes have changed very little. Gender role stereotyping reflects a simplified view of men and women in the world. Unfortunately, women are stereotyped as being less competent, which leads to lower expectations by themselves and others. This could be the result of the different perception of how women are evaluated. The bases of achievement for men are based on competition, while for women achievement is based on excellence. According to Maccoby (1988), the studies that supported the view that men and women are different have changed since the 1970s. For example, it was concluded in earlier studies of children that boys were superior in math, less active and less verbal, while girls were more active and more verbal. However, evidence now suggests that there are innate gender differences, particularly over time. Essentially, boys and girls are becoming more and more similar. An exception is the "well-documented gender gap at the upper levels of performance on high school mathematics, which has remained constant over three decades" (Santrock & Yussen, 2000; p. 421).

Stereotypes die hard. It is true that men are washing dishes, taking care of children and doing other domestic chores around the house, but women are still doing most of the housework whether or not they work outside the home. According to the Population Crisis Committee (1988), which did an in-depth study of the status of women, there is nowhere in society that women enjoy equal status with men. For example, financially, the ratio between men and women's salaries for similar work is 70 to 100. In other words, women earn only 70 cents to every dollar men earn. Based on this dismal report, it is easy to conclude that the image that men and women have of themselves has changed very little. Perhaps it is "popular culture" that perpetuates traditional stereotypes. For example, a study on how men and women from four cultural perspectives (American, Japanese, Navajo and Mexican) view themselves and the opposite sex are surprisingly similar. Both men and women view men as being "large, angular, and dark," while both men and women in all the groups saw women as being "small, round and light" (Kagan, 1969; p. 40). If men exhibit so-called feminine traits (passivity) and women exhibit so-called masculine traits (aggressiveness), they may be ostracized. The changes taking place in society will undoubtedly reduce people's perceptions of what men and women **should be**. Until that occurs, men and women will continue to be regarded as being differently psychologically and socially.

Men: In Western society men are conditioned to be unemotional, cool, detached, rational, objective and strong. Certainly they will cry and be sensitive, but are they willing to give up their power? All reports indicate that there is only lip service paid to this. The sad part of all this is that men have attempted to live up to this limited sexual stereotype and in the process have lost a very vital part of themselves, for instance their feminine part. A case in point in the theme of Robert Bly's (1991) *Iron John: A Book about Men*, is that men do not know what it is to be a man. This is due mainly to the disappearance of "traditional" role models and the criticism men have received from the women's movement for being patriarchal. Bly is not criticizing women's drive for equality, but bemoaning the lack of congruence many men feel. In short, many men are asking what it is a man is supposed to be.

Using the Jacob and Wilhelm Grimm's fairy tale, "Iron John," Bly analyzes the lost wisdom from the past to shed light on what men have lost since the Industrial Revolution. "Iron John" is a very revealing fairy tale. It is about a hairy wild man named Iron John, who is freed by a boy who is the son of the king. Iron John takes the young boy into the forest and teaches him about responsible behavior. When the boy is grown, he returns to his place and becomes king. However, as the new king, he integrates his polarities: civilized part and wild part. According to Bly, modern men have been psychologically wounded in childhood and bury, deny or sublimate their pain. Men need to bond with other men, particularly older men, and to become more vulnerable and sensitive without losing their "wild" nature. Through integrating these divergent parts, men can restore their energy and be "builders" and "creators" rather than "destroyers" and "cogs in a wheel."

One of the blockbuster films of the summer of 1991 was *Terminator 2: Judgment Day*. The hero is a robot, a computerized man, who symbolizes the "strong" male role of the "technological age." The characteristics of the robot, powerful, unfeeling and consistent, seem to reflect what many men wish to project to the world. I have observed that, in general, men have difficulty reaching out to others; attempt to be active, aggressive and striving; attempt to hide their fears and weakness; tend to see others, particularly other men, as competitors; suppress vulnerability, warmth and tenderness; view their bodies as a machine; are afraid of closeness with other men; work at winning and being successful; and extinguish traits such as nurturance and sensitivity that are identified with women. As a result of these rigid behaviors, men have had to pay a high price. Men seem to have lost what it takes to love or be loved. They have to be continually vigilant lest someone, male or female, discover who they really are. As a result, there is a chronic burden of stress and an incredible expenditure of energy. This can be easily seen in the life span of men and women in North America, 72 years for men and 79 years for women. Men do more poorly in school, are involved in more crime and have a higher suicide rate than women. Many women complain that men are emotionally constricted, sexually aggressive, unfaithful, neglectful, abusive and condescending emotionally (Buss, 1989). However, there has been a change in men's attitudes, while still being drawn to the "masculine mystique," they are trying to be more sensitive and egalitarian.

Women: The feminist movement has been waging a successful challenge to the stereotypical image of women of being "nothing but the weaker vessel" (I Peter. III, verse 7). It is true women have asserted themselves and have come closer to equality than at any time in history, yet they are still in revolt and angry at being treated in an unequal manner. While work quotas have been frowned on, government, industry, academia and business have striven to hire and promote more women to upper echelon positions. Many of the negative characteristics associated with woman, such as fragile, helpless, unambitious, unintelligent, unadventurous, unassertive, non-competitive and weak, are disappearing. However, many women are trying to "hang on" to the "positive" characteristics of being empathic, gentle, nurturing, sensitive and warm (Deaux, 1976; Buss, 1989).

According to some, even women themselves have been insensitive to each other in the quest for equality. Consider what the 19th century German writer Anne Louise de Stael said: "I am glad I am not a man, for I should have to marry a woman." It is possible to respond to this misogynist statement by saying – "Yes, but she was a 19th century woman." Yet in today's society there are still many groups who are talking about the home and the need for women to become more "traditional." In the United States one group called **Real Women** has lobbied strongly against equal rights for women. Although in the 17th century, Abraham Crowley said, women are only one of nature's agreeable blunders, it still reflects many people's attitude today. This simply demonstrates that women were not taken seriously. It implies that a woman's role is to stay home, raise children and be a "homemaker." Despite changes in attitudes, it is not easy to escape the "housewife syndrome" as described by Betty Friedan (1983) in her book the *Feminine Mystique*. What makes it even more difficult for women to find fulfillment compared to men, is that women's lives tend to be tied to the "biological clock." Some women see themselves as having 30 years to get educated, develop a relationship and have children. Once the children are grown then they have the opportunity to go back to the work force. The stress in negotiating these "phases" is not easily understood by many men, whose lives proceed in a very different way. For many women, their most productive work years often come after the reproduction cycle ends, while men, whose work lives have become more solidified, are beginning to think about retiring.

Through the home, religion, education and the media, society shapes the roles of men and women. However, no matter how powerful these influences are, they do not have to be static. Many women have not accepted the traditional view of themselves and have revolted against stereotypes. How about in the realm of sex? Men say that they are bothered most by women who are unfaithful, abusive, self-centered, condescending, moody and sexually withholding (Buss, 1989). Exploring emotions is how women generally deal with intense feelings. Women have more prerequisites than men do about sex. They simply do not want to acquiesce sexually, but want emotional closeness, warmth, conversation and a sense of worth with their sex. Sexual intimacy follows emotional intimacy for women, while it seems to be reversed for men.

Despite the lack of progress on some levels, there have been substantial gains. Women only have to look at their mothers and grandmothers to see how much they have gained. Women are moving away from the view that satisfaction can only be found only in marriage and the home. Does this mean that the earth mother is dead? Women have changed and have become more assertive, stronger and more independent. That does not mean they have to be uncaring or not nurturing. Some may say that women have become more like men, thus losing those positive qualities. I suppose this is a trade-off, but on the other hand women are freeing themselves to say "no," rather than saying "yes" when they want to say "no." They are discovering that it is possible without feeling bad to be achieving, strong, assertive, sensitive and nurturing. Most people in groups, men and women, express the hope that the nurturing quality that women possess is not lost, but becomes a model for men.

Androgyny: What is androgyny? Androgynous people have traits that are masculine or active, assertive, and self confident (yang) and feminine or supportive, helpful, and empathic (yin). Perhaps surprisingly, researchers have found that androgynous people have higher self esteem, date more, receive more recognition in society, are more adaptive, "less likely to become mentally ill and better able to handle marital problems than those who conform rigidly to the stereotypes" (Nicholson, 1984; p. 71). These types of findings have prompted more and more schools to institute courses that teach androgyny. This is a controversial step that has produced "mixed results" and created ethical problems. For example, one study found that the course created a more "liberal" attitude about gender, while another study found a "boomerang effect" that produced more rigid gender attitudes (Sandrock & Yussen, 2000). Those who advocate androgyny courses feel that traditional gender stereotyping is harmful, while those who oppose androgyny courses feel that gender roles should develop in accordance with socially and culturally approved modes.

In the final analysis, the liberation of women will also be liberating for men. Both men and women want the same things – the **freedom** to fulfill themselves. There are few reasons to suggest that the nature of men and women is different to justify stereotypical generalizations. Men and women need to be open to each other and to themselves. To be intimate emotionally and physically means sharing and accepting. Yet many men and women have wondered how to do this. Should men and women let go of what makes them men and women? Maybe it is not letting go, but adding to what they already are. Perhaps the goal for everyone is to become more androgynous. What is it about men and women that is so attractive and desirable? Are they qualities that men and women have not achieved, but hope to gain someday? Laurent Van der Post (1963) expressed this idea eloquently in his novel *The Seed and the Sower*, which applies equally to men and women:

> *It was for me a sign of how greatly [men] women long, in their deepest being, to help men [women] to bring up into the light of day what is uncertain, fearful and secret within them. So deep is this instinct that they tend to be less afraid of the unpleasant facts of human nature than are, and to mistrust profoundly only that which shuns the light of truth within us. No matter how unpleasant our secret or how awful the consequences of self-revelation may be for us, all that is best in women [men] feels triumphant because of the act of trust that makes the emergence of a secret possible (p. 171-172).*

The concept of yin and yang, that within the world and within all people there is a coexistence of both male and female characteristics, is very appealing. Jung (1964) called these aspects animus/anima, or the male and female parts of everyone's personality. Perls (1969b) was fond of the notion that "each one of us has male and female substances and that the pure male man and the pure female women are rare...in those with neuroses...there is conflict...[but] in the genius I see the opposites integrated...and...balanced" (p. 180). It is only by being aware of opposites that people can gain more sensitivity, but just because there are polarities does not mean that the male and female parts should be in conflict. While people may not be consciously aware of it, the polarities are balanced and the challenge is that any "part of the self has a counterpart that is available for knowing and understanding. Thus…behind every good little girl is a bad little girl ready to break free, and for every negative emotion there also is a positive counterpart" (Van de Riet, Korb and Gorrell, 1980; p. 14).

Can the androgynous person be attractive? There is no question about that, for attractiveness includes not only physical but personality variables. Those who are likable are often thought to be attractive. Attractive people are perceived to be kind, sensitive, exciting, strong and sociable. According to Burgoon and Saine (1978) people are attracted to those who praise them and do favors for them. The challenge is to be encouraging and help others, but not as a trade off for being liked. It is the total person, not the body, personality, mind or the spirit, but the whole person integrated into a complimentary mix of feminine and masculine parts. Perhaps attractiveness is a state of mind. As more role options for men and women increase, the greater the challenge and possibility of there being a "backlash." After all, the traditional role of both men and women has been restrictive, yet safe. It is easier to allow the old roles to become a part of people's lifestyle, but to risk trying new ones is a "leap into the unknown." "There is no upper hand in love though one is under, one above: the man who said so lied – it is a choice for human mates lacking in other vertebrates that you or I should ride" (Comfort, 1962; p. 84).

When Comfort wrote this, he was stressing the sense that no one should have power because of their sex. Despite this, however, many women are still conditioned not to be successful, for there is a real fear that success will somehow make them less attractive. Many men want women to be subservient to them, citing traditional values as a rationale. Does this mean that men want women to act inferior so they can feel superior? Is that some men only want an object (woman) to "play power games with?" That is a distressing thought. I like the attitude of Goldberg (1976) who says that men who need to free themselves must do it, however, not on the backs of women, but as a "free male…constantly reaffirming [the] right and need to develop and to grow, to be total and fluid, and to have no less than a state of total well-being" (p. 191). Is sexuality an acquisitive desire on the part of men and women to move upward to a higher order or way of being? Maybe it is, yet somehow it is possible that once people become one with themselves, they may be able to achieve perfection. On the other hand, is it an egocentric drive? Or is love simply self-assertion for the benefit of possession? Is it true that the upward tendency for sexual expression is a myth concocted by physical urges and does not lead to integration and self-actualization? Yet is sexual desire a "mask" or somehow an expression of some hidden or ulterior motive? Questions seem to beget more questions. However, group members can learn to be clearer with themselves and others about what they want. It is only as sex and gender boundaries are explored that the negative effects of sexism and the power of differentiation can be eliminated.

THE SEXUAL CONFLICT BETWEEN MEN AND WOMEN

There does not have to be a conflict between men and women, yet there is. Why is this? On one hand this is a moot question, because to have relationships is to have conflicts. According to Kopp (1972), conflicts for many people in relationships are created because of differing sexual needs and desires. This happens because of the following characteristics of sexual behavior:

❀ Dependable ("It is an instinctual drive that no matter what happens, I know it is there");

❀ Expendable ("While I may desire sexual activity, it is not necessary for me, for I will not starve if I do not have it");

❀ Interpersonal ("Sex involves another person, even when it is consummated only through imagery");

❀ Vulnerable ("I find it difficult if not impossible to fake sexual excitement, particularly when I am angry").

A major source of conflict revolves around the shame many people feel about their bodies. One way of viewing the body is as "armor," where emotional responses reside. In other words, the body contains memories of past decisions and choices. Unexpressed or distorted emotions (shame) are reflected in how people restrict their bodies. This may take the form of carrying the body in such a way as to conceal a sensual aspect (women concealing large breasts and men concealing erections). In addition, some people have the sense that somehow things connected with sensuality or the body are sinful, for example, the pain around menstruation is a punishment or that masturbation is sinful. Interestingly enough, one of the major sexual dysfunctions that seems to be occurring more frequently is Inhibited Sexual Desire. When people experience this they simply have no desire for sex. This problem affects roughly 15% of males and 35% of females at least sometime in life (Hite, 1987). The poet Ralph Waldo Emerson said that if people want sexual intimacy, then they must be sexually intimate, because it has to come together. But what happens when people cannot express their love and desire?

Most people have probably had the experience of wanting to greatly impress someone they were attracted to, only to make the opposite impression because they tried so hard. Rather than acting natural and spontaneous, they put on a performance that blocks sensual pleasure. In extreme cases, this may result in impotence or frigidity. Goldberg (1976) says that people's genitals are "not a piece of plumbing that function capriciously, but an expression of total self – it is a sensitive and revealing barometer of...sexual feelings" (p. 39). The media has played an influential role in determining how men and women interact. According to Stroller (1979), the use of sex has increased in literature and the media. For example, in television and films, the amount of time for men and women to know each other before engaging in sexual activity has decreased. Almost all characters portrayed in films and books are able and willing to have sex. While violence has decreased, it has been replaced with sex. Advertisements are full of sexual suggestions, innuendoes and flirtations. And the worst part is that, in advertising, women are the stimulus of choice for 65% of the ads. This not only emphasizes women as objects, but it reinforces negative stereotypes.

If men and women are not to suffer from sexual dysfunction, they have to be more open in communicating their wishes and desires. What is surprising is that people do not share their sexual likes and dislikes, but feel that others should intuitively understand. It is clear that the body does not lie; thus, paying attention to the body is only a first step. When people do not want sex they should not force themselves to have it, otherwise they are inviting impotence, frigidity and abuse. If people care about themselves and want to please themselves they have to feel that it is their right to express what they want or don't want. People need to ask for what they want, very clearly and very specifically, and equally as explicitly communicate what they don't want or don't like.

IMAGERY AND SEXUAL BEHAVIOR

Imagining and fantasizing takes up a major part of most people's time and energy. And a frequent subject for imagery and fantasies are sexual topics, which are timeless and Transcultural. When people remember certain experiences, it is similar to reliving them, and the more clarity in the images and fantasies, the greater the arousal. In effect, fantasies act as a source of arousal. According to Przybyla, Byrn and Kelley (1983): "creativity is all that is required to give birth to a fantasy and to nourish it over time. Depending on the fantasist's predilections, it is possible to bring about an instantaneous change of mood, partners, or activity" (p. 438). There does not seem to be much difference between men and women, for both sexes fantasize about sex, although research has found that men think about it more than females. In addition, men use more concrete visual images, which include a lot of anatomical detail, while women emphasize emotion, plot and dialogue. Not surprisingly, men's masturbation fantasies, compared to those of women, are more likely to include sex with a stranger and group sex. Surprisingly, women are more "likely to fantasize acts which they would never actually engage in" (Przybyla, Byrn & Kelley, 1983; pp. 438-439). For both men and women sexual fantasies are very egocentric, but the difference is one of explicit sex for men versus relationships for women. Fantasies for men and women basically serve a function of maintaining a sense of balance and preserve the balance of power in life. Stroller (1979) says that sexual fantasies serve as a method of playing out that which is forbidden or unknown, but paradoxically, the excitement is "between knowing and not knowing, seeing and not seeing, safety and danger...the knowledge that the story is contrived, the daydream manufactured, the pornography a myth, the prostitute a paid actress, the spouse or lover a player in one's theater" (p.18).

GENDER DIFFERENCES IN COMMUNICATION

There is a difference in the way men and women communicate nonverbally, but the differences are subtle. Women seem to be much better at judging and expressing emotions, perhaps because they are more transpersonal (e.g., they smile more, show happiness, fear, love, and anger more readily). Compared to men, women smile and gaze more, have more expressive faces, stand closer, touch more often, have more expansive body language, are less restless, more relaxed, show fewer errors in speech and use fewer pauses in speech (Hall, 1987). When women communicate they are more likely to look at others more often as compared to men who interrupt more often. In other words, women will sit and listen, while men are more likely to talk, and direct the conversation. Not surprisingly, women more than men allow their voices to go up more at the end of a sentence, which may reflect more tentativeness. The communication differences in male and female children are much less than in male and female adults.

The comparison of non-verbal behavior of men and women demonstrates once again the comparative power each sex utilizes. The power that men take is reflected in the larger amount of space they use and control, as compared to women. Women sit and stand closer to other women, while men sit and stand further away from other men. When sitting, women are more likely to sit side-by-side, while men generally sit face-to-face or separated from each other. Women touch and are touched more often, however the latter is more in response to rather than initiating touch. When women are touched, they tend to cuddle, and express a desire to be closer. Other differences between men and women are the manner in which they use their bodies to emphasize their sexuality. Men often protrude their pelvis and adopt poses that accentuate muscles. Men will wear tight fitting clothes and unbutton an extra shirt button to expose more of their chest. It is not surprising that in the 90s the most popular and attractive male actor was former body builder Arnold Schwarzenegger. The most popular female figure is pop diva, Madonna. Her sexually explicit music, films and behavior have shocked many, yet she remains an icon and a model for millions of women worldwide. The image in films and music videos show more and more women rolling their hips when they walk, accentuating their breasts, exposing their thighs when sitting, stroking their thighs, and touching in suggestive ways. There are, of course, many other popular entertainers who do not engage in suggestive behavior who are also role models for men and women.

SEDUCTION: "SPICE OR POISON"

North American society's paradoxical attitude on sexual issues is sometimes permissive (availability of sexually explicit materials) and sometimes prudish (prohibiting the advertisement of condoms on television). Faced with sexually active adolescents that hover around 90% of the population in some metropolitan areas, schools have tried to establish more explicit sex education programs, but many parents and religious leaders have protested. Educators back off, wring their hands, and try to cope with more and more teenage pregnancies and cases of sexually transmitted diseases. Sex shapes society and society reacts to it. Sex is not only the most often used sales technique in product promotion, but is a common form of entertainment and artistic expression. Seduction is accepted and promoted in all forms in the media and in everyday life. It is called flirtation by some who think of it as harmless, yet is it? Does seduction warp relationships and detract from sensuality? Perhaps it does. Seduction is not just sexual, but any behavior, whether it is conscious or unconscious, that is designed to manipulate or mislead to gain something the seductive person desires. Seduction can occur in a variety of situations and for a variety of reasons. For example, seduction occurs when someone takes advantage of another's need for closeness and warmth to gain sexual favors. In its worst forms, it becomes sexual harassment or even sexual assault. These types of cases are being reported so frequently that it is estimated that one out of five people have suffered from it. Even parents are not immune to it:

> *Seductive parents are unaware of the sexual significance of their actions, as when they kiss their children on the mouth or when they expose their bodies to children. Such behavior is rationalized as affection or liberalism, but the child senses the sexual overtones of these actions (Lowen, 1967; p. 86).*

Seduction is so pervasive that it is not given much thought until an unwanted advance takes place (e.g., "He is very flirtatious" or "I like flirting with men"). It is not only a surprise that the advance is refused, but that it was offered in the first place. Yet what can be done? Should it be ignored in the hope that it will go away? Or talked about and confronted? Seduction appears to be a way to avoid the pressure of having to deal with difficult relationship issues. While ignoring or removing oneself from situations may be the easiest way to deal with it, the most therapeutic way is to explore one's behavior. For example, when seductive behavior occurs, a person may ask any one of the following questions: "Are you being flirtatious (seductive) with me?"; "Let's talk about how we come across to each other?"; "Do you have an issue around your relationship with me?"; "What do you want?"; "I am aware that you seem to have long eye contact with me."; "Are you aware of how you are sitting?"; Seductive behavior is a "road block" to communication that leads to false and ultimately unproductive relationships. And in helping, it is vital for the helper to confront a client who displays such behavior. It is a kind of fantasy that, when brought into the "light of day" loses its allure and power. It is vital not to be seduced by seduction, because it is a lie. The Russian writer, Maxim Gorky, (1943) said that the person "who is strong, who is his own master, who is free and does not have to suck his neighbor's blood – he needs no lies. To lie – it's the creed of slaves and masters of slaves…truth is the religion of the free" (p. 245).

SEXUAL ETHICS

Openness and expression of sexuality does not mean there should be no ethical consideration. Consider what May (1974) said: "The Victorian person sought to have love without falling into sex; the modern person seeks to have sex without falling into love" (p. 46). There is something not quite right about this, because it suggests a holding back or perhaps an incongruence. People will no doubt choose to do what is right for them because they know what is best. To go into relationships without the right feeling seems wrong and incongruent, because people need to decide for themselves what are acceptable practices. They need to ask themselves if their actions are consistent with their values.

There are a lot of sexual practices that were once considered abnormal, but are now acceptable in today's society. At one time, society considered many forms of sexual expression between heterosexual and homosexuality as crimes. And even the American Psychological Association labeled homosexuality as a disease that people had to be cured of in the past. Now it is an avowed sexual orientation for many and is no longer considered illegal or abnormal by most people in society. The need to be loved and to love is the same whether people are homosexual or heterosexual. In a changing world, "gay" men and women need to be accepted and embraced by "straight" men and women. All are valuable and add to the diversity of humanity. In the end no matter what choice is made it needs to be compatible with personal values. People have the choice to do what is best for them; however with this freedom comes the obligation to be sexually responsible.

IMPLICATIONS FOR THE GROUP

What makes the group experience a stimulating vehicle for exploring sexuality and gender issues is that it is a safe place where there are a variety of people to offer feedback, with whom to establish connections and a place where a support network exists. The climate encourages the sharing of dreams, fears, hopes and perceptions. And when men and women act in a stereotypical manner they suffer; therefore, activities that help them explore their male and female identity are empowering. For example, women can experiment with behaviors which are stereotyped as male and men can experiment with behavior that is stereotyped as female. Men can experiment with being more expressive, nurturing, sensitive, self-disclosing and vulnerable. Women can experiment with being more assertive, decisive, independent and rational. To facilitate gender role exploration, the leader could ask men to take on female roles and women to take on male roles. The rationale behind doing this is not only to understand how gender roles develop, but also to add those characteristics of the opposite sex to their repertoire. Perhaps every man has a female part and every woman has a male part. When people have the use of their gender polarities, they can act in a more androgynous manner.

The gender role reversal activity has always been a powerful tool in communicating and providing group members with the opportunity to explore a unique part of themselves. Participants are asked to give themselves a name, wardrobe, hobbies and then introduce themselves to others in the group. An alternate to introductions is creating a "party" or an interactive atmosphere such as a "picnic" where people can get more into their roles. To get into differing gender roles, the facilitator can ask group members to cross-dress by wearing at least one item from the opposite sex. At the end of the activity, participants in the group share their perceptions of themselves and others. Invariably people have been amazed at how different they felt as the opposite sex. For example, in one recent group, a woman who had always acted in a quiet and self-effacing manner role played a man who was assertive and expressive. Her character was a "man" named "Bobby," who enjoyed climbing mountains and riding motorcycles. As "Bobby" her voice was forceful; her manner open in providing feedback; her body language suggested strength; and she had an infectious sense of humor. At the end of the activity the group provided feedback that was startling to her. All of "Bobby's" characteristics were the exact opposite of hers. "I never felt so free before," was one of her responses after the feedback. While she never displayed the vitality of the character "Bobby" in the remainder of the group meetings her actions were more similar to "Bobby's" than to her old self. The commitment she made to the group at the closing activity was to retrieve "Bobby" more often. Below are some suggestions people can do in the group is:

❦ Examine guilt feelings relating to sexuality;

❦ Accept sexual desires, feelings and fantasies;

❦ Discriminate between sexual feelings and actions;

❦ Be open to giving and receiving;

❦ Clearly define personal boundaries (e.g., likes, dislikes);

❦ Act in an ethical manner;

❦ Experiment with androgynous behavior.

CONCLUSION

The syndicated newspaper columnist Ellen Goodman (1991) asked an intriguing question about two 1991 summer films, *Thelma and Louise* and *Regarding Henry*. Her question was: If Thelma and Louise would have shot Henry in the head, would the media focus on male bashing? First consider the themes of the two films. Thelma and Louise are two women who decide to travel across the United States together in an automobile. They encounter various men, who all negatively stereotype them and in defending themselves they kill and maim some of the men. Their "light-hearted" trip turns into desperation when they are pursued by the police. Rather than surrender, they drive off a cliff. Henry displays the worst aspects of men by his insensitivity and aggression until he is shot by a robber and loses his memory. Henry's wife and daughter "reshape" Henry into a loving and sensitive man. Goodman suggests that "the process of change is either magical or lethal. It implies that there is nothing worth saving, nothing to build on. Want to be a new man [or woman]? The movies offer a choice: death or brain damage" (p. 5).

While great strides have been made to address gender inequities, there remains a large gap between men and women in many areas. Some people argue that the gap is not artificially created, but based on genuine differences that enable men to have the upper hand with women by natural selection. However, while there are differences in genitals, there are few inherently biological, social or even behavioral differences that would provide men with reasons to assume dominance over women. Sexual expression in men and women has long been cited as a key difference, yet new evidence suggests the opposite. While sexuality seems to be a "flash point" in the battle of the sexes, it serves and enriches life. Intimacy is craved by all, yet it confuses, intimidates and disillusions many people. In every group it is not uncommon to see sexual attractions, and gender differences are either a central focus or an important peripheral side-issue. It is a part of life, whether people like it or not. In these days of AIDS it is not difficult wanting to avoid something that promises to kill. However, there is "wisdom" in the group that can help others be less gender biased, promote egalitarian values and reduce "old fears" about sexual expression and identity. Vanier (1998) stresses that "the third aspect of love is...communication" (p. 24).

In part, the communication within the group, be it eros or platonic, needs to be respectful when expressing one's sexuality and love. When looking at desires through the lens of Maslow's hierarchy of needs, the group can examine their motives and methods of sexual expression. The passion expressed by St. Augustine is similar to Pierre's – there is no difference. Love is a need that can be expressed on a variety of levels and directions. Perhaps the expression of sexuality is a seed: how and where it is released determines what people experience and what they receive. To paraphrase the prophet Hosea: If you sow a garden, it will multiply, but if you sow a whirl-wind, that so shall you reap." When asked what the difference was between food and sex, Prather (1970) said, "Consent." The use of power in sex seems to be a dominant theme not only in fantasies of both men and women, but in everyday communication and interaction. The constant use of gratification as a thermometer of happiness is clearly self-defeating. It may be true that too much time and energy are devoted to sexuality, yet people cannot escape the powerful role it plays in life. Rogers (1973) suggests that the way to deal with sexuality is not to:

de-sex it, but to acknowledge the existence of sensuousness; accept it...accept the experience of contact, [and you] will no longer be troubled by it. If...[you] accept the responses it touches off...[you] will probably discover not fear, repulsion; but the content of the hug – love, warmth, joy (p. 64).

ACTIVITIES

1. **Measuring Androgyny:** Take the Bem Sex-Role Inventory and have group members share their level of androgyny. The items in the questionnaire ask, on a scale of 1 (never) to 7 (always) a number of items, such as self-reliance, helpful, warm, secretive, etc. [The questionnaire can be obtained from the following sources: Bem, S. (1977) On the utility of alternative procedures for assessing psychological androgyny, *Journal of Consulting and Clinical Psychology*, 45; 196-205.]

2. **Sexuality Sentence Completion:** The group brainstorms topics to be discussed by triads. Write all of the topic on a chalk board, which should then be put in incomplete sentence form (e.g., "For me, sexual satisfaction is..." or "What I find attractive in the opposite sex is..."). Twenty items that cover the broad range of topics can be used. Working in triads, each person takes turns, completing the sentences, taking only 60 seconds to respond. Once all the items have been responded to, participants share perceptions with their partner's responses (e.g., items that were embarrassing, discomforting, difficult, easy, risky, etc.). Participants can choose not to respond to some items. A large group discussion can be generated to explore gender specific values, perceptions and attitudes.

CHAPTER NINE
THE ISSUE OF
RELATIONSHIPS AND GROUP WORK

No man is an island, entire of itself; every person is a piece of the continent, a part of the main; if a clod be washed away by the sea, Europe is the less, as well as if a promontory were, as well as if a manor of thou friends or of thine own were; and every man's death diminishes me, because I am involved in mankind; And therefore never send to know for whom the bell tolls; It tolls for thee. John Donne

This part of Donne's seventeenth century poem, from *Meditations XVII*, after all these years hits a deep cord of the human condition. People need to feel "connected" to others – to form relationships. Relationships with others are probably the most central aspect of everyone's life. There is a great deal of evidence that substantiates the positive value of relationships on well-being. There is also convincing evidence documenting the negative effects when there is an absence of a positive relationship. This reminds me of a legend I heard a few years ago about the 12th century King Frederick II of the Two Sicilies (during the Crusades, the island of Sicily and the southern part of Italian peninsula up to Naples). The King apparently believed that all people were born with an innate ability to speak the biblical language of Hebrew. To prove his hypothesis, he took fifty newborn babies away from their mothers at birth and gave them to foster mothers. He commanded them not to speak to the infants, so they would be able to speak the "heavenly language." What occurred was a total surprise to the King, for all the infants died within a year. The infants simply could not live without the cooing, caressing and loving presence of their mothers. We call this phenomenon "marasmus" or the sudden wasting away of the body of infants entering the final stage of grief after prolonged separation from their mothers.

When people do not have satisfactory relationships, they experience loneliness, which is often cited as the most painful of all feelings. Yet despite the drive to "make contact" nearly all people will experience the inevitable problems and stresses that are a part of most relationships. I have often wondered: if the drive to build relationships is so strong, why are there such a large number of divorces, break-ups and disintegrating families? In groups, from self-help to work to counselling groups, I have observed that most people spend energy trying to make connections with each other. This drive for relationship development is much like the drive to quench a thirst. The feelings that a satisfactory relationship brings to me are like a "high" that has no comparison. I am reminded of a member of a previous group who shared her sensation after going home from a rendezvous with an intimate friend; "I smiled as I drove away, because I felt so complete…my body tingled and I felt totally satisfied and had the sense that I could accomplish anything…climb Mount Everest. I wanted to scream out my happiness to the night."

WHEN RELATIONSHIPS NEEDS ARE NOT MET

Lorenz (1966) argues that all mammals have a biological instinct to form relationships. The evidence of the biological basis for human companionship demonstrates that people's well-being is endangered. This is apparent in examining the population of the State of Nevada. Twenty percent of Nevada males between the ages of 35-65 are single, widowed, divorced, or living alone. This is one of the highest percentages in the United States and may account for why Nevada has the highest death rate in the United States for white males. Consider the effects of serum cholesterol and high blood pressure that are linked to stress, and as a result, are an aspect of cardio-vascular disease. From the results of a study of the residents of Roseto, Pennsylvania, who have high cholesterol levels, it would seem that there would be a high percentage of deaths as a result of cardio-vascular disease, but this is not so (Lynch, 1977). The difference here appears to reflect the supportive community and family ties rather than an individual's diet.

The lack of a satisfying relationship, along with health status, seems to be the critical factor in early death from accidents, suicide and homicide. The rate is twice as high for single males and females than for those who are married. However, it is not marital status per se that ensures a longer life, but the degree of happiness. The dissatisfaction in a marriage is correlated with heart disease. For example, when there is a "psychological divorce" in a relationship where spouses are focused more on their jobs than on the relationship, there is increased risk of early death. Nowhere can the connection between early death and lack of a satisfying relationship be seen more clearly than in children. There is a correlation between early loss of one or both parents and illness. In fact, early loss, isolation and loneliness are highly predictive of suicide. In other words, the loss of significant others seriously affects physical and mental well being and can bring about premature death. This is sometimes called the "broken heart effect."

Relationships are one of the greatest sources of positive well-being. They not only help people feel better about themselves, but being liked increases self-esteem. Along with this, high self-esteem is attractive to others. Interestingly, high social support helps to strengthen the immune system. Another aspect of relationships is that it reduces anxiety. The desire to affiliate can be satisfying by giving people the opportunity to get information by making a social comparison (e.g., how bad is it?). According to Schachter (1989) just having people present reduces anxiety about how bad a situation is. In his experiments, people had reduced levels of stress when someone else was present, compared to when they were alone. In addition, verbal assurance reduces anxiety. Social support is given in a variety of ways:

❧ Attachment (emotional support);

❧ Guidance (information; advice; feedback);

❧ Tangible assistance (material or service aid);

❧ Embeddedness in a social network (feeling a part of a cohesive, well-defined group);

❧ Opportunity to provide nurturance (helping others or having others dependent on oneself).

While positive relationships strengthen well-being, negative interactions with one's social network can be upsetting. This is particularly true if the social network or relations use a lot of criticism. And while friendship has a positive relationship, the downside is that friendship can increase anxiety by feeding on one's fears of rejection.

Table 9.1: Erikson's Psycho-social Stages		
Age	**Issue**	**Resolution Leads to...**
First year	Trust vs. Mistrust	Optimism, warmth
2-3 years	Autonomy vs. Doubt	Self-control, pride in accomplishment
3-5 years	Initiative vs. Guilt	Purpose and direction
6-puberty	Industry vs. Inferiority	Competence
Adolescence	Identity vs. Role	A sense of self and diffusion of who one is
Adulthood	Intimacy vs. Isolation	Form relationships
Middle Age	Generativity vs. Productivity and stagnation	Creativity
Old Age	Integrity vs. Despair	Meaning and accepting mortality

THE DYNAMICS OF PERSONAL DEVELOPMENT

Erikson (1963) suggested that as people pass through the developmental stages, they experience problems specific to that stage. He felt that, if people were unable to make the transition from one stage to another, they would fixate and not mature. By stressing the influence of relationships Erikson's theory of personality development differed from Freud's emphasis on instinctual and internal factors. Table 9.1 highlights the core issues in the psychosocial stages and the effect when the stage is successfully passed. These core issues span over the lifetime of a person. If a sense of trust is not acquired early, the person will not have a sense of optimism or warmth. However, the inability to resolve an issue at a certain stage does not mean the person cannot at some later point in life resolve it. It is possible that there may be an accumulative effect, which decreases the adaptability and feelings of well-being. For example, the socializing influence of a mother on the development of the infant is crucial in helping to resolve the issue of trust versus mistrust.

The primary issue in adulthood is intimacy versus isolation, which hinges in a great degree on the ability to establish a relationship. However, a relationship does not guarantee intimacy. What is intimacy? Intimacy is a closeness in which people are open to sharing their feelings and thoughts. The goal of most successful relationships is closeness, intimacy and love. It may seem as though closeness, intimacy and love is a progression when in reality they are elements of the same thing. Love is the most talked about concept in relationships. Thousands of songs wail about the joys, sorrows, dissatisfactions and excitement of love. The Greeks thought that there were two kinds of love – eros and agape. **Eros** is the extreme need for another, while **agape** is the attempt to satisfy another. There are other forms of love besides romantic love. These are maternal love, creative love, sexual love, love of friends, love of humankind and love of god. These other forms can be as fulfilling and varied as romantic love. The down side of intimacy is isolation. Those who are isolated are usually lonely, experiencing neither closeness, intimacy nor love. To live a life where there is no sharing is to experience neither giving nor receiving.

THE TRANSPERSONAL THEORY OF SELF

The psycho-social stages developed by Erikson (1963) give a general overview of those issues that people confront over a lifetime, but Gestalt provides a more coherent explanation of how those issues block maturity. As people grow they make contact internally (self) and externally with things and people in their environment (others). Perls, Hefferline and Goodman (1951) stress that contacts are necessary for self-adjustment:

> *Self may be regarded as at the boundary of the organism, but the boundary is not itself isolated from the environment...it belongs to both, environment and organism. Contact is touching something. The self is not to be thought of as a fixed institution; it exists wherever there is..."when the thumb is pinched, the self exists in the painful thumb" (p. 373).*

When people allow their external self to be incongruent with their internal self, they are communicating: "I do not trust you with my feelings, because I do not trust myself." The role insulates people, but also keeps them unaware of what is under the facade. The facilitator in the group needs to focus people in contacting the facade they have erected around themselves. Only by ridding themselves of the facade can people utilize their power. The implication is to use the symbols people use as a means of accessing their personal system. For example, in one group a person described herself as "numb," which protected her from a confusing relationship, but prevented her from developing intimacy. Pairing "numbness" with "liveliness" evoked a powerful image for her to learn to feel again. For her, the pairing was an efficient means of self-perception that helps in making sense of impressions and experiences that she lived. As a result of exploring the facade she was able to make contact at a deeper level with others in the group.

If people are not able to make contact at a deeper level, they will lack authenticity and congruence. In other words, they will not be able to determine the "rightness" of their experiences. This inability to make contact will result in a confused sense of self or a diffused self-identity, in which it becomes very difficult to be spontaneous and make meaningful relationships. For example, in a previous group, Tim, who was highly verbal, had a habit of intellectualizing when speaking about himself. His descriptions were so verbose that he would lose contact and alienate other members of the group. This occurred in part because he was not in contact with himself at a deeper level and was unable to be spontaneous and natural. His verbosity and intellectualizing reflected how out of contact he really was with his feelings. Once he was more natural with his feelings and thoughts he became more open and free with them. While still maintaining his considerable intellectual integrity he was regarded as more sincere and trustworthy.

Polarization is another crucial aspect that affects how people relate, because it reflects how people view the "world." When emotions are polarized into dichotomies like good-bad, honest-dishonest, hard-soft, ally-enemy, controlled-spontaneous or any other polarity classification, it is easier for people to organize and act on information. However, it also reinforces rigidity, inflexibility and prejudices, and immobilizes people who wish to develop or enhance a relationship. While polarization seems to naturally occur, the more defined a relationship, the greater the difference. In other words, there is only "black and white" and no gray areas or a view of things on a continuum. This translates into a block in relationship enhancement or in development as related in "you either agree with me or you are my enemy." For example, I am reminded of one woman who felt that all men were to be distrusted. Since all the men in her life had either harmed her or never helped her, her behavior was to discount all men. Yet deep inside she expressed the feeling that out there was, maybe, just maybe, a good man. Rather than just discount men entirely, which might have seemed logical given her experience, she expended much energy getting to know men who, in the end, confirmed her point of view that men were not to be trusted. In the end, it hindered any long-lasting relationships with men in her life. For Kopp (1986), the relationship style that is restrictive or protective has:

> developed early in life as necessary armor against an emotionally destructive environment. At first they served to keep the patient safe from the surrounding dangers. Additionally, they offered protection against internal anguish too overwhelming to be borne at the time. Now in adult life these attitudes are self-maintaining. In limiting the patient's experience of anxiety, they also restrict the possibilities for new experience. Ironically, in this way they prevent realization that the original danger has passed (p. 134).

In a therapeutic sense this polarization is affirmed and considered acceptable, everyone is unique. It is not surprising or strange that some people may have a feeling of attraction-revulsion toward others in the group. What Gestalt emphasizes is that the polarities need to be **owned**, "I am attracted to your energy" or "I'm not comfortable with your intensity." Only in affirming the polarities and accepting dichotomous feelings can people build a relationship based on honesty. It is entirely possible that once all the ingredients of a relationship are recognized, there exist the possibility that feelings will change. When feelings are ignored, then the potential for change is nil.

Contact occurs when the boundaries of two people meet or the boundaries between a person and a group or between two groups occur. When I say meet, I mean they come up against each other and have an effect on the person, group or environment. Sometimes people have such a habitual way of interacting that despite what seems like contact, there is no contact at all. For example, often people will meet someone and talk about the weather or some other event that has little meaning or effect. In a situation like this, contact is not really made. I think of a colleague who is personable and friendly, but who reacts in a ritualistic manner. Every time I see him, he always says: "How is it going?" It is not a question, because an answer is not expected. Usually, I am not feeling mischievous and so I answer in the usual way: "Very well, how about you?" Once I did answer him honestly, "Just terrible." It was as if he had not heard me and he continued walking down the hall. I was left standing in the hallway with my mouth open.

When contact is made and a relationship begins to develop, all of a person's awareness and senses become involved. I see, smell, hear, touch and sometimes even "taste" the other person as I make contact. In addition, I pay attention to the pattern of the interaction, looking for clues that will help me better understand this person. It is possible, if I am very aware, to even make contact in a spiritual or psychic manner. There are always limitless possibilities available. While the "boundary" acts as a division that separates, it also joins and brings the possibility of limiting or expanding the relationship. Withdrawal, the polar opposite of contact, is just as powerful in relationships. Conflict is also a constant aspect of all relationships, particularly when the relationship does not fulfill expectations or one's demands. Reliving patterns, projecting feelings, or simply withdrawing from the relationship are common signs of a communication problem. Perhaps as Kopp (1986) suggests, "it is only our attachment to wanting things our own way that makes us unhappy" (p.44). However, the key to communication difficulties according to Perls (1969a) is resentment because it is:

> *among the worst possible unfinished situations, unfinished gestalts. If you resent, you can neither let go nor have it out. Resentment is an emotion of central importance. The resentment is the most important expression of an impasse of being stuck. If you feel resentment, it is best to express your resentment. A resentment unexpressed often is experienced as, or changes into, feelings of guilt. Whenever you feel guilty, find out what you are resenting and express it and make your demands explicit. This alone will help a lot (p. 49).*

Guilt leads to "shoulds," "oughts," and a whole host of actions that lead to dishonest and distorted relationships. Through the acceptance of responsibility for the self by identifying with personal expectations, it is possible to make clear demands in relationships. This is a process of saying what one wants, desires and expects. When this happens there is personal "owning" and that means accepting responsibility. All relationships are typified by changing conditions and evolving feelings that make them interesting and satisfying. Yet people should remember that "the quality of life remains an unpredictable uneven cycle of periods of easy living disrupted by troubled times" (Kopp, 1986; p. 2). Change is always going to be a constant companion in relationships.

FORMS OF RELATIONSHIPS

All forms of relationship share certain fundamental characteristics that motivate people to pursue them and seek fulfillment through them. Basically, all people are attracted to others and seek to join their lives with them. However, not all personal needs are going to be met exclusively in one form of relationship, thus people are drawn to different relationships for different reasons. While sexuality remains a powerful motivator and force in relationships, it is by no means the only ingredient. The reasons for establishing relationships can be as diverse as the desire for security, to love or be loved, to be accepted, not to be alone and so on. It seems that if there is an ingredient that is universal in relationships – it is love. As might be expected, love not only has different definitions, it also has different dimensions (e.g., love of a mate is different from love for one's child). These dimensions of love could be applied to a variety of targets from the cosmic to the romantic. Yet how many people consider the complete field of potential relationships? Ricketts and Gochros (1987) suggest that many people are ignorant of the many dimensions of love or alternative forms of relationships, because of the strong emphasis in society on "finding the one and only rather than finding companionship, community, and emotional support through networks of extended family and lifelong friends" (pp. 7-8). While poems, songs and novels are full of various meanings on love, the one I like the best is Gibran's (1933): "love gives naught but itself and takes naught but from itself, love possesses [not] nor would it be possessed; for love is sufficient unto love" (p. 13).

INTIMATE RELATIONSHIPS

According to Schultz (1987) intimacy, through its therapeutic usage, has become in the helping professions one of the new mega-trends. Intimacy can either be short-term, as in brief encounters, or long-term, as in marriage. Marriages can be legal or common law and can be heterosexual or homosexual. All these forms of intimate relationships have similar expectations, issues and challenges. All are capable of being fulfilling and satisfying. In the past, marriage has always been perceived as the deepest and longest lasting. Yet, does the high divorce rate mean that this perception is changing? The dissatisfaction with marriage, although influenced by the changing nature of the dynamics between men and women, has not really changed the attitude of people toward the fact that it offers the best hope for achieving intimacy. During the sixties and seventies there was a lot of experimentation with differing forms of relationships, but the trend, particularly during the "age of AIDS," is towards a more traditional and exclusive relationship. The rationale for homosexual couples might be the need to be intimate, to love and to be loved; in heterosexual couples the need to have a family is most often cited as the rationale for marriage. However, heterosexual and homosexual couples also expect their marriages or relationships will fulfill the following roles.

- Therapeutic or that a mate can support and offer help in dissipating life's problems, by providing emotional and financial security.
- Recreational or that mates are to take shared responsibility in planning and participating in leisure time, by going on vacations together.
- Sexual or the mutual satisfaction of partners in the relationship, by sexual exclusiveness.

In keeping with the trend towards more equality between men and women, research has always suggested that there is only a slight difference in attitude about relationships (Hatfield & Rapson, 1987). There is no difference between the sexes in terms of susceptibility to being passionately in love, although there are some attitudes in society that suggest there might be differences. Society has often reinforced the idea that there are gender differences, but the evidence is not substantiated. Attitudes and practices are changing. In the past more men said they were comfortable initiating intimate relationships than were women. However, with more and more men and women developing an androgynous attitude, this is changing.

Perhaps what is most intimidating about intimate relationships is the perception that along with intimacy comes a loss of independence. Yet, intimacy and independence are compatible. While some people do forfeit their independence when they enter an intimate relationship, it does not have to be that way. It's a choice. Erikson's (1973) identity issue is not just a developmental task for adolescence, but something that will have to be faced again and again throughout life. People not only have the right to be themselves, but owe it to those they develop intimate relationships with to maintain their integrity. According to Hatfield and Rapson (1987) intimacy skills consist of: recognizing and accepting others as they are; eliminating automatic emotional responses; accepting that what is shared may not be accepted; and encouraging open and honest expression.

FAMILY RELATIONSHIPS

The family is the basic unit in society, although in recent years the definition of the family has changed. There are single parent, blended, homosexual, lesbian, extended and nuclear families, just to name a few. People spend most of their lives in some kind of family setting and much of their perceptions are shaped by their experiences. In a real sense, the "family" is the ultimate small group because it is the experience in the family that influences people in all other group experiences. Therefore, the manner in which people conduct themselves in the various groups they are members of reflects how they manage themselves in their family. According to Goldenberg and Goldenberg (1980), the central focus of therapeutic intervention is the family and not the individual:

> *Rather, the family begins to understand that his or her problems or symptoms are an expression of the entire family's system. Problems get related within a family framework as relationship difficulties. Within such a system's prospective viewpoint, the locus of pathology is not the individual but rather the individual in context, and the individual's experiences and subsequent behavior patterns begin to change (p. 9).*

Adler (Corsini & Wedding, 1989) uses the family system as an assessment procedure to investigate present life-style convictions. In other words, to understand others, it is necessary to look at their primary relationship in the environment – the "family." The conditions in the "family" seem to influence the life position people take in other groups, in school and with peers. Early recollections that are often related to their place in the family constellation seem to reflect the way they live their lives now. Thus, when examining roles people have had in their families it is not surprising that there are many similarities for those who were born first, second or last. For example, when asking people in a group to join with others who were first born, second born or last born and compare their experiences, I am never surprised that the groups have had remarkable similarities of experiences. The rationale for exploring family constellations and early recollections is to help people examine basic myths about their families. The family usually is where personal mythologies develop, which form the beliefs about the way the world functions. Maturation often brings these beliefs in to conflict and people are challenged to redefine their beliefs. In the group these introjected beliefs can be explored and people can either decide to confirm or change them. It is often a surprise to group members when they become aware of how early myths influence present beliefs and sometimes "block" them from satisfying relationships. Sometimes myths have developed truths and now affect relationships. The following are examples of some myths that have been explored in previous groups.

Over generalizations: "People are bad and are not to be trusted." "All men (or women) are going to hurt you."

Impossible goals of security: "You should be nice to everybody, because that is the only way you will be liked." "Once you get married you will live happily ever after."

Mis-perceptions about life and the demands of life: "You only go around once in life, so you better grab things when you have the chance." "I'm destined to repeat the mistakes of my father."

Denying or minimizing self-worth: "I'm just not smart enough." "I'm only a woman." "I'm never going to be competent enough."

Faulty values: "The only way to be a man is to be strong." "Win at all cost." "You will have to kiss a lot of frogs before you find a prince."

However, the complexities of the relationships that people have had with their mothers and fathers are at times difficult, if not impossible to separate from their present functioning. There are reciprocal influences of everyone in the family. The relationship between the mother and the father affects how children are regarded and how they regard their parents. The perception of the child concerning how relationships are supposed to be is then carried on into adulthood and is sometimes repeated. However, it is the attachment or the bond that develops between parents and children that some developmentalists think has the greatest impact. Erikson (1973) believed that the first year is a key time for forming attachments. If trust does not develop during this period, then the child may grow up feeling mistrustful in future relationships. Mothers usually have the closest attachment to children compared to fathers, although this is beginning to change. Fathers are taking greater responsibility in rearing children, but predominately take a secondary role. Interestingly, most children in families describe their mothers as warm and sympathetic, while fathers are generally described most often in relation to their jobs. All people do gravitate towards establishing some kind of "equilibrium," which the family usually provides.

FRIENDSHIP

In one of the final scenes of Erich Maria Remarque's (1931) classic novel, *All quiet on the western front*, one soldier carries his friend many miles to a hospital, despite the fact that his friend has died. For that soldier it was immaterial, for the friendship gave him meaning and was the only "real" aspect of his existence in a "world gone mad." In the end, the soldier became shaped by his friend as he took on his friend's traits. Friendships shape people and people shape friendship. Aristotle echoed the symbiotic aspect of friendships when he said: "A true friend is one soul in two bodies."

Most friendships are arrangements bonded by affection, esteem and respect. It is a relationship that is simplistic and not complicated, unlike marriage or romantic couplings, which contain more intense issues of sex, power or control. This suggests that friendship has a level of freedom that does not exist in most other relationships. There is nothing like the support of a friend, mostly because there tends to be fewer strings attached. Many people say that the greatest value friendship has is it is a relationship where people can go for advice, companionship, support and an honest opinion. Perhaps the real value of friends is they are there whether they are utilized or not. For example, I am reminded of a time I felt really at a "breaking point"; it seemed like there was no way out of my predicament, and this depressed me. The figure of my focus was my dilemma and everything else faded into the background. Suddenly, I thought of my friend Paul and my spirits soared. I made a time to go and talk with him about my concern and as I thought of what I would say, I had an imaginary dialogue with him in my head. I thought of how he would respond to me and like a "flashing light," his words brought the answer. Through this, I discovered I had some choices that I had not considered. I immediately became aware of the lightness in my body and in my spirit. The problem faded into the background, resulting in a greater feeling of well-being. Friendships also serve to affirm people's values. Most people choose friends who are like themselves, which might suggest that people need approval from others. To identify with others and become like them are very powerful reinforcers. But this can result in compromising personal values in the desire to gain peer approval. In the extreme, this can result in a sense of confluence in which personal boundaries disappear.

The result is social comparison, which has been termed the forming of friendships to gain feedback and reduce uncertainty on how to behave. While the positive side of this is being able to check out perceptions, the negative side is to adopt other people's views and perceptions through confluence or introjection. For example, I can gain insight into myself or a new perspective of the world around me by bouncing ideas off a friend. This "give and take" provides friends the opportunity to grow emotionally. Rogers (1980) utilizes this in the helping relationship, which he called "unconditional positive regard" or acceptance without any conditions. Not surprisingly, unconditional positive regard and total acceptance is one of the most important ingredients of a loving relationship.

RELATIONSHIP ISSUES

Relationships involve the whole person and result in inevitable stress. Some relationships, like people, become sick, and some even die. Thus, the tragedy of relationships is what dies inside them while they still live. I have often watched the television reruns of the *Carol Burnett Show* and the funniest and saddest characters in her repertoire are the ones in the skit called "the family." These people reflect all the negative types of interactions that make a relationship destructive. I laugh in part because it is so exaggerated and cartoon like, yet the issues that block any meaningful communication in "the family" are so very typical of my experience. "The family" includes: Mother, Eunice and Ed.

Mother, who is peevish and negative, likes to have control of the family. She includes a "put-down" in almost everything she says, including compliments. For example: "That meal was OK, but you would think there was an oil glut with all that grease you use." Her relationship with Eunice, her daughter, reflects the strange "push-pull" relationship that often exists between mothers and daughters and sons and their fathers. She does not allow Eunice to be independent of her, but regards her as an extension of herself. All her self-loathing is projected onto Eunice and Ed, who no matter what they do will never get her approval. Eunice is immature, self-centered, and angry. Her hostility is always "sugar-coated," except in relating to Ed and then it is poison. She knows that in her mother's eyes she is not valued and never will be, yet she desperately tries to please her. There is the constant plea for acceptance typified by the statement: "Mother, you have never been grateful for what I have done for you. Just once I'd like to hear a thank you." The anger is never owned and is always deflected, usually in a spiteful way at Ed, her husband. The relationship with Ed is personified as so many male-female patterns – role defined – resulting in them both being victimized and feeling angry. Ed is simple, boorish, whining and is a total projection of conventional male conditioning. A can of beer and a "ball game" is his focus in life. He has no intimacy or contact with any of the females in the family other than the false facade of "manliness" and as the target and foil of insults and sexual innuendoes. He is relegated to forever wander in the "no man's land" of Mother and Eunice's quarrels. Despite all the posturing, he is treated in a disrespectful way, yet he never confronts directly, as he always "sabotaging" potential contact. In one memorable scene, Ed goes off to a convention without her, with Eunice's parting reply in a mixed tone of "sweetness" and venom: "Go ahead, Ed, enjoy yourself, I'll be here when you get back…to make your life a living hell!"

The "family" in *The Carol Burnett Show* illustrates what is repeated again and again in many relationships. Yet the issues and themes that disrupt relationships are as varied as people. The "family" reflects communication patterns that are in all types of relationships. I have chosen to focus on some fundamental issues that affect people. What intrigues me are the polarities (opposites) in these issues. In most relationship issues there are two sides. I also believe that there is no way to happiness in a relationship, except through choosing it.

LONELINESS VERSUS ALONENESS

Escape from loneliness is often cited by people as a reason for entering relationships; however, loneliness is not just a feeling produced by not having one. It is a discomforting feeling that reinforces a perception that something is missing from one's life (France, 1984). When this is felt, life is seen as empty and worthless. This feeling of separateness from self and others does not mean that people have to be physically alone, because loneliness can occur when others are around. This occurs because there are dimensions of loneliness that people experience differently (see figure 9.1).

Figure 9.1 Dimensions of Loneliness

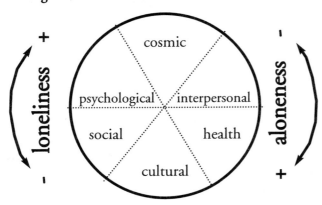

None of these dimensions of loneliness exists separately, but are interrelated producing pain and blocking people from maintaining a satisfying social network. I sometimes experience these dimensions of aloneness or loneliness when I am experiencing the following feelings:

✻ **Psychologically** separated from myself, not owning and having a self-depreciating attitude (e.g., "no one loves me").

✻ **Culturally** separated at times from my culture and language, particularly when I am abroad (e.g., "I feel like a stranger").

✻ **Socially** separated from friends and others by not belonging to any special group (e.g., "I don't have anything in common with others").

✻ **Interpersonally** unable to build significant friendships (e.g., "I am never going to find someone who can give me what I want").

✻ **Cosmically** separated from a divine being (e.g., "I feel spiritually empty at times when I wonder what the purpose of my life is").

✻ **Unhealthy** or a sense of being cut off and devalued from others as a result of my physical condition (e.g., "I can't do the things I used to").

At different times most people have experienced these dimensions, but what is significant about these is the double bind inherent in them. For example, one group member from a European country, who spoke English fluently, shared that he felt "like a fish out of water." Even though he had been away from Europe many years, he still had a difficult time coping with different customs. At times he felt different and separate from the person in his primary relationship. In times of stress in the relationship, his partner pointed out that he was the "foreigner." He tried hard to be like everyone else, to learn their language and customs, but he "never" succeeded. Sadly, he found himself feeling negative about himself for being different. The result was a narrowing of independence, decreased self-esteem and alienation from himself and others. The other side of loneliness is aloneness, which is the feeling of wanting to have solitude. For many, solitude is necessary for actualizing their aspirations, ideals and interests. Sometimes these periods of solitude or aloneness occur in periods of grief, suffering, loss and pain; this is when life's values are usually re-examined. Sometimes even the experience of pain can result in creative energy and can becomes a "springboard" for personal change. For example, another group member who had been a refugee from war, felt her adjustment had a beneficial affect. While missing her culture, the experience of emigrating from Asia resulted in a greater feeling of adaptability, independence and more opportunity for self-reliance. Being a "foreigner" was something that would always be a part of her life, but she felt it also enriched her relationships.

Everyone will experience loneliness, yet not everyone will be able to cope with it successfully. I say "cope," because loneliness is not something that can be avoided – to love is to experience loneliness. Many coping mechanisms work well, while others heighten loneliness. It is an intrinsic element of all human existence, and to live is to experience it. Relationships, like everything, will change. The more experience with relationships, the more people will experience loneliness. Thus, loneliness has to be accepted if people are to take more control of their existence. This means that people will have to feel better about themselves before they will be free to choose to involve themselves with others in whatever way they desire.

CONTROL VERSUS FREEDOM

"I'd like to feel free, but I want him there when I **need him**," remarked one group member. "You can't have it both ways," responded another. Freedom has always had a "double edge" to it. On one hand people want to "connect" with others, have them be "accommodating," but do not want them to limit their freedom. Relationships sometimes seem like a trade off – to be a part of a relationship, people must give up freedom. When that happens, they often feel controlled. It would be nice to go anywhere and do anything and not have to account to someone else. Do people ask too much in relationships? It seems many people want to have relationships with people who are agreeable to their desires, yet they do not want others to tell them what to do. [People can't have their cake and eat it too, I guess.] Since childhood, most people have been taught to deny impulses, spontaneous actions and natural instincts. The poet T. S. Elliot once remarked that so many today think they are emancipated, when in fact they are merely unbuttoned. Perhaps he is right. Freedom is a very vague notion that needs to be defined and negotiated in relationships.

People desire to have control over their destiny. In relationships where people feel a lack of control they feel negated. When people do not have control, they will become withdrawn, apathetic, depressed and even helpless. It is not easy to change patterns in relationships. In a previous group, one woman shared that she was in a relationship that did not satisfy her needs. She said: "I don't like it, but I feel powerless to change it or get out of it." Her helplessness seemed to turn into hopelessness and I suspect that she began to lose the ability to develop adaptive techniques. This is necessary if she and others are to make changes or in fact overcome any discomforting situations in the future. Those people who are adaptive to changes are generally more spontaneous and expressive. In essence, choice equals freedom.

I remember a group member who constantly monopolized the group time with his issues. Initially the group was accepting of this, but afterwards began to get tired of it and challenged him. This led to anger on his part and he blamed others for not being supportive. When offered a chance to work on the issue he "pulled" back saying he didn't trust people yet. Those who did try and reach out were rebuffed. When feedback about this was offered, he protested that "some" people in the group "picked on" him and he berated others for not being supportive. The group once again became "exhausted" with him and began to ignore him. His manner from this point on was vindictive, and the result was that he dissipated much of the group's energy. Finally, he lapsed into apathy and eventually dropped out of the group. The tragedy of this person's pattern is that he constantly undermined his power by inappropriately exercising control. Whether control is expressed in a facade of strength (perfectionism) or weakness (helplessness), it robs people of their freedom. Freedom is not controlling, but being open to aspirations, desires, creativity and spontaneous expression. Freedom is not introjecting, retroflecting, projecting, deflecting or confluencing. Freedom in relationships is being aware of personal needs, expressing those needs and accepting the needs of spouses, lovers, friends, children and parents. Freedom is not doing what one wants at the expense of others, but choosing to be what one is and to accept others for what they are. Like all important things, relationships require a lot of work, but the choice to do the work is the essence of freedom.

RELIVING PATTERNS VERSUS ESTABLISHING PATTERNS

Relating, responding and behaving in a patterned manner is a common experience that has both a positive and negative affect. That which is predictable is comforting and familiar. Yet some patterns, such as reflecting past experiences, are relived in the present, reinforcing fears, increasing discomfort and resulting in relationships being seriously undermined. I am reminded of Hector Babenco's (1987) film, **Ironweed**, in which the central character, Francis Phelan, has become a vagrant to escape his tormented past. He has tried alcohol to drown his memories of the accidental death of his young son. Yet, despite this, the ghosts of the past appear and multiply as he relives the terror when he is sober. Like the ghosts of Francis Phelan, unfinished situations will not go away unless they are "put to rest" and new ways of living are established.

I recall one person from a past group sharing that her boyfriend was to go with her to an important event. He was an hour late, although he had a good reason. During the wait she was suddenly "thrown" back to the past and remembered the unreliability of her alcoholic father. While she had a right to feel angry, the reliving of past panic was retrojected; a man had disappointed her because she was unworthy. The pattern for her was the constant reliving of feelings from past relationships transferred to the present. Her father was unreliable and she projected it onto her boyfriend. She felt unworthy and she turned it back on to herself with self-blame. To act in a way that is not spontaneous can produce behavior that is not adaptable. Conditions change, situations change and people change; thus, patterns that hamper spontaneity and dull awareness block the enhancement of relationships. Old patterns stifle creativity, while experimentation with new behaviors increases people's repertoire of communication. I think of how Kopp (1986) contrasted the differences between reliving patterns and establishing patterns: "One then has the sense of using and mastering rather than that of discovering and inventing. The senses are on the alert, on the lookout for, rather than finding or responding" (p. 379).

RESPONSIBILITY VERSUS BLAME

In relationships, the rejection of responsibility is a major factor in creating misunderstandings and blocking communication. Sometimes it seems people like to escape from personal responsibility by thinking of themselves as helpless "pawns" reacting to "accidents," rather than "players" responding to choices. Perhaps the payoff for not taking responsibility is being able to blame something that is the polarity of responsibility. It seems that most conflicts in relationships center around who is right or who is to blame. I have noticed in my relationships that "fixing the blame" is where all the energy lies. This is a courtroom style of arbitrating conflicts, which emphasizes the judicial process on fixing who is at fault. As a disagreement intensifies through the arguments, each side digs more deeply into immovable positions, with the impasse growing and the "battle" being pursued in earnest. Both sides begin to act on irrational beliefs, seemingly followed with a need to hurt as they prove who is right or wrong. Suddenly, they are thrust back into the past and perhaps unfinished business with their parents or other significant others. In reality, blame is avoiding responsibility. If something that has happened is someone else's fault, then this person is responsible, for example, "You hurt me, so now you are going to pay."

I am reminded of an incident in a group in which several of the most active members became angry with some of the inactive members. The active members blamed the inactive ones for the low energy level of the group, because of the lack of participation in a proposed activity. An argument ensued as to who was to blame. The inactive members felt they had a right not to participate in any activity, and the active members blamed them for "killing" their enthusiasm. As a result, everybody "shut down" and the energy "died." For the active members blaming was a way of avoiding their fear of self-disclosure. For the inactive members the incident only reinforced their belief that they were being manipulated. The "courtroom game" made it impossible to feel empathy or warmth towards each other. Rather than take responsibility for themselves and try to understand each other, they chose to act in a self-defeating manner. Sad to say, but it seems easier for some people to blame somebody else than to make personal changes.

CHANGING VERSUS STAGNATING

I am reminded of Rogers (1980), who had a very optimistic outlook on life. Even during his eighties, he felt that, although he could not throw a Frisbee or work in the garden any more, he could still enjoy walking. He always felt that change was a constant life theme, which is reflected in this remark: "I feel as sexy in my interests as I was at 35, though I can't say the same about my ability. Yet from the inside I'm still the same person in many ways, neither old nor young" (p. 20). Rogers took risks until his death. He attributed his ability to do so to: a well developed support group, being actively involved with others, looking for new challenges, and being open to learning new ideas. I do not believe Rogers was unique, but one thing is clear: he had a positive self-image based on involving himself with others, thinking positively and being open to new experiences. Some people's sense of well-being depends upon the feeling of fulfillment experienced in their lives. This sense of fulfillment is not just the feeling of what was accomplished in the past, but what can be accomplished in the "here and now." This means that, if people are to continue to grow, they must develop a positive self-image, trust themselves, be open to learning and accept new things in their lives. This can only happen when people remain true to their natural selves and not through materialism, blind ambitions, worldly goals or direction from others.

The aging process is just one of many changes that people in relationships will have to respond to. Their self-image greatly influences their state of well-being. This means that they have control over what happens – the choice is theirs. In essence, it is their reaction to change as a result of the events in the environment that affects their self-image, not the changes themselves. Therefore, the choice is to stagnate and fixate on something in the past, which only leads to disaster or to growth. To grow older is inevitable, but to grow, while becoming older, is a choice.

ENHANCING RELATIONSHIPS

It always seemed to me that attention, no matter what kind, is the highest form of generosity, particularly relevant in enhancing relationships. Giving myself in the form of attention goes beyond playing and working together with others in relationships. It means attending systematically to the psychological and emotional well-being of those I give attention to. Considerable work in developing a model for enhancing relationships, be they intimacy, marriage, family, friendships, or groups, has been expended by Guerney (1988). He felt that an understanding and practice of what he termed "behavior modes" could reduce the inevitable conflicts and miscommunications that are a part of all relationships. In addition, he emphasizes the ability to switch between modes as a means to help people be more versatile as communicators. Most people seem to adopt a pattern of communication that is role-related (introjected), rather than responding out of the immediate situations and circumstances. First, all people in relationships are responsible for how they feel, think and experience things. Second, people can differentiate their modes of communication by enacting them. Finally, the use of good listening skills provides an atmosphere and a mutual sensitivity to the communication process.

EXPRESSIVE MODE

In the expressive mode feelings, thoughts, ideas, perceptions or actions that are spontaneous are encouraged. The idea during this mode is for those in the relationships to be as open with each other as possible. As people become experts on everything they say and do, their expressions are absolutely argument-proof. However, Guerney is very emphatic that during this mode no one is to interpret or analyze other people's motives. As well, in this mode, people are to be specific and concrete about what they want to communicate by avoiding generalities. Being expressive does not mean being disrespectful. Expressiveness is being sincere and natural. What happens in the expressive mode is best described by Perls, Hefferline and Goodman (1951):

As one's orientation in the environment improves, as one's awareness of what one genuinely wants to do becomes clearer, as one makes approaches which are limited try-outs to see what will happen, gradually one's techniques for expression of previously blocked impulses develop also. They lose their primitive, terrifying aspect as one differentiates them and gives them a chance to catch up with the more grown-up parts of the personality (p. 150).

EMPATHIC RESPONDER MODE

The empathic responder mode is putting one's self into the position of others. The person wants to enter another's system and see things as another feels and thinks about a particular issue. The person strives to communicate acceptance through what is said and how it is said. The goal is to understand those blocks that inhibit spontaneity, responsibility and naturalness. In this mode having environmental contact awareness is primary to being an empathic responder. However, to be aware of others in their environment requires that people not only be aware of themselves, but be in tune with their surroundings. According to Passons (1975):

Interactions between the person and his environment, then, are dependent upon his awareness of that environment. The person who has a dull or fuzzy awareness of his environs will experience contact which is correspondingly unclear. Such contact renders the person less competent and unable to cope with the environment to meet his needs (p. 54-55).

FACILITATIVE MODE

The facilitative mode is essentially neutral. It can be someone outside of the relationship or group, although not necessarily. It is important that when in this mode, the person acts in a neutral capacity. The function in this mode is to assist in the communication process. In therapeutic situations the persona acts as a "facilitator," but in the group, it could be either the leader or one of the group members who takes on the role. The "facilitator" is a "referee" who not only helps the others move between modes, but also a person who uses specific skills to instruct in the use of more open communication. According to Guerney (1988), the facilitative mode has two purposes:

to help [people] teach each other relationship enhancement skills when they are in the group session, and to teach and encourage their family members to use the skills at home. The teaching skills that are taught to the participants as facilitators are essentially the same as those that the group leader must learn (p. 44).

MODE SWITCHING

The "heart" of Guerney's model of relationship enhancement is knowing when to switch modes. Communication is greatly enhanced if both "sides" know when to make the switch. The primary condition for making the switch is when both sides agree to switch or when the expresser judges the last statement of the responder to be accepting, which indicates understanding. This is a recognition that the person is finished and prepared to move to another level of communication. There is a mode switch when the expresser has shared all feelings, thoughts, or ideas about the issue. Now he or she waits for the responder to reply or share any objection or elaboration on some small point. The switch can either be suggested by the facilitator or initiated by either the expresser or responder through soliciting a response. The switch is designed to give everyone a chance to be expressive, respond and listen with empathy. There is constant airing and clarifying in a circular manner. It does not matter if there is repetition, for the process lasts as long as the "parties" wish to communicate. The facilitator remains objective, doesn't "side" with either person and keeps them in focus.

Figure 9.2: The Relationship Enhancement Model

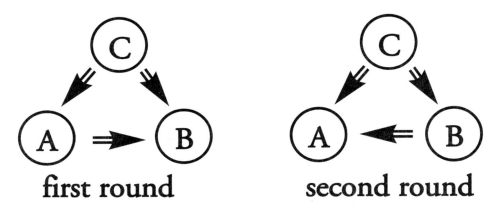

The relationship enhancement model operates in a manner similar to the "two-chair" method. What is different is that, rather than one person's moving from chair to chair based on conflicting parts of self, two people move from differing modes, experiencing how it feels from all sides of the conflict. Figure 9.2 demonstrates how the switching of modes enhances relationships. If, for example, there is a disagreement between **"person A"** and **"B,"** both will take turns in alternating modes until both feel that they have been heard. In the first round, **"person A,"** in the expressive mode, will share his feelings about the situation, while **"person B,"** in the empathic responder mode, actively listens. **"Person C,"** in the facilitator mode, keeps them on track and offers suggestions to **"A"** (e.g., "Can you experiment with 'I' statements") and to **"B"** (e.g., "Are you aware that you have been reflecting only concrete expressions?"). In the second round, **"B,"** in the expressive mode, shares her feelings, while **"A,"** in the empathic responder mode tries to understand how she feels. The process continues until a solution is found or until both feel they have been heard.

CONCLUSION

If we are to realize the richness, color, depth, and intensity of experience available to each of us, we must learn to tolerate the discontinuity of life's inevitable episodic interruptions. The return of constancy requires tolerance of change…an exorbitant emotional price is paid for a forced illusion of consistency (Kopp, 1986; p. 31).

All people depend upon relationships that are supportive and satisfying, not only from their peers, but also with their parents, children, friends, spouses and primary groups. Sometimes people have a difficult time asking for help, because self-reliance and autonomy are highly valued in Western society. Even in self-help, support and therapeutic groups asking for help or support is difficult for many people. Yet, surprisingly, social support is cited as the most compelling aspect of satisfying relationships. Many people can undertake activities with it that they might not be able to do without it. For example, Alcoholics Anonymous and a variety of self-help groups use it to motivate and support members to accomplish some common goal.

For me, building satisfactory relationships is a major focus along with personal development. In some ways these two go hand in hand. Of course, relationships are more than people building bridges to each other. They satisfy basic needs such as security, safety and belonging. Relationships help to affirm identity and are the source of people's greatest pleasure by heightening feelings of well-being. Not all relationships are the same, but are of different qualities and types. Some are based on shared interests like hobbies, while others are based on shared beliefs like church or political memberships. What people give and take in relationships depends upon the choices they make. They can use relationships to relive the past or they can grow through the experience. Thus, it is not just the fulfilling of needs but something else that goes beyond that. Relationships are mutual encounters that are based on trust, given into our hands to enjoy, to experience, to share and to give back when the time comes.

Therefore, relationships, like any other endeavors, need to be "treated like a garden." There are the inevitable cycle of the seasons (**change**), weeds (**conflicts**) and lack of fertilizers (**nourishment**). And like the seasons, relationships will change in a cyclical way: passion (**Spring**), fruition (**Summer**), decay and loss (**Fall**) and death (**Winter**). People simply have to live with the cycles and be positive, yet when problems come, as weeds do, the more attention and work devoted to dissipating them, the greater the chance that those **nasty pests** will not irrevocably destroy the **garden**. Every gardener knows that nourishment is the only way to have healthier plants in the same way relationships need to be **fed**, enhanced. And so I remember the words of Voltaire: "In the end, we have to learn to cultivate our own garden." What people have to do is decide whether they are going to involve themselves with others around them by continuing to build new relationships. The challenge is to learn to cope with the inevitable cycles of isolation and loneliness. Loneliness is a constant aspect of the human condition, for to love is to be lonely. While it is a constant feature of relationships, it does not have to kill people emotionally or physically, as it surely can. To be actively involved in human relationships is one of the most important conditions of good mental and physical health. To be understanding and help the significant others in the relationship cope, through support, acceptance and with the heart, is a necessity. There are no easy answers to enhancing relationships, because people have so many different needs. According to Kopp (1986):

The misery of human life is due to the ignorance that attributes substance to the illusion that is this life and to the attachment that leads us to try to hold on to the impermanent things of this life. To whatever extent we focus our longing on getting our own way, on doing to achieve results, on holding on to things beyond our control, to that extent we are trapped in needless suffering…suffering is not a tragedy. It is cosmic necessity…Karma is the concept that each act has consequences (p. 51).

Activities for use in a Group

1. **Birth Order:** The room is divided into four meeting areas, which are designated for the "only child," "oldest child," "middle child," and "youngest child" groups. Group members are to go to the group that best describes their birth order. People should share their experiences growing with those in their group and make a list that describes the experience (e.g., "received hand-me-downs," easy going, rebellious, etc.). The groups can then share their lists with the other groups. A discussion can follow that explores how perceived birth order affected achievement, interests and relationships. Allow enough time for sharing by everyone in the small groups and the discussion in the larger group.

2. **The Unsent Letter:** Most people have thoughts or feelings that are unsaid about "things" that have happened yesterday or 10 years before. Write a letter (that will **not** be sent) to either a mother, father, family member, wife, husband, girl friend, boy friend or best friend (e.g., "the letter is for you"). It doesn't matter if the person is alive, dead or far away. The contents of the letter should include something that has not been said that people feel is holding them back from becoming spontaneous and fully functioning adults (e.g., being freed from perceived control). After writing the letter, it should be put away for a week, reread and brought to the group. Those who **wish** to share their letters can do so, followed by supportive feedback. [Names should not be used in sharing the contents of the letters.] A discussion follows exploring relationship patterns, relationship styles, or perceptions and experiences from the unsent letter. An alternative procedure is for some of the letters to be role-played. Instead of sharing the letter by reading it, people can enact verbally saying what they said in the letter. Other group members can play any of the "letter recipients," who should be coached by the "letter writer" on how they might act. [Allow 15 minutes for reading a letter and feedback for each person. A role-play can take much longer depending on what is being communicated.]

CHAPTER TEN
THE ISSUE OF CROSS-CULTURAL
COMMUNICATION AND THE GROUP

Shallow understanding from people of good will is more frustrating than absolute misunderstanding from people of ill will. Martin Luther King, Jr.

In Kosinski's (1976) autobiographical novel, *The Painted Bird*, he fashioned the story around a metaphor that symbolized his experiences in occupied Poland during World War II. As a form of entertainment, a hermit would catch a bird and paint it in a colorful and bizarre manner. Later he would release the colorful bird and then watch as the bird joined the flock. The painted bird would fly to the flock seeking safety. At first the flock would be fearful of such a different kind of bird, but later something inexplicable would happen and the flock would reel in mid-flight and fly towards the painted bird. First they would try and scare it off, but the painted bird, not knowing that it was different, continued to try and join them. The flock's fear of the painted bird seems to turn to anger and they would attack the alien and peck it to death. The message is clear to me – to be different is dangerous. Even as a metaphor this tendency is a depressing and overpowering symbol of how those who are seen as different fare in society.

There always seem to be some in society who have been labeled outcasts, because they are different. I have often wondered about this phenomenon and why it is so. One of the aspects about group development that I have noticed is how people in some groups will exclude others. In my work with groups, I have seen people dismiss some people because of some difference or unusual personal aspect. In most cases it is a style or physical difference. When someone is rejected because they are different, I feel grief as I do when I think about the "painted bird." It is the image of pain in the "painted bird," which desperately wants to join the "flock," yet is rejected because it is different – alien. If the "painted bird" could talk, what would it say about its feelings? Imagine the incomprehensibility of one being rejected despite all that one did to be accepted. There must be an incredible feeling of pain in the outcast. Most people at some time during their childhood or as an adult have experienced the bias and prejudice of others who rejected them because they were a **new kid** in the neighborhood, fat or thin, tall or short, darker or lighter, disabled or wore glasses, had a accent or a different religion. Perhaps the word prejudice seems too hard, yet prejudice, no matter what its intensity, is still prejudice.

RATIONALE FOR THE TRANSPERSONAL
CROSS-CULTURAL APPROACH

The rationale for understanding the cross-cultural issues in group counseling is in part the growing multicultural factor in everyday life and the increasing smaller world brought about by more efficient communication and transportation systems. Broadcast reports of **ethnic** cleansing in the Former Yugoslavia fill the news on a daily basis. It brings up an important question about multiculturalism. Do societies that have a variety of ethnic backgrounds experience more ethnic conflict than those that are more homogeneous? Certainly, cultural differences in a counseling group is usually an issue in how the members communicate with each other. Even in the omnipresent O.J. Simpson murder case that dominated television news in 1994-1995, the race card or the issue of race was an important factor in how the case was prosecuted. North American society cannot close its eyes to the issue of culture, race and language. Finally, in a world where most of the world's people are not Westerners, Caucasian or Christian, a world that is growing smaller is not only enriching, but protective. All people must be aware that society, as a community, has the power to destroy our world through nuclear war and pollution. War has its genesis in society's disrespect for people who are different. People not only have to learn how to control their genocidal responses, but learn how to live in harmony with others and the environment. Everyone has heard the maxim: "If people do not learn the lessons from history, they are doomed to repeat them."

Every small group is really a microcosm of society. The transpersonal approach considers all individuals as a whole, recognizing each and every part of the being, as part of the cosmos. Regardless of one's language, race or culture, every community is interdependent with another. There is a universality in how people interact with each other in that the transpersonal approach seeks to develop the innermost source (essence) and the deeper nature of who we are, what are our roles and relationships with others. As a result, when society discriminates, marginalizes and ostracizes a person or people because they are different, then everyone suffers. Society has come a long way in being more accepting of different people, yet it has a long way to go in creating a society that respects diversity. Many cultural conflicts of the past have occurred because different people were pitted against each other. Take, for example, the experiences of the United States and Canada during their founding. Like people, they have reacted differently to similar situations. While both are more similar than different, they have developed differently historically. For example, after Sitting Bull and his warriors wiped out Lt.-Col. George Custer at the battle of the Little Bighorn, he fled to Canada. Upon his arrival with 5 000 supporters, he was met by Inspector James Morrow of the North West Mounted Police, who explained that they could stay only if they obeyed the laws of Canada. Sitting Bull remained in Canada for 25 years before returning to the U.S. in 1890, where he was killed at Wounded Knee, South Dakota. This does not mean that Canada has acted more honorably than the United States, only differently. In the United States the relationship between whites and Aboriginals was a war over the land, which the Aboriginals lost. In Canada most Indigenous people were regarded as a labor force, suppliers of fur and consumers. In fact, the Hudson's Bay Company's motto was: "Never shoot your customers" (Newman, 1989). The U.S. had 69 Indian wars in the 19th century, while Canada had only a few minor skirmishes. Tragically, Aboriginal people suffered similar fates under both jurisdictions. In the U.S. Aboriginals suffered as a result of conflict, whereas in Canada, Aboriginal people suffered through disease and abuse. But the conflict continues. In February 1973 the American Indian Movement challenged the U.S. government by seizing the village of Wounded Knee. Seventy-two days later they surrendered after drawing attention to Sioux grievances. In May l990, Mohawks blockaded the village of Oka, Quebec, to draw attention to land claims. After one death of a policeman, Aboriginals throughout North America took on greater militancy.

The world is changing very swiftly, where ethnic boundaries are changing. In the past, European cultural groups comprised the vast majority of new immigrants in North America, whereas today Asian groups top the list. According to the U.S. Census Bureau (2002), the Asian population of the U.S. increased by 79.5%, the Hispanic population increased by 38.7%, and the aboriginal population by 21.6%. It has also been estimated by the U.S. Bureau of Census that by the year 2030 the States of New York, Florida, Texas and California will have majority populations that are non-white. Already most urban areas of the United States are largely comprised of racial minorities. However, what is making a remarkable impact is the large number of immigrants settling in North American cities. This trend can already be seen in urban areas like New York, Los Angeles, Miami and Toronto where half the households are not native-born. The multicultural reality is evident in North American schools where large numbers of students do not come from the "founding" ethnic groups. However, it goes much deeper than accommodating the new multicultural fact, as is emphasized in Leviticus 19: 33-34 "love foreigners who live in your midst as yourselves…for you, too, were once foreigners."

THE HUMAN COST OF PREJUDICE

She didn't like Indians and talked in front of me as if I were deaf. She would tell her visitors that we were only good for two things – working and fucking, if someone could get us to do it. She made jokes about hot bucks and hot squaws and talked like we were animals in a barnyard (Campbell, 1979; p. 108).

The pain and anger in Maria Campbell's retelling of her experiences growing up typifies like nothing else the nature of prejudice. It is defined as "an unfavorable attitude toward an idea or people, which tends to be highly stereotyped, emotionally charged, and not easily changed by contrary information" (Poduska, l980; p. 234). It is not a natural response, but a learned one from societal norms; observations from parents, friends and neighbors. Not surprisingly, prejudice is not a result of constant negative experience with someone who is different, but through occasional contacts and reinforcers, such as a negative experience in a bar or an ethnic joke. It was the African-American activists Stokely Carmichael and Charles Hamilton (de Montigny, l972) who differentiated between individual racism and institutional racism. The most obvious forms of individual racism such as segregated schools, bars and neighborhoods, laws against interracial marriage, and job discrimination have all but disappeared. While laws have rectified many of these overt forms of racism, there are a number of attitudes that are ingrained in society that still reflect prejudice. For example, Allison Laurie's (l978) novel, *Imaginary Friends*, gives voice to prejudicial habits:

Every time one of them would talk about jewing down *the price of something, or say disparagingly that somebody was smart as a Jew I felt a twitch inside, as if they had pulled on a string tied around my small intestine. Like many WASPS…[they have] little sense of how prejudice feels when you're on the receiving end (p. 73).*

Institutional racism is reflected in a group or community attitude from habits or unwritten laws that discriminate against others. School curricula, for example, primarily reflect white heritage, "which is the history of Europeans on the North American continent" (de Montigny, 1972; p. 101). In the housing codes there are restrictions against ownership, clubs that exclude certain groups, and taboos against interracial sexual encounters. No group of people or government is totally free of racism. It exists in all countries and among all groups, including among white ethnic groups (Serbian and Croatian) and among black ethnic groups (Watutsi and Hutu).

The reason for discriminating against others is not really complex. However, when people are faced with evidence of prejudice, they tend to reject it; "I'm not prejudiced against Indians, but most of them just want to live on government assistance." There is of course some cognitive dissonance going on, because it is difficult to admit. It is easy for a society to judge situations in other nations as racist or oppressive, such as Apartheid in South Africa or the practices of the Israeli occupation forces on the West Bank. Some might respond and say "It's their fault that their culture has disintegrated." That is not an uncommon response, but it is a curious one, because it blames the victim for being victimized. Aboriginals are penalized for being culturally different, because of a system that neither allowed them citizenship nor allowed them to practice their language and culture. As democratic people, it is easy to overlook the glaring evidence of oppression, such as the scapegoating of those of Japanese descent during World War II. The government played into the hands of racists who had for years viewed Orientals as a threat to the West Coast. In 1942, 120 000 Japanese-Americans and 22 000 Japanese-Canadians living on the West Coast were forced by their respective governments to evacuate to harsh and isolated areas. At most 75% of these people were either born, raised, or naturalized citizens of the U.S. and Canada. The government admitted that there was not one report or incident of sabotage or anti-government activity on the part of ethnic Japanese to warrant this action. The internment of ethnic Japanese was simply an act of racial segregation. Kitagawa (1985) captures the hurt, anger and despair eloquently:

They do not think what it would mean to be ruthlessly, needlessly uprooted from a familiar home ground, from friends, and sent to a labor camp where most likely the decencies will be of the scantiest in spite of what is promised. They think we are cattle to be bred wherever it pleases our ill-wishers. They forget, or else it does not occur to them, that we have the same pride and self-respect as others…who can be hurt beyond repair. In short, they do not consider us as people, but as a nuisance to be rid of at the first opportunity (p. 181).

The dehumanization of "enemies" can clearly be observed when examining the emotional demonstrations of Iranians shouting "Down with America, the great Satanist" or the indifference of American leaders to the shooting down of the Iranian passenger airplane in 1989. In the Gulf War, American President George Bush constantly equated the Iraqi President, Saddam Hussein, with Hitler. It is clear that an "enemy" has to be dehumanized in order to sustain hate. This dehumanization is also evident in the paternalistic and stereotypical manner in which native Americans are viewed by North American society, which by and large sees them as "less responsible, shiftless, less intelligent and drunkards." Such an image certainly helps to alleviate any guilt we may feel for the condition of our native population and to justify our take over of their land. These rationalizations are really a facade for an attitude that Poduska (1980) says allows a group to "consider improper to cheat or lie to members of one's own race, but quite acceptable when directed towards another race" (p. 235). This exclusiveness of attitude is universal for most ethnic groups who practice discrimination.

In groups, a sense of exclusiveness is used to support superiority, for example, "This club is for people of good breeding." Even on a smaller scale, research evidence suggests that individuals need to maintain a sense of superiority over others (Higham, 1972). Sometimes people refer to this as "group pride," but why does pride hinge on a feeling of superiority? Pride in doing things well or in a feeling of solidarity with one's ethnic group are beneficial, but when it evolves into superiority, it is destructive. Perhaps people should remember the wisdom of Proverbs XVI:18; "pride goeth before destruction, and an haughty spirit before a fall." There also seems to be a relationship between people who have a disposition towards authoritarian and prejudicial attitudes. People who seem to be more prone to prejudice are overly submissive, feel inadequate or are overly suspicious. The philosopher Voltaire said that somehow the infinitely little have a pride infinitely great. While these examples demonstrate how racism is used to deprive foreigners of their human qualities, the process is the same in sexism, ageism, religious bigotry and homophobia. The kind of prejudice experienced by ethnic and racial minorities, intentional or unintentional, is the essence of the challenge of an open society. The scope of the issue associated with integrating the culturally different into society is reflected in a recent government report on the attitudes of North Americans, which asserted that 15% of people exhibit blatant racist attitudes, while another 20-25% have racist tendencies (*Maclean's*, 1989). These results are not comforting, but the insidious aspect of racism is the manner in which it is reinforced by society's institutions. In addition, people ought to be cognizant of the effect of prejudice on others. Chief Dan George (de Montigny, 1972) said:

> *Do you know what it is like to have your race belittled…? You don't know for you have never tasted its bitterness…It is like not caring about tomorrow for what does tomorrow matter? It is having a reserve that looks like a junk yard because the beauty in the soul is dead…Why should the soul express an external beauty that does not match it? It is like getting drunk for a few brief moments, an escape from the ugly reality and feeling a sense of importance. It is most of all like awaking next morning to the guilt of betrayal. For the alcohol did not fill the emptiness but only dug it deeper (pp. 162-163).*

THE CAUSES OF CONFLICT AND PREJUDICE

There has been a good deal of research examining what creates conflict and gives birth to prejudice. Is it a part of the human experience? Are people born feeling prejudice? Consider that when people compete for scarce resources, they will form groups to help them get ahead. Often, these groups are based on similarities within the group, which become the "in-group." Those who are different, become the "out-group." Differences could be based on a number of factors, including group norms, language, race, religion or even goals. On a smaller scale, even people who are very similar, but who have different goals, become frustrated with others whose goals are different. However, according to Baron, Kerr and Miller (1992), people become less aggressive, and thus, more cooperative, reducing prejudice, if goals are mutual. In fact, friendships develop and differences, regardless of color or race, are minimized when goals are mutual. Generally, people from one group are more generous or over compensate for those in their group, while conversely, under compensate for those from another group. In other words, people from one cultural group will be more forgiving for those in their group, while being less forgiving for those from another group. For some reason, there is a tendency to exaggerated similarities within group, while exaggerating differences with other groups. People react to each other based on their group membership. Since they do not know the other people, viewing the others as "face less" and interchangeable is common. It is easy to not see the others in the same light as themselves and differences become exaggerated (e.g., they don't value human life).

Is it human nature to try and simplify the environment, despite the fact that most day-to-day interactions among people are positive? A good question. One bias is that the members of one group will "naturally" see themselves as acting responsibly, but see the other group as being irresponsible. That is, according to Baron, Kerr and Miller (1992), a factor of the human experience. Also, for whatever reason, there is a tendency to promote negative views about others who are distinct and different. Thus, the bias is reinforced with each "negative" experience one has. In the end, one's attitude becomes more rigid, ideological and part of one's cultural norm. Which means, for example, if you have attitudes that are negative towards the police, you will see examples that reinforce this bias more often than if you don't have the bias. There is also the "reciprocity" rule or the "tit for tat" idea, in which if one "wrong" is done, you retaliate, causing a series of behaviors that reinforce one's belief. Social comparison is also a factor in creating a sense of anger, prejudice and aggression. It seems one group is "getting away with something," which creates anger. The fact is, when all things are equal, people get along. And finally, if there is a "triggering" event, people react on the basis of emotion and do something that has a chain of events that can last for decades. Consider the Kosovo situation in which Serbs are fighting Albanians. Historical "wrongs" were enmeshed within the differing groups, attitudes about each other. The Turkish invasion during the 16th century is played out in the 21st century. People adapted to these attitudes and made them part of their behavior, thus creating another myth that reinforces prejudice.

THE INFLUENCE OF CULTURE

Culture is a human necessity, a way of life, because it is the way people establish and maintain a relationship with their environment. As people of understanding interact with those who

Table 10.1: Cultural Value Preferences		
Preferences	Majority (white)	Aboriginal
Nature	Control	Harmony
Time	Future	Past
Relations	Individual	Collateral
Activities	Doing	Being/becoming
Humanity	Good/bad	Good

are culturally different, they must explore the socialization forces that affect behavior, values and language. All differences can be seen by being aware of differences as seen in the cultural value preferences between majority (white) and aboriginal groups in Table 10.1:

For example, notice the dichotomy between the two: control and good/bad versus harmony and good. The stress of control over nature produces a feeling of seeing other people in terms of good and bad, which corresponds exactly with how humanity ought to be treated. If they are not good or consistent with societal norms, then they need to be controlled. Taken one step further, people with this attitude also have to control those urges that they feel within themselves. Even in a relatively homogeneous population, there are cultural differences that are easier to be aware of in others than in self. According to many social scientists, culture is both a critical aspect of a person's lifestyle and an essential element of human behavior. While the clothes people wear and the attitudes they voice may reflect the dominant culture they are in, it is their cultural background that shapes their thinking and feelings, such as reflected in the analogy, "blood is thicker than water." There are strong indicators that cultural conditioning reflects how people communicate with others (Pedersen, Draguns, Lonner & Trimble, 2002).

The biological force is the most universal, because no matter who people are or where they are from, they are human beings. Some biological differences include age, shape, size, color, and gender. With the exception of a few cases, these differences are not going to change nor can they be manipulated. In all societies these biological differences have reflected attitudes relating to behavior and how people will interact with others. For example, someone large is viewed as powerful and possibly aggressive; as a result more deference is shown towards that person. A big and muscular person may be seen as a brute, or a lean and slight person as effeminate, or someone with rough features as unrefined. The cultural norms that dictate reactions to biological differences are infinite, with each group having its own interpretation about the meaning of biological characteristics; for example, plumpness is healthy in some groups. All cultures are affected psychologically by various influences on the group. People in the group are continuously subjected to pressures to conform to the norms of the group. In this respect the personality to a large extent is formed through these group norms. The family, as a primary socializing agent, is responsible for the basic values that people exhibit. This is particularly true in Asian cultural values of respect for authority, traditions and learning (Gaw, 1982; Vernon, 1982). In addition, exposure to significant others, relatives, friends, teachers and peers enhances the repertoire for the inculcation of the social mores and behaviors of the entire culture. This is obvious when a comparison is made between the way people feel, think and act in different cultures. For example, Sue & Sue (1990) found the following differences in communication styles between Whites and Aboriginals. [It should be noted that this is a generalization and does not affect individual differences among and within groups.]

Whites: Verbal oriented, adherence to time schedules, have long range goals, individual centered, emotional expressiveness, cause and effect oriented, open and intimate, rational and thinking, comfortable with ambiguity, and a clear distinction between physical and mental well-being.

Aboriginal: Action oriented; different time perspective; immediate short-range goals; intuitive and nonverbal; satisfy present needs; cooperative and not competitive; comfortable with concrete, tangible and structured approaches; uses folk or supernatural explanations.

Behavior may also be affected by ideology or the characteristic manner of thinking (e.g., assertions, theories or aims). The ideological foundation of an individual's culture will to a large degree have impact on their behavior. It is from such foundations that people derive religious, social and political beliefs that direct and govern their behavior. Being born in a certain culture causes the display of certain characteristics that are behaviorally right for that culture. In other words, people have a cultural or national way of thinking and seeing the world, which is reflected in language, values and beliefs. The ideological differences can be observed in the behavior of group members who come from different ethnic groups. For example, in one recent group, a person who was of Native American decent (Cree) put more emphasis on group responsibility and another member who was of French-Irish decent, was a great believer in individual responsibility.

The ideology of a nation dictates to people certain attitudes, beliefs and ways of thinking that frame their existence. Their beliefs about life, death and marriage determine the behavior between others. People tend to respond to their environment in consistent manners that are dictated by the attitudes in their society. Minorities have partially adopted the ideology of the dominant culture in order to survive, but the adoption may or may never be fully ingrained in their personality. According to Buriel and Vasquez (1982), even after three generations of living in the United States, Mexican-American adolescents modified their basic cultural characteristics in only a few small ways. Yet these minorities are not totally similar to the cultures of their origin. For example, an African-American or Arab-American will have more in common with each other than with people in Nigeria or Iraq. This creates a strain for visible minorities who can feel that they are "neither here nor there." It is also true that some beliefs and values are more affected by gender than cultural differences (e.g., men have more freedom of choice regardless of culture). Ecological forces refer to how the environment has influenced culture and behavior. Someone born on a isolated island may develop a different view of the world than someone born on a large continent. Climate, prosperity and population density, like terrain can also play a role in developing a distinct cultural norm. People born in a highly populated area may have to be more assertive, because that is the only way to survive, while someone born in a non-dense area can be more relaxed and quiet.

LANGUAGE AND CLASS-BOUND VARIABLES

As a primary form of communication, language is of great importance to people in groups. Language patterns are reflective of people's culture or subculture (Vontress, 1996). Even when people are speaking the same language, there is a great deal of misunderstanding, because of individual differences. Therefore, it becomes easy to understand or imagine why people who do not have the same cultural and linguistic background misunderstand each other. An inaccurate picture of another person's issue formed on verbal responses, or in some cases, what is not said, produces real conflict. There are certain phrases in a language that are either uninterpretable, or if translated literally, do not convey the many dimensions the phrase encompasses.

Some words, phrases or how the word is used have negative meanings, which is acceptable to some from one cultural group, but not others. For example, many high school and professional sports teams have names and logos like the "Braves," "Indians" or "Redskins" and so on. First Nations communities have protested on the basis that it reinforces negative stereotypes, uses their images and icons in a disrespectful manner and trivializes their ethnic background. A recent incident in greater Vancouver created controversy when the Musquem name, Spull'u'kwuks, was proposed. The problem was that authorities felt that the name, meaning "place of bubbling waters," could be used in a negative way because there was the potential for rhyming using the "F word" or "sucks" or so on. The response from the Musquem first was "it was their language…and…it should be celebrated, not made the subject of humor" (*Vancouver Sun*, Feb. 8, 2000; p. A1).

Even non-verbal gestures are relatively different from culture to culture. Touching of the head is considered an insult by many Buddhists, while for Westerns the touching of the head is a friendly gesture. Native Americans were offended when home crowds at the World Series in Atlanta used a tomahawk gesture to cheer on their baseball team. Eye contact and personal space also differ from culture to culture. In North America people are taught that eye contact communicates closeness and attention, while lack of eye contact communicates dislike, disinterest or disrespect. Degrees of eye contact might have different implications for different cultures. Sue and Sue (1990) declare that white middle class people, when speaking to others, look away (eye avoidance) approximately 50% of the time. When Whites listen, however, they make eye contact with the speaker over 80% of the time. But Blacks make more eye contact when speaking and infrequent eye contact when listening. This reinforces the idea that we should be careful when we try to attribute reasons for the amount of eye contact encountered. The amount of eye contact is not necessarily related to aggressiveness, shyness or inattentiveness, but rather it depends on cultural patterns. Each culture seems to develop specific and complex processes of communicating non-verbal messages (chroemics).

Physical distance (proxemics) is another cultural variable that is different in other cultures. In past groups I have noticed that there is a marked difference between some of the Canadian anglophone and francophone members. The francophones touched more in conversation and kissed those they felt close to. Anglophones touch far less and rarely kiss both cheeks in greeting. In my travels in Asia, the differences between Asians and Westerners in regards to distance and touching were polar opposites. For example, when I first went to live in the Philippines, a colleague from the school where I taught took me to a dance. The whole night he held my hand and I danced mostly with other men. In this society, women, like men, danced mostly with each other and held each other's hands. Heterosexual Westerns tend to touch more and be physically demonstrative with the opposite sex than with the same sex.

According to Sue and Sue (1990), socio-economic factors affect the way people communicate and interact. For example, groups with members from lower economic and educational levels appear to prefer more concrete and structured activities. These people may actually want direct advice or at least, a chance to talk in terms of concreteness and tangibles. In general, those in the lower socio-economic sphere report that counseling activities are "all talk and no action." In addition, people from different cultures may be unfamiliar with the dynamics of groups, which may be incongruent with what they expected. This inexperience may in turn block their progress in counseling groups. It is therefore essential that leaders of groups be aware of and be able to identify the values of differing group members. Members of the group are projecting their cultural values when they emphasize verbal, behavioral and emotional expressiveness as goals for growth. These characteristics of group process may be quite aversive to people of different cultures. Reluctance to self-disclose does not necessarily mean group members are intentionally preventing feelings, thoughts and beliefs from being released. Rather, it could be that group members were reared in a culture which places high priority on restraint of expressing feelings and thoughts, particularly to strangers. If members of groups misinterpret the reasons behind the reluctance to self-disclose, the results may be a block of communication, severe anxiety and extreme discomfort.

Another important culture-bound value is the family relationship. Westerners, as a cultural group, tend to center on personal responsibility, and decisions are made based on the good of the individual. If a personal decision is made by a someone from a culture that emphasizes family involvement in decision making, the family might block attempts to achieve individual goals. An example of this type of belief was stated by one woman I worked with who said: "whenever I disagreed with my mother, it seemed to her that I was questioning her character." In her family, the authority of the parents is paramount and not to be questioned by the child. When she made a decision without consulting anyone, her mother felt hurt and angry. She loved her mother, but felt a desire to assert her individuality and this produced a great deal of conflicting feelings.

BLOCKS TO CROSS-CULTURAL COMMUNICATION

I have observed in groups of culturally diverse people that there are a number of stumbling blocks in communication that can occur more frequently than others. To be sensitive and aware of another person's frame of reference is elementary, but it is particularly significant with those of diverse cultural backgrounds. In some ways the following list of stumbling blocks applies to almost any group, but they are especially intense in cross-cultural groups.

Language: Vocabulary, syntax, idioms, slang and dialects can create problems of understanding. The problem is the tenacity with which people cling to "the" meaning of a word or phrase in the new language, regardless of the connotation or the context.

Non-verbal Areas: People from different cultures employ different non-verbal sensory words. They see, hear, feel and smell only that which has some meaning or importance for them. They abstract whatever fits into their personal world of recognition, and then they interpret it through the frame of reference of their own culture.

Tendency to Evaluate: Some people from different cultures need to approve or disapprove the statements and actions of others, rather than to try and completely comprehend the thoughts and feelings expressed. This bias prevents the open-minded attention needed to look at the attitudes and behavior patterns from the others' frame of reference. This is heightened when feelings and emotions are deeply involved. Yet this is the time when listening with understanding is most needed. Group members need to examine values that are negatively evaluative towards those who are different.

High Anxiety: This stumbling block is not distinct, but underlies and compounds the others. Its presence is very common because of uncertainties present when people function in a foreign language where the normal flow of verbal and non-verbal interaction cannot be sustained. There is a sense of threat by the unknown knowledge, experience, and evaluation of others, thus bringing the potential for scrutiny and rejection by the self. There is the added tension of having to cope with the differing pace, climate and culture. Self-esteem is often intolerably undermined unless people employ defenses such as withdrawal into their reference group or into themselves, thus screening out or misperceiving stimuli, rationalizing, overcompensating or showing hostility.

THE CROSS-CULTURAL COMMUNICATION

The group experience can enhance personal power and improve communication skills. What group members say and do can either promote or reduce their credibility and attractiveness in a group. The style of self-disclosure, their perceived trustworthiness and their motivation for change emphasizes a few of the variables. In this regard, the cultural emphasis of group members is not on how effective they really are, but on how their credibility, attractiveness, and trustworthiness are perceived. In a study evaluating the effects of group member's race on perceived effectiveness in communication, people were affected by the person's race and ethnic background either in a negative or positive way (Lee, Sutton, France & Uhlemann, 1983). Some people may tend to be more indulgent or forgiving to people of other cultural backgrounds (Uhlemann, Lee & France, 1988).

In leadership and helping situations, evidence suggests that, for culturally different people, the issue of expertise is raised more often than whether the person has a similar cultural or racial background (Sue & Sue, 1990). This suggests that group members will have to be more sensitive and develop strategies that will attenuate or, perhaps, eliminate this effect, particularly if the effect is negative. In other words, using appropriate communication skills and strategies that are congruent with a person's values is more important than race or ethnic background. There seems to be no particular communication strategy which proves to be more successful with a specific population. Yet the approach used by group members from the majority culture must be consistent with the those from other cultures' life-styles, along with flexibility for individual differences within a culture; not all people with a similar cultural background behave the same. On the other hand, equal treatment in communication may be discriminatory treatment. If group members proceed on the basis that everyone is the same without recognizing differences, this may have a negative effect. If all people could be more aware and appreciate their different parts, perhaps they would be more accepting of cultural differences in others. Expansion of alternative ways of behaving comes down to being able to move and use the strengths from each part, for example male and female; Hispanic and French; white and black.

Obviously, group members who are seen as trustworthy will be more influential than those who are not. Self-disclosure by culturally different group members is very much related to the trustworthiness of group members. Perhaps group members may have to prove themselves trustworthy; this task may require more openness. This may not be as easy as it sounds, since some culturally different people may view self-disclosure as a negative and undignified way to behave. The question of whether group members can be successful with those from a different race or culture depends on the following variables: race, religion, kind of issue, group members' experiences and style, and the degree of ethnic consciousness. In other words, what differences there are between people in groups can be mediated or mitigated. There is no denying, however, that ethnic similarity does increase the probability of identification between group members from other cultural backgrounds.

SENSITIZING THE GROUP: THE FRANSAUD MODEL

The broad emphasis of the FRANSAUD sensitivity model is to create awareness, acceptance and sensitivity to cultural and personal differences (France & Persaud, 1991). While the model focuses on the culturally different, it works exceedingly well with other types of differences, such as male – female, heterosexual – homosexual and so on. The model consists of five phases of interaction and three distinct roles that are shifted in phases two through four. Each of the phases can last from five to ten minutes and can be adjusted depending on the purpose of the training, the level of awareness and the ethnic make-up of the group. There should be three groups composed of two to eight people (Figure 10.2).

Preparation Phase: In this phase the group brainstorms and makes two lists of those differences between the two target ethnic or social groups to whom they wish to become more sensitive. The aim in this phase is for the group to generate as many possible differences that can exacerbate conflict and decrease effective communication. In addition, the brainstorming offers the group a chance to accept and appreciate how differences make each ethnic group unique. For example, if the group explores differences between an ethnic minority of Native Indian extraction and a majority individual of English extraction, the list of differences might include the following: Indian people are oriented towards the land, have strong bonds to the group and use folk or supernatural explanations and those of English descent may be individualistic, espouse liberal values and use concrete and specific language.

Figure 10.2: FRANSAUD Model

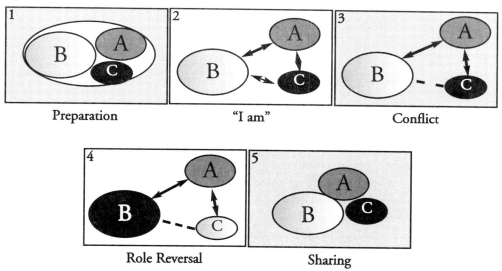

Preparation   "I am"   Conflict

Role Reversal   Sharing

"I Am" Phase: In this phase each of the three groups choose one of the roles to play. The three roles are:

A: referees whose role is to offer feedback, keep the others on task and keep time;

B: the minority group who role play the target ethnic group;

C: the majority group who role play the dominant ethnic group.

The aim of this phase is to provide "**B**" and "**C**" with the opportunity to share, uninterrupted, those qualities that make them different and unique. People in both "**B**" and "**C**" groups must use "I statements," listen carefully to the others and refrain from making any comparisons.

Following the presentations by "**B**" and "**C**" groups, "**A**" group offers feedback to "**B**" and "**C**" groups focusing on their unique qualities, verbal and non-verbal communication styles. If "**A**" offers any incorrect or confusing feedback, "**B**" and "**C**" can respond to "**A**." The purpose of the feedback is to provide "**B**" and "**C**" with a neutral "picture" of how each group comes across and reinforces what makes each different and unique.

Conflict Phase: In this phase the group decides on an issue that can be a source of conflict. The conflict should be one that is normal and minor in nature (e.g., playing music very loudly) that has the potential of bringing ethnic differences into the forefront. Once sides are taken on the issue, either "**B**" or "**C**" group confront the other group with the conflict. For example, "**C**" may complain to "**B**" about their inability to concentrate because of the loud music, while "**B**" may respond that there is a party in progress in their apartment and it is impossible to dance without loud music. Both sides are encouraged to "ham it up" to ensure that they each have a concretely different position in the dispute. Both "**B**" and "**C**" groups can use any argument or stereotype to amplify the situation and make sure that their side is heard (e.g., loud thumping noises made by dancers and inconsiderateness of loud music). At the end of the interchange, "**A**" group restates the problem concretely and offers feedback to "**B**" and "**C**," once again focusing on verbal and non-verbal communication. In restating the problem, it is important for "**A**" group to zero in on the special differences and share their perception of how these difference fuel the conflict. Also, "**A**" could draw out from "**B**" and "**C**" groups what feelings surfaced for them and what resulting negative conclusions, if any, they came to about the others. This is crucial because these conclusions may be reinforced and used to inaccurately label others of the same cultural group encountered in the future.

Role Reversal Phase: In the role reversal phase the disagreement is renewed between "**B**" and "**C**" groups, but this time they exchange roles, the minority group becomes the majority group and the majority group becomes the minority group. As the dispute continues, "**A**" as the referees can at various times ask those in "**B**" and "**C**" group to exchange roles once again. In addition, "**A**" group should ask both groups, after various interchanges, to share their feelings. It is vital that "**A**" group help "**B**" and "**C**" groups be more sensitive to the dynamics of the dispute by focusing their attention to the messages that each are communicating. For example, the "**A's**" could ask the "**B's**" and "**C's**" to reverse roles after someone in the group uses an ethnic difference in the dispute (e.g. the music is loud because we have rhythm).

Sharing Phase: In this phase all the participants from the groups share their feelings with each other during the various phases, paying attention to comparing how it was to experience the other point of view. In addition, they explore how stereotyping is used in their everyday communication and what they can do to be more culturally sensitive. This phase begins with "**A**" group providing feedback to "**B**" and "**C**" groups on their verbal and non-verbal communication styles, pointing out the insensitivity and possible biases made during the roles that they played. Particular attention in the sensitivity training process focuses on how those in the majority ethnic group can be more aware of communication that enhances, blocks, or reduces defensiveness and can be made more effective. Hopefully in this phase, cultural awareness of self and others may lay a beginning foundation for compassion and genuine respect for each other.

To be culturally skilled, people need to be knowledgeable about minority groups with whom they might work. In addition, they have to be flexible with their communication skills and strategies. It does not mean only being sensitive to the values and beliefs of those from other cultures, but also being in tune with their own values and beliefs and how they might affect those from other cultures. People should not ignore that differences do exist, because to ignore these cultural differences might be to deny the uniqueness of others and their place in society. Whatever communication approach is used, it has to be appropriate to the minority person's culture. Basic skills such as tone of voice, rate of speech, eye contact and body language must be used to different degrees depending on the culture. The same goes for listening skills, such as self-disclosure, reflection of feelings and meaning, and questioning. Concreteness, confrontations, respect, warmth, immediacy and genuineness should also be adjusted in relation to those from other cultures and cultural background.

ENHANCING CROSS CULTURAL COMMUNICATION

During the Apartheid period in South Africa, Tucker (1988) eloquently described the situation for most white South Africans in choosing sides in the black-white confrontation. She called it co-opting. Co-option refers to pressure on them to take sides, not because they choose to, but because the force to do something is so great on one side or the other that just doing nothing brings about the choice. In the beginning, the temptation for people is:

first to acquiesce, then to be co-opted, and finally to collaborate is as subtle as the proverbial serpent...[but] the essence of life and the challenge in most societies is the realization that everything we do is relevant and the consistent resistance to co-opting influences on any side other than the advancement of the causes of justice, peace, and a better society – remembering also that peace isn't the absence of conflict, but the assertion of justice (p. A5).

It was not very easy for those whites to be "out there" fighting Apartheid, when the pressure was so strong to sit on the sidelines. However, there are a number of principles that can be used to enhance cross-cultural communication.

Self-Acceptance: A fundamental principal of Gestalt is the owning of all parts of the self-including differing polarities, as well as affective, cognitive, physical, and cultural parts. Some educators emphasize that people should be taught to de-emphasize what is different and replace it with emphasis on similarities (Friesen, 1985), yet I wonder if it is not better to glorify the differences. If people can accept that differences make life interesting and add spice, then when they are faced with people who are different, they will celebrate those differences.

Openness: The idea that one approach to life or one life style is the only one fosters not only an us verses them attitude, but creates a sense of superiority and ignorance. During the Cold War period when Ronald Reagan visited the Soviet Union for the first time, many people were surprised that he professed Mikhail Gorbachev to be a nice fellow. All talk of the **evil empire** was forgotten as he stated that Russians are wonderful people, who loved their children. Many of the issues of the Cold War were still unchanged, yet once Ronald Reagan had a chance to visit and see how the Russians lived, it was more difficult to see them as different from Americans. Despite openness to new ideas, people in North America are quite ignorant of other world literature, customs and languages. The more people foster the notion that there are more explanations or sides to an issue, the less the chance that there will be fear of the unknown and ignorance. Fear, after all, is the culprit behind racism.

Encouragement of Cultural Identity: All people want acceptance, yet they are bound by their cultural roots and this affects how they are perceived by others. I believe that if people have a strong cultural identity, they will have a greater sense of control about their lives. Sue and Sue (1990) suggest that counselors' cultural identity can adversely affect how they interact with clients by reinforcing negative self-esteem if the client is having some dissonance about their cultural development. Thus, understanding of cultural identity of majority and minority people can help in enhancing interpersonal communication. The differences and similarities between majority and minority identity development (Sue & Sue, 1990) can be seen in the following manner:

Stage 1 – Conformity: For minorities, this stage is characterized by preference for the dominant culture, self hate, negative beliefs about their own culture and positive beliefs about the dominant culture. For the white majority this stage is characterized by viewing their culture as superior and others as "primitive"; that they are not racist and that minority inferiority is justified by discriminatory acts.

Stage two – Dissonance: For minorities, this stage is characterized by confusion, conflict and changing of accepted beliefs and values. For the white majority, this stage is characterized by anger, guilt and shame when experiences conflict with humanistic values or when there is recognition of the role of whites in perpetuating racism in North America.

Stage three – Resistance and immersion: Minorities experience this stage as one characterized by rejection of the dominant culture, mistrust, anger, endorsement of minority views and the desire to combat oppression. For the white majority this stage is characterized by the recognition of racism, self-hatred and a desire to identify with minorities.

Stage four – Introspection: For minorities this stage is characterized by conflict, but now there is questioning of primary loyalty and responsibility to one's own cultural group. For the white majority this stage is characterized by the knowledge that one's identity is not determined by another ethnic group, thus leading to a reduction of guilt at being white.

Stage five – Synergy or integrative awareness: For minorities and the white majority this stage is characterized by awareness of personal identity, a sense of cultural self-fulfillment, greater sense of control and flexibility, and an objective outlook on the dominant culture. As people mature they move from stage to stage until they achieve self-acceptance. Problems occur when they become stuck at stages one to three.

Self Pride: The kind of pride reflected in the comments of Jessie Jackson during the 1988 Presidential election exemplify the sense of pride in personal accomplishments: "I was born in the slums and yet my name will go in nomination because the slums were not born in me…and they are not born in you." Everyone has a part to play and something to contribute. Acknowledging even small accomplishments goes a long way in instilling pride. According to Passons (1975) the reinforcement of pride can be achieved by encouraging group members to become more aware of personal power. For example, the changing of language patterns that reflect confluence, "we" or "it" to more assertive patterns, "I" or "me." Rather than using language that is qualified, such as "I guess" or "maybe," group members can use more powerful non-hedging language, "I want" or "I need."

Tolerant: Accepting others does not have to mean losing personal uniqueness. I have noticed how incredulous people are when they hear their voices or see themselves on tape. They have a kind of constructed self-image, a reflection of society's view of them. Sometimes those stereotyped attitudes are accurate, but mostly they are not. The group can help individual members accept a more realistic self-image by providing feedback and reinforcing self-discoveries. Groups need to be more accepting of individual differences, allowing all traits, dispositions, and types. It is vital to remember that differences within cultures also exist.

TONGLEN: A CROSS-CULTURAL METHOD OF DEEP LISTENING

Tonglen is a meditation technique that is practiced widely by Tibetan Buddhists; it is a way of listening at a deep level. One meditates on what is heard. The purpose of this meditation practice is to allow one to make a deeper connection with another person, yet be introspective to one's processes. The value of being able to be open at a deep level with another and at the same time be able to see one's biases and prejudices is important in communicating across cultures. Sanford (2000) describes the:

word Tonglen [which] means sending and taking. It allows us to begin the work of getting in touch with something deeply embedded within ourselves that also lies within those we come into contact with. It is thought that Tonglen helps to awaken our compassion and to give us a deeper view of the reality of others (p. 34).

As a practice of being aware and seeing, Tonglen reflects the core of Transpersonal counselling practice. That is, one must be open continually to "self examination," address communication "roadblocks," be accepting of one's self and be open to the phenomenon of relating to life in all forms. Perhaps this Chinese proverb succinctly voices this idea: "heaven is over your head and in your heart." Now, notice the importance of the word "compassion" in Sanford's description of Tonglen. Buddha taught that compassion is wanting to relieve others of their suffering, thus "…compassion is the antidote to hate" (Brazier, 1995; p. 93). To say it another way, when one loves another person, the desire is that the loved one experiences only good things. The opposite of love is greed, since one only wants to fulfill personal desires. Therefore, "...love is the antidote to greed" (Brazier, 1995; p. 93). In a multicultural society, one must accept differences, honor the differences, and be compassionate. To paraphrase Jesus, "love one another."

Step One involves sitting quietly and opening one's heart to those loved ones that touch something inside. This could be a family member or even a favorite pet. As one thinks of and feels the goodness of this person or pet, one experiences the joy of appreciating and loving at a deep level. Perhaps an experience comes to mind or even the facial features, such as a smile, come from the image. In a counselling situation, the same feelings can happen when one listens at a deep level.

Step Two is regulating one's breathing and imagining the "power" of taking all of the sadness, pain or anger into oneself. As one breathes in, one absorbs all the negative feelings, but as one breathes out, what comes out is cool, light and pure. In essence, one takes on the "burden" of another, then releases it with the exact opposite. Sanford (2000) asks:

How frightening might it feel to walk into a store and have all eyes turn on you simply because your skin is brown? Your face feels hot and flushed and your stomach is in a knot...You feel small and insignificant, and it seems that a swirling darkness surrounds you (pp. 35-36).

That experience or similar ones have a texture that is very deep and full of emotion. So when you hear this description, you hold the pain in, but then breathe out the opposite so that the feeling of "being different" has a acceptance and love in it. This is a deep form of listening.

Step Three is "holding" these thoughts of brightness about the pain of another and feeling deep compassion. Then allow the mind to expand the brightness of the situation without judging or diagnosing. Sanford (2000) goes on to say that one ought to allow:

taking their story into every part of our being, letting it touch and move us. As we are touched and moved, we also let ourselves be with whatever might feel uncomfortable for us...we see and feel their discomfort; we are like them, we do not know what to do, we cannot fix it or make it go away. All we can do is continue to sit there, being totally with them, sending and taking (p. 36).

Step Four is accepting the feelings of the other and making a connection between what was heard and everyone down through the ages who has suffered in the manner being expressed. What should happen is a feeling of being human, making mistakes, being hurt, and knowing that is part of the human experience. What should be generated is a deep sense of compassion that "grows" as one makes human connections with another being. The symbolism of taking on the "pain" and feeling it deeply, while at the same time connecting it to one's self, takes the helper beyond just hearing what was said. According to Sanford (2000): "Tonglen does not allow us to just sit there and reflect, we become engaged with our client on the human level, sharing in what we as humans have in common...Tonglen keeps us in the room, firmly planted in our chair, listening and feeling with great curiosity and sincere caring" (p. 36).

Conclusion

The desire for self-fulfillment is a universal one. I am reminded of the main character in Ralph Ellison's (1972) novel, *The Invisible Man*, who is caught between his inner desire to fulfill himself and the outward reality of the prejudice towards an African-American in a white society. In his decision he suddenly achieves resolution:

I'm shaking off the old skin and I'll leave it here in the hole. I'm...no less visible without it, but coming out nevertheless. It's damn well time. Even hibernation can be overdone, come to think of it. Perhaps that's my greatest social crime. I've over-stayed my hibernation, since there's a possibility that even an invisible man has a socially responsible role to play (p. 568).

Ellison's character, in addition to the resolution of who he was, discovered a greater sense of awareness and appreciation of being caught between cultures. He began to see his power, some of which was culturally derived and ultimately served as a basis for focusing him. This is an example of the importance of all people exploring their culture and the alternative strategies they might use as a means for better understanding the role that culture plays in the communication process. In essence, people, like nations, have a tendency to look at the outside world from their own perspective. This is natural and perhaps, necessary, for all people are prisoners of a particular space and time. A global view of the group is that everyone is a stranger, just as everyone is a neighbor. In fact at one time all of us were foreigners, outsiders, and perhaps even outcasts. In essence, the challenge for group members is to be more culturally sensitive, yet maintain a sense of their own cultural identity.

According to Friesen (l985) "...the idea of eliminating the constant orientation of always wanting to do something for someone, may be at the very foundation of the new multiculturalism" (p. 162). In a global sense this attitude of wanting to impose what one thinks is right can result in a great deal of pain and suffering. Graham Greene's (1965) novel, *The Quiet American*, typifies the destructive power of the insensitive altruistic person who desires to be helpful by promoting democracy in Vietnam. The novel seems sadly to foreshadow later events, yet the tragedy of the Vietnam War, like so many others, is that the desire to do "good" results in the opposite. In the small arena of the group, the desire on the part of some members to help others usually ends in the same way. Not surprisingly, both the overeager helper and the acquiescent helpee end up being hurt and humiliated. To come to the rescue or to protect another person robs that person of power and ultimately of responsibility.

There are a number of different aspects of the cross-cultural experience, but rather than seeing the differences as isolated parts, the Transpersonal approach explores the pattern of the relationship in the components. It is an effective way to get a complete picture of the cross-cultural experience, because if people concentrate on the personal parts, they are likely to be misled. The metaphor of the blind men who felt only one part of an animal ending with a distorted picture of what an elephant is reinforces this idea. One, feeling the trunk, said that the elephant is "like a snake...long...thin...who is able to slither about." Another feeling the leg said, "it is like a tree...straight...solid and strong," while another who felt the tail said, "it is like a pig, only larger." All were right, but because they did not examine the relationships of the parts, they misunderstood the whole.

A multicultural orientation has tremendous implications for group development, because communication is an interpersonal interaction where every group member must be able to understand appropriately and correctly both verbal and nonverbal messages. Cross-cultural communication is concerned with the present or developmental issues with the added element of cultural differences. In an ever-shrinking world, all people are engaged in intercultural communication at an accelerating rate. If the interaction is to be significant, and if cross-cultural communication and multiculturalism are to foster increased understanding and cooperation, then people must be aware of the factors that may affect the communication process. They must avoid potential stumbling blocks that might hinder effective communication. It is axiomatic to suggest that the success of cross-cultural communication may well depend on the attitudes and philosophies people adopt. The way people in a group relate to each other is often a reflection of their philosophy towards life and themselves.

Group members can be models for multicultural ideals and for encouraging others to be culturally sensitive. Group members, like all people, are capable of change from day to day and from situation to situation. The very role of the people who enter into a group are offered the unique opportunity to act as agents of change. After all, things are changing daily. Many attitudes and behaviors are deeply ingrained in people's psyches, and many of them are subject to ethnocentrism. Group members, by role definition, may play the key pivotal role in enhancing the development of multiculturalism. It has been suggested that when people are in another country, they should adapt their ways and try to be like the dominant culture in every aspect. It is possible to understand the culture, but it may not be possible to act exactly like the people of that other culture. People cannot easily drop their own thought processes and adopt those which may not even be desirable. People must be true to themselves, but with sincerity and a willingness to understand others, people can be more accepting of differences. The changes required of people are neither simple nor easy. They require that people possess a willingness to communicate, empathy toward foreign and alien cultures, tolerance of views that differ from their own, and that they develop a more open approach to communication with others from different cultural groups. If people have the resolve to adapt their behaviors and attitudes with the desire to overcome ethnocentrism, they may begin to know the feelings of exhilaration that come when they have made contact with those from other cultures far removed from their own sphere of experience. This willingness to reach out, risk, learn and experience others is a challenge for everyone. Black Elk said: "Have you learned lessons only of those who admired you, and were tender with you, and stood aside for you? Have you not learned great lessons from those who braced themselves against you, and disputed the passage with you?" (Neihardt, 1988; p. 79).

ACTIVITIES TO FOCUS THE GROUP

1. **The Volunteers:** Five volunteers from the large group role play "volunteers" who have been sent by their country to a "third world" nation to help. The remainder of the group will role-

play "villagers" from a small rural village. The "volunteers" are given a task to perform in the village (who are unaware) that will help them (e.g., build a well with fresh water). The "volunteers" leave the room to plan their strategy for convincing the villagers that they need this "development." The "villager" should brainstorm some "customs" that are unique to them (e.g., always agree when someone smiles or say maybe, when they mean no). Since neither speaks very much of the others' language, both groups are aware that there might be misunderstandings. Allow 20 minutes for the "volunteers" to "work" with the "villagers." A discussion of the events, feelings, misunderstandings, helping strategies and differences should follow.

2. **Being Unique:** Take a survey of the differences that exist in the group, writing the list on the chalkboard. Five items from the list should be chosen for exploration. Some differences might be: sex, body shape, age, hair color, ethnic background and so on. From the list, people enter a group and develop a profile for that group. They should develop a list of unique aspects for themselves. For example, a women's group might choose these items that make them unique: clothes, posture, more conscious of defending themselves, etc. A men's group might decide on sports interest, non-verbal language, and hairstyle. Next, each group observes the other group and builds a profile of characteristics that make that group unique. Taking turns, each group shares their profile about the other group. After the group has been given feedback, they share their profile about themselves. A discussion of the different perceptions should follow. Allow 30 minutes for discussion of each of the items.

CHAPTER ELEVEN
RECONNECTING TO THE ENVIRONMENT:
<u>EMBRACING THE NATURAL WORLD</u>

The realization that we are basically the same human beings, who seek happiness and try to avoid suffering, is very helpful in developing a sense of brotherhood and sisterhood. As warm feeling of love and compassion for others, this, in turn, is essential if we are to survive in this ever-shrinking world we live in. For if we each selfishly pursue only what we believe to be our own interest, without caring about the needs of others, we not only may end up harming others, but also ourselves. (Dalai Lama, 1996; p. 38)

The idea that one can survive without any connections is a fallacy. Humans do need each other and they also need to be connected with the natural world. The world is shrinking and we cannot live according to self-interests. We need to see ourselves in a world where connections are natural, healthy and transcendent. The assumption of the transpersonal approach is that connecting with others and the environment is not only natural, but also a means of finding ourselves. In short, connecting, particularly with nature, has a healing effect. Consider that when one is in a natural environment, such as a garden or a park, the tempo slows us down. It basically takes us out of our daily routines, and reminds us that we live on a planet that we share with others. Nature has a power for healing; the way we experience reality is influenced by concepts we have or we do not have in our heads. More interestingly, by having a view of life in which one sees oneself on a continuum with the environment, one can accept the relationships of people, animals, things and nature, and then healing becomes an everyday event.

Connections with others have always been important to emotional, spiritual, intellectual and physical well-being. Damaged relationships contribute to a sense of disconnection, thus continually practicing compassion and forgiveness is necessary. According to the transpersonal approach, trying to understand the actions of others and forgiving them internally or externally is the most important way of connecting to others. In fact, the quality of our interactions with fellow humans, pets and nature has a powerful influence on our own states of mind, body and spirit. Perhaps we need to take advantage of the cultural aesthetic resources of new places, and learn what is available in places around us. As we do this, we need to keep in mind that we can help ourselves by being of service to other life forms. Service means first respecting, followed by supporting, and then giving your time and energy to improve the welfare of others and the environment. And since giving is an important aspect of the transpersonal approach, it is many times more personally beneficial if it is done without expectations or any return; whether of spiritual merit, admiration or a sense of being virtuous. For example, this can be done by being generous with those less fortunate, keeping our distance from a small wild animal, picking up garbage on the beach.

Oh God, I never listen to the cry of animals, or the quivering of trees, or the murmur of water, or the song of birds, or the rustling wind, or the crashing thunder, without feeling them to be an evidence of Thy unity, and a proof that there is nothing like unto Thee (Nicholson, 1984; p. 12).

THE PRICE OF BEING DISCONNECTED

Individualism has been honored as an important virtue to achieve by the majority in North America, yet when people do not have a partner, mate, lover, friends and pets, work or hobbies that connect them, life seems worthless. Many people pride themselves on their independence and habitually distance themselves from others. Some may indulge in isolation as a defensive strategy possibly developed in reaction to painful emotional experiences in childhood. If solitude is not balanced by connectedness, it is often productive of illness, first on the spiritual level, then on the mental/emotional level, and finally crystallizing into the physical structure of the body. Others may never have learned how to connect meaningfully to anyone or anything beyond themselves. Therefore, it is fundamental to build connections beyond the self. As human beings we are highly social communal creatures; when we lack those connections, we suffer. However, as people involve themselves in groups, they are challenged by people with different ideas or communication styles. Many people distance themselves in a variety of ways, but the most profound way is at the inner level. When this happens, the suffering it brings can be all more intense when it occurs in the midst of a life apparently full of other people. Western, industrialized societies have substituted the nuclear family for the extended family, glorify individualism and independence and foster a spirit of every person for him or herself in many of their endeavors. This creates a deep, unsatisfied longing in people that may be at the root of much of our social malaise - the prevalence of addiction to drugs that numb feelings, for example, the growth of gangs among the youth, and rising violence everywhere.

Human relationships are complex, often marked by upheavals that have an impact on the environment and our surroundings. The pain of separation and estrangement often balances the joy of intimate connections. To take the first step towards reconciliation is difficult, requiring maturity and skill; it can also put people more in contact with their higher self. By forgiving, people can lessen their own emotional pain and experience increased inner peace, no matter what the response of the other person is. This idea is reflect in the words of Black Elk, who reminds us to not be thankful only to those who helped us along the path, but even those that blocked the path. Thus, we need to be reminded that developing meaningful connections with humanity, with our family and friends, neighbors, pets, plants and the earth, is the only "road" in transcending our selfish impulses. Weil (1997) coined the term "Disconnection Syndrome" to reflect the "fallout" from being self-contained and independent. He goes on to stress that men are more likely than women to suffer from the Disconnection Syndrome. The answer from transpersonal perspective lies in reconnecting, which from an elemental standpoint is eloquently expressed in the words of Black Elk: "The earth does not belong to us, we belong to it!"

CONNECTING WITH NATURE

In *Walden, or Life in the Woods*, Thoreau (1970) showed that connecting with nature could heal the mind and provide people with a sense of meaning, because by going to the forest, one could "live deliberately, to feel only the essential facts of life, to see if…[one]…could not learn what it had to teach, and not when…[one]…came to die, discover that…[one]…had not lived" (p. 25). From earliest time, going out and experiencing nature, particularly through what First Nations people call the Vision Quest, has been a common feature of humankind (Deloria, 1995). Interest in nature and its healing effects continues to grow as the world sees that the well being of the planet is directly linked to the well being of humankind. Cohen (1994) eloquently states the view that humanity has always been part of the environment's consciousness; that as the earth has evolved, so have people, and so the earth responds as an animate being if treated with respect. What reinforces the value of nature is the importance many people put in how nature helps them reinforce their values (France, 1997; McCormick, 1997).

In North America the "frontier spirit" which helped European settlers develop the land into cities and farms, has given rise to an attitude of dominance over the land. It is not surprising that these early European settlers felt that way, for the land was dangerous and hostile to the European way of life. What these people built in North America is what is now the "bread basket" of the world. The USA and Canada export food around the world with a productivity that is matched by few countries, but there has been a cost. Cultural values coming out of this "conquering" of the land have affected Eurocentric North American views on a variety of cultural value preferences. Sue and Sue (1990) describe the dichotomy between the Eurocentric North American majority culture and Indigenous cultures, in which the majority views nature in terms of control and relationships in terms of individual concerns versus indigenous cultures' emphasis on harmony with nature and emphasis on collateral relationships. As people become aware of the connection between individual health and a healthy environment, more and more people, regardless of their ethnic backgrounds, are accepting the indigenous view. The stress of control over nature produces a feeling of seeing other people in terms of good and bad, which corresponds exactly with how humanity ought to be treated (Cohen, 1994; Glendinning, 1994; McCormick, 1997). If they are not good or consistent with societal norms, then they need to be controlled. Taken one step further, people with this attitude also have to control those urges that they feel within themselves. Thus, control becomes a major issue for society and the individual. The way to control nature, it is thought, is not to leave it to its natural cycle, but to "bend" it to the will of humanity.

EARTHWEEK: A DIARY OF THE PLANET (Newman, September 24, 2000): "A troop of furious monkeys in India's northeastern state of Assam brought traffic to a standstill after a baby monkey was hit by a car on a busy street. At least 100 of the animals quickly mobilized in the city of Tezpur and encircled the young injured primate. Rajib Saikia, a government information officer, said, "Its hind legs were crushed and it lay listless on the road. In no time, more than 100 monkeys descended on the street from all directions and blocked off traffic." The angry monkeys kept traffic at bay for more than a half hour as they tried to care for the infant. A local shopkeeper said: "It was very emotional....some of them massaged its legs. Finally, they left the scene carrying the injured baby with them." (p. A2).

DOES THE CONNECTION WITH NATURE ENHANCE VALUES AND WELL BEING?

There are a number of positive results that I have observed in the work I have done with group members or individual clients and through the reports of others using nature in counseling. Glendinning (1994) states that democracy is encouraged by one's contact with the environment. Does this connection bring one closer to values? Perhaps love and a sense of belongingness, as a basic of values, can be reinforced as a means to overcoming evil and mean spiritedness by humankind. I believe that being open to nature makes one more respectful to others and increases an attitude that nature is not to be controlled, but is a part of the connection with others. As such, being connected makes one more sensitive to differences. Perhaps, according to McGaa (1990), we need to "be turning ourselves against the darkness around us so that we can be free enough to get a glimpse of the higher plane. But when we become spirit, we will learn immeasurably more than we can comprehend now" (p.103).

VALUES CLARIFICATION AND INCREASING PERSONAL AWARENESS

It is my belief that when people's awareness is sharpened, people are more in touch with their senses, emotions, thoughts and perceptions. As such, they are more capable of clarifying and getting in touch with their values. People are after all, the sum total of all of their parts and, by being in touch with their values, they can become more responsible and integrated. In other words, people are not their different parts, but are a whole. Thus, the self cannot be examined without looking at the context; looking at the whole, which is being in touch with nature. If people are to live an effective life, they must be open to experiencing things in their immediate environment. The acceptance of responsibility and the recognition of their powers occur through awareness. To this end, being aware is focusing on what is there and what is not there. What is not there is also a part of what is there. For example, a silence occurring in a conversation is just as important as our verbal and nonverbal communication. To suggest another example, as people go outside and into the forest, they can not only see what is in view, yet there exists life beyond that which cannot be seen nor even be sensed; yet it is there. There is nothing in nature that is empty. When using nature to increase awareness, I ask people to experience all aspects of their environment, including all the temperature changes, sounds, tactile awareness, and movement around them, just to name a few. It requires discipline to be observant, immediate and open, yet not to try to make things happen. When one does, one tends to open all of one's perceptions to the sensations around. What group members or individuals expressed is that they can increase their ability to be aware of other aspects in their life at home and work.

Two aspects of this process of awareness assist people in understanding and putting into perspective what is happening. The first aspect is that it allows them to keep up to date with themselves, because at any given time they know how they feel and what they think. Meaning is not something that has to be processed before they can act for themselves as people who are acting as themselves – authentic. The second aspect is the interaction people have with their environment. Boundaries become clear, and they react more spontaneously to their environment. They see more, experience more and are aware of more in their surroundings. If people try to split feelings and thoughts, they will find that it is difficult, if not impossible. Nature orients rhythms between awareness and the frequent interruptions that exist in day-to- day activities in the environment. In essence they start to think and analyze, and cannot be completely aware of what is going on around them. To attend simultaneously to two things with the same degree of awareness is difficult, because they will always miss out on something. If people can just be aware of what is happening and let it flow, they will experience it, not in parts, but as a whole.

INCREASING SELF ESTEEM

It has been well documented both anecdotally and quantitatively that being out and involved in nature, whether passively observing it (e.g., sitting in a park) or actively involved in action-oriented activities (e.g., hiking or gardening) brings about a sense of well-being. I believe that there are two important aspects of this phenomenon, which are described as "natural rhythms" that reflect life in general (e.g., like one's heartbeat). And, I believe that the sense of being connected to something greater provides a sense of empowerment. Part of the sense of well being is the peacefulness of nature compared to most people's stressful existence in the home and at work. Nature to most people seems somehow slower and thus more relaxed, producing a mirror effect in people. When people sit in a natural setting, they physically and psychologically slow down, producing a positive sense of well being. Also, there is a sense of being connected to something that is greater than oneself, that one's existence is part of a "larger self."

STRESS REDUCTION

"As I worked in my garden, I felt a sense of relief from the stress of the day," reported one of the participants. This response to some involvement in a nature-oriented activity is typical of the kind of responses that are reported by a variety of people (Cammack, 1996; McCormick, 1997; France, 1997). Going for a walk or sitting in a park or going camping seems to help people defocus their attention from the stress in the home and at work. It is the natural rhythm in nature that is quite the opposite of the kind of drive and energy that push people to the point of increased stress. Thus, by re-focusing on these natural rhythms, people can slow down and move at the same speed as everything around them.

TWO EXAMPLES OF USING NATURE WITH COUNSELING

Person 1: A. is an adolescent who was referred to counseling because she was "feeling restless, unhappy and lonely." A. confessed that she is selfish and rebellious and went on to say that she had few friends. In fact, she said she was not able to maintain steady relationships with people of her age. A. was "invited" by the counselor to go out for a "walk of life" in nature. She was asked to attend to everything she saw, heard and felt while she walked. In the following session, the counselor asked A. these questions: What did Nature "tell" you? What did you sense while you were out? How do you feel after the experience? A. reported that on this "walk of life," she had felt vulnerable, more aware of her senses, and attentive of her surroundings. She gave these responses to the counselor's questions: "Nature 'spoke' to me and I felt I was part of it; I knew I was not alone and I felt that I belong to the Earth as the trees and the other creatures." To the second question regarding what she had sensed, A. replied: " I touched the trees and some little animals, I heard the sound of falling leaves and hungry squirrels; I smelled the fresh unpolluted air and felt it go down to my lungs." To the last question, A. responded that she felt "empowered" by the experience and stated that in the future, to put things in perspective and to give herself "space" she would go for walks in nature and ensure that she was always in touch with her environment.

Person 2: R. is a professional male who came to counseling reporting extreme stress related to his work. According to R., the stress of a changing workplace put stress on his professional life and work life. In discussing his issues, R. reported dissatisfaction with the verbal interaction between himself and the therapist. Because of R.'s interest in the out of doors, he was encouraged to go out into nature, but to keep a journal and undertake a series of structured activities during his hike. Afterwards, he returned to face-to-face counseling with the therapist, where the experience was processed using his journal. The following are some excerpts from his journal that the therapist used to focus the face-to-face encounters. "I want to become more authentic and natural and that means moving away from what is polite and ritualistic. Again, I drank greedily from the pristine stream. The water had such a sparkle and clearness that, when I drank from it, it became like "champagne." My taste buds are used to chlorinated water and were surprised by fresh, natural water…The message is clear, I want to live life in a respectful way, because that is nature's way."

IMPLICATIONS FOR GROUP PROCESSES

As demonstrated in the two cases presented, nature can be extremely useful not only as a metaphor for well-being and healing, but also as an arena or environment for personal change and clarification of values. Glendinning (1994) feels that the first step to healing using nature is very similar to that used by Alcoholics Anonymous – admitting that people are powerless and our lives are unmanageable. This creates a sense of being able to direct the next steps in re-connecting to nature, by not denying the trauma, which "is individual…is social…is historic" (p. 126). Once healing begins, people must be open, focused and alert to the wealth hidden within and between the environment and ourselves. A different and more natural way of thinking of oneself, that Cohen calls (1994), "old brain" thinking. According to Cohen (1994) people involved in activities in which they must look for a supportive connection in nature report that "they feel intelligent, connected and contributory (community), responsibility, powerful (self), respect for other beings (spiritual)" (p. 11). Thus, people work towards reuniting with the wilderness in nature and in the unconscious self in a holistic way.

How does one reconnect to nature? As was demonstrated with both clients in the case studies, they went out to become more aware of nature. This occurs by sharpening the senses, by listening to or witnessing the natural phenomena that occur in nature. As the clients became more aware, they gained a greater sense of safety and trust with their environment, which translated to them by accepting their place in the ecological process. The recounting of the hike by client # 2 assisted him in finding a connecting and meaning in his life. When people start to tell their stories, parts of the trauma come up, while parts will be suppressed. The task is re-defining oneself in relation to the environment, so they can come into an alignment with the wholeness of the universe. In essence, people participate in a natural setting in nature, telling while working through their pain and fragmentation (e.g., metaphorically tearing down the chain link fence and restoring the land to the wilderness). Coincidentally, a whole new discipline has evolved that reflects the physical, spiritual and psychological worlds - Ecopsychology. This new discipline emphasizes that scientific models be integrated with ancient philosophies, non-Western knowledge of indigenous cultures and spiritual teachings.

"Heal the earth, heal each other" (an Ojibway prayer) personifies the healing process. People need to develop an unfamiliar sense of reintegration of themselves by trying to live in harmony rather than trying to maintain a sense of control in all aspects of life. When this happens, paralysis and despair can be transformed to a sense of passion and connectedness (with the Earth). The primal self, reflected by many Indigenous and Asian people, can be re-discovered. Healing, through active participation with nature, becomes possible once denial is dissipated (Deloria, 1995).

SEARCH FOR MEANING: CONNECTING TO WHOLENESS

Everything is one. All things in the physical world originate in the spiritual world. Success depends upon effective communion between the two realities. When our people seek spiritual power, call "7uusimch" in our language, they visit a sacred pool where they use special medicines (Out of the Mist, Treasures of the Nuu-chah-nulth chiefs, Royal BC Museum, 2000).

One of the most effective ways that the natural world can be utilized in group processes is as a means of finding personal meaning. The central element of personal meaning is found in a person's worldview, which according to Ibrahim (1991) consists of the presupposition and assumptions that we hold about the world, while Horner and Vandersluis (1981) maintained that because worldviews are culturally based variables, they influence the relationship between two people and they way in which they interact. Our worldview directly affects and mediates our belief system, assumptions, modes of problem-solving, decision-making and conflict resolution (Ibrahim, 1991).

Everything that a person experiences, including trauma, socio-economic and personal situation, ethnic background, gender and spirituality, influences worldview; and what motives people in life is finding meaning in the world. Consider other theories about what motivates people put forth by a variety of psychologists. Sigmund Freud said it is personal gratification. Alfred Adler said it is the achievement of power. Carl Rogers said it is the need to ascend beyond what we are. Viktor Frankl said that it is the desire for meaning that motivates us. Interestingly, this theory of Frankl's comes the closest to the traditional view of First Nations people. Why? It is Frankl's emphasis on spirituality that sets it apart from the other theories. Essentially, Frankl said that everyone is motivated to find meaning in life. The will to meaning is not based on faith, but on fact. The search for meaning in life seemed to be a powerful motivating force, which all people experience regardless of their circumstances. Nietzsche expressed it this way: "He who has a **why** to live for can bear with almost any **how**." However, Frankl did not envision the circular nature that First Nations people have in their dealing with each other, their environment, the spirits and all living things. Meaning is not just a question between one and some power beyond the self, but the connectedness of all things. Meaning is derived from realizing one's connectedness. Consider the words of Black Elk:

> When I was standing on the highest mountain of them all and around about beneath me was the whole hoop of the world. And while I stood there I saw more than I can tell and I understand more than I saw; for I was seeing in a sacred manner the shapes of all the things in the spirit, and the shape of all shapes as they must live together like one being. And I saw that the sacred hoop of my people was one of many hoops that made one circle, wide as daylight and as starlight, and in the center grew one mighty flowering tree to shelter all the children of one mother and one father. And I saw that it was holy [Black Elk Speaks, Neihardt, 1988; p. 133].

When Black Elk spoke these words fifty years ago, he was expressing the most fundamental belief of all First Nations people of North America: The idea that all living things are related – brothers and sisters. The philosophical essence of this idea can be expressed in one word – respect. Respect for the land, respect for the animals, respect for the plants, respect for other people and finally, respect for the self. This is the essential ingredient for living life. According to Russell Means (Smoley, 1992), the development of respect among First Nations people can be compared to the idea of love for Christians and enlightenment for Buddhists. The notion of respect is that humankind is not separate from any other thing in the world, but just another living, breathing creature among many. Thus, the environment, as a brother or sister, is not something to be exploited or harmed, but is to be considered an integral part of everyone. When this does not exist, then nature is separate. As a separate entity, nature becomes like a machine – something to be mastered – something to be exploited.

Disease is caused when people are out of harmony with the land. First Nations people believe that humankind has a choice of two roads: the "road" to technology or the "road" to spirituality. What is the meaning of one's self without the whole – without the connectedness of all living things. To First Nations people, humankind has custodianship of the environment. For European settlers in North America, the land was something to conquer and subdue. The land is something that is a part of each person. This idea of the connectedness with the land is eloquently expressed by Carl Jung (Smoley, 1992), who said: "children born there [a foreign land] would inherit the wrong ancestor – spirits who dwell in the trees, the rocks, and the water of that country....that would mean the spirit of the Indian gets at the [person] from within and without" (p. 85).

The "road" to technology, strongly associated with European civilization, has led society to pollution and a "scorched Earth policy." The "road" to spirituality, while less scientific, reflects traditional native people's beliefs; the belief that the environment is reflected in how natives relate to God. There is one Supreme Being, the Great Spirit, and there are also spirits of locality, spirits of natural forces and animal spirits. All have distinct powers. In some ways the animal powers are greater that the Great Spirit. In fact, the Great Spirit is rarely invoked, while the spirits under the Great Spirit are routinely involved. Among the Salish people, "almost every action in life is centered around the Spirit Power" (Ashwell, 1989; p. 68). One spirit is not greater than another, but they are omnipresent, in Mother Earth, Father Sky and the four directions. God is everywhere. The spirit is in the trees, in the universe, everywhere in life. The Nuu-chah-nulth believe that "the ocean is our front yard and the mountains are our backyard" (Out of the Mist, Treasures of the Nuu-chah-nulth chiefs, Royal BC Museum, 2000). Thus, our beliefs about the world that shape how we view ourselves and how we interact with others relate to our world view, interconnectedness, balance and spirituality. Among First Nations people are beliefs about the world that shape how they view themselves and how they interact with majority culture. Among the most important are the worldview, interconnectedness, balance and spirituality. An understanding of these beliefs can help the educator work more effectively with First Nations people.

WORLD VIEW

According to the transpersonal approach, it is important to understand differing world views and be able to incorporate them into a helping and learning framework. Despite the naive wish to be seen as 'value free', the Western educational system makes inherent assumptions. These assumptions are rooted in philosophical views of human nature and people's place in the world. Our worldview affects our belief systems, decision making, assumptions and modes of problem solving. People understand worldview as the way in which individuals relate to things and each other. Thus, worldview and personal value systems will vary according to a person's ethnic background, levels of acculturation, experiences and other personal characteristics. McKenzie (1996) says that, "when united in a conversation in which understandings and worldviews are shared, we stand a better chance of reducing the limitations and narrowness of our existing worldviews"

(p. 123). But how, then, can educators assess worldview? Ibrahim (1984) has developed a scale for assessing worldview across cultures based on a scheme developed by Kluckhohn and Strodtbeck (1961). The common themes are: 1) People – nature orientation, 2) Time orientation, 3) Activity orientation, 4) Relational orientation and 5) Modality of human nature. An examination of these schemes would further our understanding of any culture or individual's worldview. For example, aboriginal people attempt to live in harmony with nature, whereas non-aboriginals attempt to control nature to meet the needs of the people. Time orientation also differs. According to Sue and Sue (1990), time orientation in traditional native culture has always been towards the present, as compared with the western tendency to focus on the future. In terms of activity, native culture honors "becoming" rather than the idea that one has to produce. In regards to relationships, native culture stresses a collective view of the world rather than an individualistic one. Finally, the view of humanity is that it is neither good or bad, as in a western view. This is often confusing to those who have not shared this perspective.

BALANCE

The Medicine Wheel is a ready-made model of the First Nations Worldview. The Medicine Wheel shows the separate entities of the emotional, mental, spiritual and physical part of man as being equal and part of a larger whole. This reinforces the concept of interconnectedness and the lesson that one part cannot be the center, but must instead learn to work in harmony with all of the other parts. The medicine wheel represents the balance that exists between all things. Aboriginal people seek out balance and equilibrium. The First Nations worldview as represented by the medicine wheel has balance as one of the basic tenets of healthy living. The medicine wheel represents the all-encompassing cycle of creation, from birth to death, in which balance between animal, nature, humanity and spirits co-exist.

Traditional medicine incorporates the physical, social, psychological and spiritual being. It is difficult to isolate any one aspect, because these parts exist in a harmonious balance. Aboriginal people become ill when they live life in an unbalanced way (Medicine Eagle, 1989). Balance is essential for the First Nations person, because the world itself is seen as a balance among transcendental forces, human beings and the natural environment (Hammerschlag, 1988).

INTERCONNECTEDNESS

The idea of interconnectedness is reflected in the ecopyschology approach that closely matches the aboriginal view and the transpersonal approach. Consider that the role of healing in traditional aboriginal society or other nature oriented societies has been not only to reaffirm cultural values, but also to consider the individual in the context of the community (Trimble & Hayes, 1984; Lafromboise et al., 1990). The goal of the transpersonal approach is not to strengthen a person's ego, but to encourage people to transcend the ego by considering themselves as imbedded in and expressive of the community. This means that the individual considers him or herself in relationship to nature and all living things. Transpersonal helping and learning approaches, unlike other psychological approaches, usually involve more than just the teacher/counsellor and the student/client. All aspects of the person's relations and the environment need to be part of the healing process, because everything is interconnected. For example, when one wants to lose weight, the successful dieter needs to not only change what and how much is eaten, but be involved in physical exercise. To become a better human being, one not only needs to change one's attitude, but how one interacts with others and the environment. In short, "Life is made up of interdependent parts…dominated by a network of interdependent passions (complexes). When one changes, they all change. When a new one comes into being, all the others have to adapt. When one is given up, all are weakened" (Brazier, 1995; p. 127).

SPIRITUALITY

From a transpersonal perspective, developing a spiritual dimension or "higher states of consciousness" is vital in working with individuals, organizations, communities and cultures. One of the processes of accomplishing this is through "decentering" or moving people away from identification with the individual ego, or "smaller self," to identification with that which encompasses self, culture and environment, or "larger self." The assumption is that this helps people become more responsible for the self and to become responsible and aware of the impact on the environment and society. The spiritual dimension is closely aligned with moral development, which in turn becomes "wholeness" and the development of a higher state of consciousness. In turn, taking care of the self is the same as taking care of other life forms and increases social responsibility. Thus social responsibility becomes closely associated with self-responsibility. The result is a greater sense that taking care of the environment or nature is fundamental in well being.

In pre-industrialized European societies and in traditional First Nations beliefs, mental health was much more spiritual and holistic than present day western psychology would suggest. Consider that many traditional aboriginal healing ceremonies emphasize the spiritual aspect of healing. It is to the Great Spirit, perceived everywhere, that the Indian turns to in times of need (Dugan, 1985). Different ceremonies stress the need for reconnection with one's spirituality. In the Vision Quest ceremony, the First Nations person makes contact with his/her spiritual identity. The Medicine Wheel symbolized by the circle represents spiritual ties that bind human beings to each other and to the natural world (Bell, 1991). This spirituality or holiness is seen as the essence of healing for Native people. This means to manifest wholeness in spirit and to bring it into our bodies, our families, our communities, and our world (Medicine Eagle, 1989). There is a oneness in the First Nations life philosophy that is reflected in the Salish belief in the creation of the world. Ashwell (1989) emphasizes that the Salish believe that the human soul is characterized by that:

indestructible spark, which once departed went to the sunset, where it remained forever, that which was left behind was the earthly body and its shadows these shadows held a threepart existence and remained on the earthly scene with either good or evil intent, depending on the characteristic of the person in life (p.60).

This continuity of life is often represented by the circle, which appears in many of the symbols used in First Nations ceremonies (e.g., the drum, the Ghost Dance, etc). According to Smoley (1992), this idea of spiritual power is conceptualized in "si si wiss, which means sacred breath or sacred life" (p. 85). When humanity respects everything, there is love of all things, because people can see God in the trees, animals and rocks. Everything has experienced the same sacred breath. Because when there is respect, which is the essence of the healing spirits, then people feel "love of God in our hearts" (Smoley, 1992; p. 85).

USING NATURE IN REFLECTION OF MEANING

The major function of reflection of meaning is to explore what an event or experience means. One experience may mean something very different to different people. Therefore, the facilitator focuses on deeply felt thoughts, feelings and behaviors in an experience as it relates to life in general. One of the positive effects of being outdoors is that as a metaphor it expands the possibilities in problem solving. Clean air invigorates and provides a sense of being connected to something greater than one's body and mind. Much of this grows in a subliminal way. For example, walking in a natural setting, our steps become slower and more relaxed. It is easier to flow with the natural surroundings and begin to identify with the grass, flowers and trees. Most importantly, there are lessons to be learned about living and one can begin to reflect on the meaning of life. According to Ivey (1983), reflection on meaning has some secondary functions: facilitating a person's exploration of values and goals in life and an understanding of the deeper aspects of a person's experience.

The natural world offers healing by just being in it. When watching a stream or river, one becomes aware of the way waters flows around rocks, constantly changing course. Nothing obstructs water. A facilitator can instruct the group to go out into nature and just be there for a period of time. Later, the facilitator can engage the group in a dialogue about the experience with an open ended question (e.g. "What did you see?" or "How did you feel when you were outside?"). Any answer given could be followed with a meaning probe or question (e.g., "What does that mean to you?"). The facilitator would then begin to substitute "you feel" for "you mean." This might be followed by paraphrasing the main idea that is being discussed. The facilitator tries to identify the meaning through values and needs. If, for example, a person is talking about being unable to do the things he or she wants to do; the facilitator might do the following:

PERSON: "My job and the people I am involved with at my work place are basically nice, but I don't feel any great connection there."

FACILITATOR: "Tell me the types of things that you enjoy most?"

PERSON: "Well…I love working in my garden."

FACILITATOR: "How do you feel after working in the garden?"

PERSON: "It brings me a sense of peace and makes me feel like I'm doing something positive."

FACILITATOR: "What are these positive things that bring you peace?"

PERSON: "Well, it is fabulous when the flowers I planted and nurtured bloom in the spring. The color and beauty of these flowers are indescribable."

FACILITATOR: "Helping in the growing process gives you gives you a sense of being involved in something greater than just making work. You are nurturing. Nurturing means a lot to you."

PERSON: "Yes, it is a great feeling. Do you know what I mean?"

FACILITATOR: "I think so. In what way is your gardening important to you?

PERSON: "I felt complete . . ."

FACILITATOR: "Being in your garden means being nurturing and sense of being a part of something greater than yourself. In fact nurturing means a lot to you."

PERSON: "Yes, that is why we are here, aren't we?"

FACILITATOR: "Let us say that your work is a garden. In what other ways can you be more nurturing at work?"

PERSON: "Well, gardening is watering and providing for the plants. Humm...so at work, I could give to those around me things that help them...such as positive comments for work well done..."

The facilitator first focused on an activity that the person felt positive about. After reflecting the feeling and subsequently paraphrasing what was said, the facilitator focused on what made that activity a positive experience (e.g., nurturing). Nurturing came out as providing a sense of meaning, which was then redirected towards the work place. In other words, the meaning is arrived at by the connectedness to all, including our emotions, minds, bodies and spirits. One, with everyone and everything around us. The effective facilitator could use the exploration of the meaning of the gardening to get at the strengths the person possessed (e.g., what was meaningful). This exploration could reveal to the person that those needs and reinforcement of values that the work meant could be achieved through other means. The focus of the facilitator would then be on identifying how this might be accomplished.

A THERAPEUTIC PROCESS

To gain insight one must be a "seeker" in a completely open and sincere manner, and embrace the lessons that abound in nature. For example, Henry David Thoreau (1970) reminds us that: "every part of nature teaches that the passing away of one life is the making of room for another. The oak dies down to the ground, leaving within its rind a virgin mould, which will impart a vigorous life to an infant forest" (p. 52). Thus we begin to see ourselves in relationship to everything around us and become purified by transcending individual desires (e.g., to become innocent). There are three stages of this process: the illumination of the cultural self, identifying qualities of self and developing positive self-essence (the natural self without pretensions). The process follows two interlocking steps. First, there must be a disintegration of social-self, self-intellect, and partial soul. In other words, a letting go of selfishness brought on by materialism and becoming "ecologically grounded," which has been described in ecopsychology literature as having a sense of wonder and belonging within nature as the result of carrying out a gradual and profound communication with the larger natural world: the soil, the landscapes, the wind, the creatures (wild and tamed), as well as with friends, family and the cultural practices that shape our identities.

Secondly, there must be a reintegration of the cosmic or universal self. This happens when people begin to see themselves as a part of everything around them, including the natural world. According to McGaa (1990), "a nature-based orientation and life style supports the concept of extended family and discourages prejudice" (p. 28). A nature-based orientation is the desire to live in harmony with everything around us. Since everyone possesses the power to be a positive or negative force for personal development, the choice is to live in harmony or to live in disharmony. The struggle for everyone is to get beyond either emotion or reason and harmonize these discordant elements of being. According to Arasteh (1989), "Disharmony appears most often between (1) the force with us that commands regressive and evil acts and reason; (2) reason and that which confirms certainty; and (3) intuition and reason in the final state of personality growth" (p. 153).

The result of disharmony causes people to act in self-serving ways (e.g., lust robs people of intelligence and reverence and materialism robs people of growth). The purpose of life is union with all and comes only after the abandonment of the "social self" and the embracing of the "universal self." In a sense, each person has the potential to develop "god like" qualities of compassion, self-lessness, generosity and respect. That is, everyone possesses the power for bringing about good if they so choose. Yet it is not so easy for some to understand what is beyond themselves. It may require a great deal of effort or it may appear suddenly. The answers are always elusive, but it is clear that awareness can only be found within and not through someone else. It is important, therefore, to be introspective and remove the mental barriers that have been interjected through socialization. With awareness of the universal self comes a realization of what one is – a creature of the earth. According to Thoreau (1970):

> *Live in each season as it passes; breathe the air; drink the drink, taste the fruit, and resign yourself to the influences of each. Let them be your only diet, drink and botanical medicines. Be blown on by all the winds. Open all your pores and bathe in all the tides of nature, in all her streams and oceans, at all seasons (p. 45).*

CONCLUSION

"I ran to the spring to fetch water for them when they were thirsty...by these little services I won their affection" (Playful Calf in Hiffler 1992; p. 248). I have always thought of how the act of helping and the way of being are so closely connected with one's sense of self in nature. In March, 2002, I had the opportunity to participate in a Healing Circle for Residential School survivors, and be privileged to take a bath with like minded others, at dawn early one morning in a stream next to the healing lodge (Tsa Kwa Luten). A place for immersing oneself in the water had been created, but I lay facedown in the cold stream, and let the waters run over me to not only cleanse my body, but my spirit. I arose out of the water with the mutual cry of shock and praise to the Great Spirit for allowing me to understand that there are basic rules for being and living in the world. Consider, "if you are going to learn to swim, then you have to immerse yourself in water" (McGaa, 1990; p. 133). However, whatever I do, I can never take my place on this land for granted nor can I forget that I must immerse myself in living. I am eternally connected to it and as such, the "road" to good living is being respectful to the land. Indigenous and people around the world who live close to the land have always stressed the sacredness of humanity's connection with nature, not only for spiritual well being, but also physical, social and psychological well-being. The most important element is a respect and sensitivity to the land. When one becomes respectful and sensitive to the land, then one can communicate with the spirits that inhabit the land and everything in it. Recent research reinforces these practices and suggests that humankind's separation from nature in the modern world increases stress and leaves people with a sense of psychological, social, and spiritual isolation. More importantly, nature offers an obvious focal point in that there are many messages that can teach lessons in living in a transcendent manner. Connecting with the environment can help humanity tap into the "higher power" wisdom inherent in nature. The major counseling strategy is helping people reflect on meaning and how "nature" is a metaphor for values that underlie everything in existence.

Perhaps the origin of personal and collective pathology and dislocation often reported in Western society, such as increased stress and mental illness, is a result of the lack of connection between people and nature. Those who do connect with nature in a deep way stress that they have increased sensory awareness, a better sense about themselves, and that involving themselves with nature has reduced levels of stress. This suggests possibilities of how nature can help people maximize their potential and create infinite possibilities of helping people improve their overall levels of responsibility for themselves, each other, and the environment. Furthermore, Glendinning (1994) indicates that nature can also help people deal with issues such as workaholism, sharpen their sense of identity, increase their respect for values, increase tolerance for others and respect for all living things. It may also help increase levels of self-validation, trust in the self, others and nature, thus obtaining a sense of balance and values clarification. In essence, nature teaches that people can live in greater harmony with all living things and increase the levels of peace between them. As a process, nature is the primary vehicle for coming to grips with spiritual, personal, social and physical problems. Re-connecting to nature can help people reach a state of enlightenment, which is non-discriminative, because no element is valued over any other. In the same way, there should not be a separation of self, including the physical, social, psychological and spiritual, from nature. The basic practice of nature re-connecting starts in the body, for the body epitomizes the natural process of living. "Only when you drink from the river of silence shall you indeed sing. And when you have reached the mountaintop, then you shall begin to climb. And when the earth shall claim your limbs, then shall you truly dance." (Kahlil Gibran, *The Prophet*, p. 81).

ACTIVITIES FOR FOCUSING A GROUP

1. **Walking Meditation:** Meditation is a process of focussing on something, thus, with a walking meditation, one goes outside to walk among the trees or in a garden. Walk for 15 minutes not thinking about anything; just see the beauty of nature paying special attention to everything with your senses. After returning to the group, share the experience. With the group sitting in a circle, each person in turn has the opportunity to share their awareness. Take turns facilitating each other. The facilitator can focus them by asking questions. For example, a person can start out by saying: "I was aware of the many shades of green outside...I was amazed at the number of birds there were...and how peaceful I felt...I like the fresh smell of the grass and the wind on my face..." The facilitator can then ask: "What are you feeling as you share that?" or "What did you learn?" or "What were the lessons you learned while you were walking?" The dialoguing can continue, following up on the response of the group member sharing the walking meditation. Provide feedback to each person who facilitates.

2. **Stargazing:** With a close friend or loved one, go out on a clear night to a beach, meadow or hill, with a blanket. Lie down together and hold hands and simply gaze at the stars for 15 minutes without saying anything to each other. Next, begin a dialogue focussing on what each person feels or sees as both gaze at the stars. Finally, each should share how greater connections could be made with the stars in the cosmos.

CHAPTER TWELVE
SPIRITUAL DIMENSIONS OF THE GROUP
EXPERIENCE: HONORING AND LETTING GO

Do not stand at my grave and weep. I am not there I do not sleep. I am a thousand winds that blow; I am the diamond in the snow. I am the sunlight on the ripened grain; I am the gentle autumn's rain. When you awaken in the morning hush, I am the swift uplifting rush, of quiet birds in circled flight. I am the soft stars that shine at night. Do not stand at my grave and cry. I am not there...I did not die. (Hopi Prayer)

When my daughter died on Friday, December 1, 2000, there was a great pain in my heart that I felt in a deep physical way. I could not believe she was gone. She seemed to be here one day and gone the next. I was with her when her doctor told her that she had only three months to live. We both cried and held each other. Finally, she said that she didn't want to die and that she was afraid. As a father, I wanted to comfort her, but I did not want her to go either. The end was near and in fact she was gone in two weeks. I did not want her to suffer with the cancer that was eating her up inside, since she had experienced so much in the four years that she lived with it. Deep in my heart, I wanted to give her some hope, as her mother and I did at each stage, even when the news was bad. To comfort her I said that I did not believe that when one dies, one goes away. The spirit never dies, I told her. I was with her on the last night of her life and watched as she peacefully passed on. Her loved ones and I spent the next few days saying our goodbyes at her side before she was interred. We all pass on, some of us sooner than others, but it is never easy. Death is probably always unexpected. If the spirit of a person never dies and lives all around us in nature, then why is it that we have such a hard time letting go of someone we love? In a more general sense, every loss is a kind of "death," whatever it is. It is never easy, but then neither are many things that are part of being human. The Hopi prayer was passed on to me and it gave me great comfort. In this final chapter I want to explore what letting go is all about, particularly in reference to a group. I like the way that the Transpersonal approach honors saying goodbye and letting go.

In the Transpersonal approach to groups, the inclusion of the spiritual dimension of human behavior only completes what it is to be human. In other words, humanity can never be understood without looking at the wholeness of what it is to be human. In aboriginal spirituality, the medicine wheel is used to demonstrate the importance of balancing the emotional, mental, physical and spiritual. The first three dimensions are straightforward, while the spiritual is more difficult for most people. What is spirituality? It pertains to the innate capacity and tendency to seek, to transcend one's existing locus of centricity, where transcendence involves increased knowledge and love. Spiritual wellness is humanity's ability to strive for meaning and purpose in life. In order to transcend, people need to question everything and to appreciate the abstract life, which cannot be explained or understood right away. In other words, the pursuit of harmony of the spiritual as well as all the other parts occurs when there is a balance between what lies within and that which exists outside ourselves as human beings. A different angle on the same theme is that "the spiritual life is part of the human essence (the contemplative, religious, philosophical, or value-life)...a defining characteristic of human nature" (Maslow, 1971; p. 47). However, it is when we have experiences of trauma, such as a near death experience or the death of a loved one, that we are forces to look at our lives with different lenses.

- ❦ Near death experiences reinforce and often act as catalyst for spiritual growth;

- ❦ The world needs what we have (everyone is special and can offer something to the community);

- ❦ "Spiritual drives or urges are real, basic and fundamental" (Groff, 1965);

- ❦ The choice is moving towards greed/consumption or doing good deeds;

- ❦ Spirit in action or living compassion through actions (Wilber) or the spirit is all around us waiting for us to connect;

- ❦ Model:

  Touch the sacred; (authentic self);

  Systematic form of self-reflection: (find the true calling);

  Commitment to loving service (serve a higher reality).

IS THE GOAL IN LIFE TO ASPIRE TO ACHIEVE WHOLENESS IN LIFE/CAREERS?

While we may say good-bye without much visible pain, in reality most of us find it a difficult process. As a result in individual and group relationships, we resist the termination process. Is it because a great deal of our energy is put into making a commitment to share, support, play and work together during relationships? This is especially true when the experience has had a lot of "heart," which is enthusiasm, positiveness, energy and intimacy. To think about the relationship in terms of "heart" makes more sense than to think about it in relative terms of good or bad. All people involved in relationships, whether they are work or play related, have different ways of resolving the loss involved in disengagement. The ways people deal with it range from denying that it was important to hanging on desperately. Most of us have experienced both of these, even though we knew endings were inevitable. Coming to terms with endings is one of life's great lessons. Yet we linger and drag our feet even when the relationship has ceased to be exciting or happy. William Shakespeare's (Shoenbaum, 1971) Romeo reminds us: "good-bye, good-bye, parting is such sweet sorrow, I'll say good-bye till it be tomorrow." Thus, in this final chapter, the termination process is explored and its implications for groups (e.g., saying good-bye and letting go). Disengagement and coming to terms with ending the contact with others is as much a vital part of the group processes as the beginning. It is the chance to be reminded of one of life's great lessons – accepting that everything will end.

Disengagement in the Group

As I think of letting go, I think of a member of a past group who shared that he despaired because of the breakup of his marriage. Hunched over, he stunned the group by saying that he was contemplating suicide. He went on to say that he could never find another relationship like the one that he lost. His description of his experiences with his family were sometimes funny, inspiring and sad. It was easy to see in his face the pleasures and the pain of the relationship. He concluded that life without his wife and son was dreary at best. When questioned about it, he shared that cognitively he knew they had so many differences, and these differences made the relationship quite impossible at times. But emotionally he did not want to see those differences. He saw that his wife ended the relationship and it hurt very much. He did not want to say good-bye, and as he found over the next couple of months, coping with the loss was very difficult. Many people in the group offered advice and support, which over the life of the group had an effect.

He learned to "let go" of what was "passed" and redirected his energy towards rebuilding "connections" with others and his environment. Through a process of learning to refocus his attention away from the loss into daily activities, he found joy in living. He shared that as he worked in his garden he noticed that he did not feel the pain of his loss. His mind was engaged. The group members, sensing that an impasse had been broken, were eager to know how he had done this. One excited group member asked him to share with her the "secret of gardening." Thereafter the group devoted ten minutes of each group meeting to this topic. He took great pride in sharing his newly developed skill. In a sense, he stopped looking at his loss, which he had fixated on, and began to become aware of the life around him in a way that was totally new. Paradoxically, what had been a nightmare was now a leap into the unknown, which brought excitement and hope. His hope for himself at the end of the group was that he would continue to develop his awareness, accept life the way it is, accept the responsibility of living, and enjoy every minute of life as if it were his last.

Helping people cope with endings in groups and in everyday life is a chore that has implications for their future relationships. Usually in relationships, whether group or individual, people want to ignore the ending, but that goes against all that being responsible and self supporting is all about. I understand this, because I too want to "hang on." Perhaps it is the final ritual of good-byes that I, like others, fight against. Departures should always be sudden, said the nineteenth century British politician, Benjamin Disraeli. I like this because it seems to appeal to the part of me that does not like to see things end. Endings and good-byes are universal in friendships, marriages, partnerships, projects and a host of other situations. As a fact of nature there is no choice about it. But why does one fight against it? Is it because people do not want to let go? Or is it because as people, we want to control what happens? It might be that, for me, I cannot see beyond what is immediate, and in my fear, I fight against the natural process of endings. The mystery of it reminds me of something Castañeda (1972) said:

> *Don Juan spoke to me almost in a whisper. He told me to watch every detail of the surroundings, no matter how small or seemingly trivial. Especially the features of the scenery that*

were most prominent in a westerly direction. He said that I should look at the sun without focusing on it until it had disappeared over the horizon (p. 45).

DOING VERSUS WHAT HAPPENS

The message of Don Juan is to simply let go, yet people want more answers. In the dulling of our grief we have forgotten something about living. According to Watts (1958), this is not surprising, for even when Buddha, the enlightened, was on his deathbed, his disciples wept and cried out in their grief – "why?" Buddha was disappointed in their refusal to let go, because he had taught that life is suffering. Buddha's message was that one cannot escape disease and suffering. A bad state of mind is the "core" of disease. It can be seen through our cravings, lust, attachments and selfishness. While Buddha's prognosis is that it is possible to cope with suffering, it isn't easy. And what is the remedy? Buddha said we can overcome it by being ethical, keeping a pure mind and developing wisdom. The world is full of suffering and it is not easy to forget the face of suffering. All of us can only cope with the suffering that will eventually kill us. Interestingly, we say have to suffer and die, but why do we react as if death, like all other partings, happens against our will. It is difficult to let go of things in our lives, because we do not know what else is out there. Ever so slowly we will age and even though we think from time to time that we can stop this aging process, the inevitable will occur. According to Brazier (1995):

The road to happiness involves freeing ourselves from attachments to things, which will inevitably let us down. Everything changes. Sticks on the fire burn and disappear. Although they disappear, they have not ceased to exist. They are now ash, smoke, and heat...put the ash in the soil...[and] perhaps one day a tree will grow in this soil and the ash will have become sticks once again (pp. 237-238).

To say good-bye to friends is similar to saying good-bye to life. It is something we want to avoid, yet to ignore dealing with it is to suppress our feelings. Does all this have something to do with our early experiences? One group member shared with the group that as a child, he moved so often it was difficult to recount all the different places he had lived. Every time he felt "at home," his family was on the move again. The group member wondered if perhaps it was the emptiness he felt in saying good-bye. Does it have to do with something unsaid or unfinished? Do we need to mourn over the ending of each relationship? Is that what we want to avoid? Watts (1958) said that people divide their experiences into two parts: what they do and what happens to them. This is life's great illusion, according to Buddha. There is really no difference, as the protagonist found out in Herman Hesse's (1951) novel *Siddhartha*. There is a kinship of all "seekers" with Siddhartha, because like him, seekers leave their home and go in search of the meaning of life. Siddhartha, a Hindu prince, tried the life of an ascetic with the Samana tribe and the life of love and gratification in Kamala. He found no satisfaction until he met Vasudeva, a ferryman of the river. With this ferryman, Siddhartha learned happiness, heartbreak and peace by not fighting or even searching. He found that "The river has taught me to listen; you will learn from it too. The river knows everything; one can learn everything from it. You have already learned from the river that it is good to strive downwards, to sink, to seek the depths" (pp. 107-108).

What Siddhartha found in the depth and the rhythm of the river was Siddhartha. He learned that the interpretations of others only lead to answers to others, for hope only resides within the self. Buddha taught that no one finds salvation through a guru, or a dogma, or another person, but only through letting go. This concept is beautifully illustrated in the parable of the Zen monk Tanzan. In this parable Tanzan and his disciples are crossing a river when they come upon a beautiful woman trying to cross it. Offering help, Tanzan picks her up, carries her across and then sets her down. Continuing on their journey, the disciples are agitated, but do not say anything until their evening meal. The disciples ask Tanzan why he took the woman in his arms. Without thinking, Tanzan replies: "I left the woman back at the river, but you are still carrying her!" The secret of non-attachment is accepting things as they are and letting the mind be still. When this happens the whole universe surrenders. In Buddhism, karma is what happens to people, which means the force generated by actions. It comes from a Sanskrit word, which means doing. In other words, what happens to people, as well as what they do, is fundamentally their doing. When Buddha referred to doing or the actions people take, he was not referring to the ego or conscious mind, but about a deeper part of self – a self at which point people become one with nature. When people are at one with nature they do not try to control or pollute it. That would be like polluting themselves. Another way to put it – which is appealing – is what the great Arab philosopher, Kahlil Gibran (1933) calls the larger self: "You are not enclosed within your bodies, nor confined to houses or fields…that which is in you dwells above the mountains and roves with the wind…it is a thing free, a spirit that envelops the earth and moves in the other" (pp. 91-92).

ON LETTING GO

Being able to let go is a challenge all people must face. The inability to say good-bye is primarily the result of unfinished business. There are a number of reasons that people in groups have given for not being able to do it. My experience matches what other helpers have said about it, which leads me to believe that it is a universal phenomenon. The most obvious reason is that some past experience is not resolved and it just keeps returning and interfering in the present. For example, I have seen many people express the view that, because their father (or mother) was absent, others in their lives will be absent. Somehow events in childhood keep being played out again and again, like a never-ending soap opera with the same plot. And if you look at people who fear letting go, you will notice the first sign in their bodies. Most common are the incongruities of the verbal and non-verbal messages. In their minds, they are saying that everything is fine, but in their bodies they are saying that they are angry. Surprisingly, many people are unaware of their body and its capacity to store feelings.

People do receive some gains for not letting go of a pattern, relationship or a part of self. This may be that the pattern is serving a function or that the consequence of change is considered too disruptive or scary to be worth the effort. For example, one woman told the group of her obsessive pattern in her relationships, yet to change seemed like too great a task. While she saw the down side of her pattern, she also viewed it as a virtue, "I love too much." A seductive aspect of unfinished business occurs when things are seen in terms of "black and white." Something is either good or bad with nothing in between. This eliminates doubt, but makes it impossible to deal with change. The function of unfinished business serves to help people deny loss, vent feelings, and avoid pain or dishonor. All of us have experienced illness and death in our lives. We know that it can rob us of our ability to be positive and generous. Death does not happen to teach us a lesson, it happens because it is a natural phenomenon. Accidents happen without reason. Illness occurs to the young and the old. It still shocks us and will continue to do so many years afterwards. It is our inability to let go which sometimes results in physical and emotional symptoms. Physical attributes, like scars, or the manner in which people carry themselves, become the embodiment of people from the past. However, emotional symptoms like whining or a negative attitude are most common. People use the past to justify their behavior. For example, one person usually justified his inability to change because he had a deprived childhood. After a lot of work in the group, he was surprised to admit that his past deprivation was also a source of pride. He got a great deal of "mileage" out of being the victim. When he was able to let go of the vision of himself as victim, he stopped from blocking the contact with himself and others.

On Being Aware

I remember a conversation I had many years ago with a former teacher, who asked me what I wanted to do when I graduated. I told him, in all seriousness, that I wanted to be a tree. He looked at me with incredulity and then with anger. I thought he was going to hit me; instead he walked away as if I were a madman. Years later I met him at a reunion and he laughingly asked me if I had become a tree. As if swaying in the wind, I stretched out my arms and, before I could answer, he literally ran from the room. What I thought of when he asked me was something expressed in William Shakespeare's (Shoenbaum, 1971) play, *Troilus and Cressida*: "One touch of nature makes the whole world kin." Perhaps for me what Shakespeare means is that this is the point where nature and I form a single pattern of energy. For me the "tree" was a metaphor for how I wanted to be in my life – a continuous extension of everything in nature. In a sense, the group is a logical extension of that which is found in nature. For example, if the group is a "forest," with each member being a "tree," they form a "chain" in the ecosystem of society. As a system, their beginnings and endings are a part of the process of **birth** and **death**. There is only the process and there is no difference between them and all that is in nature. It is true that they think and perhaps they are a little more complicated than the trees, but they are partners with nature. They are not better or worse than anything else, but a part of the ecosystem. In effect, I believe they must understand that the whole world is just one single process. I like to think of the process as the potential of trees, because like a tree, in each member of the group there is a seed, which is a silent promise, and the promise is always Spring. Therein lies the challenge for group members, such as saying good-bye.

"You say good-bye and I say hello. Hello, hello…I say hello and you say why and I say I just don't know…good-bye, good-bye" goes a Beatles song (Lennon & McCartney, 1966). These lyrics epitomized the confusion that people have in endings and saying good-bye. Is it that there is more that they want from others? Is it more intimacy in the relationship? Is this unfinished business? Perhaps people should address these questions when they first meet? On the other hand, does this mean that they should approach each relationship as if it were going to end soon? In the process of communication, as the Beatles imply, hello and good-bye are the same thing, because to say hello is to say good-bye. Does this mean that nothing has a beginning or an end? It is confusing thinking about all these questions and so easy to wonder if everything is a paradox. If you look around your environment you may wonder if you are living in a world made so fantastic with questions that may never have answers. Could it be that we have become estranged from reality? Are we now so estranged in our heads that we talk about things that have no practical value? Perhaps it is that we have become unromantic versions of the appealing protagonist in Hesse's (1929) novel *Steppenwolf.* In this novel Hesse pictured a man, Harry Haller, who has come to know some frightening things about himself. As a result "he has decided to live in the world as though it were not the world, to heed the law and yet to stand above it...Haller will live in the world, but it will be a fantastic world" (p. 4). Is it that, like Harry Haller, we are living in a "magic theater" where we have made reality? If so, are we centered enough to see it, not as a prison that limits us, but as a place where we can be creative and grow beyond ourselves?

ON BEING COMPASSIONATE

To have an open heart that lets the waters of compassion, of understanding, and of forgiveness flow forth is a sign of a mature person.... Then we...will walk towards greater freedom and let waters flow onto others, healing them and finding healing through them (Vanier, 1998; p. 102).

From a transpersonal perspective, compassion for others is one of the most empowering characteristics that we can wish for. To be compassionate, means to wish others not to suffer the indignities of pain and sorrow, socially, intellectually, psychologically, and spiritually. However, compassion that emanates from the heart and embraces all of nature's creatures is the transcendental sense that unites us with everything in existence. When we empathize we are separate, but when we feel compassion that goes beyond ourselves we are joined with the cosmos. That happens when we realize that we are not a separate ego or self, but part of a collective identity that unites us. Brazier (1995) says that "Compassion is to understand the other person's subjective world without stealing anything. Stealing means taking over...In compassion one sees through the eyes of the other, and feels with their heart, without any private agenda" (p. 195).

In a world that is characterized by oppression, people become burdened by the lack of acceptance, thus they lose one of life's most precious gifts – love. Oppression robs one's opportunities for being compassionate and without compassion there is no love. When one is compassionate, one gains meaning, lives with purpose, and has understanding for the welfare of other living things. This is the ability to see one's self in a context of all living things and to understand that one is related to the birds and the trees. When one is compassionate, every experience is full of meaning, reminding us that even bad experiences help us along the "road" to greater awareness. That is, that one is a part of a great family that loves every member, no matter how small. This is living with the humility that one has survived because another has given to you; it means that to be humble is to receive a reminder of one's humanness. Even disappointments become opportunities for growth. Brazier (1995) goes on to say that compassion:

may begin as a set of observational, empathic and caring skills — thoughtfulness, giving time and attention, listening, helping and generous in action — which we can all improve with good effects upon both our professional work and our private lives. As it grows it becomes, inexorably, a challenge to us to overcome the obstacles to life within ourselves and to flow with the boundless Tao in which we lose our attachment to separateness. The world needs kindness (p. 200).

On Assessing the Personal Journey

As the group ends, everyone needs to assess their personal journey. Personally, I want to remind myself of the words of philosopher Aristotle, who said that all art and education are merely a supplement to nature. Could the natural process that I see in nature get subverted in my desire to be creative? Is it possible that my creativity can get out of hand? Could I risk so much in the process of experiencing that I destroy my environment and myself? How far can I go? There are many exciting and also depressing things going on in this world. One of the most exciting is the new discoveries that open new possibilities to exist. However, in the process of discovering many new different things, the environment is changing. One of the most frightening changes is the depletion of the ozone layer, the layer that filters out harmful rays of the sun. This is strange because the sun also brings life. It is similar to my outer surface or armor covering my inner core of vulnerability. Once again, I have found a paradox. If I let down the protective "armor" that has developed, I will be vulnerable and then hurt or destroyed. I think: "So what makes life exciting can also kill me!" Perhaps more importantly, living life, whether positive and negative, is vital, because living is experiencing. One question everyone has to ask him or herself is, "Will the experience be worth it, whatever the outcome?" Victor Frankl (1972), who experienced terrible and unspeakable hardship in a concentration camp during World War II, put it this way to his fellow inmates: "Whoever was still alive had reason for hope…whatever we had gone through could still be an asset in the future. And I quoted from Nietzsche: "that which does not kill me, makes me stronger." What you have experienced, no power on earth can take from you" (pp. 130-131).

In trying to control the environment, people are about to destroy it. Perhaps this is also the case within their inner selves. Does this mean that they have been forcing nature into their image as they have forced themselves into the image that is acceptable to society? Maybe so, but that gives me an uneasy feeling. If people, like Siddhartha, try not to control, but keep their eyes open and are awake to their surroundings, they can discover more than just beauty. It means looking at surroundings as if for the first time instead of looking with introjected perceptions. Society has introjected acceptable ways of thinking and feeling, which often denies creativity. In Buddhism, when surroundings are looked at with freshness, it is called tatata, which means "suchness" or just like that.

When relationships end or when death comes, they simply occur like the changes of the seasons and each of us are faced with an opportunity. And so I think about the past, and it is hard to believe that I am now as old as my father when he died. I only knew him through pictures, talking to my mother and some other relatives. The other relatives came much later and for many years I was only able to talk to my mother about him. He was a man who allowed no pictures and for many years I was unable to find out anything about him. Eventually, I found a baptismal certificate. That probably does not sound like a great discovery, but for many years I wondered whether he was only an invention of my imagination and my strong need to have a real father. Now I know more things about him, and what surprises me is that as I have found descriptors of him, I have found descriptors of myself. My mother told me that I have become as inscrutable and mysterious as my father. Somehow that makes me smile. The German philosopher Rainer Maria Rilke (1964) said that the future enters into all people, in order to transform itself, long before it happens. Rilke's idea is a very appealing thought when I realize what it means to the group – endings are always with us, even in introductions. There are so many parallels that people in the groups discover from their pasts that somehow surface in the present. I believe these are the patterns that make up everyone's living routine. However, they do not have to repeat the past, only understand it, explore the patterns, and rectify that which needs to be rectified. Letting go really means understanding the past and choosing how to live life in the future. It is all a choice!

ON EXPERIENCING CHANGE

It is said that everything changes but change. That makes me wonder. For example, how strange not to have different seasons. That would mean that the winter season, when the leaves turn brown and fall and the snow and rain come, is some kind of defeat. People in their right mind would not say there should not be a winter, that it ought to be stopped. No, the seasons, whether winter, spring, summer or autumn, are part of the natural process of events. If there were no winter, then there would be no summer. If there were no darkness, there would not be any light. If there were no wet, then there would be no dry. If there were no women there would be no men. If there were no bad there would be no good. If there were no mountains, there would be no valleys. In the group as in life, people experience the good with the bad. Without the inevitable problems, there would be no ecstasy. Problems are a part of the group and people learn not to run away or deny them, but to let go of the notion that the group must be blissful. The way to do that is for them to be open to change. "Change for the sake of change, even though directionless and unformed, reawakens the energy in the system and shows that a live organism is reviving" (Polster & Polster, 1973; p. 78).

Everything has its opposite, which causes it to be enhanced or emphasized by the contrast with its counterpart. I have the "high plains drifter" and the "bodhisattva" in me. This concept of polarity is an important concept in Gestalt, because problems arise when polarities are not reconciled and not because they exist. I do not want to get rid of the "high plains drifter" or the "bodhisattva," because they contrast each other. No, I want to utilize both parts because the polarities are the energy field for understanding attractions and conflicts. This is the source of personal power, which helps me adapt and cope with change.

I have always been impressed with the polarities personified in another of Hesse's (1971) novels, *Narcissus and Goldman.* The two protagonists represent the dual sides of nature: Narcissus the ascetic, disciplined monk and Goldman the erotic, renegade monk. Narcissus convinces Goldman to leave the monastery to find out about life. Goldman, in one of the most moving parts of the book, discovers a village that has been wiped out by the bubonic plague. All the people have died after great suffering. What he notices is that the face of death is very similar to the face of sexual ecstasy. Pain and pleasure are just opposites of the same coin. More importantly, Goldman, who eventually becomes a wood carver, discovers that life is transitory, "that all men trickle away, changing constantly, until they dissolve, while their artistic-created images remain unchangeably the same" (p. 176). When Goldman dies early from living life "close to the edge," his face reflects the blissful smile that Siddhartha had when he died. Like Goldman and Narcissus, I too am split, and healing that split takes a lot of my energy. Healing is not only patching up the rift and integrating the parts, but also having the parts work together in partnership and turning what is a weakness into a strength.

One of the aspects of the group experience that I have noticed is the tendency to avoid issues that produce dissension. My hope for the group is that they will "let go" of this desire to "smooth the edges" to create harmony. There is a metaphor in nature for this tendency. When I look at the mountains it would be strange to blame them for being high or praise the valleys for being deep. Neither would it make sense to praise straight trees for being straight or curvy trees for being curvy. To look at another person and blame that person for being what he or she is also makes no sense. People, like nature, are. Every person must define him- or herself and choose to be what they are. So it is in nature or to put it as the philosopher Emmanuel Kant said, "everything in nature acts in accordance with the law, because nature is the law." In other words, nature is a pattern and it can be seen everywhere in the environment. Recognizing this pattern is essential to letting go, because once this happens the group will understand that they have choices.

I remember the first time I heard my daughter say "papa." I was so excited by the recognition, until I heard her call other people and things with the same sound. As I watched her look in wonder at the things around her, she was not calling me or anybody else. She was not saying anything specific, but just making sounds, listening and watching. Now I think she was saying, "there . . . look at that . . . see it . . . there . . . pa . . . pa." She seemed to have a quality of looking at something, not to determine what its use might be, but just focusing. Piaget (1965) calls this process of focusing on a single aspect of an object as **centering**. That makes me laugh, because after many years of meditation I was able to relearn centering. The ability to focus on patterns in the environment starts with being aware of sensations. Letting go is being aware of the immediate. For example, if group members have the awareness of feeling hunger and sexual desire, their stomachs growl and their excitement increases. Unlike the infant, they do not act on their awareness, for it might not be polite or appropriate. They also fear the risk of rejection. Maybe they introject (swallow ideas without understanding them), retroflect (turn on themselves), deflect (push things away), project (invent what is there) or experience confluence (lose themselves in their surroundings). When they let go and do not think or feel that it is bad, but just let it develop, it becomes a flowing pattern and they experience their awareness like music. What this means to the group is that they can learn to look at things in their lives and see "things" as they are and not as they **wish** them to be. Letting go is adopting the freshness of the infant and looking at things as if it was the **first** time.

On Reflecting on Patterns in Life

I have observed over the years that many people involved in the group experience have habits and routines that result in avoidance of the unknown. The paradox is that these patterns bring a sense of safety, but they also can bring about the asphyxiation of excitement. I have always liked the simile of the group experience and music. The group, like music, does not have an objective other than the process, nor is there anything that is supposed to occur, except what does occur. The group, like music, has no destination; if music had a destination then the best singers would be the ones that reached the end of the song first. Music is not played to get anywhere. Music is a pattern that is listened to and enjoyed as it unfolds. Relationships with others are just a part of the wholeness of life and not to be held on to. As relationships develop they unfold offering possibilities. Watts (1957) said that "we must all build our lives upon a fathomless abyss - so to discover that what we are is not what we are bound to be, but we are free to be" (p. 35). As I look at the ocean, I marvel at its beauty and power. And I wonder where is the water going? I smile at my silly question, because it is not going anywhere; all nature understands that the point of all life is to be here. Perhaps to be widely awake intensifies the only reality – which is to be aware in the here and now. As a facilitator, I want to understand what people are experiencing right now, by observing what is said, how it is said and the patterns. Yet, no matter how much I understand or how much I try to help others, ultimately people must feel the truth of their actions. In a way, communicating or even living is like listening to music. As the people in the group listen to music, they do not try to hold in their memories that which is past or to think about what is coming, but just to listen to the pattern as it unfolds. When I listen to the driving saxophone of John Coltrane, my body wants to move – dance. When I dance I do not aim at a particular place on the floor, which is the destination of the dance. I do not worry about making the right dance step. I listen to the music and I move my body to it, just as my eyes follow the pattern of my partner's body or the waves of the ocean as they move; it seems as if everything is a rhythm, a beat, and so my eyes do not see what is there, only the movement, and my ears hear the sound.

When I imagine in my mind's eye the ocean, my eyes follow the movement…see it move…see the ripples. My eyes know that the water is not going anywhere. The idea that something should happen, that there is a goal or purpose to it all, is just a thought, words, a mind game. Therefore, in order to see all of this, people in the group have to stop thinking. If they are to hear what anyone else has to say, they sometimes have to stop talking. In Gibran's (1933) book *The Prophet*, he said that in much of people's talking, thinking is half murdered. So thinking is talking inside of the mind. A diversion. If people are going to have anything to think about they sometimes have to stop thinking. In the same way, if people are going to have things to talk about, they sometimes have to stop talking and listen. "From listening comes wisdom and from speaking comes repentance," stresses the Italian proverb.

On Being Open to the Rhythms

If I tried to achieve complete mastery in my breathing, the only way I could do this would be to stop breathing. Of course, I have to do this without dying. Perhaps this is the answer, because Nirvana is a Sanskrit word meaning "breathing out" (Watts, 1957). It requires that I be spontaneous, but when my anxiety is up my spontaneity is down. Is the rhythm that which determines how the organism regulates itself? Then how can I achieve rhythm in my life and in my relationships? In constructive living, like the helping process, there is a release that enables everyone to move out from a preoccupation when their personal condition is experienced as a catharsis or a climax of emotions. However, this does not mean that the ego should be suppressed, as Siddhartha tried to do. No, it means accept that people are. Because ego, as confidence, is maturity itself. There are many ways of doing this, but one natural method I have used is similar to what is practiced in meditation and reflects the Buddhist, Christian, Muslim or any spiritual view of life. In Zen Buddhism, this is called zazen, which Watts (1957) described as:

> seeing reality directly, in its "suchness". To see the world completely as it is concretely, undivided by categories and abstractions, one must certainly look at it with the mind, which is not thinking – just sit, with a blank mind which excludes all impressions because that can only come when you do not try and make it happen – it is just a quiet awareness, without comment, of whatever happens to be here and now (p. 155).

Is this yet another paradox that each of us faces in life? This does not mean that people have to sit in the lotus position or go to a dojo to do it. It means that they could spend some time every day when they do not think, but just watch; a time in which they do not form any ideas about life, but just look around. People must listen, smell, feel, taste and then get rid of all the talking in their heads and all the ideas about what they do as distinct to what happens to them (Watts, 1958). When this is done they will discover something very rare and precious, a meaning so profound as to be indescribable. No longer will it matter what others think about them, or what others do, or what is the difference between what belongs to me and what belongs to them. It matters little what is different between people and nature, because it will all go away anyway. People cannot stop things from changing. Relationships are bound to change and ultimately end. No matter what people do, they are bound to die. So they have to let everything go...

Albert Schweitzer said that the tragedy of life is what dies inside people while they are still alive. I think of a colleague who killed himself a few years ago. But every time I think about him, I feel so angry. How could he be so stupid? How could he have so much despair? The only consolation is that perhaps his suffering is over, but is it? The poet Sylvia Plath wrote of the freedom of death, and the Japanese writer, Yukio Mishima, celebrated the beauty of Seppuku of the Samurai (ritual suicide). Sylvia Plath sent her children off to school and then turned the gas on and put her head in the oven. Leading his private army, Yukio Mishima, took over a military base in Japan. When the troops did not heed his exhortations to restore the Emperor, he cut open his belly and asked his lover to cut off his head. Mishima "courted self-destruction and longed for the greatest sensation of all…death's swiftly flapping wings beating upon his brow" (Thomas, 1973; p. 60).

That view saddens me, because suicide is a process of controlling life through death, which ultimately limits it. Sadly, limiting is a human condition. I cannot imagine a tree or any part of nature doing that. Nature lives until it dies. I want to approach life and each relationship as if it will end tomorrow; I have made a choice to get as much out of relationships as humanly possible. After all, life and relationships are so fragile. To paraphrase the philosopher Desiderius Erasmus: no one has to experience despair as long as there is breath, for while there is life, there is hope. Imagine if, rather than looking back and feeling sad, people looked back and remembered what was meaningful in their relationships. Tobin (1975) says that a person could discover that he or she had a:

meaningful relationship with the person when [he/she] was still around and [he/she] would have been continually enriched and changed through the relationship. The lost person then would really have become part of the one who is left and live on in a much more meaningful way – as part of that person's being – instead of as an introjected lump of dead matter that comes between the person and his world (p. 122).

Standing Bear said that: "in the Indian, the spirit of the land is still vested; it will be until other men are able to divine and meet its rhythm" (Hifler, 1992; p. 249). Life, rhythm and relationships are just a dancing pattern that changes and transforms us for more opportunities. Patterns exist in everything in life. A great Nuu-chah-nulth carver, Harold Lucas, told me that when I am carving I must never go against the grain of the wood, but always with it. Wood patterns or grains in the wood are the flow of growth and are similar to the way a stream flows. You will work harder going against the "grain" or "flow" of nature. He went on to tell me that "what is in the heart flows out through the hands" (in conversation, March, 2002). This idea of patterns is a very comforting thought. When I think about the ocean, I can see it – the pattern. And it is just like the pattern in music or as the rhythm in dancing. The pattern in music and dancing are a process in which the pattern brings out our emotion and fills our spirit with life's rhythm. I am drawn to Prather (1976) who said: "The way for me to live is to have no way. My only habit is to have none. Because I did it this way before is sufficient reason not to do it this way today" (p. 25). Rather than letting old patterns and habits dictate interpersonal relations, I want to encourage those in the group to be open to change, be open to what is new. For soon even the new will be old. What I admire in Kazantzakis' (1952) novel, *Zorba the Greek*, is the unabashed sense of freedom. He said, "liberty is to have a passion, to amass pieces of gold and suddenly to conquer one's passion and then throw the treasure to the four winds" (p. 30).

FINDING MEANING IN THE GROUP EXPERIENCE

We knew out of our own suffering that life cannot begin for the better except by us all for-

giving one another. For if one does not forgive, one does not understand; and if one does not understand, one is afraid; and if one is afraid, one hates; and if one hates, one cannot love. And no new beginning is possible without love (Van der Post, 1974; p.413).

This thought in Laurens Van der Post's novel *a far off place*, brings me back to the meaning of the group experience. I want to focus people in my groups on the shared energy. The experience, like any relationship, speaks itself, because the time spent together is like a Zen journey. It is like traveling without a point or destination, with nowhere to go. Watts (1957) says that to travel is to be alive, but to get somewhere is to be dead. That is very similar to an old proverb, which says, that to travel is better than to arrive. It is the process of being together and making all the time we have together dynamic, meaningful and pleasurable.

Most people come into counseling or self help groups with the idea of resolving personal issues that are blocking them in living their lives satisfactorily. However, because of the very nature of group involvement, as members of groups they have been practicing for behavioral changes. This occurs in the exploration of how they adapt to group norms and pressures, use problem solving strategies and communicate with others, and of how the dynamics of interpersonal interaction affect their self-perception. For example, in this process they were able to examine how they own what they say, how they use their body in communication and how they develop relationships others. In the Transpersonal approach to groups, there is emphasis on modifying patterns of behavior and thought, because people cannot change others, only the way they react to others. I believe this helps people maximize their power in their personal lives outside the group and allows them to achieve their fullest potential as human beings.

The dynamics of the group provide the best opportunity for giving and receiving feedback, which is one of the most potent tools of helping people understand how they communicate. One of the advantages in the group experience is that people can receive a greater variety of feedback from a greater variety of people. As the group begins the process of disengagement, there is a strong desire on the part of members to get answers to questions they have had about themselves. Even people who have been quiet during the experience suddenly begin to make more contact. In effect, endings produce a desire for complete gestalts and letting go. However, I do have mixed feelings about using this energy in the last stage of the group. While the "final burst of speed" accomplishes a great deal, it is possible that new issues can be raised. Therefore, helpers and group leaders need to caution the group about raising new issues and ensuring that the final feedback process is one of closing. While a favorable response may give a momentary lift, feedback that is constructive, specific, and concrete – whether negative or positive – is better. "I like you" or "I feel close" or other non-specific feedback is not as helpful. Group members can be encouraged to experiment with giving feedback to each other using some of the following:

"My greatest fear for you is . . ."

"I hope that you will seriously consider . . ."

"I see you blocking your strength by . . ."

"I hope you will think about . . ."

"My hope for you is . . ."

Albert Einstein often said he never worried about the future, because it would come soon enough. But maybe the way to bring together what people have experienced in the group is have them image what would happen if the group were to have a reunion after one year. One year is not very long in time, yet what would the people share with each other about what their life had been like since they were together? According to Napier and Gershenfeld (1999):

> *Many work groups end their task work in a frantic, pressurized fashion, leaving little time for interaction or reflection. Yet the termination stage, when approached in a plainful way, can provide a rich opportunity for evaluation, reflection, and closure. It gives members a chance to collectively assess what was learned and accomplished during their time together (p. 435).*

Many people in the various groups make arrangements to meet, although few actually do that. But what if they did meet again? What would it be like? All of the people would be a little older, a little wiser, and certainly more experienced. What would they want to know about each other? Perhaps they would wonder how they have handled the issues that plagued them during the group. Or maybe they would wonder how they have used their newfound power? What notable memories from the group would they share with others? Did anything stand out for them that seems to typify the experience? It is not surprising that people have issues around their separation from the group. They may have developed relationships that can carry on outside the group. It is sad when something ends, and to mourn is only natural. So I ask people in the group to reflect on what the relationships and insights that occurred in the group mean to them. Maybe there is some unfinished business from the group that is in the foreground of their thinking. If people have some unresolved feelings about the group leader that they want to complete, it is vital that they take care of it before the group ends. It never seems like enough time is available, and they may have to take care of some important unresolved issues after the group ends. I want the group to remember *Ecclesiastes III* (1): "To everything there is a season, and a time to every purpose under the heaven."

One important aspect of saying good-bye and letting go is reviewing what has been learned in the group. For me, that means reviewing what I have learned, those issues that I still wonder about, and how I am going to implement new insights. Maybe behavioral patterns have become clearer, or new alternative behaviors people have been practicing need more work. If there were any turning points in the group, what were they? It is not enough to say, people have "grown" or they will do things differently next time. Brazier (1995) feels that "endings can provide an opportunity to experience loss in a more conscious way" (p. 154). As people recall the past experiences they have had, they may want to share with others what has been learned, how they have perceived others, and what they appreciated about others. At the same time people need to be open to any feedback from others. Perhaps some things have become clearer or through the experience with others, they have learned something about their own behavior. However, they need to remember that positive and negative feedback are of equal importance. It is always nice to end on a positive "note," yet I personally want to hear about others' doubts and concerns. If I have grown during the group, negative feedback is really no "big deal."

Finally, I want the group to consider how they are going to carry the learning from the group to the next stage of development. That is, knowing how to build a harmonious community, which Buddhists call **sangha**. The essential element of a sangha is that all members of the group positively support everyone else in the group. Interestingly, Thich Nhat Hanh (Brazier, 1995) says "Without an intimate, deep relationship with at least one person, transformation is unlikely. With the support of one person, you have stability and support, and later you can reach out to a third person, and eventually be a brother or sister to everyone in the sangha" (p. 259).

Maybe members of the group need to make a "resolution" that includes specific dates, times and places on how they will continue the learning if necessary. For example, I might say "I have learned that I introject a great deal, so I have decided to never agree to anything without first considering whether it agrees with my values. In addition, I will work on being more assertive and expressing my personal power by exercising more, taking up a martial art, and attending a personal growth group." The excitement about making that kind of contract with oneself is that a person can become active – even passionate. In Kazantzakis' (1952) novel, Zorba reminds us that the way to live is to be "consumed with one desire: to touch and see as much as possible of the earth and the sea before [we] die" (p. 160). Maybe Albert Einstein was right about the future but, as people reflect on what has occurred since the beginning of the group, I reinforce the following about the experience:

❧ The group has been only a **means to an end** or a process of experiencing what people do and what has happened to them. The real benefits of the group experience are not the resolution of immediate issues, but the learning that occurred in the dynamic context of the group.

❧ What happened in the group has only to do with the group and it is **intimate sharing that should be treated as confidential and private**. To share the intimacy with others outside the group is similar to sharing with others the intimacy of the "bedroom."

❧ The **change in people can be slow and subtle**, which may not be recognized until much later. People will continue to recall experiences from the group, trying to make sense of them. This is a natural process of learning that occurs over time.

❧ People should not expect that the group experience will renovate or **change their lives radically**. The group experience is similar to other experiences, in that one experience builds on another experience and so it goes like "building blocks."

❧ People may want to deny or reject some things, but **they should not forget the feedback**, and the experiences from the group. It could be that what has occurred in the group only relates to the group, yet to deny what occurred may be to miss important aspects of learning.

🌿 People need to decide what they are **going to do about what they have learned** and then make a commitment to change. It is not enough to desire change; people have to make the effort to do so.

🌿 People need to speak up, be themselves and **reclaim their power**. To do this means taking responsibility for personal choices in life. To live life the way they want to live it.

Conclusion

As the relationship of the group comes to an end, people need to review the idea that the "group is more than the sum of its parts, and group process is more than the sum of the principles and elements" (Kepner, 1980; p. 23). What the group has become is not because of some individual powerful member or the leader, but through input from all of the members of the group. All of the group members have been responsible for what has happened and what has not happened. If the experience has been positive, it is because of what they did. If it has been negative, again it is because of what they did. If it has been negative, I do not think that is something to feel bad about, but only an indication that something happened that "stirred the pot." Areas in need of exploration have been identified for the future; thus, people have become aware of the meaning of the whole, because it is "meaningful in the sense that the whole explains the parts" (Perls, Hefferline & Goodman, 1951; p. 258).

There are some things in life which are riddles that may never be answered or resolved. In the search to find meaning in life it is easy to despair in this chaotic world. Camus (1947) referred to this as rolling the rock up the hill after it rolls down. In other words, life is a matter of "plugging away" as a way of finding meaning. If nothing else, the "plugging away" serves as a means for directing energy. However, when self-doubt occurs, and it is inevitable that it will, answers are not easy to find. Camus dealt with this by romanticizing about the absurdity of life. Of course, the tragedy for Camus was that the "struggle" became too great or the absurdity of it all was too much and he drowned himself in the River Seine one rainy evening. My hope for people in the group is that they will not despair, but will see the impasse as a challenge as the group was also a challenge. Support is always there in the hearts and actions of the group members as it is in everyday life. One gets support by simply asking for support. The group experience is a place for helping people become more assertive, aware, spontaneous, responsible and integrated. Henri-Frédéric Amiel (2001), the Swiss philosopher and poet, said that "it is by teaching that we teach ourselves, by relating that we observe, by affirming that we examine, by showing that we look, by writing that we think, by pumping that we draw water into the well." Yet I hope that people in the group will adopt the attitude that change is something to be embraced. If they have the will to change, they will endure, survive and go on to higher levels of learning and living. This is the only way to reclaim their lost power, utilize their polarities, and accept the freedom that inner liberation brings. Perhaps the challenge is as Hesse (1929) describes:

I knew that all the hundred thousand pieces of life's game were in my pocket. A glimpse of its meaning had stirred my reason and I was determined to begin the game afresh. I would sample its tortures once more and shudder again at its senselessness. I would traverse not once more, but often, the hell of my inner being (p. 248).

Therefore, as people look back on the group experience, I want them to consider how they utilized the learning that took place. While it is possible and even desirable to apply what they have learned in clinical, educational and employment sectors, I believe that the greatest area of learning will be in their everyday living. It is not that these other areas are not important, but that the personal is primary. They can always learn new strategies and gain techniques for dealing with situations, but the personal goes much deeper (i.e., the you that is one with nature). If people incorporate into their style of being the idea of engaging others in the here and now with awareness, they will gain the positive contact with bodily experience (e.g., being one with the self).

This thought stated in *Job (XII.8)* eloquently provides us with advice: "Speak to nature and it will speak to you." But does it speak so clearly? It is really difficult to put one's finger on what is order in nature, because it is not symmetry. Nature is hardly ever symmetrical. Nature is something that can never be defined like the ridges of the mountains we have seen at various places in our lives. And as we contemplate the shape and beauty of the mountains, we will never quite put a finger on what it is about the mountains that is so inspiring. And not surprisingly, it can bring similar feelings that we feel for someone we love, because they always escape exact definitions. Yet when we let go of the definitions, of the attempt to try and pin down friendship, love, and nature, they flow. When we try to define life in our mind, so that we understand and feel in complete control of it, we only get confused. What happens is that we go into our head, because we base our thoughts on the idea that we are different from it. When that happens, we have limited friendship, love, nature and ultimately, ourselves. Perhaps that is an indication that we are trying to master our lives. Yet, when we let go, life has about it a sense of flowing, like water. So as I close my eyes and see the reflection of the water, I stop thinking, analyzing and just accept what is there. It is the attraction of the river that provided wisdom and peace for Siddhartha; and as people move towards one polarity and back again, they must remember that there is no guarantee that there will be no pain in life or in relationships. They will experience pleasure, but also pain. And like water, they always go away, but they always come back. We need to remember that going away and coming back are two sides of the same thing.

Say hello, let it grow. . .

Say good-bye, let it fly. . .

Say hello, let it flow. . .

Say good-bye, let it die. . .

Say hello, and let it go. . .

ACTIVITIES FOR FOCUSING A GROUP:

1. **The Gift:** Group members are to think of three adjectives that describe the other group members. The adjectives should be one or two words that characterized the other person (e.g., accepting, honorable, energetic, strong, etc.). The words should be written on a sticky label and then given to the person. It is better to have a writing round, where all the people compose their "gift" followed by the give away round. The "gifts" can be handed to the people, stuck to their shoulder or glued to a piece of paper with their names on it.

2. **The Campfire:** This activity simulates the "final night on a camping trip" in which everyone in the group must say good-bye. The activity is composed of four rounds. Put a lighted candle in the middle of the circle to simulate a "campfire." In the first round everyone sits in a circle and reminisces about some of the "challenging" aspects of the "camping" (group) experience (e.g., fear of self disclosure, discomfort in being confronted, difficult activities, etc.). The second round consists of reminiscences about some of the "high" points in the group (e.g., sudden insight, observing resolution to a problem, etc.). The third consists of nicknames or symbols for other group members (e.g., "master of the universe," "wonder woman," "the owl," etc.). The fourth round consists of each group member sharing one "thing" they will accomplish in the coming year. After each person speaks, everyone should clap or show some affirmative response. The final round consists of a large group hug, followed by the departure of everyone when they are ready to leave. The "last one" to leave the room should "turn off the lights."

REFERENCES

Allport, G. (1959). *Study of values.* Boston, MA: Houghton Mifflin Company.

Amiel, H. F. (2001). *Encarta Encyclopedia.* [Computer program]. Redmond, WA: Microsoft.

Arasteh, A. R. (1984). *Anxious search: The way to the universal self.* Bethesda, MD: Institute of perspective analysis.

Arland, D. [Director], R. Malo & R. Frappier [Producers]. (1987). *Le dèclin de l'empire Americain.* [Motion Picture]. Canada

Ashwell, A. (1989). *Coast Salish: Their art, culture and legends.* Surrey, BC: Hancock House.

Babenco, H. [Director], K. Barish, C.O. Erickson, G. Kirkwood & M. Nasatir [Producers]. (1987). *Ironweed.* [Motion Picture]. Burbank, CA Universl Pictures.

Baron, R., N. Kerr & N. Miller. (1992). *Group process, group decision, group action.* Pacific Grove, CA: Brooks/Cole.

Bem, S. (1977). On the utility of alternative procedures for assessing psychological androgyny, *Journal of Consulting and Clinical Psychology, 45:* 196-205.

Berne, E. (1966). *Games people play.* NY: Bantam.

Bernard, J. M. (1986). Laura Perls: From ground to figure. *Journal of Counseling and Development, 64:* 367-373.

Blatner, A. (1985). The dynamics of catharsis. *Journal of Group Psychotherapy, Psychodrama, and Sociometry, 37*(4), 157-166.

Bly, R. (1991). *Iron John: A book about men.* Reading MA: Addison-Wesley Publishing Company.

Boorstein, S. (1980). *Transpersonal psychotherapy.* Palo Alto, CA: Science and Behavior Books.

Brazier, R. (1995). *Zen therapy.* Boston, MA: Allyn & Bacon.

Buber, M. (1970). *I and Thou.* New York: Scribner's.

Burgoon, J. & Saine, T. (1978). *The unspoken dialogue: An introduction to nonverbal communication.* Boston, MA: Houghton Mifflin Company.

Buriel, R. & Vasquez, R. (1982). Stereotypes of Mexican descent persons – attitudes of three generations of Mexican-American and Anglo-American adolescents. *Journal of Cross-cultural Psychology, 15*(1), 59-70.

Buss, D. (1989). Seeing is believing. *Journal of personality and social psychology, 30,* 205-220.

Cammack, M. (1996). *A rite of passage with outward bound: Transpersonal perspective of the solo from 16 wilderness guides.* An unpublished MA thesis, University of Victoria, Victoria, Canada.

Campbell, J. (1962). *The masks of god: Oriental mythology.* New York: The Viking Press

Campbell, M. (1979). *Half-breed.* Toronto, Canada: Seal Book.

Camus, A. (1957). *L'exil et le royaume.* Paris: Gallimard.

Camus, A. (1947). *La Peste.* London, U.K.: Penguin Books.

Camus, A. (1946). *The outsider.* London, UK: Hamish Hamilton.

Carroll, L. (1946). *Alice in Wonderland.* Grimm Books.

Casteñeda, C. (1972). *Journey to Ixtlan.* New York: Simon and Schuster.

Cohen, L. (1983). *Song of the soul.* NY: Atlantic Records.

Cohen, M. (1994). *Connecting with nature: Creating moments that let earth teach.* Eugene, ON: World Peace University.

Comfort, A. (1962). *After you, madam.* New York: Harold Ober Associates.

Conrad, W. (1962). *Victory.* London, UK: Penguin.

Corey, G. (1985). *Theory and practice of group counseling* (2nd ed.). Monterey, CA: Brooks/Cole.

Corey, G. & Corey, M. (1987). *Group process and practice.* Monterey, CA: Brooks/Cole.

Corsinni, R. J. & Wedding, D. (1989). *Current psychotherapies,* Fourth Edition. Itasca, IL: Peacock Publishers.

cummings, e. e. (1953). *Six non-lectures.* Cambridge, MA: Harvard University Press.

Dalai Lama (1996). In A. Weil (Ed.). *Eight weeks to optimal health.* New York: Alfred A. Knopf.

Das, Lama Surya (1997). *Awakening the Buddha within.* New York: Broadway Books.

Deaux, K. (1976). *The behavior of women and men.* Monterey, CA: Brooks/Cole.

de Montigny, L. (1972). Racism and Indian cultural adaptations. In Waubageshig (Editor), *The only good Indian* (pp. 97-111). Toronto, Canada: New Press.

Deloria, Jr., V.(1988). *Custer Died for Your Sins.* Norman: University of Oklahoma Press,

Drory, A. & Gluskinos, U. (1980). Machiavellianism and leadership. *Journal of Applied Psychology, 65,* 81-86.

Dugan, K. M. (1985). *The vision quest of the plains Indians, Its spiritual significance.* Lewiston, NY: Edwin Melin Press.

Earley, L. C. & Rutledge, P. B. (1980). A nine step problem solving model. In J. W. Pfeiffer & J. E. Jones (Eds.), *The 1980 annual handbook for group facilitators* (pp. 146-151). San Diego, CA: University Associates.

Egan, G. (1970). *Encounter: Group processes for interpersonal growth.* Monterey, CA: Brooks/Cole Books.

Egan, G. (1973). *Face to face: The small group experience and interpersonal growth.* Monterey, CA: Brooks/Cole Publishing Company.

Egan, G. (1986). *The skilled helper.* Monterey, CA: Brooks/Cole Publishers.

Elliot, T. S. (1968). *Four quartets.* NY: Random House.

Ellison, R. (1972). *Invisible man.* New York: Vintage.

Enns, C. Z. (1987). Gestalt therapy and feminist therapy: A proposed integration. *Journal of Counseling and Development, 66,* 93-95.

Enright, T. (1975). Thou art that: Projection and play. In J. O. Stevens (Ed.), *Gestalt is* (pp. 149-156). Moab, UT: Real People Press.

Enright, J. (1970). An introduction to Gestalt techniques. In J. Fagan & I. Shepherd (Eds.), *Gestalt therapy now* (pp. 107-124). Palo Alto, CA: Science and Behavior Books.

Erikson, E. (1963). *Childhood and society.* (2nd Ed.). New York: Norton.

Fadiman, J. (1980). The transpersonal stance. In M.J. Mahoney (Ed.). *Psychotherapy process: Current issues and future directions*. New York: Plenum Books

Faraday, A. (1974). *The dream game*. NY: Perennial.

Forsyth, D. (1999). *Group dynamics*, Third Edition, Belmont, CA: Brooks/Cole.

France, M. H. (1984). Responding to loneliness: Counselling the elderly. *Canadian Counsellor*, 18(3), 123-129

France, M. H. (1997). First Nations: Helping and learning in the aboriginal community. *Guidance & Counseling*, 12 (2), 3-8.

France, M. H. & McCormick, R. (1997). The helping circle: Theoretical and practical considerations of using a First Nations peer support network. *Guidance & Counseling*, 12, (2), 27-31.

France, M. H. & McDowell, C. (1983). A problem-solving paradigm: A preventive approach. *School Counselor*, 29(3), 224-227.

France, M. H. & Persaud, S. (1991). FRANSAUD cross-cultural sensitivity model: Training counsellors and teachers to be effective communicators. *Guidance and Counselling*, 7(1), 14-23.

France, H. & Rodriguez, C. (1999). Reconnecting with nature: unpublished paper presented at the ACA World Counseling Conference, April 15-19, San Diego, California.

Frankl, V. (1963). *Man's search for meaning*. NY: Bantam.

Friedan, B. (1983). *Feminine Mystique*, 20th Anniversary Edition, NY: Norton.

Friesen, J. (1985). *When cultures clash: Case studies in multiculturalism*. Calgary, Canada: Detselig Enterprise.

Gaw, A. (1982). *Cross cultural psychiatry*. Boston, MA: John Wright.

Gibran, K. (1932). *The wanderer*. NY: Alfred A. Knopf.

Gibran, K. (1933). *The prophet*. New York: Alfred Knopf.

Ginn, A. (1973). *Dramatic methods in therapy*. NY: Gardner Press.

Glendinning, C. (1994). *My name is Chellis, and I'm in recovery from Western Civilization*. Boston, MA: Shambala Press.

Goldenberg, I. & Goldenberg, H. (1980). *Family therapy: An overview*. Monterey, CA: Brooks/Cole.

Goldberg, J. (1976). *Hazard of being male*. New York: Nash.

Goldman, E. E. & Morrison, D. S. (1984). *Psychodrama: Experience and process*. Dubuque, IA: Kendall/Hunt Publishing Company.

Goodman, E. (1991). Men: Looking for a role. Victoria, BC: *Times-Colonist*, A14.

Gorky, M. (1943). Lower depths. In B. Cerf & V. Cartmell (Eds.). *Sixteen famous European plays* (pp. 197-258). New York: Random House.

Greene, G. (1965). *The quiet American*. New York: Penguin.

Guerney, B. (1988). *Relationship enhancement*. New York: Jossey-Bass.

Hall, E. T. (1971). *Beyond culture*. New York: Anchor/Doubleday.

Hammerschlag, H. (1988). *The dancing healers: A doctor's journey of healing with native Americans*. San Francisco, CA: Harper & Row

Happold, F. C. (1963). *Mysticism*. Baltimore, MD: Penguin Books.

Harris, R. (1978). *I'm OK, you're OK*. NY: Bantam.

Harstad, D. (1998). *Eleven Days*. New York, N.Y.: St. Martin's Paperbacks

Hatfield, E. & Rapson, R. (1987). Gender differences in love and intimacy: The fantasy vs. the reality. In W. Ricketts & H. Gochros (Eds.). *Intimate relationships: Some perspectives on love.* (pp. 15-26). NY: Haworth.

Hesse, H. (1929). *Steppenwolf*. London, UK: H. H. Edition.

Hesse, H. (1951). *Siddhartha*, New York: New Directions.

Hesse, H. (1971). *Narcisus and Goldman*. London, UK: Penguin.

Hifler, J. S. (1992). *A Cherokee feast of days: Daily meditations*. Tulsa, OK: Council Oak Books.

Higham, J. (1972). *Strangers in the land*. New York: Atheneum.

Hilger, L. (1997). Earth-friendly therapy. *Self*, September, 70.

Hite, S. (1987). *Women and love*. New York: Random House.

Hollander, C. (1971). Auxiliary ego: Definition, form and function. An unpublished paper. Denver, CO: Colorado Psychodrama Center.

Hollander, C. (1978). A process for psychodrama training: The Hollander curve. A paper presented at workshop on Psychodrama at the University of Winnipeg, Canada.

Hoover, T. (1980). *The Zen experience: This historical evolution of Zen through the lives and teachings of its great masters*. NY: New American Library.

Hopi Prayer. http://www.accesshelp.org/mar00/spring00hopiprayer.html.

Horner, D. & Vandersluis, P. (1981). Cross-cultural counselling. In G.Althen (Ed.), *Learning across cultures*. Washington, DC: National Association for Foreign Students Affairs.

Humphreys, C. (1968). *Concentration and meditation*. Baltimore, MD: Penguin Books.

Hunt, H. (1995). *On the nature of consciousness*. London: Yale University Press.

Huxley, A. (1936). *Brave new world*. London: Panther.

Huxley, A. (1977). *The devils of Loudun*. London: Panther.

Ibrahim, F. (1984). Cross-cultural counselling and psychotherapy: An existential-psychological perspective. *International Journal for the Advancement of Counselling*, 7, pp.559-569.

Ibrahim, F. (1991). Contribution of cultural worldview to generic counseling and development. *Journal of Counselling and Development*. Vol.70 p.13-19.

Immortal poems of the English language: An anthology. (1966). NY: Washington Square Press.

Ivey, A. (1983). *Intentional interviewing and counseling*. Monterey, CA: Brooks/Cole Publishers.

James, M. & Jongward, D. (1973). *Born to win*. Reading, MA: Addison-Wesley Publishing Company.

Jilek, W. (1992). *Indian healing: Shamanic ceremonialism in the Pacific Northwest*. Surrey, BC: Hancock House.

Johnson, D. & Johnson, F. (1991). *Joining together: Group theory and group skills*, Fourth Edition. Englewood Cliffs, NJ: Prentice Hall.

Johnson, D. & Johnson, F. (1999). *Learning together and alone: Cooperative, competitive and individualistic learning.* Boston, MA: Allyn & Bacon.

Jong, E. (1977). *How to save your own life.* New York: Pocket Books.

Jung, C. (1963). *Memories, dreams, reflections.* NY: Pantheon Books.

Jung, C. (1964). *Man and his symbols.* NY: Doubleday.

Kagan, J. (1969). Check one: Male - female. *Psychology Today.* July, 39-41.

Karp, M. (1968). Catharsis: Its occurrence in Psychodrama and psychoanalysis. *Group Psychotherapy and Psychodrama*, 26, 7-22.

Katz, R. & Rolde, E. (1981). Community alternatives to psychotherapy. *Psychotherapy, theory, research and practice*, 18, 365-374.

Kazantzakis, N. (1952). *Zorba the Greek.* NY: Ballantine.

Kellermann, P. (1984). The place of catharsis: Fact or fantasy. *Group Psychotherapy and Psychodrama*, 21, 137-139.

Kelly, P. (1980). Identity house – A Gestalt experiment for gays. In B. Fedler & R. Ronall's, *Beyond the hot seat: Gestalt approaches to groups* (pp.). New York: Brunner/Mazel.

Kepner, J. (1980). Gestalt group process. In B. Feder & R. Rondall, *Beyond the hot seat: Gestalt approaches to groups.* (pp. 5-24). NY: Brunner/Mazel Publishers.

Kepner, J. (1987). *Body process: A Gestalt approach to working with the body in psychotherapy.* NY: Garder Press.

Kitagawa, M. (1985). *This is my own: Letters to Wes & others' writings on Japanese Canadians.* Vancouver, Canada: Talonbooks.

Kitzler, R. (1980). The Gestalt group. In B. Feder & R. Rondall, *Beyond the hot seat: Gestalt approaches to the group.* (pp. 25-36). NY: Brunner/Mazel Publishers.

Kluckhohn, F. & Strodtbeck, F. (1961). *Variations in value orientations.* Illinois: Row, Peterson & Company.

Kopp, S. (1972). *If you meet the Buddha on the road, kill him!* NY: Bantam.

Kopp, S. (1975). The trickster-healer. In W. L. Smith (Ed.), *The growing edge of Gestalt therapy* (pp. 69-82). NY: Brunner/Mazel Publishers.

Kopp, S. (1986). *Here I am wasn't it!* New York: Bantam.

Kosinski, J. (1976). *The painted bird* (2nd Ed.). Boston, MA: Houghton Mifflin Company.

Krammer, E. (1971). *Art as therapy with children.* New York: Schocken Books.

Krantzler, M. (1979). *Learning to love again.* New York: Bantam Books.

Krishnamurti, J. (1954). *The first and the last freedom.* London: Gollnacz.

Kumar, V. K. & Treadwell, T. (1986). Identifying a protagonist: Techniques and factors. *Journal of Group Psychotherapy, Psychodrama, and Sociometry*, Winter, 155-163.

Lafromboise, T., Trimble, J. & Mohat, G. (1990). Counseling intervention and American Indian tradition: An integrative approach. *The Counseling Psychologist*, 18, 628-654.

Lamb, C. S. (1982). Negative hypnotic imagery/fantasy: Application to two cases of "unfinished business." *American Journal of Clinical Hypnosis*, 24(4), 266-271.

Landy, R. (1984). Puppets, dolls, objects, masks, and make-up. *Journal of Mental Imagery*, 8(1). 79-90.

Langley, D. (1983). *Dramatherapy and psychiatry.* London: Croom Helm.

Latner, J. (1973). *The gestalt therapy book.* NY: Bantam.

Lathrop, D. (1976). Jung and Perls: Analytical psychology and Gestalt. In E. Smith (Ed.), *The growing edge of Gestalt therapy.* (pp. 103-108). NY: Brunner/Mazel.

Laurie, A. (1978). *Imaginary friends.* New York: Penguin.

Lee, D. Y., Sutton, R., France, H. & Uhlemann, M. (1983). Effects of counselor race on perceived counseling effectiveness. *Journal of Counseling Psychology*, 30(3), 447-450.

Leiberman, B., Yalom, I. & Miles, M. (1973). *Encounter groups: First facts.* NY: Basic Books.

Leggett, T. (1978). *Zen and the way.* Boulder, CO: Shambala Publications, Inc.

Lennon, J. & MacCartney, P. (1966). *Hello, good-bye.* London: Apple Records.

LeShan, L. (1974). *How to meditate.* Boston: Little Brown.

Lieberman, N. (1980). An organismic formulation of the Gestalt group, In B. Feder & R. Rondall (Eds.), *Beyond the hot seat: Gestalt approaches to group* (pp. 37-40). New York: Brunner/Mazel Publishers.

Lorenz, C. (1966). *On aggression.* New York: Bantam.

Lowen, A. (1967). *The betrayal of the body.* New York: Collier Books.

Lueger, R.J. (1986). Imagery techniques in cognitive-behavioral therapy. In A.A. Sheikh (Ed.), *Anthology of imagery techniques* (pp. 61-83). Milwaukee: American Imagery Institute.

Lynch, J. (1977). *The broken heart: The medical consequences of loneliness.* New York: Basic Books.

Maccoby, E. (1988). Gender as a social category. *Developmental Psychology*, 24, 755-765.

Maslow, A. (1964). *Religions, values, and peak experiences.* NY: Phi Delta Kappa.

Maslow, A. (1971). *Further reaches of human nature.* London, U.K.: Penguin Books.

Matheson, L. (1996). Valuing spirituality among Native American populations. *Counseling and Values* (41), pp. 51-70.

May, R. (1974). *Love and will.* New York: Norton.

McCormick, R. (1997). An integration of healing wisdom: The vision quest ceremony from an attachment theory persepctive. *Guidance & Counseling*, 12, (2), 18-21.

Mc Gaa, E. (1990). *Mother earth spirituality.* New York: Harper Collins.

McClintock, E. (1999). *Room for change: Empowering possibilities for therapists and clients.* Boston, MA: Allyn & Bacon.

Mc Kenzie, L. (1996). *Adult education and worldview construction.* New York, New York: Random House.

Medicine Eagle, B. (1989). The circle of healing. In R. Carlson & J. Brugh (Eds.). *Healers on healing*, (58-62).

Mohler, J.A. (1975). *Dimensions of love: East and west.* Garden City, N.Y.: Doubleday and Company.

Moondance, W. (1994). *Rainbow medicine: A visionary guide to Native America shamanism*. New York: Sterling Pub.Co.

Moreno, J. L. (1953). *Who shall survive? Foundations of sociometry, group psychotherapy and sociodrama*. Beacon, NY: Beacon House.

Murry, M. (Ed.). (1927). *Journal of Katherine Mansfield*. London: Constable

Napier, R. & Gershenfeld, M. (1999). *Groups: Theory and experience*. Boston, MA: Houghton Mifflin Company.

Neihardt. J. (1988). *Black elk speaks*. NY: Pocket Books.

Nevis, E. (1987). *Organizational consulting: A Gestalt approach*. NY: Gardener Press.

Newman, P. (1989 July). Bold and cautious. *Maclean's*, pp. 24-25.

Newman, D. (2000). Earth Week: A Diary of the planet. *Times Colonist*. September 24, A1

Nicholson, J. (1984). *Men and women: How different are they?* Oxford, NY: Oxford University Press.

Noone, R. & Holman, D. (1972). *In search of the dream people*. NY: Morrow.

Orcutt, T. (1977). Roles and rules: The kinship and territoriality of psychodrama and Gestalt therapy. *Journal of Group Psychotherapy, Psychodrama and Sociometry*, 30, 97-107.

Passons, W. (1975). *Gestalt approaches in counseling*. NY: Holt, Rinehart and Winston.

Pedersen, P. B., Draguns, J., Lonner, W. & Trimble, J. (2002). *Counseling across cultures*. Thousand Oaks, CA: SAGE Publications.

Perls, F. (1969a). *Gestalt therapy verbatim*. Moab, UT: Real People Press.

Perls, F. (1969b). *In and out the garbage pail*. Moab, UT: Real People Press.

Perls, F. (1973). *The gestalt approach & eye witness to therapy*. Palo Alto, CA: Science and Behavior Books.

Perls, F. (1975a). Group vs. individual therapy. In J. O. Stevens, (Ed.), *Gestalt is* (pp. 9-16). Moab, UT: Real People Press.

Perls, F. (1975b). Resolution. In J. O. Stevens (Ed.), *Gestalt is* (pp. 69-74). Moab, UT: Real People Press.

Perls, F., Hefferline, R. & Goodman, P. (1951). *Gestalt therapy*. NY: Dell Books.

Piaget, J. (1965). *The moral judgement of the child*. NY: Free Press.

Pirandello, L. (1943). Six characters in search of an author. In B. Cerf & V. Cartmell (Eds.), *Sixteen famous European plays* (pp. 623-665). NY: The Modern Library.

Poduska, B. (1980). *Understanding psychology and dimensions of adjustment*. NY: McGraw-Hill Book Company.

Polster, E. & Polster, M. (1974). Notes on the training of the Gestalt therapist. *Voices*, Fall, 38-44.

Polster, I. (1966). Imprisoned in the present. *The Gestalt Journal*, 8(1), 5-22.

Population Crisis Committee (1988). *Poor, powerless, and pregnant*. Washington, D.C. U.S. Government Printing Office.

Prather, H. (1970). *Notes to myself: My struggle to become a person*. NY: Bantam Books.

Przybyla, D., Byrn, D. & Kelley, K. (1983). The role of imagery in sexual behavior. In A. A. Skeikh

(Ed.). *Imagery: Current theory, research, and application* (pp. 438-457). New York: John Wiley & Sons.

Ram Dass, B. (1975). *The only dance there is.* NY: Double Day.

Ramaswami, S. (1989). Yoga and healing. In A. Sheikh & K. Sheikh (Eds.). *Eastern & western approaches to healing: Ancient wisdom and modern knowledge.* NY: John Wiley & Sons.

Remarque, E. C. (1931). *All quiet on the western front.* New York: Random House.

Ricketts, W. & Gochros, H. (1987). Introduction: What's love got to do with it? In W. Ricketts & H. Gochros (Eds.). *Intimate relationships: Some social work perspectives on love* (pp. 1-14). New York: Haworth Press.

Rilke, R. M. (1964). *New Poems.* NY: New American Library.

Rogers, C. (1973). *Carl Rogers on encounter groups.* NY:Random House.

Rogers, C. (1980). Growing old or older and growing. *Journal of Humanistic Psychology*, 4, 5-16.

Rogers, C. (1983). *The freedom to learn.* NY: Holt, Rinehart, and Winston.

Rumi, J. (1898). *Masnavi.* (E .H. Whinfield, Trans.). London: Clarendon Press.

Sanford, G. (2000). Compassionate curiosity: A transpersonal bridge in multicultural counselling, *Guidance & Counselling*, 15(3), 33-37.

Santrock, J. & Yussen, S. (2000). *Child development: An introduction*, Fourth Edition. Dubuque, IA: Wm. C. Brown Publishers.

Schab, F. (1990). Odors and the remembrance of things past. *Journal of Experimental Psychology: Learning, memory and cognition,* 16(4), 648-655.

Schachter, D. (1989). *Disociable memory and consciousness: essays in honor of Endel Tulving.* Hilsdale, N.J: Erlbaum, pp 355-389.

Schoenbaum, S. (1971). *William Shakespeare: A documentary life.* NY. New American Library.

Schultz, L. (1987). A note on brief intimate encounters. In W. Ricketts & H. Gochros (Eds.). *Intimate relationships: Some social work perspectives on love* (pp. 39-44). New York: Haworth Press.

Secharist, E. (1974). *Dreams: Your magic mirror.* NY: Warner.

Shaffer, J. B. & Galinsky, M. D. (1974). *Models of group therapy and sensitivity training.* Englewood Cliffs, NJ: Prentice-Hall.

Sheikh, A. & Jordan, C. (1983). Clinical uses of mental imagery. In A. A. Sheikh (Ed.), *Imagery: Current theory, research, and application* (pp. 4-24). NY: John Wiley and Sons.

Sheikh, A. & Sheikh, K. (1989). *Eastern and Western approaches to healing.* Toronto: John Wiley & Sons.

Shorr, J. E. (1978). Clinical use of categories of therapeutic imagery. In J. L. Singer & S. Pope (Eds.), *The power of human imagination* (pp.89-99). NY: Plenum.

Shulman, S. (1979). *Nightmare.* NY: Macmillam.

Simkin, J. (1974). *Mini-lectures in Gestalt therapy.* Albany, CA: Wordpress.

Skinner, B. F. (1948). *Walden two.* NY: MacMillan Company.

Skinner, B. F. (1976). *About Behaviorism.* NY: Vintage.

Smith, E. (1976). *The growing edge of Gestalt therapy*. NY: Brunner/Mazel.

Smoley, R. (1992). First nations spirituality. *Yoga Journal*, January, pp 84-89, 104-108.

Softley, I. [Director] & G. Lawrence [Producer]. (2001). *K-Pax*. [Motion Picture]. Burbank, CA: Universal Studios.

Spranger, D. (1928). *Types of man*. Berlin, Germany: Halle Max Niemeyer Verlag.

Stanislavski, C. (1969). *An actor prepares*. NY: Theatre Arts Books.

Sterling, S. (1997). Skaloola the owl: Healing power in Salishan mythology. *Guidance & Counselling*, 12(3), 9-12.

Sinclair, S. (1992). *Courageous Spirit*. Vancouver, BC: Mowet Press.

Stevens, B. (1975). Body work. In J. O. Stevens (Ed.), *Gestalt is* (pp. 157-184). Moab, UT: Real People Press.

Stevens, J. O. (1971). *Awareness: Exploring, experimenting, experiencing*. NY: Bantam.

Stroller, R. (1979). *Sexual excitement*. New York: Pantheon.

Sue, D. W. & Sue, D. (1990). *Counselling the culturally different: Theory and practice* (Third Edition). New York: John Wiley and Sons.

Suzuki, D. T. (1962). *Zen Buddhism*. Garden City, NY: Anchor Books.

Tart, C. (1975). *Transpersonal psychologies*. New York: Harper & Row.

Thomas, S. (1973). The warrior who chose death: Yukio Mishima. *Psychology Today*, 59-64.

Tobin, S. (1975). Saying good-bye. In J.O. Stevens (Ed.), *Gestalt is*. (pp. 371-383). Moab, UT: Real People Press.

Thoreau, H.D. (1970). *Walden*. New York, NY: Harper Collins Publishers.

Trimble, J.E. & Hayes, S. (1984). Mental health intervention in the psychosocial contexts of American Indian communities. In W. O'Conner & Lubin (Eds.). *Ecological approaches to clinical community psychology*. (pp.293-321).

Tucker, B. (1988). Failure to act individually. *Times-Colonist*, August 7, p. A-5.

Tyler, D. M. (1979). Gestalt movement therapy in groups. In B. Feder & R. Rondall (Eds.). *Beyond the hot seat: Gestalt approaches to groups* (pp. 105-115). NY: Brunner/Mazel Publishers.

Uhlemann, M., Lee, D.U. & France, H. (1988). Counsellor ethnic differences and perceived counselling effectiveness. *International Journal for the Advancement of Counselling*, 15, 1-7.

Underwood, W. (1973). Roles that facilitate and inhibit group development. In R. Golembiewski & A. Blumberg (Eds.), *Sensitivity training and the laboratory approach* (pp. 123-127). NY: F. E. Peacock.

Upanishads. (1962). London, UK: George Allen & Unwin.

United States Census Population Bureau. Retrieved in January 10, 2002 from the World Wide Web: http://www.census.gov/main/www/srchtool.html

Van de Castle, R. L. (1973). Ancient theories of dreams. In S. Lee & A. Mays (Eds.), *Dreams and dreaming: Selected Readings* (pp. 17-32). London, UK: Penguin.

Van de Riet, V., Korb, M. & Gorrell, J. (1980). *Gestalt therapy: An introduction*. NY: Pergamon Press.

Van der Post, L. (1963). *The seed and the sower.* London, UK: Hogarth Press.

Van der Post, L. (1974). *A far-off place.* London, UK: Hogarth Press.

Vanier, J. (1998). *Becoming Human.* Ontario: House of Anansi Press.

Vaughn, F. (1989). *The inward arc.* Boston, Mass.: New Science Library/Shambala.

Vernon, P.E. (1982). *The abilities and achievements of orientals in North America.* New York: Academic Press.

Vontress, C. E. (1996). Racial and Ethnic Barriers in Counseling. In P. Pedersen, W. J. Lonner and J. G. Draguns (Eds.), *Counselling Across Cultures.* Honolulu, HI: The University Press of Hawaii.

Walsh, R.N. & Vaughn, F.E. (1980). Comparative models of the person and psychotherapy. In S. Boorstein (Ed.). *Transpersonal psychotherapy.* Palo Alto, CA :Science and Behavioral Books.

Warr, P. & Wall, T. (1978). *Work and well-being.* London, UK: Penguin.

Watts, A. (1957). *The way of Zen.* NY: Pantheon.

Watts, A. (1958). *Nature, man, and woman.* NY: Pantheon.

Vancouver Sun , (2000). "School violence," Feb 8, p. A1.

Weil, A. (1997). *Eight weeks to optimal health.* New York: Alfred A. Knopf.

Williams, S. K. (1982). *Jungian-Senoi dreamwork manual.* Berkeley, CA: Journey Press.

Willis, R .J. (1979). Meditation to fit the person: Psychology and the meditative way. *Journal of religion and health.* 18 (2), 93-119.

Wolf , F. A. (1999). *The spiritual universe: How quantum physics proves the existence of the soul.* NY: Random House.

Yablonsky, L. (1981). *Psychodrama: Resolving emotional problems through role-play.* NY: Gardner Press.

Zajonc, R. B., Heingartner, A. & Herman, E. M. (1969). Social enhancement and impairment of performance in the cockroach. *Journal of Personality and Social Psychology*, 13, 83-92.

Zinker, J. (1980). *Creative process in Gestalt therapy.* NY: Vintage.